Anna and Tranquillo

Anna and Tranquillo

Catholic Anxiety and Jewish Protest
in the Age of Revolutions

Kenneth Stow

Yale

UNIVERSITY PRESS

NEW HAVEN AND LONDON

Published with assistance from the Annie Burr Lewis Fund.
Published with assistance from the foundation established in memory of
Henry Weldon Barnes of the Class of 1882, Yale College.

Yale University Press books may be purchased in quantity for educational, business, or promotional use.
For information, please e-mail sales.press@yale.edu (U.S. office) or sales@yaleup.co.uk (U.K. office).

Set in Fournier MT type by Integrated Publishing Solutions.
Printed in the United States of America.

ISBN: 978-0-300-21904-3 (hardcover : alk. paper)

Library of Congress Control Number: 2016935684

A catalogue record for this book is available from the British Library.

This paper meets the requirements of ANSI/NISO Z39.48-1992 (Permanence of Paper).

10 9 8 7 6 5 4 3 2 1

For Roni, Ilay, Or, Halleli, Sarai, Tomer, and Yuval

Contents

Acknowledgments

This book is the fruit of research and thinking that has spanned many years. Work began in earnest as I prepared three lectures titled "Anna and the House of Converts," which were delivered during my tenure as the Shier Distinguished Professor of Jewish History at the University of Toronto in 2008, where I was warmly received by Derek Penslar and my friends Nicholas Terpstra and Natalie Zemon Davis. Subsequently, I had the great fortune to spend extended periods in two very special places: first, the Diamond Library of the Columbia University School of Law, one of the great collections of medieval and early modern law, whose possessions, as cited in this study, have been previously unknown. I had the privilege of using this collection for my doctoral dissertation decades ago, and now I was privileged to return, in 2011, as a Bodini Scholar of the Italian Academy for Advanced Study at Columbia. I thank the entire staff of the Academy, particularly David Freedberg and Barbara Faedda, and so very much my colleague at the Academy and lasting friend, Francesco Cioffi, for making my time there so profitable, as well as pleasant. In the Law Library, I enjoyed the unflagging day-by-day help of the reference librarian for rare books, Sabrina Sondhi. I cannot thank her enough. I thank Michael Widener at the rare book library at the Yale Law School for allowing me to use his splendid collection.

The second special place, where I was also welcomed with great generosity, was that archival treasure the Archivio Storico of the Jewish Community of Rome, ASCER. Silvia Haia Antonucci and the late Giancarlo Spizzichino, along with Gabriella Yael Franzone and Claudio Procaccia, were constantly at hand to resolve perplexity and show me the way. The documents from this archive, which have nourished this book, with the exception of those copies in ASCER made from originals in the Archive of the Roman

Inquisition, the ACDF, have never been used before. Finally, my appreciation goes out to all those who have had to put up with my constant reference to my project and to those who have helped me by reading its sections. I thank Francesca Trivellato in particular for pushing me to perfect arguments, but also for finding what would have been unacceptable flaws in the translation. Christine Cooper-Rompato was the first to read the manuscript, and her encouragement was invaluable.

I thank Erica Hanson of Yale University Press, who on first inspection saw this project as worthwhile, and who has guided me in restructuring the original manuscript. Paul Betz's sharp editorial eye perfected the prose and eliminated errors. So many others at the press have smoothed the book's way into print, including Margaret Otzel, Clare Jones, and Chris Rogers. I thank the Press's anonymous readers, whose challenging comments were reasons to make the arguments so much the more precise, including the fuller integration of the diary into the whole. And I thank Micol Ferarra for her reconstructions of Anna's route from the Ghetto to the House of Converts, but even more for locating the del Monte home and its insertion into topographic depiction. Anna Foa, Francesca Bregoli, Federica Francesconi, Angela Groppi, Katherine Aron Beller, Debra Kaplan, Manuela Militi, Manuela Bragagnolo, Magda Teter, Maurice Kriegel, and Isabelle Poutrin read the text and gave good advice. Jeannine Horowitz read the text time and again. Special thanks to Mitchell Duneier for his support, to Robert Somerville for enduring friendship and good advice, and to Robert Stacey for the same, even in his most difficult moments. To my wife, Estela, who has patiently, and lovingly, had to listen to more than all the others combined, my greatest appreciation and affection.

It is to my seven grandchildren—Roni, Ilay, Or, Halleli, Sarai, Tomer, and Yuval—that I dedicate this book. May they grow and thrive in a land of peace and harmony between peoples.

Abbreviations

ASCER   Archivio medievale e moderno, fondo AMM, Università degli ebrei di Roma, Archivio Storico della Comunità Ebraica di Rome

ASR   Archivio di Stato, Rome, Tribunale del Governatore

CAJP   Central Archive for the History of the Jewish People, Jerusalem

JTS   Jewish Theological Seminary, microfilm 4026a, Copies of Roman documents

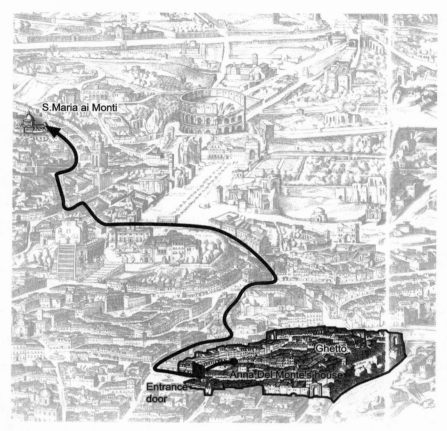

Route from the ghetto to the *Pia Casa dei catecumeni e neofiti* (Pious House of catechumens and neophytes), set against *Veduta di Roma* (View of Rome) by A. Tempesta. Revised and enhanced by G. G. De Rossi in 1693. Reconstruction by Micol Ferrara.

Introduction

Our laws have applied the only antidote to this vice, protecting our religious,
as they do our civil rights, by putting all on an equal footing.
—James Madison to Mordecai Emanuel Noah in 1818

The subject of this book is the transformation in Jewish life that *failed to occur* in late eighteenth-century Rome. Everywhere else in Western Europe, as well as in the young United States, Jewish life was being transformed. The French Revolution and the U.S. Constitution had established in principle (fact would take time to catch up and sometimes never did) that Jews were citizens with full and equal legal rights, the same as those enjoyed by all others in the state. In Rome, the capital of the then Papal State, which, until 1860, occupied about one-third of the Italian peninsula, no such thing occurred. Although Rome's approximately 4,000 Jews possessed rights in civil law, the law of everyday life, and were officially denominated citizens (*cives* or *cittadini*), religiously, the discrimination determined by canon law was great.

Roman Jews were forced to live in a closed precinct, the ghetto decreed by Pope Paul IV in 1555, tightly packed into an area no larger than about two-and-a-half modern city blocks. On one side, the Tiber River bordered the ghetto, which flooded annually, inundating ghetto houses. The ghetto endured until 1870. The establishment of the ghetto and its regulations were part and parcel of a vigorous conversionary drive. Preaching was instituted and owning Hebrew books deemed blasphemous and inhibiting conversion prohibited. Tight limits were placed on the use of Jewish law to regulate wills and testaments, and sometimes on marriage, spheres where Jews had always enjoyed self-rule. The conversionary program, essential to the Church's dream of uniting all peoples under "one flock and one pastor" (John 10:16), was maintained uninterrupted for three centuries, although from the end of the sixteenth century and well into the seventeenth, it seems to have been largely dormant.

In the later seventeenth, and into the eighteenth century, the program came back to life. Its principal manifestation were attempts virtually to co- erce conversion by allowing those considered spouses or endowed with what was termed legally "parental power" "to offer" young children or women to the Church. These people were taken, at times forcefully, to an institution known as the *Casa dei catecumeni*, the House of Converts, where they were held for periods of time, sometimes twelve days, and sometimes forty, or even eighty, "to test their mettle." Most converted.

Some did not. The best-known example is that of Anna del Monte, who not only remained a Jew but also left a "diary" recounting her thirteen days in the *Catecumeni*, as Rome's Jews called this hated place. There were others (we do not know exactly how many) like Anna, but only Anna left a personal record. The title on the single surviving manuscript copy is chilling: *Ratto della Signorina Anna del Monte*, The Kidnapping of Signorina Anna del Monte. The kidnappers were papal police. The kidnapping took place in May 1749.

As it has survived, the diary's text is far from the original. Very likely, Anna herself prepared a draft shortly after she returned home, but at some point, Anna's brother Tranquillo reworked it to suit his own perspective. External evidence and the diary's introduction suggest the editing was done in 1793, which was also when Tranquillo shared the diary, privately I believe, with others. The diary as we have it, therefore, has two protagonists: Anna and her brother. Tranquillo was a communal leader, and we have some infor- mation about his life and doings. Apart from the approximate dates of Anna's birth and death, in 1731 and sometime before 1779, respectively, and that she belonged to one of the ghetto's leading and very few well-to-do families, as we learn from a census made in 1733 and a note in the diary's introduction, we know of Anna only what Tranquillo wishes to disclose.[1] We can recon- struct what she experienced and felt only by peeling back imaginatively the layers Tranquillo added. Readers of the diary, whose full translation is at the heart of this book, will be free to picture the real Anna as they will.

Yet it is as much with Tranquillo's world as Anna's testing in the *Cate- cumeni* that the reader of this study will be asked to grapple. To read the diary without Tranquillo constantly in mind is to read only half the story. To think of Anna alone would be to pass over Tranquillo's protest, whose underlying motivations, including his informed grasp of the forces, new and old, that shaped his world, we must set out to know. Otherwise we will not read the diary well.

The text we have conveys the message Tranquillo wanted his readers to absorb; and that, I will argue, was his animus against the absurdity of Roman Jewish life at the end of the eighteenth century. This, of course, was at the same time that the French and American Revolutions granted Jews full legal equality, while Rome remained mired in the discriminatory past. What was affecting Jews decisively when Tranquillo circulated the diary were changes in the legal definition, and perception, of what makes a citizen. Changed, too, was the definition of the proper relationship between the citizen and his or her state, especially as religion affected the citizen's life.

In the confessional Papal State, where Anna lived, religion was decisive and laws were imbued with religious principle: the study of law becoming a study of values. Had Anna lived in Pennsylvania in 1749 (or in any other of the thirteen American colonies), there would be no story to tell and no diary to read. It would have been the same had she been living in post-Revolutionary France. In both places, people were under no duress to change their religious identity, and civil rights were no longer legally contingent on religious affiliation. Confessionalism had been formally eliminated, and no one religion or religious sect was given precedence over another in law—although, to be sure, one might argue that in France (and even in some states of the United States), it was decades before theory became reality and theoretical legal equality became identical with equality in fact. Some might argue that with respect to certain groups other than Jews in the United States, theory still remains unrealized.

Anna's diary portrays the ills of the confessional state at its worst, one in which civil needs bowed unexceptionally to the demands of religion. Well aware of the revolutions that had just taken place, late-eighteenth-century readers of the diary would see it as the protest Tranquillo intended. It is not overly exaggerated to call the diary as Tranquillo has bequeathed it to us a "political tract." His objection was not alone that the Papal State insisted on remaining a confessional one. It was—and on this Roman Jews concurred— the utter confusion of one and the same political body affirming, on the one hand, that Jews were *cives*, citizens, with full public rights, yet, on the other, that when "spiritual" issues were involved, Jewish rights were to be curtailed. In the words of the late-seventeenth-century legal giant Cardinal G. B. de Luca: "Jews are *cives* in all matters, both with regard to privileges and responsibilities, except where spiritual matters intervene." This was a halfway house, located somewhere between the old and the new (post-Revolutionary) worlds, an anomaly that was demonstrably flawed and in whose shadow it was maddening to live.

The end to this anomaly required more than the simple disestablishment of a state religion. That option worked well, if imperfectly, in the early United States, with its many Protestant sects and few Catholics. In the Catholic Papal State, the obstacle was the integral nexus, the essential link that had existed for close to two millennia between citizenship and faith. In 1558, the highly quoted legist Marquardus de Susannis had written that one became a full citizen through "regeneration," rebirth, at the baptismal font. As a Jew, one could never be a full citizen; a full citizen could never be a Jew.

Régénération again became an issue at the time of the French Revolution. However, its meaning had altered radically. Historians of the Jews at this time normally identify the term with new thinking that demanded Jewish moral and social improvement. This was the "price" Jews would pay in exchange for their emancipation, the acquisition of equal rights. This perspective has great value, as does a second one, which perceives a steady incrementation of rights that ended in equality for Jews settled in states bordering both shores of the Atlantic.

This view of Atlantic commonality is reinforced by the content of this book. But its investigations will move the discussion a step forward. George Washington caught the essence best. Writing in 1790 to the Jews of Newport, Rhode Island, he said: "The state demands no more of you than that you observe the law." Observing the law, reading Washington backward, creates the citizen. Legal change and observance had become the agent of *régénération*, no longer baptism. *Régénération* would move hand in hand with the implementation of the uniform system of law inaugurated by the Revolution, gradual and halting as that implementation was.

That new law attained its full measure (in western Europe) in Napoleon's *Code civil* of 1804, which, as the legal scholar Antonio Padoa-Schioppa has observed, occurred "in one [swift] blow," displacing all previous law and, no less importantly, doing away, as far as the state was concerned, with legal confessionalism. This included outlawing the highly Christianized *ius commune,* the Roman Law–based legal system that for centuries had provided the theoretical backbone, if not the foundation, of law as applied throughout

Europe. Without this legal revolution, de-confessionalization and the subsequent implementation of principle and acquisition of rights would have gone only so far, just as prior to the legal revolution, some rights would never have been attained. Most notably, as long as laws upholding confessionalism held sway, Jews would never have been able to vaunt that most evident badge of equality, the right to hold public office, which, in a confessional state, always required taking a religious oath at the moment of swearing in. It was also the Jews' good fortune that *régénération* by way of a legal revolution had to be universal, applying equally to all. It could exclude neither Jews nor anybody else, lest the system fail for want of perfection.

Yet legislation and application are rarely the same thing. Likewise, legal emancipation must not be confused with social acceptance and integration, as the history of Jewish social integration and its failures and of the impediments put in legal equality's way has made clear. The history of emancipation's demise in Italy and Germany during the 1930s, with the rise of Fascism, Nazism, and the racial doctrines that replaced equality with severe discrimination, and worse, has been told. So has that of Eastern Europe, where emancipation came late and was always equivocal. These stories will not be repeated here. Rather, we want to investigate what people were thinking and saying leading up to the moment of emancipatory change.

Till now, the study of events leading up to emancipation has focused on the debates about Jews and the nature of Jewish citizenship that took place between 1789 and 1791 in the French National Assembly created by the Revolution.[2] Similar debates, which had been going on since the late seventeenth century in the Papal State, have not been studied. These debates will occupy much of our attention. They are found in legal briefs, papal responses, and petitions by the Jews of Rome. They provide the background to Anna's diary, as well as to the ideas Tranquillo wished to instill in the minds of the diary's readers. Their invariable subject is whether canon law should take absolute precedence over civil law, and in making their case they expose with unparalleled clarity the kind of thinking that would be instrumental in shaping the late eighteenth-century rebellion against confessional regimes in both France and the United States.

In Rome, where the effects of confessionalism were a fact of Jewish daily life, the terms of the clash were pragmatic, as well as ideological. Was it, both sides queried, legal to kidnap a Jew, usually a young child, but also a spouse—or somebody said to be a spouse, as was Anna del Monte—and hold him or her in the Roman House of Converts until he or she gave in? Those defending these kidnappings claimed that they were acting for "the good of the faith," *favor fidei*, a venerable legal principle, which, from about the twelfth century, the Church had made supreme. It was on this principle that confessionalism hinged; it will be examined in depth.

Later eighteenth-century popes did all they could to augment *favor fidei*. It was their way to defend against detested rationalist Enlightenment thinking, against associations considered dangerous like the Freemasons, and against successful attempts by lay rulers to gain control over traditional Church functions and powers, in particular, marriage, which was at once a sacrament, but also a source of social control. All three of these novelties were classed as *favor*'s opposite, *odium fidei*, hatred of—in the sense of "a war on"—the faith. The popes were fighting for what they considered of utmost importance, which made the battle so much the fiercer. Papal strategy was seconded by lawyers like Giovanni Riganti, who held fast to de Luca's and de Susannis's definition of citizenship and advanced their case by identifying as one and interchangeable the concept of *favor fidei* and what they called the "highest good" of the state. Their ideal political body would be a modern, centralized, but still confessional one, in which pressing baptism on Jews was deemed good, proper, and legal.

Not everybody agreed. Carlo Luti insisted that it was civil, not canon, law that must be decisive. To promote canonical supremacy was arbitrary and the naked exercise of "papal power." It was also the height of the confessionalism that he and other legal thinkers more and more opposed.

The pain of those trapped between the protagonists of this debate is what the reader of Anna's diary is intended to feel. It lies at the heart of Tranquillo's protest. Though the diary concentrates on Anna alone, contemporary readers unquestionably read it with the discordant theorizing of their day squarely before their eyes. The effects of this discord they often knew only too well from personal experience.

They knew also that Anna represented the many others ensnared in the House of Converts, the majority of whom had capitulated and converted. Their empathy with Anna's mounting despair, but also their frustration with their own essential powerlessness—other than to plead through the agency of hopefully sympathetic lawyers—had to have ballooned as they relived Anna's distress, which, as Tranquillo portrays it, grows ever more terrifying with each passing day.

The joy readers no doubt felt with the diary's "happy ending" following Anna's release was also marred. They were under no illusion that anything in the Papal State was about to change, just as they knew that Anna's sojourn in the House of Converts destroyed the rest of her life, as was the lot of others who survived the same testing. Many Christians, too, were uncomfortable with this inevitable outcome, which they criticized openly. Yet for all the anger, so long as the Papal State continued to exist, trials like Anna's and the Jews' maddening confusion spawned by being at once citizens, yet still disenfranchised, would not end. That would happen only with that state's demise and the founding of an Italy united by a monarchy on September 20, 1870, the day on which the ghetto itself became a thing of the past.

These are the themes treated in the following pages. With little fanfare, apart from some introductory pages, the reader will meet the diary in its full translation head on. The succeeding chapters will elaborate on the diary's background, setting, and implications, discussing the Roman Ghetto, the confessional state, the travails of the Roman Jewish Community as a body, and the growing opposition to the papal stance. The book closes with some brief reflections on what came after. Did the century after the diary's release bring with it substantial and lasting change? My hope is to have furnished today's readers with the tools they need to understand the diary in the same way that readers did in Anna and Tranquillo's day.

1. The Diary

On May 6, 1749, papal police seized Anna del Monte and carried her away from the ghetto, where Rome's Jews had been forced to live since 1555. They brought her to the Roman House of Converts, the *Casa dei catecumeni*— Roman Jews called it the *Catecumeni*—where potential converts were instructed and baptized. Anna was urged repeatedly, but unsuccessfully, to accept baptism. On the thirteenth day, she was released, to return to the ghetto a Jew.

To us, in the twenty-first century, for whom religion is a question of individual choice, this scenario is perverse. However, Anna del Monte lived in the mid-eighteenth century, in Rome, closed within ghetto walls; and like all other Jews in that city, she was constantly pressed to renounce Judaism and accept Christianity. Conversionary activities in Anna's day were intense, and, at times, violent. When preachers, accompanied by the papal police, the *sbirri*, came knocking at her door, Anna had no option of closing it, however politely, in their face. But she did resist. She also left us a record of her experiences, which her brother Tranquillo del Monte heavily edited and began to circulate in a handwritten copy in 1793, years after Anna's death.[1] This record, properly titled Anna's *Ratto*, her kidnapping, but often called her diary, furnishes unique testimony to Roman Jewry's late eighteenth-century plight.

Anna was not alone. Others, too, were dragged into the *Catecumeni*. We have no precise count, but theoretical discussions make it clear their

---

1. On Tranquillo, see *Archivio mediovale e moderno, fondo (AMM)*, *Università degli ebrei di Roma (Archivio Storico della Comunità Ebraica di Roma)*, henceforth, ASCER, b. 2Oe 7 sup 3, fasc 1, 1799; 2Sd 9 sup 3, fasc. 1, 1793; and 2Vm 10 sup 2 fasc. 04.

number was not small. The common fortune of these women is instructive, an unhappy fate, which even Christians lamented. Jewish men, the ghetto's chosen leaders, struggled to defend them, however, mostly, but not always, in vain. Tranquillo del Monte went a step further. He used his sister's story as a vehicle for making a protest. He had had enough of what, for him, was Roman Jewry's absurd condition. Through his correspondence with Jewish communities as far away as London and Amsterdam, he had learned of the enormous gap separating the increasingly desperate straits of Roman Jewry from the vast improvements in rights and civic standing recently won by the Jews of Western Europe and the new United States.

Tranquillo also witnessed the struggles going on in the contemporary Church as it was being put upon by modernizing states seeking to acquire for themselves powers once judged to belong exclusively to the Church.[2] Part of the reaction, part of the Church's drive to reassert itself, was a series of restrictive edicts against Jews, alongside a renewed emphasis on the conversionary policies that it took to symbolize its invincibility. It was only a matter of time before somebody in the Roman Jewish Community spoke out, which is what Anna's brother Tranquillo did by circulating his sister's diary.

That Tranquillo, or somebody like him, would speak out in 1793, four years into the French Revolution, might have been expected. How, Tranquillo must have asked himself, can Jews be as they are in Rome, while in France, north of the Alps, they have been granted equal legal rights along with all other citizens? Even in the German lands ruled by the Austrian Habsburgs, Emperor Joseph II was revising and, in his mind, bettering Jewish privileges. The Habsburgs were also the rulers of the Italian duchy of Mantua and the city of Venice, not to mention Tuscany, so physically close to Rome, where traditional prohibitions began to be relaxed about 1780. This was a changing world, and Roman Jews were keeping track of the changes. Collected in their communal archives are copies of the expanded privileges accorded Jews elsewhere,[3] liberalizations of which Roman Jews could only

2. The most recent full-length study of the Mortara case is David Kertzer, *The Kidnapping of Edgardo Mortara* (New York, 1997). See also JTS microfilm 4026a, pdf, page 163, for brief references to this episode.
3. For this collection, see ASCER, b. 2Za 10 sup 2, nn. 121, 158, 162, 163, 179, 184. Communications were also maintained with various communities, for instance, Livorno, which reported in 1800 the results of an unsuccessful appeal to Amsterdam; ASCER, b. 1Zi 2 inf 4, 17 Feb 1800, Livorno: *"nella quale vedranno la risoluzione di quel congresso di non trovarsi presentemente in stato da poter soccorrere alli loro bisogni, tutto contrario di quello che fecero sapermi con altra loro precedente lettera del 20 settembre anno passato...."*

dream. In the meantime, the order of the day was to hold fast and mount a defense. Never to yield is one of the diary's central messages, which it does by recounting the fine points of Anna's incarceration, a term she herself uses repeatedly. Anna's experience in the House of Converts as told by the diary may make us think of the kind of pressures to which prisoners of war are subjected and of how easily they can be made to adopt their captors' ideologies.

Anna's kidnapping also took place at a trying moment for the kidnappers themselves. New eighteenth-century thinking that promoted the "inalienable rights of mankind" was threatening not only ecclesiastical power, but, even more, the Church's claim to possess the single, absolute truth. A prime defense was in the accession of new believers, especially Jews, which, for the Church, was a font of reassurance. Eliminating the perpetual "affront" posed by the refusal of the Jews to enter the Christian fold would also validate the Church's claims to supersession, of having replaced the Jews as God's chosen.[4] All the more reason "to kidnap" young women like Anna and hold them in a place like the *Casa dei catecumeni*.

Little is known of what went on in this place. Its doings were not on the public record. There are only third-hand accounts of resistance and, mostly, capitulation. Anna's diary conveys details, especially about what potential *neofiti*, new converts, heard. She was told that Jesus is the messiah, that she should convert and save her soul, and that Judaism is the source of eternal damnation. The message was straightforward, but its particulars, the content of the preaching, for preaching it was, can be pieced together only from the published writings of catechizers, themselves usually converts.[5] As for Anna, the diary ascribes to her feelings of exquisite horror, but also detestation. There was nothing in her experience in the *Casa,* whether it be the surroundings, the people, the preaching, and its manner of delivery, but especially the preachers' message, that she did not find repugnant.

Anna's stay at the *Casa* was divided into a series of interviews. She saw preachers, she saw high clerics, she saw converts, especially women, and

4. On the continuity or break in these older motifs at this time, see Marina Beer and Anna Foa, eds., *Ebrei, minoranze e Risorgimento: Storia, cultura e Letteratura* (Rome, 2013), esp. the three closing essays: Valerio De Cesaris, "Cattolici, gli ebrei e l'«ebreo»: Note su antigiudaismo e filogiudaismo in Italia"; Gabriele Rigano, "Antigiudaismo e antisemitismo: elementi per un dibattito storiografico"; and Renato Moro, "Antigiudaismo e antisemitismo: continuità e/o rotture." My own feeling is that the older motifs were transformed, not replaced. The constant is the threat to the body of the faithful, however this term is defined.

5. See the full summary of the tract of Lorenzo Virgulti in Appendix IV.

she saw nuns. They appeared and preached and preached some more. Some were conciliatory, but one visitor threatened physical violence. There were ultimatums: today, she was told, you will convert. There were promises of riches and a fine marriage to someone of a social state to which even she, the daughter of a well-off ghetto family, could otherwise never pretend. An ornate carriage with riders and elegant ladies would carry her to the baptismal font. This last, which is a motif in many tales of anticipated baptism, may have been accurate. Baptismal ceremonies were often grand affairs, attended by the cream of society, with a high prelate, even the pope himself, or a direct representative, in attendance, sometimes serving as godfather, or spiritual protector, creating, ideally, a lifelong bond of commitment to the new Christian.[6]

What Anna experienced most was the attempt to outwit her, to trap her into professing what she neither felt nor intended. Today, one thinks of conversion, whatever its motives, as an act of will, of a person abandoning what was and electing a new future, achieving a sense of spiritual peace, and becoming confident about an unknown future. This is not what conversion meant for most in the past.[7]

Anna, who was about seventeen or eighteen years old at the time of her kidnapping, is presented telling her story in the first person.[8] Of the two other people she mentions, one was the man who claimed to be her fiancé and had "offered" her to the *Casa*. The second was his sister. Both, as we know from the register of converts prepared by Rudt de Collenberg, had willingly converted, although, unusually, the sister preceded the brother.[9] Men in a family normally converted first, followed by the women, who were often cajoled or left with no choice.

We know Anna's family. Her grandfather Angelo Zevi was once one of the Roman Jewish Community's three *Fattori*, as would be Tranquillo in 1793, and it was in this guise that he shaped his sister's diary into an instrument for fighting back, a manual for those who might find themselves

6. See Kenneth Stow, *Catholic Thought and Papal Jewry Policy, 1555–1593* (New York, 1977), 198–210.

7. See Kenneth Stow, "Church, Conversion, and Tradition: The Problem of Jewish Conversion in Sixteenth-Century Italy," *Dimensioni e problemi della ricerca storica* 2 (1996): 25–34.

8. Giuseppe Sermoneta, *Ratto della Signora Anna del Monte* (Rome, 1989), 47, that "the manuscript continuously passes from direct to indirect discourse," a problem I have tried to overcome in the translation to avoid readers' confusion without distorting the actual text.

9. For the names of converts, including Sabato Coen, but not Anna, see W. H. Rudt de Collenberg, "Le baptême des juifs à Rome de 1614 à 1798 selon les registres de la 'Casa dei catecumeni,'" *Archivum Historiae Pontificiae* 24 (1986): 91–231; 25 (1987): 105–262.

in Anna's place.[10] The message is blunt: expect the worst, but hold fast and, if incarcerated in the *Casa*, admit to nothing, not even to believing in God. They will say that God is Christ and that your admission is one of Christian belief. You will be baptized on the spot. Yet however much Anna herself was aware of the dangers, when preachers and others in the House of Converts came to persuade Anna to turn her life upside down—to become a *sacco revoltato*, a bag turned inside out, as Jews in Rome often sarcastically referred to converts—she must have panicked.

To complicate matters, Anna probably had little historical sense. She knew her present. She may have known that the ghetto had not always existed, but surely she did not know what things had been like two hundred years earlier. Her present was composed of Jews living in a ghetto, many of them poor, yet firmly Jews. Abandoning Judaism was the act of traitors, albeit the traitors were many. As for Catholicism, like most ghetto Jews, Anna probably thought of it as a jumble of unfathomable ceremonies and magic. Tradition called it idolatry. She was unquestionably bewildered. Nonetheless, as the diary testifies, her vague knowledge of saints and Christian salvation was about to undergo an intensely distasteful thirteen-day "crash course."

The "Ratto"

The bulk of what the diary has to tell us is real. Thanks to a census of 1733, we know what till now has been a matter of speculation, that Anna was a real person; she was born in 1732 and died sometime before (shortly, it seems) 1779.[11] The names in the diary are those of actual people, playing their real-life roles, and the core of the diary is no fiction: One could not purport, even in a work of polemic or literary intention, to say that a young woman who came from a prominent family and was known to all had been kidnapped

10. ASCER, Varia, contain the following names for Del Monte family members at this time. I thank Katherine Aron-Beller for eliciting: Angelo del Monte, Angelo di Salvador del Monte, Angelo di Prospero del Monte, Consolo del Monte, Crescenzio del Monte, Donna del Monte, Gabriel del Monte, Jacobbo del Monte, Israel di Leon del Monte, Israel di Sabbato del Monte, Moise di Giuseppe del Monte, Rubbeno del Monte, Ricca del Monte. Some of these people's names appear in the 1733 census, but we know little, if anything, else about them, although it is known that Anna's grandfather Angelo Zevi was once a *Fattore*, as was her brother Tranquillo in 1785, 1787, 1791, 1793, 1796, 1798/99; see Sermoneta, *Ratto*, 39; also ASCER, b. 2Vm 10 sup 2, fasc. 4, and b. 2Oe 7 sup 3, fasc. 4, n. 222, for 1799.

11. According to the 1733 census, transcribed by Manuela Militi, "Descriptio Hebreorum, Trascrizione," in *Gli abitanti del ghetto*, ed. Angela Groppi (Rome, 2015).

and taken into the House of Converts, had such a kidnapping never occurred.
Nor could one say that Anna did not emerge still Jewish after her sojourn in
the *Casa dei catecumeni,* had she converted. The particulars to which we are
made privy of what Anna went through in the *Casa,* however reworked and
probably reordered to create dramatic tension, are also too vivid to imagine
that they are the product of a writer who had *not* spent many days within its
walls. It is entirely plausible that Anna, as the diary's introduction states, did
write down her recollections when she returned home.

However, to accept at face value the events as the diary tells them is
another matter. Tranquillo's additions to Anna's original are patent, subtly
addressing the hurdles she, as an individual, would have had to cross over;
they also point to additional trials the Roman Jewish Community as a whole
was forced to undergo each time it confronted a crisis like Anna's. The reader
is asked to read not only the text of the diary, but the accompanying explan-
atory notes, which explore vocabulary and other technicalities. The essence
of the introduction is as follows:

> My dear one, may her memory be for a blessing, with her own hand
> wrote down in great detail what had happened during those days [of
> May 1749 while she was in the *Casa*]. But as soon has she had done
> this, she never wanted to hear or speak about it again. And once,
> when she was pressed to give us the book, she nearly fainted in my
> arms. So we decided to leave the matter behind, thinking, after she
> had passed to her eternal repose, that we would find [the book] in the
> house. But all our efforts failed. We would have asked the celebrated
> Signor Dr. Sabbato Moisè Mieli (a second-generation member of
> the academy founded by Tranquillo Corcos, the most famous rabbi
> of the ghetto period), who had assisted my dear one as she made her
> transcription, but [just before we did] he died, suddenly. [His books
> passed to his maternal brother David Calò, who also died, and then
> to a third brother, Abram Elia, a total boor, who sold the book to a
> certain Caciaro Amadio di Segni, who, in turn, was about to dispose
> of the book when I came running after him, *mi portai nell'istante,*
> and bought the book, to discover it was what my heart was search-
> ing for.] There were four fascicles, each with eight folios, and one
> of them, I discovered upon reading, contained my sister's tale retold
> in *ottava rima* and in the hand of R. Sabbato Moisè Mieli, may the

memory of the righteous be for a blessing. But four days [of events] were missing, which I then filled in [hopefully without errors].[12]

Giuseppe Sermoneta, the diary's modern editor, was rightly uncomfortable. It was a mystery why Tranquillo would have concocted the "treasure hunt," hinting that the rest of the diary was invented as well. Nonetheless, Tranquillo writes that the diary was to be preserved as a family chronicle. This was a style of literature well known from the time of the Renaissance, and there was also a distinguished Italian Jewish predecessor, the *Megillat yuhasin* (the family tree) known as the *Megillat Ahimaaẓ, The Scroll of Ahimaaẓ*, composed in the eleventh century in southern Oria, halfway between Taranto and Brindisi, although it is doubtful Tranquillo knew of its existence. Yet as a family chronicle that may have survived in no more than a single copy even after Tranquillo circulated it, it stretches credibility to imagine that Anna's diary was created out of whole cloth.

We may also be certain that what Tranquillo says of the parallel, poetic rendering that follows the prose diary in the surviving manuscript is correct. It is the product of two authors, Moisè Mieli and Tranquillo. The break in styles is sharp. Tranquillo, though he writes as an educated person, does little more than follow the diary in poetic strophes. Moisè Mieli, whom the diary says helped Anna transcribe her original notes, introduces embellishments, which also demonstrate his knowledge of classic vulgar (Italian) and Latin literature by way of frequent classical allusions.[13] Possibly, the poetry came first and then the prose, the latter being a reworking of the poetic original. Mieli's text was accessible only to the ghetto's very limited elite. So depleted intellectually was the ghetto, certainly with respect to *halakhic*, Jewish legal, expertise, that shortly after the diary's circulation, a foreigner, Leon di Lion, from Hebron in the Land of Israel, was appointed chief rabbi.[14]

12. Eight iambic lines, usually pentameters, namely, five poetic "feet" of an unstressed followed by a stressed syllable, frequently, for example, found in the work of Shakespeare.

13. On Mieli, including bibliographical references, see Sermoneta, *Ratto*, 22, n. 2, and for classical references in Mieli's poem, *Ratto*, 110–11, among others. Mieli died in early 1779. For women, as well as men, actively involved in Italian and Italian Jewish culture, see recently, Dan Harrán, *Jewish Poet and Intellectual in Seventeenth-Century Venice: The Works of Sarra Copia Sulam in Verse and Prose*, along with *Writings of Her Contemporaries* (Chicago, 2009). Sara was exceptional, but many Jewish women were apprenticed to learn fine embroidery; their mistresses were to teach them to read as well, which may have been not only for saying prayers, but in order to embroider biblical verses on Torah covers and cloths made to cover the *bimah* (reader's stand in the synagogue).

14. ASCER, b. 2Sd 9 sup 3, fasc. 5, for November 8, 1795, describes this rabbinic appointment.

Both Tranquillo and Mieli, but especially the former, could have drawn on, and enhanced, a number of authenticated parallels, just as they may have also read and taken advantage of contemporary biographical fictions and romances to embroider Anna's own account by adding suggestive phrases, irony, suspense, and tension, as well as structuring the tale so that these qualities stand out ever more greatly as the narrative progresses. Theology, Jewish and Christian, even canon law, Hebrew Psalms, and folk beliefs are there, too, as will be pointed out in the notes to the translation.

In at least two critical moments toward the end of the diary, there is clear manipulation. First, the "happy ending," which is so contradictory to what many Christian commentators were saying about the sad lot of kidnapped young women; Anna's triumphant return home is "too good to be true." It is also almost assuredly copied from a similar story told about a young girl in the city of Cuneo in northern Piedmont.[15] Second is the interview Anna has with the Vice Regent—the bishop or archbishop responsible for running the city of Rome and its institutions, including the *Casa*—in which the latter apologizes. We are taken back to the world of Renaissance Jewish "historical writing" and memory, in particular to the dialogues found in Ibn Verga's *Shebet Jehudah* between Jews and high ecclesiastical officials or even between Christian theologians and royalty.[16] Jewish writers of the past had always added details and sometimes imagined events.

One may also, if most tentatively, refer to a Jewish genre. In 1788, a tale similar to Anna's was composed in Hungary; the surviving text is in German, but the original may have been in Yiddish, or even Hebrew. It is the story of a young girl, baptized as a baby by a midwife or nurse, but whose baptism came out only when a local priest related the events eleven years later following an edict by the king (which king is not said, but neither was the edict real) demanding the forcible baptism of all Jews. The girl is taken to two or three locations and pressed mightily, but she never yields, while all the time, like Anna, she cries out that she be returned to her family.[17] It

---

15. We will soon discuss this story and its origins.
16. Solomon ibn Verga, *Shebet Yehudah*, ed. A. Shohat, intro. Y. Baer (Jerusalem, 1947), chapters 12 and 13, among others. Most recently on the literary qualities of the Shebet Yehudah, see David A. Wacks, *Double Diaspora in Sephardic Literature: Jewish Cultural Production before and after 1492* (Bloomington, 2015), 151–75, who also summarizes previous literature in this vein.
17. H. Flesch, "An Eighteenth-Century Narrative of the Attempted Conversion of a Jewish Girl in the Time of Maria Theresa," *Jewish Quarterly Review*, n.s., 15.3 (1925): 389–407; I thank Michael Silber for this reference.

would be tempting to generalize, but for the moment, we must hesitate. It is hard to imagine that Tranquillo knew this text. Not only was its setting far removed from Rome, but to assume Tranquillo knew German or Yiddish (neither of which was known or spoken in Rome, where the Jewish jargon was Judaeo-Romanesco) asks too much. Besides, even had he known the tale, it was a pure fiction (except for the report of a secret baptism, of which the examples in Rome were many).

In the event, Jews did not slavishly copy what they observed "outside," which was a great deal. Rather, they adopted what suited them, often modifying it to give it a "Jewish identity." Anna's diary follows this formula well: selective appropriation, then modification to meet the narrative's needs. By its very existence the diary testifies to Roman Jewry's continuing cultural integrity, matched by its awareness of a world beyond the ghetto and the Papal State that was so quickly changing its spots, while Rome, Jewish and non-Jewish alike, remained immobile, unchanging with the times.

At the start of the introduction, Tranquillo writes that Sabato Coen (pronounced Co-en), motivated by his hatred for Tranquillo's father, converted and, armed with two false testimonies, went before the Vice Regent and "presented Anna as *Sua Sposa*," his wife.[18] The year was 1749; Tranquillo at one point writes 1795, but this was most likely a slip of the pen, not an esoteric signal as has been conjectured.[19] The Bargello (the sheriff), we are told, showed up with pistols drawn, and despite the protests of the *Fattori*, Anna was taken away: at the start of the diary itself, Anna says the Bargello pointed the gun at her father's chest to keep her from talking to him. The tension is palpable, as are the emotions. This fellow, comments Tranquillo, was "contrary to the Nation."[20] If the Bargello was doing his legal duty, he

18. Tranquillo is confusing here. He had to have known that as a "wife," Anna would have been "offered" and held for forty days, about which the diary has no hint. We would do well to take this inconsistency as demonstration that the diary as we have it is highly edited.

19. Anna begins her tale with May 20. One could spend a goodly chunk of time on these inconsistencies, but I believe there is no easy resolution, and the "slip of the pen" remains a possibility. See Giuseppe Sermoneta's full edition of the *Ratto* for a thorough examination of the issue. Caffiero's *Rubare le anime* says plainly that it is a reprint of Sermoneta, not a new edition. The diary appears on pp. 49–105 (about 20–25 pages of text without notes) of Sermoneta's version; the page numbers in Caffiero are perforce different. To avoid confusion on the part of readers in Italian using one edition or the other, I follow the diary and refer to days.

20. "Nation" as used here derives from *natio*'s original meaning as "birth group." The term was then common among Jewish communities for self-reference. Historians are most familiar with this term as applied to themselves by the Jews of early modern Amsterdam. However, note that at the sixteenth-century Church Council of Trent, we are informed that the delegates sat in *nationes*. In the event, the term has no relation to its current use referring to a country.

was doing it with animus. Tranquillo proceeds with the account we just read of how the diary was rescued from oblivion, miraculously saved after having been lost for years. At this point, the diary commences.

What follows now is a full translation, with copious notes, some to parallel literature, but most reflecting on either the meanings of words or the import of the ideas in the text. Standard punctuation will be applied. Double quotation marks are for quotations *marked as such in the original diary transcript,* not added by me, which signify the words of preachers or of Anna herself as she recalls and cites them.[21] Italian words, Hebrew that appears in the original text and is here translated, or an occasional simple meaning appear in parentheses; the rare paraphrase is, by convention, set off by square brackets.[22] The diary's text:[23]

21. See again Sermoneta, *Ratto,* 47, on language and punctuation in the diary.
22. Sermoneta's notes often point these meanings out.
23. I have chosen to set the text in normal typeface because of its length, rather than in italics, as opposed to the one long comment on the following page, which is set in italics to alert the reader.

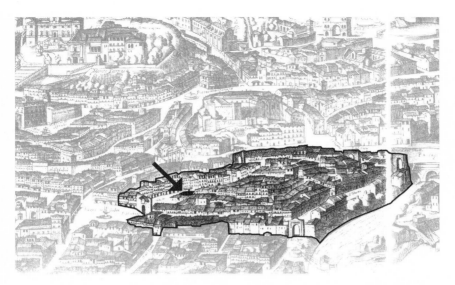

The Roman Ghetto with probable location of the Del Monte home superimposed on Tempesta's *Veduta di Roma*. Reconstruction by Micol Ferrara.

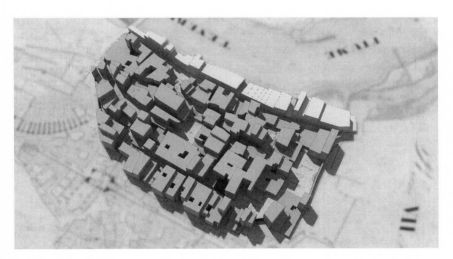

Visual reconstruction of the Roman Ghetto with the Del Monte home, in a unique two-story structure, prominently marked. Reconstruction by Micol Ferrara.

The probable location and dimensions of the home of Anna del Monte have been deduced by examining the census of 1733 and contrasting this information with what is known from a full survey (*catasto*) of the Rione S. Angelo (the St. Angelo district) of Rome from 1816. The results have been superimposed on a map, the *Veduta di Roma* (View of Rome) by A. Tempesta. The house is located in the upper quadrant of the Ghetto. Despite known changes in buildings in this area, this building was never amplified in height, which allowed searching a nineteenth-century land-registry to determine the building's exact location, which was near the main entrance to the Ghetto's principal square, the Piazza Giudia.

The Kidnapping of Anna del Monte

Without warning, on the 20th of April, 1749, at the end of the Pass-over Festival, Sunday, at about 17 hours,[24] I was kidnapped and taken away by force thanks to a false denunciation made against my family by a scoundrel (Hebrew original in the diary's text *rash'a*). I was totally innocent,[25] but he tricked the Vice Regent into issuing an order that led straightaway to the Bargello and his men bursting into my home and seizing me. They sandwiched me in between them with their pistols drawn. They did not even give me the courtesy, or the time, to change my clothing, or to say a word to my mother and father, as though I were a whore, slapping everybody around, and paying no attention to people's rank or even their state of health.[26] They snapped me up like a *guitta* (a buffoon) in such haste that I still had on my *abito di cucina* (my apron).[27] When my father tried to speak to me, they shoved a pistol into his face. Only God saved his life. I was pushed into a carriage next to the Bargello and taken with the speed of the wind to the *Casa dei catecumeni*. When we arrived at the *Casa*, I was put into the hands of the Prioress, who took me by the hand. She led me into a small room, which had a small bed, for one person, a little table, with a drawer for food, which could be locked.[28] I was left alone, until the Prioress appeared for the first time to visit me, telling me to pray to God that I be illuminated [to convert], and to be contrite. I responded boldly, and with pluck, that I had already been illuminated, and I had no intention of being deceived to desert the religion into which I was born. Each time she approached me, with the same priest,[29] I told her that I was

24. About noontime: days were divided into two twelve-hour periods determined by day and night. For precise equivalents between Italian and common hours, even well into the modern period, see Roberti Colzi, *Che ora è?*, privately distributed. I thank the late Giancarlo Spizzichino for providing me with a copy.

25. I had not done what was said of me, namely, expressed a desire to convert.

26. Though Jews were forbidden to be treated as *signori*, the ghetto did have its upper crust, which expected to be treated as befitting this state.

27. The precise meaning is "as a miserable person," but in a disparaging sense. One dictionary gives "buffoon." The word will repeat toward the end of the diary. Anna may mean they took me while I looked ridiculous, since she was still wearing a house-dress.

28. Anna's immediate surroundings, composed of "small" and "little" things, reinforce her sense of being hemmed in.

29. Likely, there is an error in the text, for previously, no priest has been mentioned.

committed [to be faithful] to His Divine Majesty, praying that He give me the strength and grace to return to the arms of my parents and to their belief, and that I would be happy should I be considered worthy in the true light of our Holy Sabbath. Ignoring me, the Prioress brought with her some young woman convert to disturb my peace [and shake my faith]. However, imagining the great damage such company might bring, I made up my mind to carry on alone, should I be allowed it, rather than share the company of that awful class of person.[30]

That same day, after *pranzo*,[31] I was visited by the Vice Regent,[32] who asked me whether I had ever had [sexual] relations with a young Jew in the ghetto. I replied that I was immune and innocent. He repeated his question, saying, "Dear Child, do not be embarrassed to tell me the truth. This is common. It is found in all girls, including [you] Jews, and possibly you yourself. Here, you are no different from anybody else." I said: "We do not have young men in the house, and no one can claim to have conversed with me, whether in the house or outside, or even to have seen me at the window talking with another living

30. A comment here is appropriate to help the reader grasp the diary's structure. The Prioress was only the beginning. The madness of the House of Converts had its method. On Monday, the second day, Anna had but two visitors, a (parish) priest and an arch-priest, a high official, who told her how important her conversion was—for herself, but also for the Church. On Tuesday, she saw the arch-priest again. On Wednesday, she was left on her own, to think. This was the strategy in the first stages; let Anna wonder: about her Judaism, her future, but especially her whereabouts. Then, at the height of her mental anguish, Anna was bombarded: four days in a row, three or four visits each day, a total of fifty-four in all, by thirty-eight different people. Each visit lasted hours, about eighty in all—the most strenuous accompanied with endless preaching, at suggestive hours of the day like sunset. These were well-designed psychological games.

Anna was told that the pope himself had decided she must convert. This was an argument that Anna may have taken seriously. The highest authority in Rome in all matters, the pope had always been the Jews' last refuge, albeit at the price of submission to his strict (sometimes overly strict) regime. When Anna heard there was an order from the pope, the inertia of centuries of obedience may have led her to think twice.

Anna records what happened to her day by day. The theme is straightforward. Repeatedly, Anna was asked, first by the Prioress of the House of Converts and then a preacher, himself a convert: "Did she not want salvare l'Anima?" But Anna knew better than to respond. "I zipped my lips," she tell us, "[which infuriated the preacher], who jumped at me, saying why didn't I say something, that I believed in the God of Israel (a trap, since this would be taken as belief in the Trinity, and she would have been baptized). Leave me in peace," I said: "I was born a Jew and want to die the same. Please be silent and go" (as they always did. This performance took place daily, and more than once).

31. Luncheon, the main meal—and what in the world did Anna eat; the food was not kosher, and the probability that Anna had ever eaten non-kosher food was almost inexistent; the reference may also be only to the time of day.

32. The official actually in charge of all of Rome's Jews, a monsignor, Cardinal de Rossi; he answered directly to the pope and was responsible for many municipal services.

soul.[33] Here, we are different from you [Christians]. Our young women never leave the house [unaccompanied] before they are married. It should be clear to Your Illustriousness that I ever never had anything to do with anyone." He then took his leave, telling me that I should pray for God's illumination.[34]

At the 24th hour (about 7:30 p.m.), a neophyte I did not know entered.[35] He looked to me like a *stregone* [a male witch], and he let me know that not only was he originally a Jew, but that he had preached to the Jews every Sabbath in the synagogue in Ancona. "But then I was illuminated by the true faith, and I left my first Law to become a Catholic, for this is the true faith; and I have come here so that with my help, you, too, can recognize the truth."[36] He then began to preach, accompanied by two other priests, trying to confute our most Holy Torah and our Prophets.[37] I, for my part, stood silent and did not respond.

Seeing me like this, he was infuriated and jumped at me, putting his hands on my eyes, saying why didn't I say something, that I believed in the God of Israel.[38] I, fearing his arrogance, answered in a whisper: "Please leave me in peace. I believe nothing, just what my parents believe. I was born a Jew and want to die the same, and I don't need your preaching, so please be silent and go." This *rasha*, this villain and scoundrel,[39] boasted: "I have had the good fortune to convert others, and so I hope to convert you, too." I, with the help of God, behaved courageously and told him he could go on all he wanted, night and day. It would be a waste of breath. Then I grew quiet and stopped responding while he continued expounding prophecies, saying that had he not seen and touched the truth with his own hands, he

33. By *outside* she must mean *unaccompanied;* compare the story below of Olimpia Pippi.
34. The Vice Regent was no doubt aiming at getting Anna to admit to a relationship with Sabato, allowing a claim that she and Sabato were actually betrothed and, hence, entitling authorities to keep her for a full quarantine (forty days), and likely more. Anna cleverly avoided the trap.
35. What does Anna mean by "I did not know"? I suspect it refers to the *neofiti* who preached to the Jews regularly in Rome, and, as such, *were* well known. Otherwise, we may suspect she had previous knowledge of the *Casa* and its familiars, which would be a whole new twist, but one I believe is doubtful.
36. Here, as elsewhere in the diary, and as Sermoneta himself observed, the text switches from third to first person with no punctuation. The reader should be alerted that this is the pattern of the original, not a flaw of the editor or translator.
37. Was this fellow the same Jew—now *neofito*—whom Benedict XIV mentions, as we shall see, in his bull *Postremo mense?* Very possibly.
38. Again, the same trap.
39. This is the same term, written here in Hebrew, that Anna uses when she first refers to Sabato.

would not have taken up the true Catholic faith, because of which, he
said: "I have come here to show you the light, to save your soul, *salvare
l'Anima.*" For my part, I let him go on, while I never answered, and he,
seeing me so obstinate, began to threaten. He said he would go to the
pope, which caught me off guard (*a me fece molto specie*). After about
three hours, he left menacingly, along with the two other priests, saying that if I did not make an effort to believe in the God of Israel,[40] I
could stay that way [in the *Casa*] for one hundred years. He turned on
his heels and left in bad spirits.

The Prioress reentered as they left and spoke sweetly, asking me
what I wished to eat for dinner. I requested two eggs,[41] even though
I did not have the strength to drink even water. To keep count of the
days, I saved an egg a day.[42] The Prioress then returned with a lamp.
It had enough oil to burn for two hours, and I was able to say my de-
votions.[43] Then, finding myself alone without light, I burst out into
tears, calling out contritely: "Keep from me you evil doers, for God
has heard the sound of my lament."[44] Then I threw myself on the bed,
desperately, without undressing, but I could find neither peace nor rest.
The great sorrow and pain I felt in my soul made sleep fly from my
eyes the whole night, and bitterly I saw daylight appear.

It was the next (the second) morning. I arose and trusted myself
to God. (Another priest, called) the Padre Curato, came and began to
preach about the three boys thrown into the furnace by Nebuchadnez-
zer, Hananiah, Misha'el, and Azariah, just as Daniel was thrown into
the Lion's den (lit., *pozzo*, or well) and saved miraculously by His Divine Majesty through the agency of an angel, thanks to their goodness
and faith in Divine worship. Just so (he said) you can be (saved), finding yourself in this place of holiness (the *Casa*) and in our hands, we
who are here to pray for the salvation of your soul. It will be for your
good, just as it was for them. My child, take my words to heart, if you

40. "Israel" is written in Hebrew letters. Note the play. They mean Christ as the God of Israel.
41. Always kosher, especially if consumed raw.
42. Count of the days, of course. Tranquillo is possibly suggesting a strategy for those ensnared. He may also be warning Jews to be prepared, to know, for example, the rules of detention, whether twelve or forty days. Anna easily could have lost count on her own, increasing
resignation and the chance of capitulation. Can we assume this much? I think so.
43. The link between the light and the prayers is vague; Anna did not have a prayer book in
the cell.
44. Psalm 6:9: the diary brings the original Hebrew.

wish to be in the grace of God like these four. And with this I take my leave, praying to God to illuminate you and that you follow this way (lit., and you do the same). Respond to me, at least. If you say what I now recite, I will be beholden to you. Respond, I ask you. To whom I said acerbically, I never miss an opportunity to pray to God: to get me out of this jail and allow me to return to my family as a Jew.[45] At which, he left in a bad mood, stamping his foot and berating my obstinacy. So much for the second day.

The third day, a Tuesday, the Archpriest of San Celso began again to preach a new sermon, starting with the verse (from Genesis 12:1) telling Abram to leave his land of birth and all he would inherit in order to be in God's grace, to leave behind his faith and to recognize the true belief in the Divine cult.[46] And good father Abram, disregarding all he had acquired and all that was coming to him from his fathers, obeyed the Divine precept.[47] So, dear daughter, do the same. Leave your possessions, Father, Mother, and all they own in this world to recognize the true God and save your soul. I understand how you feel, how much it disturbs you to leave your home and parents, but (know that) all you leave is nothing compared to what you will have from the Christians. Whatever you have now, you will have twice,[48] indeed, a hundred times more than what you leave behind.[49] You will have enjoyment not only in this world, but in the future one, too, among the angels in Paradise. Do you not see the misery of your nation, which is endlessly vexed, abandoned by God and man? No priest, no altar or

45. Note the chutzpah [the cheek, gall] of Anna, saying, yes, she would pray, but for just the opposite of what was asked. Note, too, the plea to return to her family. The plea reappears many times and is continuously paired with her insistence on remaining Jewish. More than nostalgia, this is a reminder that Anna was still a young woman—as we now know, about eighteen years old. Sequestrations like hers were destroying families besides threatening Jewish survival.

46. Likely a neophyte who had achieved success.

47. The verse is cited in Hebrew.

48. Experience, even the limited one of observing the economic straits of the *neofiti* who lived just outside the ghetto, told her this promise, which had been made for centuries, was patently false.

49. Promises of economic advantage appear as early as the thirteenth century, on which see William Chester Jordan, "Learning about Jews in the Classroom: A Thirteenth-Century Witness; UCLA Library, Rouse MS 17," in *Envisioning Judaism: Studies in Honor of Peter Schaefer on the Occasion of His Seventieth Birthday*, ed. Ra'anan Boustan, Klauss Herrmann Reimund Leicht, Annette Yoshiko Reed, and Giuseppe Veltri (Tübingen, 2013), 1258. On convert poverty and pleas for subsidies, see Solomon Grayzel, *The Church and the Jews in the Thirteenth Century*, vol. 2, ed. Kenneth Stow (New York and Detroit, 1989), e.g., 82, 191.

sacrifices, dispersed to the four quarters of the world, slaves, subject to the powers and the nations and the peoples.[50] If your religion were true, as you believe, you would be honored and respected by all the nations, as you once were when you were in God's grace in Jerusalem, before the messiah came, in whom you do not believe.[51] Though you see the truth with your eyes and touch it with your hands, why do you still wish to lose it? I pray, with tears in my eyes, that God illumine you, to remove your obstinacy, which is the cause of your fall. Were it not for God and the Princes of the nations, the ground you are standing on would fall away. I beg you not to forfeit your soul as have the other Jews, to see in yourself and in your visage something of the angelic and to reside with our saints in Paradise should you embrace our true faith with a true heart. Take my words to heart, and this I tell you as I take my leave.

The fourth day, the same preacher arrived with a new sermon, beginning with our Mothers, Sarah, Rebecca, Rachel, and Lea, as well as Miriam the prophetess, trying to show that each of them had neglected the pleasures of this world for the salvation of their souls, starting with Sarah, who left father and mother and all her goods to flee from idolatry and embrace the Divine cult. And so he spoke about each, until he arrived at Rachel, how she stole the Terebinths from her father,[52] to keep him from idolatry.[53] You should do the same to make yourself a good Catholic and to persuade your family, too. I [Anna] do not want to go on and on, so I will not repeat all I was forced to hear during three hours, while, all the while, I prayed that God save me from being ensnared, as I recited Psalm 25:15: "My eyes are ever on God, who will free my limbs from the net."[54] But when the preacher left, I was in shock and half dead. I took care to avoid a slip of the tongue that would prejudice my soul to say, and struggle to say, as little

50. As the Bible predicts and as your life in the ghetto tells you.

51. This is a cross between the traditional theology based on Genesis 49:10 that the scepter will depart from Judah when Shiloh comes—Shiloh is read by Christians as Christ—and hence Jews have no political rule, and the actual state of Jews is directly subject to ruling authorities. How the term *slaves* applied to Jews we will soon discuss.

52. The possessor of these statues held the title to all family property, but this is something known today, not then.

53. Implying Judaism is idolatry. Or is this Tranquillo's subtle way of reminding readers that Jews, for centuries, had called Christianity idolatry?

54. Here in Hebrew.

as possible, watching my words, so that I did not condemn myself.[55] I could think only of how my parents and family were suffering, compared to which, my incarceration and martyrdom, however weighty, paled.[56] I was afflicted even more by not being able to know, or to be told by anyone, what they and my poor Nation were going through after my departure. This fear was causing my greatest despair.

Thursday, the fifth day. This day a preacher presented himself to me, dressed shabbily, and with his hair falling in front of his eyes. His aspect was so fearful and ugly that he seemed like the devil emerged from Hell. He was like a Fury from Averno (the underworld), come to seize my soul.[57] I was so afraid that I shook from head to toe and looked down so I would not have to see him. He was haughty and warned me, saying, "Get it out of your head. You are in our hands, and either you be like us and believe in the true God, the one we believe in, or you are going to finish your days in our cloister. Forget about seeing your father, your mother, or any of your family.[58] If I wish, I will get the entire College of Cardinals and the pope himself to ensure you do not walk out of here as a victor, *vincitrice*." That said, he took a pitcher of *Acqua Santa* and threw it over me, saying that "this water has the power to make you convert." For my part, I struck my face with my hands and began to shout. "It will never happen that either my flesh or my face will accept a drop of this water as long as I am a Jew. I will have nothing to do with your water, nor with your superstitions. For my part, a dog may just as well have pissed on me."[59]

---

55. Words, which pronounced, would have exposed Anna to baptism, even against her desires; but note how she says the same thing in three different ways, to emphasize the danger, a note that is repeatedly hit in the diary.

56. By this point, Anna is terrified, a terror that grew when the preaching began to incorporate, as we are about to see, tactics verging on sadomasochism. Kindness is counterpoised by an assault on Anna's essence, hence the frequently repeated phrase *rubbare l'Anima*.

57. Averno; actually, a crater south of Naples thought to be the entrance to the underworld. The phrase *furia d'Averno* is a common one in Italian literature. The reference may also be to Mt. Aetna; Semoneta, *Ratto*, 43.

58. This threat, a reference to the rules prohibiting contact between Jews and converts, especially when Anna was told her family had abandoned her, might have shaken her; however, it may have worked in reverse to reinforce her resolve to remain a Jew, reminding her that conversion portended a total break with one's past. Admittedly, the rules prohibiting contact between converts and Jews were routinely violated, but Anna would have thought only of losing loved ones.

59. The legal plea of Olimpia Pippi's father, telling of untoward behavior: "ha patito sugestioni tali e è stata soggetta ad attioni e condotte così improprie," that she suffered from untoward comments and was made to put up with improper actions and conduct, suggests the picture of

To make me even more desperate, he took a chain out of his purse, which he called the Crown, and passed it again and again over my face and head, saying, "this is the chain that will bind your heart to our faith, and this is the water, which I now pour upon you a second time, which has the power to smother the infernal fire that has been prepared for (all) Jews. There is no way to make it grow cold other than by accepting this Holy Water with love." He repeated this performance nearly twenty times. Then he got down on his knees and began to pray, saying: "I now pray for you to throw off the dark cloud that throws shadows on your mind and intellect in the darkness of your belief. I hope that this very morning I will not leave without having converted you, and you will be [together with me] as one." I, hearing these words, began to fear very greatly and to shout bitterly, crying, with my eyes facing heavenward. I prayed to God that he give me the strength and save me from the hands of this rapacious, infernal, monstrous bear, who was trying *rubbarmi la Anima*, to steal my soul and rob me of my essence by force.[60]

For his part, not knowing what to do, he began again to spray me with water, saying he would convert me that very day. It was as though he had *impazzito*, gone crazy, repeating ugly verses. I could not get rid of him.[61] I could do nothing but cry and pray for release, saying from Psalm 119:134, "Redeem me from human oppression, that I may obey your precepts."[62] I was stunned, half dead, and that whole day I

Anna in the diary is true. Even if Tranquillo is manipulating, it is to warn or cry out for relief. What we cannot know is how close Anna, the real Anna, came to succumbing. Was she as convinced as the diary makes it seem that Christianity was a chimera, or was the thought of losing her identity and family the overwhelming emotion holding her back? What, moreover, is the goal of using words like *jail* and *incarceration*, or in calling the experience *martyrdom*? Perhaps, and most simply, because it was precisely that!

60. The diary spells *rubbare* with two *b*s. Caffiero, *Rubare le anime*, speaks perplexingly of stealing Anna's "free will" (*libro arbitrio*). The *exercise* of free will may be denied, but innate quality that it is, it itself can never be *stolen*. Rather, the meaning is as here. See also Malkiel, *"Ebraismo, tradizione,"* 38, who says Lampronti uses the very similar phrase *perdita di un'anima* in the simple sense of a convert; when conversion occurs, there is a "loss of a soul": in other words, a loss of identity. *Rubare l'anima* may mean nothing more than "to convert," which implies "losing identity." We must note in this context the letter from Paul III, of November 30, 1542, where he ordered the pregnant wife of the convert Alessandro (formerly Hananel, Nello) of Foligno to be brought to Rome, where "libera eius voluntas de via salutis. . . . scrutari potest"; Simonsohn, *Apostolic See*, no. 2197. The emphasis is on her expressing her "free will," not its theft ("stealing"), since baptism could be valid only if she willed it, at least with regard to rigorous theory.

61. See again the case of Olimpia Pippi on improper behavior by adepts of the *Casa*.

62. The diary itself inserts the Hebrew original, which again raises the question of Anna's intellectual preparation and the extent of Tranquillo's editing.

spent in tears. Moved by my piety, God made this fellow leave. If God had not gotten him out of there, with his bad humor, he would have brought me to kill myself. God liberated me from this diabolical *Mongibello* (inferno).[63]

Later on that day, six more priests came in, bringing with them the cursed sister of Sabato Coen, *yesh'u*.[64] Sabato was the one who made the false denunciation so that I might be robbed (of my identity: *rubbare*), but it was only after my release that I found out about him and that he was in cahoots with his sister. Seeing this grand flock, the Prioress welcomed them all and made them wait until one of the priests, [as always] a *neofito*, began to ask whether I believed in the God of Israel (written in Hebrew). I was fearful of answering, and he asked again, demanding to know why I remained silent. "I want to know only whether you believe in the God of Abraham, Isaac, and Jacob, and all the Prophets." Did I not know that God was the same for all? The statues in the Churches were only symbols of the real saints. Don't believe the rabbis who say the worship of saints is idolatry. You Jews do not want to believe that God (Jesus) is the messiah, whom you made a martyr and put on the cross, but who was the one your Sainted Ancestors as the Prophets recognized. Rabbinic charlatanism in the Talmud obscures the sun (*sole*) of the true faith, which these rabbis now recognize while they roast in eternal suffering, condemned because of their incredulity, with no hope.[65] The same will happen to you,

63. He was like [the still alive Sicilian volcano] Aetna, the mouth of Hell, on which term see Sermoneta, *Ratto*, 43, n. 18. The two references to Hades in this chapter are a reminder that Roman Jews considered Christianity an inversion of the truth, a path to perdition, not salvation.

64. This is an abbreviation with a *double entendre:* It is for *yimakh shemo vezikhrono*, may his memory be blotted out, but it also reads *Yeshu*, or Jesus. By contrast, Christians read the abbreviation as *yavo Shiloh velo* [Gen. 49:10], the messiah will come and [peoples will flock] to him. Coen is pronounced *Co-en*, with a long *e*.

65. The irony here is that Jews in Rome had not possessed copies of the Talmud (openly) for over two hundred years, since its burning in 1553. The priest is rehearsing the principal points of attack on Jewish literature that had been made beginning in the late twelfth century, indeed, as they had recently been repeated by Lucio Ferraris's *Prompta bibliotheca canonica, juridica, moralis, theologica* (1756), on which see Kenneth Stow, "Expulsion Italian Style: The Case of Lucio Ferraris," *Jewish History* 3.1 (1988): 51–63; Stow, "The Burning of the Talmud in 1553, in the Light of Sixteenth-Century Catholic Attitudes toward the Talmud," *Bibliothèque d'Humanisme et Renaissance* 34 (1972): 435–59; and especially Fausto Parente, "The Index, the Holy Office, the Condemnation of the Talmud, and Publication of Clement VIII's Index," in *Church, Censorship and Culture in Early Modern Italy,* ed. Gigliola Fragnito (Cambridge, 2001), chapter 7, which repeats Parente's essay in Italian in Corrado Vivanti, ed., *Storia d'Italia: Annali; Gli Ebrei in Italia,* vol. 1 (Turin: Einaudi, 1996).

if you ignore my prayers. Turn, therefore, and enjoy the eternity of
Paradiso. If you do as I say, you will believe in the same God who said
at Sinai I am the Lord your God (Exodus 20:20, in Hebrew). Because
you had that merit when you were in the grace of that God who said:
I (Hebrew), you were destined to obligate His Divine Majesty to do
wondrous things for you, as he did for you holy fathers. But you were
shockingly haughty, saying: *Giudio,* Jews, *gioja di Dio,* the joy of God.
This is a true heresy, for you are no longer those [in God's grace]. It is
we, who venerate him and adore him, and recognize the true God and
true messiah, whom you serve neither with your hearts nor your souls.
You do the opposite of all that He said through the mouths of the ancient prophets. You dare say that we believe in a God different from
yours, but this is all a lie that you Jews have made up, since we believe
in none other than Him who is found in heaven, earth, and the whole
world, as it is read in your Scripture: Who is in the heavens above and
the earth below, and in the waters under the earth (Exodus 20:4; in
Hebrew).

You call us idolaters. The idolaters are you, who falsify Scripture and interpret it as it suits you, wholly contrary to what God commanded. Were it up to me, I would burn all the Talmudists and their
books and false teachings, which are at the root of the flagellation of
your souls. Consider what I say, if you do not wish to consign your
soul to Hell. Others can say before the Divine Tribunal that they had
no one to teach them the true religion [but you cannot].[66] Dwell on this
well. And he left.

Friday evening, the same monster came back, to ensnare me just
at the hour, as he so well knew, that I had intended to welcome the Sabbath. After an hour and a half of preaching, which left me destroyed,
he took a little pail of water in his hand, which he said was blessed, and
began to spray it in every direction, on my back, my face, on the bed. I
could feel my flesh curling up, as though I were standing in the middle
of a fire. When this *stregone* finished making me miserable, another
frate arrived, whom they called the *Parrocchiano.* I did not know him,

---

66. This is a theological issue based on Psalm 18:5: *exivit sonus eorum,* read as the word of the
Gospel has filled the Earth. This verse galvanized missions following the New World discover-
ies of the sixteenth century. Now it was being applied to Jews in the *Casa,* if obliquely; see Stow,
Catholic Thought, chap. 11, passim.

but from the way he talked, he was clearly a *neofito,* who began to make me uneasy again, for about an hour.[67] Finally, one of the two left, and I was alone, in a solitary place, with the second, in the dark. I felt totally beaten down by these two *resha'im* (evil ones), one after the other. The great bitterness and passions they aroused created in me inexpressible pain. I was certain I would become ill.

Lacking the power to find some remedy, I threw myself on the bed. I begged the remaining curate to cease. I had no strength to listen to anybody. My head was spinning, and this was hardly an hour to try out catechisms. I was not about to convert, however long they kept it up. They could preach days and nights, but I would never renounce the faith of my mother and father. Speechless and unable to respond, the *frate* left, desperate (for his failure), while I was beside myself, this being the first time (I was alone) on a Shabbat. I tried to rest, but I was not granted repose.

Saturday morning, I awakened at the crack of dawn, after barely resting, dismayed, and confused about where I was. At that hour, my habit was to arise and prepare my clothing for the Holy Sabbath. But I was outside my home and far from my beloved parents and sisters who treat me not like a *femina,* but *even more* than a *maschio.*[68] Alone this way, jailed in this solitary place, despoiled of every hope, I could turn only to the Divine Majesty, as I did by throwing myself into prayer, asking Him to help me and free me from the hands of those Lions, who were plotting not to devour my flesh, but to steal (*rapirmi;* lit., rob) my soul.

Then, after my usual prayers and having said *Shema Yisrael* (Hear O Lord, the Lord is One), I recited Psalm 31:

67. She must mean he used some words in *giudeo-romanesco,* an allusion that is revealing about the limits of acculturation: "al parlare mi parva Neofito." Sermoneta's notes point time and again to Judeo-italiano/romanesco expressions in Anna's language. Or maybe the allusion is to a manner of expression, how the *neofiti* addressed Jews or spoke of Christianity. Or, and likely, it was both.

68. Sisters, but where is Tranquillo? Though in fact, at the time of the 1733 census, Tranquillo was not yet born, it does seem odd that he is not there in 1749. Still, this is possible, making him no more than 44 in 1793, which is a reasonable age; the census also mentions one sister, a year older than Anna, Allegrezza, but afterward, there could have been more. As for the reference comparing her to a *maschio,* Anna is telling us—if we believe, as perhaps we should here, that these are truly Anna's words—that she is responsible, educated, not easily duped. More, she is punctilious about prayer at the proper hour, an obligation that applies to men alone.

In thee, O the Lord, have I taken refuge; let me never be ashamed; deliver me in Thy righteousness. Incline Thine ear unto me, deliver me speedily; be Thou to me a rock of refuge, even a fortress of defense, to save me. For Thou art my rock and my fortress; therefore for Thy name's sake lead me and guide me. Bring me forth out of the net that they have hidden for me; for Thou art my stronghold. Into Thy hand I commit my spirit; Thou hast redeemed me, O the Lord, Thou God of truth. I hate them that regard lying vanities; but I trust in the Lord. I will be glad and rejoice in Thy loving kindness; for Thou hast seen mine affliction, Thou hast taken cognizance of the troubles of my soul, and Thou hast not given me over into the hand of the enemy; Thou hast set my feet in a broad place. Be gracious unto me, O the Lord, for I am in distress; mine eye wastes away with vexation, yea, my soul and my body. For my life is spent in sorrow, and my years in sighing; my strength fails because of mine iniquity, and my bones are wasted away. Because of all mine adversaries I am become a reproach, yea, unto my neighbors exceedingly, and a dread to mine acquaintance; they that see me without flee from me. I am forgotten as a dead man out of mind; I am like a useless vessel. For I have heard the whispering of many, terror on every side; while they took counsel together against me, they devised to take away my life. But as for me, I have trusted in Thee, O the Lord; I have said: 'Thou art my God.' My times are in Thy hand; deliver me from the hand of mine enemies, and from them that persecute me. Make Thy face to shine upon Thy servant; save me in Thy loving kindness. O the Lord, let me not be ashamed, for I have called upon Thee; let the wicked be ashamed, let them be put to silence in the nether-world. Let the lying lips be dumb, which speak arrogantly against the righteous, with pride and contempt. Oh how abundant is Thy goodness, which Thou hast laid up for them that fear Thee; which Thou hast wrought for them that take their refuge in Thee, in the sight of the sons of men! Thou hidest them in the covert of Thy presence from the plottings of man; Thou concealest them in a pavilion from the strife of tongues. Blessed be the Lord; for He hath shown me His wondrous loving kindness in an entrenched city. As for me, I said in my haste: 'I am cut off from before Thine eyes'; nevertheless Thou heardest the voice of my supplications when I cried unto Thee. O love the Lord, all ye His godly ones; the Lord preserves the faithful, and plentifully repays him that acts haughtily.[69]

Saying this psalm revived my spirit [but then] the Archpriest of S. Celso appeared with a new sermon. . . . You observe the Sabbath as it says 'Observe the Sabbath (Exodus 20:8),' and we, too, preserve the festival as do you. The only difference is that you observe on the Sabbath, while we recognize the day when God created the world, which is Sunday, and was so destined by God to be the true festive day. I will now demonstrate what I have said with a text from Jeremiah (Lamentations 2:6, cited in Hebrew), which says: "God has let the memory of the Sabbaths and festivals be lost in Zion. So you see that God does not wish you to celebrate the Sabbath, but Sunday." I, upset at hearing such heresy, told him: "You may be a theologian, but those (like you) who do not have the True Light, are not equipped to understand this verse as it should be read, allegorically.[70] If God wished us to forget the Festivals and Sabbath, it was to punish us for all our wrongdoing in offending him. Since we did not observe the Sabbaths and festivals properly, God desired to forget them himself to chastise us justly on those days. That is what Jeremiah said."[71]

He went on with other preacher's arguments, to which I did not respond. He interrogated me once more: "Do you believe, my daughter, that God can do everything and that everything we do depends on him. It pleased God to change the old, first law of rigor for the new one of *caritas*, clemency, and *amor*. Just so, it pleased God to lead you to our hands so that you will know the true faith. We have taken you out from the filth of your ghetto, so that you may purify yourself with the waters of baptism, which are the font and the key to Paradise. He who is not sealed with that seal cannot enter Paradise or enjoy the Divine presence."[72] I in a low voice, and very slowly, responded: "It

69. Cited in full in Hebrew. Translation is from the Jewish Publication Society version, the most accurate English rendering. The Psalm number follows the Hebrew Masoretic text. This psalm could easily be read as a polemic against the Christian cults of saints that the preacher is about to justify.

70. "Allegorically" is the diary's own word. Another inversion, of course: what do you mean that you Christians have the true light? Rather, it is we Jews who have it. God has not abandoned us and chosen you, as you claim, in our place.

71. On too sophisticated a level to expect from the real Anna, unless she had an education advanced even for a *maschio*, as she claimed above.

72. As opposed to the waters of the Tiber floods, which fail to wash the dirt from Jewish souls; a trope, and see again Stow, "Was the Ghetto Cleaner?"

seems to me otherwise than you sir say. God commanded Abraham to circumcise himself, for him and his heirs for eternity. Had he meant it for a fixed period of time, the Scriptures would have said so, set a limit, and revealed the moment when this precept should [no longer] be observed. They would not have said 'forever' (in Hebrew).[73] God is eternal and His law is immutable, so how is what you claim true. The law written by God, as opposed to yours, which is manmade, does not have equal weight. You can preach as much as you like and say what you want, but you will not convert me. You will do well to take me back to my home, to my parents, from whom I was stolen; you don't really care whether I am damned." Hearing this, the archpriest went off in a huff.

I thought I might rest a bit that day (the Sabbath), but after the shortest time, my peace was doubly disturbed by another damnable priest, again one I did not know, who came on Saturday evening at the first hour of the night (about 8:00 PM), just when I was saying 'arvit [the evening prayer]. He came with more preaching and proposals and discourses, all of which I had already heard, which had made me sick. To avoid dragging the story out, I will not repeat him. If I were to go on at length about everything, this book would be three times longer than it is,[74] which I have kept brief to avoid boring the reader.[75]

Sunday, the eighth day of my "martyrdom."[76] The Curate (the official priest of the *Casa* who oversees conversions) entered and recommenced his endless sermonizing; and then the Preaching Father (the monster), and then another *Frate*, and six more priests. I was scared

---

73. That is, God has not changed direction, for example, he has not replaced circumcision with baptism and, of course, Jews with Christians as His people. This idea is *not* to be read as though Anna sees circumcision as a key to Paradise. She is saying only that baptism signifies nothing. In the event, the Jewish *Gan Eden* is not the Christian Paradise.

74. Here is a hint that the diary has been reworked with an eye to readership. Note the term *volume*, in Italian, which can mean book, volume, or perhaps to Anna, pamphlet. In the event, it indicates a plan to circulate the text and thus its editing to instruct readers.

75. The reader does, though, need to question how Anna, the real Anna, knew enough to delve into the myriad allegorical interpretations offered by Christian exegetes. A further question is why these exegetes thought they could convince Jews with these subtle arguments. The Church had impugned the Talmud for giving God human attributes, like feelings and the ability to rescind harsh judgments. Anna is responding that God maintains His principles fixed.

76. Note how the pressure keeps escalating, signaling the diary's plan of construction and the secret of its power. Anna compares herself to victims of Kiddush HaShem, those who "sanctify God's name" in martyrdom. Perhaps this is an intentional inversion of the ideal Christian martyr, who suffers to hold on to his or her Catholic faith, Anna suffers to stay as far away from Catholicism as possible. Christian martyrs are also identified with the Eucharist, of which Anna wants no part.

to my depths, there, alone in that room with ten *'Arelim*.[77] The preacher recommenced his preaching and then, as before, sprayed water (*spruz-zare*), everywhere, all over me, and on my face, which made my whole being shake.[78] Praise be to God, may His name be blessed, I began to scream at them, saying your ugly acts and your water are useless, except to make me firmer in my own religion. Your water games are only making me think about returning to my family, to live with them and die.

The Preacher turned acid: "You think you will return home. You can die first. I will keep you here for twenty quarantines.[79] The Cardinal [the Vice Regent] has ordered me to bring *zitelle* [maidens, *neofite* all] to teach you our doctrine to save your soul. If you think you are going to go back to the ghetto, get it out of your head; and don't think you are hearing only what I think. I have full authority, orders from the Sacred Congregation, to do exactly what I want to produce your conversion.[80] You say, 'I want to return to my home.' Quiet down. This is impertinence. I am telling you again that I am not going anywhere unless you declare yourself (a Catholic)." I became mute. I was afraid to prejudice myself. I was alone, and they were ten.

Then, at that very moment, that cursed Coen woman showed up. She, too, said things I did not want to hear. She told me how happy she was, body and soul, and how sorry she was she had not become a Christian earlier (in life). She had brought herself here to me to tell me I should follow her example, to make myself happier than any other creature. But if I did not, and failed to do what the Preacher insisted, I would rot in that *Serraglio*.[81] "Were I to convert, I would be treated

---

77. This is one more than mentioned. *Arelim* means the uncircumcised, *Goim*, a common Judaeo-Roman usage.

78. Water pressed Anna's clothing down upon her, revealing the outlines of her figure in the presence of ten strange men, each of them no doubt calling out threateningly. Emotionally, if not physically, Anna must have felt ravished.

79. Even three, as might have happened were she "offered," rather than "denounced," would have been excessive.

80. Sacred Congregation may refer to the Holy Office of the Inquisition.

81. Meaning "enclosure," but *Serraglio* is also the term first used in the later 1550s and 1560s in papal documents referring to the ghetto; the adoption of the Venetian *ghetto* came only about thirty years later. There is punning going on here, to say the real place of enclosure is the *Cate-cumeni*, not the ghetto. I suggested in *Theater of Acculturation*, 105, that when a Jewish mystical confraternity began to meet at night while the ghetto doors were locked, the goal was to turn "closure" into an intellectual and spiritual "opening." Anna completes the picture. The *Casa dei catecumeni* is the real enclosure, the ghetto the place of Jewish freedom. In this spirit, too, Tranquillo wrote, at about this time, a poem on Purim, whose subject is Jewish redemption in

with reverence by more than one Dama, courted by princes and *cav-alieri,* and find myself in the company of the elite, even the Episco-pal hierarchy, rather than in the *canaglia* (the den of crime) of your (*Vostro*)[82] Ghetto." They hammered this message into me for over two hours, until finally they left in bad humor.[83]

On the ninth day, a Monday, the Abbot Cavalli, *Maestro di Lin-gua Sacra,* arrived to play his part.[84] He began saying: "My dear child. I have come to visit you not only on my own volition, but by order of Our Signor (the pope, Benedict XIV).[85] I wish to have the honor to convert you by arguments from your own Law, to show you the truth of our Religion, for the good of your soul. Please listen to me. I wish to persuade you with courtesy, and with pleasing speech. So, please, listen politely. Do you not say every morning just after washing your hands, the benediction, 'who created bodily orifices' (citing the Hebrew bene-

---

the Diaspora; see Enzo Sereni, "L'assedeo del Ghetto di Roma del 1793 nelle memorie di un contemporaneo," in *Scritti in Memoria di Enzo Sereni,* ed. D. Carpi and A. Milano (Milan and Jerusalem, 1970), 168–97.

82. "Your" is certainly intentional here, to point to the distance between the apostate (from Judaism), the Coen sister, and Anna, with her faithfulness and wish to remain a part of the Jewish whole.

83. Once again, the idea was to exhaust her, to get Anna to say "yes," yes to anything, which would have been taken as "yes," I believe. Yes, I want baptism—which would have been admin-istered at once—that "indelible mark" from which there was no return. This was a game of cat and mouse with very high stakes, which only a small number won, in the sense that they emerged as Jews. The game was also being played by alternating hysterics with soothing entreaty, as in the following section. Milano, *Il Ghetto,* 283–304, says up to 25 percent succeeded in avoiding baptism; I have seen lower estimates. The number of converts from Judaism is 1,195 between 1634 and 1700, and 1,237 between 1700 and 1790. From that point until 1870 116 men and 80 women. Milano notes nine instances where Jews were freed by the Community (between 1720 and 1736), mostly cases like Anna's. See JTS Mic 4026a, *Copies of Roman Documents,* pdf 173, for the case of Aron di Binyamin de Benedetti, near Purim, 1761. In dire economic straits, Aron promised the Duchess, a Corsini, the wife of the Duke of Sermoneta, to convert, along with his family. He escaped, and fled, but was brought back by the *sbirri* and clapped into the *Casa.* Somehow, the mediation of Giuseppe Baraffael, a onetime *Fattore,* including a large sum of money, got him out; we hear nothing of the family. Another way out was because, when push came to shove, as even Benedict XIV realized, it was hard to make good on "offerings" by a fiancé, despite a ruling of 1635 by Cardinal Barberini on their legitimacy.

84. This made of him, as were many of his fellows, a "professional convert." I thank Anke Koeltsch for this categorization and expression, which applies perfectly to converts who made a living by teaching Hebrew and related subjects and whose fame depended on their playing the role of convert permanently, and also on being perceived permanently as such.

85. Cavalli wrote a conversionary tract, whose arguments echo those in the diary, and which Sermoneta discusses in the introduction to *Ratto.* The tract dates to 1730. A *neofiti,* Cavalli was born in Verona, converted at about age sixteen, moved to Venice and then Rome, where he died in 1758. He taught Hebrew and biblical exegesis.

diction, '*asher yasar*), so that the body may be kept pure—and the same for the soul; and what better cleansing than with the water of baptism? This is the true purification, which removes every possible stain from the soul, whether of sins committed or eventually to be committed, provided, of course, that baptism is received with a true heart. It is certain and sure that without baptism, one may not enjoy the heavenly good of Paradise as do the angels and the Holy Fathers. You know that in the daily prayer you are bound to recite three times *kadosh, kadosh, kadosh* (Holy, Holy, Holy), which you repeat in the *Kedushah* (prayer) and in (that other prayer) *uva-leZion*—this is the Trinity, one God in three persons? You cannot deny it, and it is the foundations of your prayers; and we, too, believe the same.

"We differ only about baptism and the messiah, and I will teach you from the 'twenty four (books of the Hebrew Bible).' This is what one reads in the Torah, the Prophets, and the Writings. It is crystal clear. All three demonstrate beyond a doubt the truth of our faith, which is what your ancient Fathers believed, the Prophets as well, and so I wish you to believe, too, for your own good. You will be protected and favored by God, and by the pope himself, who wishes to be the mediator of your salvation. Think and reflect well, my dear child, and resolve (to make the right choice), while I pray to God to illumine you. I will now leave you with my spirits upraised. I hope to persuade you within a few days, although the pope himself has given orders (just in case) that you stay here the whole quarantine. As for me, I greatly hope to gain the honor of converting you. We can do nothing less, since the pope himself has decreed it. However, if you resist, the Prioress, whose words I am now repeating, has given orders that a *staffetta* be sent at once,[86] who will find a way to pressure [*forza*] you to convert, if you fail to do so out of your own accord." At this, he left.[87]

Shortly afterward, three more priests came in, who asked me whether I believe in the God of Israel. I was numb from hearing Abbot Cavalli's derision and then (that of) the three priests of our Prophets. Arrogantly, they placed their hands almost over my eyes, like men pos-

86. A baton, as in a relay race, but this is probably a disciplinary officer: *Lui*, hence, a man.
87. "Sweetness of lips," to use Augustine's expression, had ceded to open threat; Augustinus Aurelius, *Adversus Judaeos*, trans. Fathers of the Church (Washington, D.C., 1965), 27: 391–416, final chapter.

sessed. They made an infernal noise, and jarred by the disturbance, I lost control. I did not know what to say. And when they kept demanding, one of them in particular, whether I believed in the God of David, Solomon, Aaron, and Moses, with me not thinking of the 'insidious net' they were casting to ensnare me, the word they were looking for slipped out: *Sì*, yes. It was no help that I kept telling myself to say nothing.[88] But after so many interrogations, I blurted it out. So that they should see that I was not a disbeliever in *my* true God, I said, "*Sì*. Certainly, I believe." At which, one of the three began yelling desperately, "Quiet you others; with just this one word, *è fatta*, it is done."

I froze and became senseless. Still, I gathered my wits and began to scream: "What do you think, that you have persuaded me, that I would leave my holy religion? You are not going to get anywhere with lies, saying, *È fatta*. I am more firm (in my Judaism) than before. Don't pretend to yourselves that you are going to choke me with falsity and lies. You are not going to get out of my mouth something I would never dream of saying or being, to get me to do what you believe. I will not subject myself to exaggerated and shocking ideas just because you say: It is done, it is done. Preposterous. I was born a Jew and will die one. Do not think you will trick me. I will tell the Monsignor [the Vice Regent], who will not put up with any insolence, and who has no plan to conquer anyone by force. Nor it is it right for you to consider 'forcing' a soul, if only for scruples of conscience."[89]

When he heard this, the priest (*sic*) became silent. He reverted to flattery. I told him this wouldn't help. "What you could not achieve with arrogance, you won't achieve with sweet talk. You are deluding yourselves. I know no one (of you) and just want to return home.[90] What I am saying now is no different from what I said the first day." Hearing this, he became agitated. He was like a demon from the inferno,

88. The repeated theme of say nothing, or it will entrap you.
89. In real life, very likely there would have been no going back. The question of what constituted force would have been moot. Nor can anybody be sure how the Vice Regent would have reacted. Is, then, Tranquillo suggesting that appeal to the law works? He may still have had some hope. Or is this irony and satire? Perhaps he knew Pier Paul Pariseo's arguments from the 1530s against force. Pariseo had declared the forced conversions in Portugal in 1497 to have been illegal and void.
90. "Io non conosco nessuno." The meaning is a bit opaque. Perhaps it should mean I refused to recognize anything you say.

shaken by my firmness.[91] But to no avail; and two hours later, they left in desperation.

Tuesday, the tenth day. They brought me before two priests, who asked again [whether I wanted to become a Catholic]. These words made my heart jump, for just then I was grieving to see myself reduced to this terrible state, far from my parents and my beloved grandmother. I felt my blood freeze, and I was unable to respond, while they, seeing that I was wholly beaten down, began to interrogate me. He (*sic*) said he could see from my face that I should convert and die devoted and a good Religious.[92] God helped me to revive, and I answered with force: "All of this is nothing. I was born and will die a Jew."

After tormenting myself for quite some time, a short time passed, and the Illustrious Vice Regent (de Rossi) summoned me and questioned me. With great finesse, he took me into a room and asked whether I was being treated well and was courtesy being used. Did the preachers realize that it was he who had sent them with the sole aim of converting me, to save my soul and perceive the darkness of the Jewish religion, and the clarity of our (Catholic) faith? To save my soul from perdition. "Think well of your circumstances, my child, and accept that whatever we are doing is only for your good, and which we hope you will put to the best use. Know well, that nothing is important to us, not your wealth, nor your person, but that you embrace the true faith.[93] Otherwise, what we are doing has no meaning for us, nor do we have any other interest. It will be a waste and a rebuff. But for the sake of your soul we are obligated to do all that is possible. You, then, think well and think of saving your soul. There is no recourse once you die and are called before the Divine Tribunal, especially you, to whom the faith has been preached. You have no hope (unless you convert). Remember that this world is only a short passage. Eternal joy is forever, but you cannot possess it unless you enroll under the banner of St. Peter. We do not want to convert you by force, only from the spontaneous will of your heart. I never imagined you would be so obstinate. I myself will be your protector and hold you with my own hands at the sacred font."

91. Again the theme of the priests as the devil, meaning idolatry.
92. Does he mean a nun, or just one who observes? Likely the first.
93. Tranquillo is probably alluding to the opposite, that, in Anna's case, they did indeed care for more than her soul. Through her conversion, they would snare a notable person of means.

Hearing this, I wanted to die, and I had no breath left to answer. Yet I had enough breath left, with the assistance of the *Divin Motore* to speak out:[94] "Do listen, Illustrious Signor. I am imprisoned in this place innocently, without knowing why.[95] Finding me in your power, you can order my death, however unjust. But the true patron of my soul is God, and God alone. I would rather die a thousand times before I changed my God and Holy Law (the Torah) or (deserted and betrayed) my parents. This is my firm resolution. It was my first response, and it will continue to be my response until I die." To this, the Monsignor replied: "Quiet yourself! From me, you will receive the justice you deserve, for you are obstinate"; and with that, he left.[96]

Wednesday, the eleventh day. Two priests appeared and gave me an ultimatum. You have no choice. The Cardinal (the Vice Regent) says: Either you convert, or you will be jailed here at his will. Either you persuade yourself to recognize the true light, or you will be held here forever. Forced or willingly, you will bend to his will. "You are trying to scare me," I said, "with these false claims. I know that the Cardinal will act justly and not burden his conscience.[97] But if things are indeed as you first said, you can strangle me before I change my mind." I shocked him by saying this. Then he said he wanted to say something in my ear, which he knew would bring me to convert. I was upset, but held back: "What do you mean by speaking into my ear? This is not our [Jewish] way. I don't want this confidence anyway." He said: "I do not intend to use you badly, only instruct you, and illumine

94. Roughly, the philosophical prime mover, the initial [divine] agent, which is the cause of all things. Why Tranquillo decided on a philosophical term is perplexing. Nobody would speak this way. It may be a play on *Divin Redentore* for Jesus. To say that Catholics have confused God with a human is a traditional Jewish attitude.

95. Remember, she reports only afterward her discovery that Sabato had denounced her.

96. The Vice Regent is a central character in the story. He appears three times: at the start, here, and toward the end. His persona keeps changing, from concerned to stern, to inquisitorial, to threatening, to apologetic. This is no accident. As the representative of higher powers in the Church, he takes on all the varied faces of that institution. Yet more than once Anna says the Cardinal will be "just," as eventually he is (made out to be) in the apology. Is this dreaming, or irony? Or is it Tranquillo's warning that yes, he is "just," but in ecclesiastical terms and within the unpalatable limits of citizenship and law in the Papal State, which Jews must grasp? The diary, as I have said, is artfully constructed. Tranquillo, as we shall see, was building these visits and the eventual summons to Anna to meet with the Vice Regent in private on the 1792 story of Grazia di Iachetto.

97. The question is what did the Jews really think: of the threats or the possible justice, or could they never be sure?

your mind to your benefit and advantage, whether for the soul or the body."

He sent the Prioress out and the other priest, too.[98] We were left alone, and he said he would not use force. He was laboring to convert me, he said, because he had been charged with ensuring I marry a prince of rank, who would give me a grand dowry. I would go about in a carriage and be served as a *dama* [a lady] and a princess. And thinking all these temptations would move me, he awaited my answer anxiously.[99]

But I availed myself of what our great scholars (*Hakhamim*) wrote in *The Sayings of Our Fathers*, and I told him the story of R. Yossi ben Kasma.[100] A demonic spirit offered R. Yossi everything, gold, money, and precious jewels, if the rabbi would remain with him (said in Hebrew). R. Yossi responded that he would not desert his Judaism. Material riches were evanescent; all he needed in the next world was the Torah, and good works.[101] "I, too, have no interest in riches and material things. They are momentary. I care only for the eternity of the future life God promised to us, his people, the children of the Patriarch Abramo, the one who saw the true religion, and through whose merit, we are God's elect. How can you think I would exchange my soul for wealth?[102] Leave me alone; invest your time better elsewhere. Your efforts are wasted!" And furious with me, he left.[103]

That same day, the *tsorer*, the enemy, that Preacher appeared with another *frate*, who began to flatter me.[104] Would I entrust myself to God so that He would illumine me? I said that all my desires were that God would help me not to lose my soul. With his mind going in the opposite direction of my heart, the preacher missed the point. He

---

98. The Prioress seems to be there, or very close by, most or all of the time.

99. But she already was from a well-to-do background, which may explain the special attention she gets from the higher ups; the Cardinal himself indirectly confirms this later on when he tells Anna that he rarely intervenes.

100. *Sayings of the Fathers* is a short mishnaic tractate filled with moralizing statements and tales. The reference to good works may be a retort to the notion that baptism alone is sufficient and may reflect some Protestant teaching.

101. This is the cited text of the Hebrew story.

102. Once more the idea that Judaism is the way to eternal life, but again the reminder that however much Roman Jews may over the centuries have absorbed Catholic thinking on this topic, the Jewish *Gan Eden* is a place of study, and the real future world is that of Ezekiel's valley of dry bones, a mass, simultaneous resurrection of soul and body of all mankind (Ezek. 37:1–14).

103. Here again is the refrain of the frustration and anger of the preachers.

104. Presumably the wild one noted above.

flattered himself that he had convinced me. "Oh no," I said, "do not believe that your words and false prayers have convinced me. No man will change my mind, nor will he repress my Free Will (*Libero Arbitrio*).[105] Kindly leave me, and let me return to my parents."

You are so obstinate, he replied: I wish you to pray with me. You pray on one side and we two on the other. You in your prayer must say with all your heart may God lead me (Anna) in the path of Your commandments.[106] They threw me down on my knees for about an hour, with the Prioress, and then they arose and asked whether they had softened my spirit.[107] Not in the slightest, I said.

They then threw me onto my knees in front of the Prioress for over an hour. They arose and asked me if their prayers had softened my obstinate heart, to which I answered: not at all. He then said he would go home and do something [prepare?]. He had to convert me, even by force. Never had a woman so obstinate passed through his hands, a woman so incapable of reason.[108] Still, he would use all his powers to convince me within the twelve days.[109] He threatened me. If I did not accept his words by my own will, I would not get out of this place. It was clear that God Himself had willed that I arrive here, so that they could preach to me salvation. I should not contest them, but be obedient and pleasant. Otherwise, the Cardinal would become vexed. Instead of protecting me, he would hold me here at his pleasure, for two or three quarantines, or even more. Dear child, think of your plight in order to save your soul.[110]

---

105. She means deny me the use of my free will. The use here of the technical term for Free Will warns us not to confuse it with the repeated phrase *rubbarmi l'Anima*. Sermoneta here paired the term with *divin motore* to suggest Anna had some philosophical training (*Ratto*, 100, n. 97). More likely, this is Tranquillo. Sermoneta spoke of the "internal liberty of choice," a concept much favored by Augustine and his followers. This is indeed the theological heart of the text. You Catholics, the diary is saying, promote *libero arbitrio*, but when it comes to the *Casa* and converting Jews, you throw your scruples to the wind; you are phonies. And look at your methods, throwing water, ravishing Anna emotionally! It is as though turning Catholic theology into a *comedia dell'arte*.

106. Which, ironically, is precisely what Anna had been doing, only the path was that of Judaism, which is also signaled by the verse being cited in the diary in Hebrew; Psalms 119:35.

107. Genuflecting is something Jews never do in prayer; rather, standing at more sanctified moments.

108. Reason, as Thomas Aquinas put it, meant belief in Christ. It was also a sign of humanity. The end of the syllogism with respect to Jews is obvious.

109. Twelve days of my incarceration.

110. Anna was probably thinking: of her freedom.

"The Signor Cardinal is the *Patron*," I said, "to do what he wishes, but not injustice." At that, the priest thrust his hand into a cup and sprayed water everywhere, the bed, my face, in the food and drink. He did it two or three times, saying: "With this blessed water, I will convert you." What a mess he made, and I, observing it, began to call out loudly that this was hardly the way to preach a religion. If he kept it up, I would report him to the Cardinal.[111]

Then he changed his approach, saying: if you wish to be liberated, think of your quandary.[112] I want to go home, I said. I do not want to hear any more of your preaching. To make me more desperate, he said: "I can and will spray the water wherever I wish." He put his hands on my head, saying: "It is of no value to keep calling Father and Mother, because I am your father, the Prioress your mother, and the Holy Father is the Patron and King, who commands all kings and emperors."[113] Forget your parents. They are no longer your support.

Hearing this, I threw myself on the ground in great pain. As one possessed, I said: "I will never abandon my law, my parents, my Nation. I would rather die a hundred times rather than desert them.[114] You do not know how to act. Take a knife and kill me. I will die with the name of God and my parents on my lips, and one day you will have to justify this exaggeration before God and to your superiors."[115] I said this in tears, while, for their part, they departed *in malora*.[116]

Thursday, the twelfth day. Three priests appeared to ask me whether I would prefer the Inferno or Paradise, where only the baptized can enter. Think of the eternal suffering, if you do not embrace our faith, instead of the eternal blessings of Paradise. Seeing me remain silent, they said: Answer! I said I would rather suffer in the In-

---

111. The Vice Regent again changes face, but the irony also increases, with the preacher made to appear ridiculous, if not absurd; coarse comedy enters here, too, with the water. Yet it is against a backdrop of fear, one step short of torture.

112. Is he now afraid?

113. Another layer to the irony. This is high medieval papal theory; anybody spouting it in Anna's day would have been questioned. Even Leo XIII did not go that far. When Pier Paul Pariseo said the pope was right to challenge the forced conversions ordered by the king of Portugal by saying that papal acts were the equivalent of acts by God, the issue was really about power, both within and over the Church.

114. By now a motif.

115. Again, but with the knife, more graphically and historically reminiscent of medieval Jewish martyrdom, *kiddush hashem*.

116. The refrain of bad humor.

ferno in the company of my parents than to be in Paradise with Christians.[117] To this, they answered: "O you poor thing. Don't you see the precipice?" But after a long sermon, just repeating what they had said before, they left.

The Padre Predicatore and the Prioress again appeared about the 21st hour (4:00 PM), at whose sight I froze from head to toe. "My child," he began, "you see how many times I have visited you for the good of your body (person) and the salvation of your soul. I went to the Signor Cardinale and told him of your obstinacy. He instructed me to tell to you that this is the twelfth day, and he is certain of your conversion (*conversione*). If you do not convert through my efforts, the pope has ordered the Cardinal himself to come and baptize you. Willing or unwilling, you will be a Catholic."[118] Breathless, and aided by His Divine Majesty, I told them I would die the way I was born, whatever they did.

Hearing this, the preacher became like a viperous lion. He told the Prioress to fetch what he had given her. She left and soon brought back a big cross. The preacher put it on my bed, yelling like a dog.[119] Then crying and making loud noises, he again took the water and sprayed it on the bed, my face, the back, my head, saying: "Now is the hour for you to convert.[120] Tonight, you will dream of the C[ross]. This is why I have put it on your bed." The Prioress said, "If you are moved to convert, as you should be, I will be sleeping here (in the room) beneath you. It is enough to knock with your shoe on the floor, at any

117. Note the constant emphasis on family, balanced by a heavy insult that could never have been published.
118. Once more, the theme of illegal absolute force. The message could be dual, that the Church really did refrain, or that it only pretended to refrain.
119. Dog, an inversion, I doubt accidental, of the image Catholic polemicists had often used for Jews. The word "cross" is written in Hebrew, as though it was spelling the word "Cherub," but it can be read as *qarov*, someone near, or a relative, hence, parodies that express distaste for Christian objects. Sermoneta explains arguably, *Ratto*, 92, that to avoid saying words that smacked of idolatry, Jews made intentional distortions. For instance, *san* becomes '*an*. In 1568, Rabbi Ishmael Haninah was accused by the Papal Inquisition in Bologna of using '*an* to signify *agnello*, or "lamb," as though in mockery of Jesus. Yet '*an* appears with absolute regularity for *San*, Saint, in the Roman Hebrew notarial texts, as in the gate of '*an Pancrazio*, San Pancrazio, and so forth. Further sophistication is the "yelling, *strepitando*," since Jewish prayer, from the time of Pope Gregory the Great in the late sixth century, had been characterized by precisely this word. On these inversions, see Stow, "Medieval Jews on Christianity."
120. That the adepts of the *Casa* are made to look like psychotic savages over and over again is surely intentional.

hour, and I will embrace you like my child. I loved you from the very first. Do not leave me disconsolate. Here is a cross to hold with you till you become a Catholic, just as I am."

Hearing this, my heart burst with tears. I began to shout: never will you leave me with this piece of wood, which I turned upside down. This is not the way to preach. If you love me as a daughter, do not do me this disservice. Seeing me so distraught, for the mercy of God, she took the cross away. The preacher renewed spraying water over the bed and my face, calling out, as he did so, the names of many saints. "Tonight," he said as he left, "the saints I have named will appear to you. They will have you summon the Prioress, and you will profess to her your freely willed conversion."[121]

After three hours of this, they went away *in malora*.[122] I was trembling, more dead than alive. I thought the earth would open and swallow me up; I was afraid; and the light had gone out. I took my shoe to call the Prioress, but some "unknown force" inspired me to desist.[123]

With sobs I called to my dead ones, especially my *Nonno* Sabato, may his memory be blessed, that he should pray to God to liberate me from my pain.[124] Then, with tears flowing, I recited the following Psalm (86):

121. There is again knowledge of canon law here. The Italian is *spontanea*, which should be read as "of your own desire," following the requirement of canon law that all conversion must be free willed. The tone is mocking, for after all this pressure, how could Anna's conversion be freely willed? The image of saints appearing may have been enough to make some readers laugh. Indeed, failure seems to be making the preacher, if not the Prioress, too, delusional, as the burlesque of water sprayed with abandon brings out. They likely know this was the last chance to convert Anna, assuming the twelve-day rule was going to be observed.
122. By now, this oft-repeated phrase is parody.
123. How is this to be read? Anna wanted what? To call for light or to convert, which is always referred to as "illumination"? There is a play here. The suggestion is that even Anna, with all her forces, was on the verge of breaking down, at which point, all that remained to aid her was the power of a dream, an inversion of the vision of the saints the preacher said she would have. See *Epistola Ludovici Caretti ad Iudaeos* (Paris, 1554). Ludovico Carrito, a.k.a. Todros haCohen, converted when he was fifty years old. He tells of how stubborn Jews are, how he had to suffer so much loss after he converted, and how he came to convert through dreams. The famous Abner of Burgos also spoke of many dreams, which he outlined in detail. It is clear that mystical visions moved him—much as Anna sees her grandfather, but with the opposite result of remaining faithful. On Abner, see Y. F. Baer, *A History of the Jews in Christian Spain*, 1:327–54, 2:141–51.
124. The chain of inversions continues. Rather than seeing the saints, she summons her "saintly" late grandfather, Sabato (in Hebrew, Shabbetai, which is the name that appears in the census). That her beloved grandfather and the villain have the same name is purely coincidental, the part of the diary that is indeed "true to life."

A Prayer of David. Incline Thine ear, O Lord, and answer me; for I am poor and needy. Keep my soul, for I am godly; O Thou my God, save Thy servant that trusts in Thee. Be gracious unto me, O Lord; for unto Thee do I cry all the day. Rejoice the soul of Thy servant; for unto Thee, O Lord, do I lift up my soul. For Thou, Lord, art good, and ready to pardon, and plenteous in mercy unto all them that call upon Thee. Give ear, O Lord, unto my prayer; and attend unto the voice of my supplications. In the day of my trouble I call upon Thee; for Thou wilt answer me. There is none like unto Thee among the gods, O Lord, and there are no works like Thine. All nations whom Thou hast made shall come and prostrate themselves before Thee, O Lord; and they shall glorify Thy name. For Thou are great, and do wondrous things; Thou art God alone. Teach me, O Lord, Thy way, that I may walk in Thy truth; make one my heart to fear Thy name. I will thank Thee, O Lord my God, with my whole heart; and I will glorify Thy name for evermore. For great is Thy mercy toward me; and Thou hast delivered my soul from the lowest nether-world. God, the proud are risen up against me, and the company of violent men has sought after my soul and has not set Thee before them. But Thou, O Lord, art a God full of compassion and gracious, slow to anger, and plenteous in mercy and truth. O turn unto me, and be gracious unto me; give Thy strength unto Thy servant, and save the son of Thy handmaid. Work in my behalf a sign for good; that they that hate me may see it, and be put to shame, because Thou, Lord, hast helped me, and comforted me.[125]

I threw myself on a chair, determined not to enter the bed.[126] Exhausted, I drifted in and out of sleep. I had a vision of my [late] *Nonno*, his *Siman* brilliant, illuminated, sewn onto his hat.[127] He spoke to me: "*Hannah* (Hebrew for Anna), I am walking with other dead, for you. Be

125. This psalm is presented in its entirety in Hebrew. The English is again the recent translation by the Jewish Publication Society. The psalm captures perfectly Anna's perspective on the preachers and her will to be saved from their grip.
126. The memory of the cross resting on the bed was too much to bear. Anna must have feared lest possibly she embrace it unconsciously in her sleep, grasping the arch-symbol of Christian idolatry, or, worse, lest the embrace be considered an expression of Christian belief.
127. The yellow hat Jewish men were made to wear.

constant with God, saying *Shema Yisrael* (in Hebrew letters), for your suffering will soon end." I went on calling out: *Nonno,* when will the suffering end. Very soon, he said. I ran rabidly to kiss him, but in that instant, I awoke, feeling more afflicted than ever. I looked out the window and saw the dawn. A bird alighted on the window, and it seemed like it wanted to speak. It began to sing with a song sweeter than any I had ever heard. My pleasure was enormous. The song, short as it was, revived my spirit, and I began my prayers with great devotion.[128]

Friday (the thirteenth day), at 16 hours (11:00 AM), the Father Curate returned. As soon as he walked in he asked: "Are you resolved to embrace the Holy Faith?" I responded that from the first, I had set my mind on going back to my parents.[129] This was impossible, he said. The Cardinal has decided I would have to remain for two or three quarantines, until by my [own] will, or even force, I became a Christian.[130] The Cardinal, I said, may be the *Patron,* but I cannot believe he would force a poor soul in this way. It would be the same as murdering an innocent person.[131] In the event, should he force me, I would nonetheless die in the grace of God a Jew, and he who did me ill would have to answer before the Almighty.[132]

128. Birds often appear in dreams as good omens. Here, the meanings may be multiple, as in the dreams of the biblical Joseph, where once they are a good sign, and once they augur personal disaster.

129. As a convert, when Anna would have had to leave her home forever.

130. Here was the great fear that a denunciation would be manipulated into an offering. What is more, there is further mockery of the idea of freely willing to convert, now admitted to be, in the minds of the adepts of the *Casa,* a "choice" that could be brought about by force.

131. We ask again whether the ambivalence is real or ironic. A subtheme is the neophytes who keep saying the Cardinal will approve force, while Anna responds over and again that the Cardinal would never stoop to it. How is this counterpoint to be perceived? As a hope, however justified, that there were malleable forces within the Church and that subtle pressures would keep them from yielding to extremists like the Curate, or "the monster," or specifically Francesco Rovira Bonet, the rector of the *Casa* in Tranquillo's day? Perhaps; Tranquillo was a clever writer.

132. There are two ideas at play here. First, and implicitly, in response to the threats of force, that force was not only canonically illicit, but that absolutely forced baptism was also invalid, perhaps again thinking of the arguments of Pier Paolo Pariseo. Closer to home, absolute force was discussed again by Benedict XIV in *Postremo mense* by mentioning Innocent III's bull *maiores,* which defines absolute as opposed to conditional force and was treated as a benchmark ruling ever after. It is marvelous how well informed were the Jews, no doubt by people like Carlo Luti. Yet it is no less marvelous that Tranquillo was able to work these ideas in so subtly. Tranquillo also managed to display both sides of the coin: the second idea. For not only did the canons say that force did not confer legitimate baptism, but Jewish tradition, certainly in the event of force, would still call Anna a Jew, as she protests, this time, directly. She rests on the teaching "even though a person sinned [by converting]," he or she remains a Jew, on which see Jacob Katz, "Even though a sinner, he is still of Israel" (in Hebrew), *Tarbiẓ* 27 (1958):

The Curate replied that God was like a good physician, who sometimes must make the patient suffer to effect a cure. How much the more will God work to save your soul,[133] which otherwise would go to the Inferno. Make up your mind to go to Paradise with the holy fathers who have embraced the true faith. After about two hours more of this sermon, he left.

At 21 hours (about 4:00 PM), the Curate returned, bringing the sister of the *Rasha*, that evil fellow, Coen, who began flattering me, saying, "Dear child, do something to save your soul, while there is time. Thanks to your obstinacy and cruelty, your suffering in the Inferno may begin at any moment. Hear me out, and then I will leave you."[134]

The Curate left and that bastard (*mamzerata*), the Coen sister, stayed.[135] She urged me to desert my faith. "Believe me," she said, "to be a Christian is the true faith." And she began to embrace me and kiss me and to say it would break her heart to leave me. Holding me to her, to bring me to her side, and kissing me closely, she beseeched me again, saying: "Heart of my soul, become a good Christian, to save *your* soul in this world and in the next, and to gain the glory of eternal Paradise." She held me so tightly that she did not know how to free herself.

Then she turned to the Prioress and said, believe me, my dear Prioress, that from the moment I began to believe in the true faith I never had an hour of despair. I have become the member of a good family with riches; my mother-in-law is an angel, better than my own mother.[136] His Divine Majesty has given me a husband who loves me. What greater felicity could I have? Before, I had nothing to eat.[137] I had

---

203–27. See also Edward Fram, "Perception and Reception of Repentant Apostates in Medieval Ashkenaz and Premodern Poland," *AJS Review* 21 (1996): 299–339.

133. . . . and, by implication, make you suffer.

134. This is her third appearance. Is this a statement about treacherous women?

135. The term means fruit of adultery—not simply illegitimate—or the fruit of incest; the term here, however, is Italianized.

136. Really? Once more, if by implication, the theme of Anna's parents and the mockery, since most converts had economic problems, although not all. But, then, the Coen woman was, as she is about to say, poor, as we have suspected, and being able to eat regularly and sleep in a bed may have been a sharp improvement in her lifestyle. Anna, by contrast, had no such worries as a Jew.

137. There is a great deal here. First, an indication of who is susceptible of converting; second, the inversion, because in Anna's case, it is precisely the opposite. She has plenty, and rather than gain a well-off husband, she gets a poor one, Sarra Coen's brother. It is he, not Anna, who will be able to put food in his mouth. Third, this is a warning, to be concerned about the poor. Ignored and unprotected, they may convert and prey upon well-off girls.

thought about converting for five years, until the Madonna inspired me. There is not an hour of day or night that passes that I do not express my thanks. I am content and satisfied, better off than a queen. So my sister [dear Anna], think well about what you are doing. Once your soul is lost, it is gone. I was a Jew like you are, but when I saw that this was the true religion, I desired to save my soul. If you convert, I will visit you daily. You know I love you so, more than if you were my own blood.[138] You will enjoy Paradise in this world, as well as in the next. The Curate then entered and observed, "what good advice, this dear child has given you; her reasoning is true and pure. I would never have imagined such obstinacy from you." For my part, I stayed quiet, offering no response.

At that instant, I was again called by the Monsignor Vice Regent, and when the others knew he was there, they fled, like a pack of lions.[139] I went to him with the Prioress. The Monsignor, who was waiting to examine me, saw me desperate from all the importuning (the threats) of those *resha'im* (*evil ones*). They had exhausted my patience (*stratziata*) and frustrated me with their three-hour sermons. I was deaf, without sensation, no longer able to stand on my feet. Seeing me so distraught and frightened, he said: "Dear child, do not be upset by my presence. We do nothing here by force.[140] You know, I have come three times, and although hundreds and even thousands have passed through here, I have never honored them with my own presence.[141] You have had this privilege far more than others.[142] But you have spurned us again and again. From the first day, I sent the best theologians in Rome, true prophets. Yet you held back. What is the source of this cruelty? I wish I could baptize you with my own hands."

Hearing this, I shook from head to foot, but I screwed up my courage. "Hear me, your Illustriousness. It will never be. I would rather die a thousand times than convert. You may be the *Patron*, and you may have the power to ruin (*far strazio*) my life, but I must offer my soul to

138. Allusion to the marital plans of her brother, no doubt, but also to the wretched mess in which girls like Anna with a suitor/fiancé like Sabato found themselves.
139. Why, because they had been threatening her, and the Vice Regent had heard about it—all, of course, as part of a script Tranquillo had written, or so it convincingly seems?
140. Is Anna supposed to believe this, a line that completes the circle of force/no force?
141. About 2,500 of these "others" in 300 years, not all Romans by origin.
142. Most likely, the status of Anna's family made the special effort worthwhile. Her conversion, it must have been hoped, would stimulate others to follow. In which case, one may ask, speculatively, but reasonably, whether Sabato had not been goaded on to lure Anna.

the one God.[143] You cannot compromise my free will (*libero arbitrio*).[144] You cannot get me to say something with which my heart, mind, and will disagree. You, Signore, know very well that I was brought to this place innocent (without cause). I do not know why I was imprisoned and why such unjust torments came raining down on me. I was in my home, behaving honestly. My parents permitted neither visits, nor (improper) conversations in the home, nor did anyone see me peeping through the blinds.[145] If only I knew the reason and the identity of the person who had me seized (by the Bargello) with such force.[146] It was surely an imposter, a fraud.[147] Please, let me go back to the home it was so bitter to leave. I was dragged here like a sheep, a *guitta*. Oh poor me. I have passed thirteen days here, in this prison, closed in and not allowed out, even though I have done no wrong."[148]

Seeing me so afflicted and tearful, the Monsignor was moved to compassion. "We are required," he said, "to act out of *misericordia*. I am in charge of the salvation of your soul, and if I must do justice, I must do what is necessary.[149] You say your heart tells you *not* to become a Christian, that you wish rather to return to your mother and father. You have said that every minute here is like a year. I understand this. But the inspiration (the initiative) to send you home must come from me. And I will indeed release you." It distressed me to hear this arrogance; and with that, he left.[150]

---

143. Most distinctly not the triune God. There is much subtle polemic here.

144. Note: compromise, not steal.

145. *Sfesitura di gelosia*, which Sermoneta renders in modern Italian as *"fissura di persiana,"* as in my translation here. Is this a case of "my lady doth protest too much"? Had Anna flirted through a window? She would not have been the first; as seen in the case of Miriana in Modena, where something definitely had gone on, although likely much less frequently than the Inquisition in that city claimed.

146. This is the second time she feigns innocence about Sabato. Is she to be taken at face value? She knows the Coen sister, and she knows she has been denounced or possibly "offered." Could she not have put two and two together? Or, again, is it Tranquillo, describing a generic condition?

147. The constant fear of false denunciations emphasized again.

148. A question is whether any of this was legal formulae. At this period (as today) defendants often wove legal formulae into purely emotional pleas; see Natalie Z. Davis, *Fiction in the Archives: Pardon Tales and Their Tellers in Sixteenth-Century France* (Stanford, 1990).

149. Alluding to the options of force or of holding Anna, unwarrantedly, for a full quarantine? Or is this, as suggested, reminiscent of the ironies about "good" prelates in the sixteenth-century *Shevet Yehudah* of Ibn Verga?

150. Namely, his sanctimonious posturing—even as the Vice Regent insists he is a paladin of law, which no doubt made Anna, as well as Tranquillo, furious. The absurdity of living in a society where religion confers such authority was unbearable.

The Vice Regent then called the Prioress, who came, and with whom he spoke for about a half hour, leaving me alone, perplexed and wondering.[151] She came back to me with venom in her eyes, like a snake. Her face was black, and she frightened me when she looked at me. She tried to preach to me, even though she knew that I was to be sent home.[152] She had the orders, and she was crying. "This is the hour to save yourself from eternal damnation," she said. "Do it now, for later there will be no time, and while (you are suffering) infernal pain, you will recall this precious moment (of opportunity), but in vain." She kept this up until the first hour of the night (about 5:00 PM). Then she was called away and left.[153]

In a few moments, the Prioress returned saying: "It is like this. Either you declare (your desire to convert) or you go home." To my home, I answered, to the arms of my parents. Go miserably, she added. The devil will have your soul (*farà a palla*).[154] The Prioress then brought me down (to the entrance), where I found a domestic, whose identity I asked. "I," he said, "am the Dean of Monsignor the Vice Regent. I have come to put you into the hands of the *Fattori*, who have arrived to take you home." I wanted to say something nice to the Prioress, but she disappeared.[155]

I went down into the street with the Dean, and, a few steps ahead, I saw the *Fattori*, eager to receive me. One was my uncle Angelo Zevi, who threw himself upon me, crying and embracing me so tenderly and hard that he could not let go. Then the other two *Fattori*, Samuel Corcos and Moise Modigliani, did the same, kissing my hands, as I did

151. Perplexed, that is, about the Vice Regent's sincerity.

152. Hence, her anger; the inmates of the *Casa* had failed. Whatever else concerned them about failing to persuade Anna, they must have been equally upset that the enterprise of the *Casa* had been compromised.

153. But as Anna herself put it, she was a viper, a snake, a lion, a predator, like all the other preachers. This was Anna's perception of Christian missionizing, and no doubt Tranquillo's, too. To this, add the charge of idolatry, symbolized by the cross on the bed and its unspeakable invasiveness.

154. Literally, to make a ball of your soul. Not only had the Prioress been defeated, but as a *neofita* herself, she had suffered mockery. Her protestations here were a last-gasp attempt, using intimidation as a ploy, to get Anna to give any minimal sign of acceptance, which would have been grounds for a full quarantine. Anna, the real Anna, besides the one in the diary, gave no such sign, which is certain, since there is no record of Anna in the registers of the *Casa*.

155. Again mockery.

theirs.[156] They led me to Piazza Colonna,[157] where the Vice Regent was waiting to speak to me before I returned to the Ghet[to].[158]

I could no longer control myself. "Aren't my sufferings ended," I queried.[159] They [the *Fattori*] gave me courage, telling me: "Have no fear. We are with you. He said nothing more than that he wanted a word with you. So be of good spirit, and do not sully yourself, for you are in our hands."[160]

We went in and waited in the antechamber, thinking the Vice Regent would come out. Instead, we were amazed to hear a voice say, "Kannà [Anna, Hannah in Hebrew], come in." The *Fattori* wanted to enter with me, but the chamberlain kept them out. "The Monsignor wants only the young woman." The *Fattori* gave me courage, telling me to be strong, *ḥazaq*, and to have no fear, *pahad*.[161] Then I was escorted through three rooms. There was the Vice Regent, seated. He said: "My dear Kannà, accept my *scusa* (my apology). Your unacceptable treatment has taught me. As long as I am Vice Regent, nobody else will suffer this way."[162] More dead than alive, God inspired me to reply that I was innocent and that I had been seized and maltreated with no justification. Yes, he answered. Pardon me. Go console your parents and relatives, who are awaiting you. I went back to the arms of the *Fattori*, who were overjoyed to see me.[163] They were de-

156. Modigliani is the family of the famous early twentieth-century artist.

157. Piazza Colonna was then the location of the Vice Regent's *palazzo*, as contemporaries would have known without need to explain. This meant the Cardinal had traveled a considerable distance, about a mile or more, three times in twelve days, to visit Anna, a gesture meant to emphasize the importance of the del Monte family and its status. Or is it part of the parody about the absurd methods of preaching and the flip-flop of the Vice Regent that is the *obligato* of the diary?

158. Written in Hebrew, *gimmel tet*, as in a bill of divorce. Caffiero's edition—not Sermoneta's —has an incorrect *gimmet tav* (109), an error that is repeated two pages later in *tov*, spelled with a *tav* rather than *tet* (111).

159. Wondering why she had to speak again to the Vice Regent.

160. Sully, in the sense of a last-minute change of heart and conversion, which would have been seen as self-pollution. On the other hand, why a promise to stand alongside her should have cheered Anna is not clear. The diary begins with the Bargello commanding these same *Fattori* to hand Anna over. If they could not help her then, why should she think they could save her now?

161. The use of Hebrew: how much did Anna know?

162. This is an amazing statement, but certainly not true, considering incidents like unorthodox offerings accepted in 1751, 1763, and 1782, that is, after Anna's trials of 1749. And why the intimacy? Was a true apology possible? One final time, we have a troubling burlesque. This apology is also unique to Anna's diary. Grazia di Iacchetto is summoned to the Vice Regent, but only to test her intentions.

163. Their bravado likely masked their fear of a last-minute trap.

lighted with the apology and that nobody else would experience my torments.[164]

We then happily went back to the street and reached the ghet[to]. My parents greeted me—I was more dead than alive—while my (blood) relatives gave a shout of joy. After which, all of them embraced (me). With effort (on the part of my parents), I was taken into my room[165] to change clothes,[166] while the whole populace awaited my appearance. The rooms were jammed with people of every sort, who did not tire awaiting me, nor did they want to leave. I was told to say nothing, not a word about what had gone on (in the *Casa*), lest people hang about to hear what I had to say and not give others a chance to see me that evening.[167] It still took a lot to get them to leave. We did not eat dinner until *doppo la mezza note* (probably about 10:00 PM). We had to replenish the lamps twice.[168] Finally, we got rid of everybody and retired to sleep.

On the Sabbath morning, after synagogue, the whole Greater Council of Sixty came to visit me, along with the excellent Signor our teacher Sabato di Segni.[169] To them, I was obliged to tell something of my sufferings. I asked who was the cause of it, and they told me it was a beggar named Sabato Coen, a rascal, may his memory be blotted out. Then I understood what his wicked sister had been doing. They were amazed, and even cried, when I told them how she had pressed me. God had given me the strength to escape the ferocious lions who wished to

---

164. Assurance, which no Jew at the time would have—or should have—dared believe.

165. In the ghetto, to have a private room was extraordinary privacy, and a sign of wealth. Anna's home, as calculated by Micol Ferrara, was about 65 square meters (700 square feet) in size, huge by ghetto standards.

166. *Mutarmi*. Does this take the standard meaning, as here, of changing, or is it also *mutare*, to be silent, as in *muto*, dumb? They did not want her to talk.

167. The diary says this, but, I believe it really meant that Anna was told to say nothing lest some snitch, and one could never know when one was present, might try to turn the account into an expression of a desire to convert, whereupon Anna would instantly have been hauled away for a full quarantine. An unstated theme in her agonies is that if it took an act of enormous will to survive twelve days, who would have made it through forty or eighty, as few did, without succumbing to the conversionary pressure?

168. Following the diary, she returns home on the eve of the Sabbath. But if so, who refilled the lamps? Adding fuel is the same as lighting the fire in the lamp, which is forbidden. Perhaps this is another slip, suggesting it was only a stylization to have her return on the Sabbath?

169. Women are not obligated to attend services, but in the ghetto, there was such a thing as a women's synagogue with a woman prayer leader. Just where this synagogue would have been located in the single building housing the *Cinque Scole*, the five ghetto synagogues, is a problem.

steal my soul. As if in one voice, they called out, *Hodu l'adonai ki tov* (praise God for He is good).[170]

Once they had left, every kind of person came to visit me, and in the following week, my uncle Moshe Zevi sent me ten cuts of cloth, from which I was to choose one to make a dress that would suit me. I selected a white cloth with turquoise flowers, then very much the *moda,* the fashion. The following *Shabbat,* there were more gifts. From the two *Fattori* Corcos and Modigliani, I received two silver candleholders and from the third, my uncle Angelo, a psalter covered in silver. From Rabbi di Segni, a box with silver filigree, and from Gabriel Ambron (a member of another important ghetto family), a miniature fan, whose handle was covered with gold-plated mother of pearl. From Moses Panzieri, leggings of red silk, and from Alessandro and the brothers (not otherwise mentioned) del Monte, a swatch of the richest brocade (woven) with a golden thread to cover a blouse. All of my blood relatives presented me with gifts.[171] "On the third Sabbath, I went to the Scola (synagogue) to say the blessing *haGomel* (recited by persons who have survived danger) and then returned home. Even though the hour was late when I went, the Scola Tempio (the main synagogue) was filled with people, while others, awaiting my return, lined the Piazza and the Street, while still others watched from their windows."

This then is my sad and pitiful story. It could not have been worse (*funesto*), and let us all say Helleluyah. "Who can recount the wonders of God / who can sing His praise?"[172]

---

170. An integral part of holiday and other prayers.

171. This list of gifts at the end of the diary fittingly stresses the oxymoron of the entire presentation. Anything but frivolous, as we might at first think, and turning Anna into just another stereotyped young woman, the list affirms the great discontinuity in Jewish life. Though fully acculturated, sometimes highly cultured, and, like Moisè Mieli, even up-to-date (the word *moda*), Jews were nevertheless threatened for their constancy to Jewish beliefs, as well as their social structures. Return me to my parents is Anna's dominant refrain. Let me live a normal life, enjoy gifts of rich cloth. Do not make my existence pitiful, *funesto*, as is her last word in the sentences to follow. Our life in the Papal State, as we now are forced to life it, is insupportable and absurd. These tensions continued even in contemporary Livorno with its much more favorable conditions; again, see Francesca Bregoli, *Mediterranean Enlightenment: Livornese Jews, Tuscan Culture, and Eighteenth-Century Reform* (Stanford, 2014), 64.

172. Psalms 106:2.

2. Crises

All's well that ends well, or did it? Anna's story is a very human one, that of a believable individual struggling to maintain integrity despite her horrific situation. At the same time, the Anna of the diary is the intentionally composite and, to some extent, artificial figure created by her brother, which enriches the way we see her.

To emerge from the House of Converts a Jew was a mixed blessing. Regardless of the supposedly enormous joy at the reunion with her family, Anna had been permanently scarred, while the fear among other Jews that she might be taken back into the *Casa* must have ruined her marital prospects. The days she spent in the *Casa* likely destroyed her physical health, too; she died at the age of 47, shortly before 1779, not unusual for her day, but many lived longer.[1] We must use our imaginations to wonder what Anna's life was like following her sequestration. Besides remaining unmarried and childless, she may have been chronically depressed, staying within the walls of her house and room, fearful of what would be said, or what might happen should she venture outside, even within the ghetto. In her case, the chance of a true "happy ending" was virtually nil.

Anna herself must have been plagued by the possibility of a repeat performance. Would she be remanded to the *Casa* on the flimsiest of pretexts? There were clergy in Rome who objected to these sequestrations, a patent violation of the rule of free will in conversion. Yet just what was free will in these matters? Anna, at least, could not be threatened with the loss of her children. So many times, a woman whose children had been "offered" by a converted husband, despite all her attempts to be steadfast, finally gave in.

The choice between staying Jewish and her children smacks of no choice at all—as King Manoel of Portugal first demonstrated in March 1497, when he sequestered the children of Portuguese Jews and conditioned their return on their parents accepting baptism. The tactic remained in vogue. Mazaldò, a rough contemporary of Anna, was taken into the *Casa* twice. In the end, overcome by motherly feelings, she converted.[2]

There is also something counterintuitive about the means that were used. How could those in charge of the *Casa* have imagined that they had something attractive to offer to those who entered its precincts in total denial and against their will? No wonder there was resort to intimidation, and worse, which often worked.

Anna's Fate

Anna's experiences must be seen against the background of what has been estimated to have been, on average, ten conversions a year that took place in the *Catecumeni:* about half were Roman Jews; the other half came from outside the city. This number may not seem great, but, considering the ghetto's size, on average about 4,000 people, conversion must have touched just about every family. In addition, individuals from the various groups composing Rome's Jewish community married each other freely. The hundreds of immigrants who entered Rome about the year 1500, from Spain, Germany, and Sicily, all the victims of expulsions or attacks, quickly amalgamated through marriage with older Jewish families, mostly Italian Jews, some of whom had lived in the city for over two millennia and whose members were in many ways more culturally Roman than many of Rome's Christian inhabitants—their Judaism apart. By the mid-eighteenth century, most, if not all, Roman Jews were somehow related, a fact that with regard to the House of Converts, was a source of preoccupation. If even a distant relative could make an "offering," all of Rome's Jews were somehow threatened—as well as outraged when a sequestration was ordered. To prevent riots on such occasions—they had occurred—the papal police orchestrated kidnappings to occur in the dark of night.

The growing threat to Jewish security no doubt heightened Tranquillo's resolve to make Anna's story known, even if this required embellishing on the details, including by borrowing from similar stories. This includes the scene of the final glory, when Anna is returned to her family on a Friday eve, May 19, for a joyous Sabbath celebration; the particulars are Tranquillo's invention—and to some extent, the exact dates. In 1749, May 19 fell on a Monday, and to confuse matters further, the original dates on the manuscript of May 3–16 have been written over and replaced by 6–19; yet even the 16th would have been the Sabbath itself, not Friday eve.[3]

Apart from the perplexing dating, Tranquillo's portrait of joy is problematic. The real Anna almost surely did not convert, or her name would appear in the House of Converts' records, along with her baptismal date and the name of her godparent(s). This was the norm. Yet the diary's "happy ending" stretches the imagination, with Anna sent back to the ghetto and her family after thirteen days, there to continue her life as a Jew unhindered.[4] Tranquillo has left to the reader the task of reading between the lines to perceive how Anna's experience must have left her deeply scarred in both mind and body. The reader does well to think of two young women named Anna, the real one, who was likely destroyed by the pressure, even without converting, and the ideal and idealized one, who held her own and kept her head high. The great pathos in the telling is in the tension between the "happy ending" of the diary and the gloomier one of probable fact.[5]

Women's Predicament

The mental torture Anna suffered was without question the harshest strain of all. Young women who had been denounced, taken to the *Casa*, and then released without converting were "marked" for life. Their sojourn "in the lands of darkness" had made them permanently suspect, at an impasse the legist Domenico Fiorello—who wrote to the court of the Roman Inquisition not as a paid advocate, but as an expert consultant—addresses sympathetically.[6] Suspicion of possible future infidelity to Judaism made these women unmarriageable. Who could guarantee that following marriage they might not one day convert, or, worse, that they might be returned to the House of Converts arbitrarily, especially if they were mothers or carrying a child?[7]

This scenario, as Fiorello's brief reveals, was no fantasy.[8] Nor was he the only one to point it out. The later seventeenth-century Giacobo Pignatelli, whom Fiorello cites ad verbum, went on at length about the dangers of denunciations.[9] And my suspicion is that at least one explanation of why Anna's brother Tranquillo decided to make the diary known was his reflecting on similar episodes, which, as will be seen toward the end of this study, were still occurring in the earlier nineteenth century.

Tranquillo may have also reflected on the collateral damage that was the lot of those who did convert. For if Anna was a casualty, so was Sarra, the probable name of the sister of Sabato Coen, Anna's denouncer.[10] Sarra is a pitiable figure, a part of the equipe of the House of Converts, most likely keeping her head above water by reciting a fixed script, including about her "wonderful marriage and mother-in-law." She had little choice. Like all converts, she was under constant supervision, her behavior monitored in the supervised converts' confraternity she was obligated to join. This was a victimization of another kind, which more than one Christian writer protested.[11]

One is left to wonder what provoked the Christians who raised their voices and quills in protest. Possibly, as suggested by Salo Baron with respect to earlier events in Portugal, they were disturbed by the violation of human values endemic to the Church's conversionary apparatus. They were beyond a doubt uneasy about the modes the Church had adopted to produce conversion. Its application of force, or near-force, offended their appreciation of the law, of the right order of the state, and perhaps, too, as we shall eventually see, of citizenship and its nature.[12]

The Casa

Anna's contacts in the *Casa,* which was located about a mile from the ghetto, were almost exclusively with converts.[13] Inmates in the *Casa* were physically cut off, but even afterward, the convert was isolated, no longer physically —complaints about converts entering the ghetto are legion—but emotionally. Converts were promised entrance into Christian society, yet in the end, thanks to excessive supervision, full entrance was effectively denied.[14]

Converts were not trusted; discrimination against them went back to the early Middle Ages. They might "backslide," as it was put, openly returning to Judaism, or they might resume Jewish practice and contaminate others. If we can trust the words of Lorenzo Virgulti, himself a convert and a leading preacher in the *Casa,* who died just fourteen years before Anna's enclosure, the *neofiti* were also a demanding, reprobate bunch.[15]

There were efforts at integration, including through translations into

Hebrew of Christian prayers like the Office of the Blessed Virgin, the *Ave Maria*, and the Our Father. The texts of these translations survive.[16] The goal was to ease the transition from the former religion to the new, making the break with the past *seem* less severe. Yet precisely here is the sign that *neofiti* would remain just that, converts for life, even when married to a Christian—and usually far less well than they, especially women, had been promised. One suspects that the writings of "convinced" converts, often full of spleen against Judaism, may sometimes have been cover-ups, transferring and projecting disappointment onto another.

How could Anna not despise the *neofiti* she encountered in the House of Converts, especially the women, who were, in effect, professional prose-lytizers? In the depths of her struggles, Anna cannily rejected their tales of the material glory awaiting her. Perhaps she knew that after the exquisite baptismal ceremony—staged for the benefit *of the Church*, not the *neofità*—there was invariably a letdown. One wonders whether Anna could have also known that going back well over five hundred years, the annals of papal letter-writing are full of requests for stipends from converts living in misery.[17]

Anna possibly had heard about what happened to family fortunes when a younger member, especially a son, joined the convert army. His inheritance would be demanded immediately. And were he, as he so often was, a minor, it would be invested in his name in the *Monte di pietà* (the Catholic loan fund that had so successfully competed with Jewish lenders). Conversion thus might lead to family ruin; and, unless the convert hated his or her parents and had converted in "adolescent" rage, conversion had to bring with it a sense of guilt for disobedience.[18]

Was there nothing appetizing about conversion? Barring conviction of Christian truth, a wish to escape dire poverty, or perhaps some personal motive, even love, there was, as Anna saw it, nothing at all.[19] This nothing-ness was enlarged by the *neofito* preachers Anna met in the *Casa*, including the terrorizing tyrant, full of fury, who would not countenance his quarry's escape—the same *stregone* who threw holy water on her, threatened to tie a huge cross to her bed and could not imagine there were those he could not persuade. Who could possibly reject what he himself had come to believe—or persuaded himself he believed?

Anna was also a woman, evoking even greater zeal. For were not women the incarnation of Eve, and were they not veiled in Church to hide their seductive charms?[20] Undominated—and in Anna's case, unconverted—

they were a social danger that needed blunting. But mostly, in the minds of the preachers in the *Casa*, these women needed baptism; and one asks what precisely were they saying to women like Anna, words that had sometimes persuaded others. What was the content of the too many three-hour sermons Anna was forced to endure?[21]

Anna, as the diary reveals, was told of the absolute certainty of Catholic truth and of the Jews' dismissal as God's chosen; the catechizers were well trained. They may have also conjured up the frequently voiced degrading imagery of the Jew as a dog, the rejected child (of God), covered, as contemporary popular Roman verse relished in saying, with the Tiber's—read: human—filth.[22] The preachers trotted out verses from the Bible, the prophecies of Isaiah and Daniel that reportedly tell of the coming of Jesus, all of which, they said, gave the lie to the Jews' Talmudic "nonsense." Humans should seek to unite eucharistically with God. The God of the Jews was humanized, sullied, and blasphemously brought down to earth. Jews had lost all political power and been placed under Christian rule, their laws long ago superseded.[23] Did Anna not know that (contemporary) Judaism was the corrupt fruit of a demon (named Bentamalion, as the Catalan Ramon Martí had written in his late-thirteenth-century *Pugio Fidei*)?

Anna, in the diary, rejects claims like these out of hand. But was the real Anna so truly constant? Is it not possible that in her state of bewilderment, Anna began to believe what she heard, rationality cast to the winds? She might have been impressed by the rudimentary kabbalistic arguments found in the tract of the *neofito* Ludovico Carrito.[24] Besides, were not these horrid *neofiti* really Jews? In Jewish law, the renegade always had the possibility of coming back,[25] while many, if not most, Christians thought that converts had never left. As a noted eleventh-century priest said of even the *descendant* of one famous convert: "He was a Jew, and he spoke like one, too."[26] But so did the converts who confronted Anna, who spoke to her in Italian, but, perhaps intentionally, injected a word or two of *ebraico* into their speech; not "Hebrew"—as the word means in normal Italian—but local "Romanesco" into which Hebrew words, often Italianized, might slip. This "in talk," paradoxically, might mitigate her disgust.

Familiar, too, were the biblical images the preachers evoked, like the one of the three boys in the furnace in the book of Daniel. Much as these boys, Anna was told, she had been tossed into a burning trench of purification.[27] Baptism would set her free. She should see herself like Abraham, leaving his homeland and people to become a person of God, founding a dynasty of believers, and she should compare herself to the Mothers of Israel, a term with a *double entendre*. Did not the Church call itself the True Israel, *Verus Israel,* as opposed to the Jews, who were no longer Israel? And did it not also call itself the Holy Mother Church (*Sancta mater ecclesia*), anticipating Anna's fusion with the wider Christian corpus? She must fulfill her dual motherly role, as Mother of the Church and in union with it. Do not, moreover, Jews mention the Trinity itself three times a day in their prayers, saying *Kadosh, kadosh, kadosh,* meaning in strict Hebrew, not only the normal holy, holy, holy, but Godly, Godly, Godly, which, she was told (and as Christian Kabbalists were fond of saying), referred to the Trinity's triune nature.[28]

Sincere Conversion

This kind of argument may have made Anna ponder. Not all Jews reacted negatively to conversionary drives. If Anna's story was one of refusal, and if to persuade her, she was made a captive—and captive she was, as the name of her account, the *Ratto,* "the kidnapping," tells us—we must put the narrative in proper perspective. Not all conversion resulted from force. There were sincere converts, some of whom turned on their past and through sharp verbal and written attack acted out their rage at having once been Jewish. They were angry, because, as they saw it, Judaism had stood between them and salvation. They had a point. Precisely where the churches of all denominations offer the sincere believer hope for the soul, and in a personal future life, Judaism does not. It speaks of a general day of judgment, one of glory, and of corporeal, as well as spiritual, resurrection for all mankind. But this is for a distant time, following the arrival of the messiah—not the Second, but the *first* Coming. Judaism offers none of Christianity's immediate reward. Nor does Judaism promote equivalents of Christianity's great mysteries. There is no union in the body of Christ or insertion into the mystical unity of the Church and its people. Judaism offers community and a way of life, often rigorous, certainly different, very little understood by observers.[29]

For the believer, the mystery of the Trinity, and especially incarnation, is a great marvel. For one wholly outside the Church, it is incomprehensible myth. Thus the Spanish Jew Alfonso de Espina in the fifteenth century was persuaded to convert, or so he reports, by a dream; a dream persuaded another convert, Hermann of Cologne, too, five centuries earlier, although more than likely the contents of Hermann's dream, as it has come down to us, are a product of monks who wished to set down in writing ideals to which they hoped others would aspire.[30]

Yet those whom belief overwhelmed were the few. More often—most often—people converted because they were hungry or despairing. There were also, if rarely, women like Rachel Carmi, a prostitute or simply promiscuous, who freely had sex with Jews and Christians alike, until one Christian partner fathered a child, which would surely be baptized, and so would Rachel, too, if she wished to rear the child herself.[31] When one parent was a Christian, offspring were invariably made Christians, as the canons had established for well over a thousand years.

However, Rachel was never tricked into accepting baptism—which could have easily been Anna's lot had she not, as her diary says, had her wits about her always during her stay in the *Casa*. It is most likely that even sheltered in her privileged life in the ghetto, Anna had heard both sides of the story. It was not only the resistant Anna but also the knowledgeable one—a point Tranquillo was so set on making—who held out despite the enormous pressure. Anna held her ground and emerged from the *Casa* a Jew, although, as Tranquillo wants us fully to absorb, a person terrorized and shattered. The escalating terror built into the structure of the diary, more frightening as the days succeed one other, is designed—was designed, by Tranquillo— to make us empathize with Anna to the fullest. Tranquillo was also clever, planting hints here and there in the diary, to make us aware that as much as he depicted his sister as triumphant, in reality, she had been shaken to her roots. What kept her from saying, Yes, I will be baptized, may have been simply good fortune, a tirade, for example, that ended two minutes too soon.

Tranquillo, His Sister, and the Times

A half century later, the diary was circulated. It was a family chronicle, but also a source for raising Jewish morale. To accomplish this, Tranquillo borrowed. Anna's experiences seem to be overlaid with those of an otherwise unidentified young woman in northern Piedmont, who, too, had been the victim of an "offering" or "denunciation" sometime in the opening years of the eighteenth century, and whose fortunes are recounted by the Turinese jurist Giuseppe Sessa. The details of the two episodes are so alike that it is hard to imagine the overlap is coincidental, most notably, the young woman's festive release from the House of Converts in Turin, which was celebrated in the synagogue.[32] Sessa had reported the events in 1716, years before Anna's reclusion. Whether Tranquillo learned about them from reading Sessa's tract remains unknown. Possibly, he discovered it much later in a different source, prompting him to rework Anna's story to make it more poignant and instructive to its readers.

Yet why did Tranquillo not reveal Anna's story until 1793? As he writes in the introduction, he seems to have gained physical possession of the diary sometime after 1779, but kept it private. Some spark in 1793 made him change his mind. Possibly it was the word of happenings in France, especially the guillotining that year of Louis XVI and his consort Marie Antoinette, which had spread like wildfire through Rome, and, in response to which, a mob murdered the liberal, Jacobin-leaning noble Giuseppe Hugo di Basville and then laid siege to the ghetto. After some injuries, although only to Jews caught outside the ghetto walls, the authorities intervened, preventing the ghetto's being engulfed in flames. As reports tell us, the Jews were shaken. A charge of Jacobinism (supporting the radical Revolution) and of secreting arms had been laid at the ghetto's door. Would not an account of Jewish survival in the *Casa* allay fears? This is more than fanciful speculation. The presenter of that tale of survival, Tranquillo del Monte, was also the author of our most detailed account of the siege.[33] In 1783, it was again Tranquillo, along with one Salamon Ambron, who had approached the Jewish community of London, seeking help during the Terracina episode, to which we shall return, when Roman Jews were defended by the lawyer Carlo Trenca.[34] Shortly afterward, Tranquillo had unsuccessfully petitioned this same community to admit three hundred Roman Jews.

Most likely, though, it was another incident, one with an element that rings perfectly with Anna's, that persuaded Tranquillo to share the diary's contents. This incident could be described only with reserve: its memory was too recent; the active players were still in office. On November 29, 1792, the three current *Fattori*, of whom Tranquillo was one, were receipted for paying the expenses of Grazia, the *nuora* (daughter-in-law) of a certain Iacchetto. Grazia, an *Ebrea gravida* (she was pregnant), was being held in the *Casa*, denounced by unnamed Christians and under orders *da consegnarsi il feto doppo sgravata ai Cristiani*, to hand over her baby at birth to Christians for baptism.[35] However, after the *Fattori* had *esperimentati le loro ragioni*, undertaken a vigorous defense, Grazia was released, and *il feto resti alla madre nell'ebraismo,* both the mother and her fetus were allowed to remain together as Jews. Grazia had apparently promised to become a Christian and then reneged, although when she made the promise, she was in jail (for reasons unknown). The *Fattori* argued that she had acted under duress, depriving her vow of legal value, not to mention that, as they demonstrated calendrically, Grazia was not pregnant at the time of her incarceration and promise. How could she offer to give something (the fetus) that did not yet exist? The Vice Regent, no doubt to the surprise of all, agreed.[36]

Had Tranquillo been reminded of his sister, despite the differing circumstances? Or were the circumstances really that different? In a *Memoriale* composed by a member of the Jewish community—as insertions in the text in the Hebrew script common to Rome attest—we learn that the *Fattori* had been forced, under the threat of the enormous fine of 1,000 scudi, to bring Grazia to the *Casa dei catecumeni* by themselves; usually *Birri*, papal police, did the job. The *Fattori* were both embarrassed and afraid of the mobs that had attacked the police on similar occasions. The Curate of the *Casa* meanwhile protested that he had the testimony of five witnesses that Grazia had promised the child, which she vigorously denied, affirming her determination to remain a Jew. To resolve the matter, the Vice Regent himself— whom twice the *Fattori* say was motivated by justice—summoned Grazia to his chambers; the *Fattori*, as we learn from a marginal note, waited in the *anticamara*. The Vice Regent tells Grazia that he has accepted the reasoning presented on her behalf. She can go home, which she does, to give birth six weeks later, to a boy, who is ritually circumcised—by Tranquillo himself.

With one exception, the apology of the Vice Regent (along with his many protestations to Anna that he has honored her with his presence, as he would do for no other), matches the diary of Anna, including the refrain that the Vicar is just. The exclusion of the *Fattori* from the Vicar's presence during the interview is the "smoking gun" that makes it certain that there has been copying. There is also the happy end of the festive circumcision, reminiscent of Anna's putatively joyous welcome home. Grazia, of course, was married; she would not suffer Anna's lonely fate. The diary's intimations about Anna's moral probity would also have been inapplicable. As for the diary's unique apology, I suggested—and still believe—that it was modeled on Ibn Verga's fictional narratives, supplying the irony that accentuates the central message of Roman Jewish absurdity.

Grazia's misadventure, which occurred just months before the diary's release, gave Tranquillo both the impetus to speak out, but, even more, a model with which to say it. This model, amplified by the invented apology, crowns the diary's narrative. Here was the material Tranquillo lacked to make Anna's diary so very poignant, crying out his pain for his sister, but also the unbearable frustrations created by the conundrums of Roman Jewish life. The Jews, as all legal authorities agreed, were *cives,* citizens, living under the law; and the law might actually work in their favor. Yet just as often, it did not. The Papal State they inhabited was a confessional one, with distinct laws discriminating against those not of *the* dominant (Catholic) confession, as Tranquillo understood well, provoking his irony. Irony, too, underlies the remarks in the *Memoriale* about justice always prevailing, if not cynical double entendre. For was it not lawful in the confessional state to maintain the Jews' second-class status?

Irony among Rome's Jews was not unknown. It appeared in a protest from 1720, that as citizens, Jews should not be forced to buy wheat for bread that would be offered to no others,[37] and it comes out once more in 1793, with aplomb and sophistication, in a demand for respect as citizens, in whose composition again Tranquillo likely had a hand. Jews passing the headquarters of the Roman Civil Guard, or encountering a patrol, had been forced by the guardsmen *cavarsi il cappello,* to doff their hats. Once, when this happened to a poor Jew, Moise Zarfadi, out trying to find some way to earn money, he dropped his hat on the ground. It became soaked with rain, which, somehow, the guardsman took as an insult, and he gave the Jew four *piattonate puntate di bajonetta,* four hits with the sharp blades of a bayonette. That happened ten days before, and Zarfadi was still languishing near death in a hospital. To make matters worse, other guardsmen had entered the pub where Zarfadi's companion, Angelo Frascati, was inside drinking a *foglietta,* a measure, of wine at the invitation of *due cristiani suoi amici,* two Christian friends. The guardsmen poured the wine over Frascati's head.

Indignant, the Jewish leadership addressed the head of the Guards. This outrage, they said, insults *i principi della legge naturale,* natural law, and even more the *Carità* that every Christian must embrace, obligating him *deve amare ogni suo simile,* to love all those like him, every other human being, *sia Nazionale, sia estero, sia della stessa religione, sia diversa, sia amico, sia anche nemico,* regardless of whether that person is a co-national, a foreigner, of the same religion, or another, whether friend or foe. More urgent, it was *un miracolo from Dio,* a miracle, that nobody struck back. It is only a matter of time [if things go on like this] that somebody will lash out. Imagine the tumult. First, troops in the ghetto, then the populous united with the soldiers, sparks, and fire. And then. . . . (The suspension points are in the original text.)

Are we not, the Jews demand, citizens? We are not slaves, even in this church-state *stato ecclesiastico [gli ebrei] non sono . . . schiavi, ma sudditti a paragone di tutti gli altri cittadini?* We are subjects on a par with all the other citizens; and here they cite the Code of Justinian (C. 1, 9, 7), which says precisely this. Indeed, they were paraphrasing the formal definition of Jews as citizens with full civil privileges coined by the great seventeenth-century jurist Cardinal Gian Battista de Luca. And just to be sure, they added the words of Lucio Ferraris, a recent judge on the Roman high court the Rota, saying Jews were not enemies and were to be treated peacefully; Ferraris was referring to Alexander II's dictum of 1063, enshrined in the canon *Dispar nimirum est,* which the Jews themselves had repeated for emphasis in a petition they had made only four years earlier. For good measure, they also cited a well-known decision of the Rota and, finally, the prohibition on treating Jews with *contumelia,* contempt, found in Benedict XIV's bull of 1747 *Postremo mense,* whose subject was legitimate "offerings," which also cited *Dispar nimirum.* The Jews, as I said, were clever in throwing the pope's words, even in this most disheartening of texts, back in his face.

They were even cleverer in doing so in the context of the reality of 1793, and that of France, in particular, where, since 1791, in theory, if not yet fully in fact, being a citizen meant legal equality in a non-confessional state. Why, the Jews of Rome in 1793 may have been intimating, is our lot so radically different from that of our brothers in France. But since it was so different, and since, as they knew all too well, French thinking was completely foreign to ecclesiastical minds, their only possible resort was to rehearse notable citations of *Dispar nimirum est.*[38]

A group of lawyers, charged in 1789 by the pope but actually representing the Jews, was of the same mind. The call they issued to lessen restrictions choking the Jews rested squarely on *Dispar nimirum,* although they introduced a novel reading. They explained the bull (and canon's) critical clause, "Jews are always ready to serve (*servire*)," to mean not only, as its originator Alexander II intended, "ready to accept Christian dominion" and not, as some had said, that Jews were true slaves. Rather, they said, "to serve" meant to serve the state, which Jews did through their commercial activities, meriting them fair treatment. To sustain their position, they produced a stream of laws and canons, including fleeting references to the Law of Nature and the Law of the Nations. These laws were not signs of the Enlightenment. As the lawyers themselves emphasized, they were medieval and were being applied even prior to 1555 and the innovations of Paul IV. As the Jews they represented knew all too well, to go beyond this, to introduce, possibly, Enlightenment rhetoric, or even hint at the idea of emancipation, served no purpose.

Or do their numerous references to *Libertà* and *Cittadinanza* bear an otherwise hidden message that they dared not put down on paper? Whatever they themselves thought in their hearts, their written argument had to be one, as all good lawyers' arguments are, that might persuade the papal judges. And for the latter, the only valid frame of reference, the only judicial and civil structure, they would—indeed, were equipped to—consider was that of the past, the one defined by the canons and the highly confessional common law of the *ius commune*.[39]

Entrenched as it was in this traditional structure, the Papal State might (but, in fact, failed to) respond to pleas to lighten the Jews' burdens; going further was impossible. As long as that state continued to reinforce its confessional roots, the Jews could never achieve what at least knowledgeable leaders like Tranquillo must truly have wanted: citizenship and rights without discrimination. A second petition from 1793, read together with the two we have just seen, is transparent; its demand was to maintain recently granted commercial privileges outside the ghetto in Piazza Navona, now threatened with revocation. "Once it was," the petition states, in fact borrowing language from the lawyers' petition of 1789, "that the Jews, who live by *ius commune*, enjoyed full *libertà*" to practice whatever craft they desired, to own fixed property, and not to be subject to the rule of the guilds. But Paul IV upset everything with his commercial restrictions, which his successors renewed. Now, the moment to revoke these restrictions had arrived.

At the same time, Rome's Jews understood perfectly the role commercial limitation played in conversionary policy. They had observed the increase in the number of conversions that followed the closing of Jewish banks in 1682. What they were asking to repeal, therefore—especially as they coupled their request with a reference to *ius commune*, and with the petition itself coming on the heels of the other reminding the pope that they were *sudditti a paragone di tutti gli altri cittadini*—was conversionary policy itself. This was tantamount to calling for an end to all canonical constraints and the establishment, in their place, of equality before the law.[40]

Our status, the Jews were saying, floats between living as full-fledged *cives* and those relegated to second-class, subject to canonical limitation and dependent on *Dispar nimirum est*. We are members of society, but also its abjects, forced to depend on *caritas,* the rule of divine justice, as much as on civil law. Attuned as we are to the world around us, this troubles us. We have collected and digested the charters of privilege being given in the Empire and in other Italian cities, and we are versed in the principles of the Enlightenment, which call for the equality of all mankind, and to which, however implicitly—we dare not mention them outright—we are appealing. It is as though the Jews of Rome had read the latest documents of political and revolutionary thought. Our condition, declare the two extraordinary Jewish texts of 1793, whose authors in both cases were the very same leaders of the Roman Jewish Community, verges on the incongruous. In this sense, Anna's diary, as reworked by Tranquillo, is the arch-statement of what in a properly ordered polity, free from confessional bias, should never be.

3. The Roman Ghetto

But perhaps we should step back before reengaging the discussion of Anna as her tale reflects Roman Jewry's political condition and examine the scene of the drama, its setting, and its background. To vivify Anna's story, we do well to paint a picture of the heart of Roman Jewish life, the Roman Ghetto. By the eighteenth century, the ghetto had become a wretched place. What had set the decline in motion were policies begun in 1555 by Pope Paul IV and continued by his successors, often with greater rigor. Deterioration in papal-Jewish relations occurred slowly. Over hundreds of years, there was an incremental hardening of limitations on Jews that the canon law of the Church had established as early as the eighth and ninth centuries.[1] Still, the establishment of the Roman Ghetto by Pope Paul IV in July 1555 was a jolt. The bull *Cum nimis absurdum* set policy not only for Rome, but for all places under direct papal rule, too, which meant most of central Italy. It also put pressure on adjacent principalities to follow suit.[2]

Yet there was as much continuity in 1555 as rupture. As stated by *Cum nimis absurdum*, the Roman Ghetto was established to bring the Jews to convert *en masse*. This goal had long been desired, but until shortly before 1555, it was pursued in starts and stops. After 1555, conversion became, and remained, prime. Its pursuit would include burning Jewish books and preaching to Jews on the Sabbath in their synagogues or in churches just outside the ghetto wall. The House of Converts, founded even before the ghetto, in 1542 into 1543, would instruct and care for its inmates, the *catecumeni*, who, upon baptism, would become and were called *neofiti*, new converts. Most of all, Paul IV, a devotee of "discipline" in the Church,[3] had persuaded himself that strictly supervised regulations, even if they were nearly all traditional ones, now tied to residential restriction, would achieve what past, yet phlegmatically applied conversionary policies had not.[4] Paul IV had taken to heart the advice given by the Camuldulese monks Pietro Querini and Paolo Giustiniani in the *Libellus ad Leonem decem* of 1513. The Jews were to be brought to the faith by *piis verberibus,* a phrase taken from Gregory the Great, *Deus qui culpas nostras piis verberibus percutis ut nos a nostris iniquitatibus emundes,* God, punish our sins with pious lashes so that you will cleanse us from our sins, a citation found many times over after his time, whose meaning with respect to Paul IV's policies is transparent.[5]

To promote his policy—and demonstrate its legality—Pope Paul IV, the ghetto's founder, made common ground with the well-known jurist Marquardus de Susannis, whose detailed summary of canon law and *ius commune* as they affected Jews was so successful that it went through five editions in fewer than sixty years. To clarify his intentions, de Susannis added a conversionary sermon he himself composed.[6]

From now on, Jewish life in Rome was conditioned by the ghetto, which, among other things, had revolutionized the structure of Jewish residence. For nearly two millennia, Jews had mingled freely with Rome's other inhabitants by day or night, admittedly (but not always consistently) limited by restrictive canons. After July 1555 and the bull of Paul IV, *Cum nimis absurdum,* Jewish life would take place for the most part behind a wall, especially at night when the ghetto gates were locked.

The timing of the ghetto's establishment was no accident. The mid-sixteenth century was the moment when religious and political axioms that had endured seemingly from time immemorial were shattered and the rise of Protestantism ended the monopoly the Roman Church had held for centuries over Christian belief. The Church had been in difficult straits since the early fourteenth century, when important ecclesiastics had said the pope should be subject to a council; and there were constant charges of corruption, matched by an articulate call for internal reform. The goal was purity and unity. However, as reforming tracts, like the *Libellus ad Leonem Decem*—composed, note, before the outbreak of Protestantism—never tire of stressing, achieving this end required the conversion of the Jews. Convincingly, the reforming tracts argue that the fate of the Jews and the universal Church were intertwined,[7] so that the modern historian following the fate of one, the Jews, gains insight into the overall structures and programs of the other, the

Church. And the Jews still resident in Europe in the early sixteenth century were gathered largely in Italy, under direct papal rule or influence.[8]

Jews had been expelled from nearly everywhere else in Western Europe, and, even in Italy's North, expulsions occurred, like that of 1597 from the area around Milan; Liguria (Genoa) never allowed a fixed Jewish settlement. Jewish life in Italy continued principally in Venice, Ferrara, Mantua, Modena, and Tuscany, with the greatest concentration in the Papal State, which, by the end of the sixteenth century, stretched from Bologna and Ancona (on the Adriatic) in the North to just above Naples in the South. The largest Jewish community was that of Rome, so that the pope ruled politically over more Jews than any other monarch in Western Europe.

Papal Maneuvers

As of the mid-sixteenth century, no pope had expelled Jews or enacted laws delegitimizing their presence. The popes also treated as inviolable the Jews' right to due judicial process; this term is medieval, not modern. Even the otherwise draconian—toward everybody—Pope Paul IV took special pains to ensure that the law be observed, including when he ordered the Roman Ghetto established, although his concern was as perverse as it was obsessive. Propelled by the shocks of the sixteenth century and reformist sentiment, but also by his personal conviction (not to be discounted) that the End of Days—the Last Judgment and the Second Coming—was upon him, Paul IV chose to ignore the failures of the past and disregard the perennial anxiety churchmen and others had expressed about converts reverting to Judaism.[9] It is not that the popes before the sixteenth century had *opposed* conversion, but, with the short-lived exception of Benedict XIII (officially an anti-pope) in Iberia, they themselves had done little to forward it beyond applauding missionary activities like those of the thirteenth-century Louis IX of France and the fitful James I of Aragon. Nor were their policies consistent.

But in 1555, when Paul IV ascended the papal throne, there was a desperate need for rejuvenation, the most unmistakable sign of whose achievement would be throngs of new Jewish converts. During the reign of Paul IV and for over three hundred years, the popes dedicated energies, sometimes greater, other times lesser, to reaching this end.[10]

Even prior to Paul IV, papal letters had begun to insist that all matters touching Jews must be directed toward their conversion, adopting, in their salutation, at the start of the letter, the formula: *via veritatis agnoscere et agnitam custodire,* may you recognize the way of truth; and once you have recognized it, preserve it. From about 1550, it was going to be said repeatedly that the Jews are allowed to live among Christians *only in anticipation (ad hoc ut)* of their mass conversion,[11] which would signal the absorption of all mankind into a single spiritual body, the *unis panis,* as well as the purification and perfection of society. The reassertion of the Catholic Church would become reality in one fell swoop.

Yet Paul IV's preferred method of promoting conversion through restriction had already been tried, although its history was anything but straightforward. Heavy taxation, said Pope Gregory the Great, at the end of the sixth century, would persuade rude country bumpkins, pagans, to approach the baptismal font. Paul IV applied this principle to Jews, urged on by contemporary writers like the Jesuit Francisco de Torres, who said that Jews would convert when they were made literally "to suck at husks [for sustenance]." Pope Paul also raised taxes sharply and imposed heavy fines on Jewish lenders, claiming they were charging excessive rates of interest. The squeezing of Jewish lending eventually bore fruit. The closing of Jewish banking in Rome in 1682 induced large numbers, including families, to approach the baptismal font.[12]

The ghetto, the mainstay of the papal program, was conceived as a site of social ostracism, but also as a limbo. The Jews would be forced to reside there until they "saw the light." However, the Italian ghetto as such was not a papal invention. That "honor" belongs to the Venetians, who, in 1516, allowed Jews to settle on a small island called "the ghetto," where a copper foundry had once stood and where workers cast, or threw, *gettare,* the molten metal.[13] There are variations on the theme, but this explanation of the term *ghetto* and its origin is almost certainly the correct one. The Venetians were clear about motives. It was dangerous to mix with the Jews and inadvisable to allow them to dwell in Venice proper, on the islands of the lagoon. Previously, Jews had lived in Mestre, on the mainland, and could reside in Venice itself only for brief periods of a few weeks. In the debate held in the Venetian Senate preceding the ghetto's establishment, it was said that God would punish the city if it allowed a permanent Jewish residence (which, technically speaking, it never did).[14]

In Rome, the ghetto was called the *serraglio,* the place were one is closed up. The name *ghetto* was adopted only in the later 1580s. Rome's Jews, and papal officials, first called the precinct the Courtyard of the Jews (*ḥaẓer ha-yehudim; serraglio [or] claustrum iudaeorum/claustro degli ebrei*). But in 1589, following an increase in the Jewish population, the area was expanded rather than allowing a select few to live outside. The implication was unambiguous: the ghetto was here to stay, to which the Jews responded by starting to speak of *nostro ghet*. They were punning on the Hebrew *get*, a writ of divorce, which, from their perspective, is what they had been given. The *get*, moreover, is "delivered" to the wife, the divorcee, and belongs to her by right. By invoking the idea of *nostro ghet*—*our* writ of divorce—the Jews were declaring themselves the cast-out woman. Indeed, this is what the Hebrew word for divorce, *legaresh*, strictly means. Besides, regardless of whether the Jewish image, from within or without, was masculine or feminine, no one would question whether in the balance of powers pitting the Jews against the papacy, the former were the weaker party.[15]

The area of the Roman Ghetto was not new. Most Jews already lived in the S. Angelo Quarter, which is still the center of Roman Jewish life. Roman Christians saw the quarter as squalid. And some deprecatingly observed that the periodic floods of the Tiber that inundated the ghetto's streets and ravished its homes might remove the filth from Jewish bodies, but not the dirt from Jewish souls.

Jews saw things differently. Until the late eighteenth century when the ghetto had sunk into deep poverty, its physical reality was not the unsanitary place Christians imagined. Jewish documents from the seventeenth century reveal a ghetto population highly sensitive to its physical surroundings. They built latrines, washbasins, and sewers and stipulated regularly in contracts of rental the need for the presence of a toilet and the terms of its use.[16]

Spiritually, Jews were wont to picture the ghetto as a refuge, not a place of confinement. To the Jewish mind, the ghetto walls had an aura of sanctity, replicating the enclosed holy space of Jerusalem; passage through the ghetto by disrespectful gentiles was intensely disliked. A Christian miller who galloped his wagon through ghetto streets at breakneck speed in 1621 was stopped, assaulted, and eventually kicked to death.[17] The term *nostro ghet* implied that others would enter on sufferance, or so the Jews would have wished. The *sbirri*, the papal police, like those who abducted Anna del Monte in 1749, reminded them to think otherwise.

Jews also had to confront the reality of the ghetto's limited physical space. Within three decades of the ghetto's founding, it was becoming ever harder to find lodgings or a place to start a family. The Jews were so tightly packed that they often went to court to decide who had legal rights to a dwelling.[18] Moreover, beginning about 1570, the papacy launched a campaign to disenfranchise Jewish self-governance. Its principal weapon, closing down internally managed consensual arbitration, left Jews with no alternative but to turn to papal courts. There, *ius commune*, not halakhah (Jewish law) or simple equity, decided the outcome. Disenfranchisement was complemented by a policy of pauperization, both individual and collective. Regardless of Jewish commercial activity, communal debts grew inexorably, with the papal treasury owed ever greater sums, until the Community defaulted. Sometimes it seems that the only official function the Community, the *Università*, exercised was collecting taxes, which went to pay off debts.[19]

To compound difficulties, the early eighteenth century witnessed what amounted to an orchestrated progression of batterings. The offensive began in 1731 with a new confiscation of Hebrew books, including the financial records of the Community, only some of which were ever recovered. In the same year, a petition to enlarge the *Cinque scole* (the five synagogues of Italian, Sephardi, and Sicilian Jews housed in one building) was not only denied, but, in proceedings that dragged on for a decade, judges of the Roman Inquisition demanded that the five synagogues be unified; Roman Jews formally had permission to have but one place of worship. This move was paralleled with the simultaneous closing of a small area outside the main ghetto known as "the *ghettarello*," the small ghetto, where Jews had maintained storehouses, and also the Porta Leone synagogue, which, against all odds, had survived for nearly two centuries after the ghetto's founding.[20] The next steps would be bulls issued by Pope Benedict XIV in the later 1740s and the 1750s and, in 1775, by Pius VI, whose texts we will revisit and analyze more thoroughly later on.

In addition, Roman Jewish leaders were warned that they would be held responsible personally should someone be persuaded not to convert. Rather than being a source of power, or pride, the office of *Fattore* became an unwanted burden, which sometimes remained empty for years; at one point a revolving triumvirate of three *Fattori* at a time, each holding office for three months, was instituted. The laments of the *Fattori* were multiple. They petitioned the papal Vicar not to jail them for intervening to help other Jews, they protested when communal members publicly berated them at meetings of the Council of Sixty, the Community's large deliberative body, and they begged for assistance when Jewish rowdies began sitting in front of the Talmud Torah, the communal school, and the *Piazza Cinque scole*, joking, laughing, and creating a general nuisance, which the *Fattori* said they were powerless to stop.[21] Most poignant was the petition of 1716 to reopen the banks shuttered in 1682; an attempt in 1689 to engage in commerce outside the ghetto had proved insufficient to revive Jewish economic health. The Jews, the petition says, were becoming destitute. Since the bank closure, capital had dried up, with the result that nobody was able to work, whether in commerce or the crafts.[22]

Misfortunes multiplied. The *Fattori* were especially wary of heavy punishments should they be accused of actions like assisting a pregnant woman whose unborn child had been "offered" to the *Catecumeni* to slip out of Rome. The body designated to mete out punishments in these cases was the meddlesome Papal Inquisition. Fortunately, the Inquisition's principal concern was often to levy fines. The one imposed on the father of Miriana Sanguinetti of Modena in the earlier seventeenth century went into the Inquisition's coffers. Sanguinetti had been charged with dissuading Miriana, who had been denounced as wishing to convert, from taking this step. Miriana, as the questionable Inquisitional transcript says, had been nearly wooed into converting to marry a Christian rather than her Jewish fiancé. Just like Anna del Monte, Miriana, too, was promised that lovely ladies would come to fetch her in a coach and escort her to her baptism.[23] Visions of opulence, it was hoped, as opposed to the helplessness and despair that the papacy had made into the real Jewish lot—much as the elegance of baroque Rome contrasted with the squalor of the ghetto—would surely persuade many to approach the baptismal font.[24]

Roman Jews needed means to counter papal designs. One, I believe, was the creation of tight-knit families. Anna del Monte's longing to return to her family as a paramount value is a central refrain in her diary.[25] Families themselves were small. Rarely did they have more than two to four (living) children, while husbands and wives were often close in age, both of which factors no doubt encouraged emotional bonds.[26] With communal powers severely reduced, and with the waning of the confraternities, basically self-help organizations that had offered succor in the past, the family was the only steady institutional source of comfort Roman Jews had left. Keeping the family small and affective also reduced the probability of "offerings" by numerous collateral relatives, such as uncles and cousins.[27]

Baptismal Pressure

We must not overestimate the number of those who were "offered." It is all too easy to make too much of the clamorous cases that were contested. Yet, we should remind ourselves that just about every Roman family had a converted relative, who ipso facto was a source of latent danger. Nonetheless, until Pius VI opened the potential floodgates, which he did in 1783, by admitting "offerings" by distant relatives, the strategy, however conscious, of warding off conversionary threats through maintaining tight-knit nuclear family groups worked reasonably well. Anxiety, though, must have been high. Jurists like Giacobo Pignatelli and Giuseppe Sessa had explained how improbable "offerings" by distant relatives could be canonically justified, although they had also cautioned against making them. An uneasy papacy, however, stimulated by outside events like those of the 1780s and '90s in France, the Empire, and even the United States, eventually decided to turn possibility into fact and to permit what had not been allowed before. Growing anxiety in a Church much alarmed by new challenges to its spiritual supremacy had given impetus to conversionary maneuvers that went beyond strict discipline and began to verge on force.

There was one crucial reservation. Every element of this policy had to be justified by demonstrating its roots in long-standing legal traditions. In particular, the guarantee that parental wishes be respected when it came to baptizing offspring had to be honored, as it had been over the centuries. With the exception of Visigoth Spain in the seventh century or Portugal, in 1497, when all Jews were forcibly converted, the canons had determined that one parent at least, mother or father, had to consent to a child's baptism. The Jews should have been protected. They were not. Beginning in the later sixteenth century, and drawing on a precedent from the thirteenth, to which we shall return, expansive legal interpretations were vouchsafing the power of parental consent in an ever-widening circle of relatives: first, with a small step, in 1583, to the paternal grandfather, then, in 1751, with a large jump, to the paternal grandmother, and, eventually, by 1783, to paternal uncles and aunts.[28]

Ghetto Insecurity

Living in the ghetto had to have created insecurity vis-à-vis the world outside. Previously, Jews and Christians had lived cheek by jowl, and, sometimes, despite rabbinic and clerical wrath, cheek to cheek, at least for fleeting moments. The ghetto had *not* cut off all Jewish-Christian contact.[29] Christians entered by day to have clothing repaired or to buy secondhand goods, and some of them entered not only the ghetto precinct, but also the homes of Jews themselves, in particular, on Jewish festivals like Sukkot. Social transgressions of every kind occurred, which made Church officials fume and impose fines.[30] Nevertheless, acts of disrespect multiplied. During the Carnival season, the fish sellers, whose *pescaria* was located at the Portico di Ottavia, which abutted the ghetto walls, staged parodies (*beffi*) of Jewish funerals, while in 1771, the rabbis and *Fattori* were ordered to abase themselves inside the halls of the Campidoglio (the Roman city hall) in lieu of the centuries-old humiliation of (Jews) running half-naked and being mocked in Carnival races.[31] There were also the famous *giudiate,* plays that poked fun at all that Jews did.[32] No less disconcerting, and the source of many complaints, were the intrusions of *neofiti* into their parents' homes, principally to extort money, no doubt by threatening offerings and denunciations.

Were, then, Christians who visited the ghetto during Jewish festivals coming in friendship or were they out to "observe" and "deride," as contemporary writings on Jewish customs throughout Europe were increasingly doing?[33] Moreover, were these ostensibly social contacts—the measure of whose frequency in real time cannot be known—spontaneous or a remnant of what previously to 1555 had been casual? Interaction with Christians, once the norm, now seems too often to have become artificial and, possibly, awkward. Suspicion was rife. A petition made by "all the heads of Roman Jewish families" in 1770 to the Holy Office specified that *negli ultimi tempi* [they have found] *insopportabile la licenza e libertà de' plebei Cristiani d'ogni sesso in battezzare furtivamente le creature che trovavano nelle Case del ghetto da loro pratticate,* that recently, the license taken by various Christians, both men and women, secretly to baptize the little creatures they find in ghetto homes they frequent [likely for reasons of employment or trade] has become insupportable.[34] By any definition, the act of Christians entering a Jewish house was not a sure sign of friendship. For their part, the Jews must have been desperate. Of all things, the petition of 1770 was asking to have enforced the clauses prohibiting this practice found in Benedict XIV's bull *Postremo mense,* which defined appropriate "offerings."

This does not mean that Anna and her fellow ghetto Jews had ceased being Romans. Is not her diary written in Italian? And were not rabbis like

Moisè Mieli and Tranquillo Corcos well versed in rhetoric, the writings of classic authors, and even civil and canon law?[35] Roman Jews *never* relinquished their dual Jewish and Italian identity.[36] Still, Roman Jews must have struggled to know just where they stood vis-à-vis Roman society. Events like Anna's *Ratto*, the constant redefinition of who was authorized to make an "offering," the clear submission of civil to canon law, and the growing gap between Jewish life in the Papal State and elsewhere in Europe (and the new United States) could only have evoked protest, if not perplexity. Rome's Jews were left ever more bereft of a sense of security.

In this atmosphere, one might think that a politically astute papacy would sit by, waiting for the birds to come home to roost at the baptismal font. Despair by itself would multiply conversions. Yet in the turbulent eighteenth century, quiet waiting is the last thing the popes contemplated. The process of reaction that typified the Roman Church from the start of modern times was peaking, where it would remain for a century, if not longer. The idea of "freedom of conscience," for one, was considered so inimical and despised that two nineteenth-century popes, Gregory XVI and Pius IX, called it a "delirium." "Freedom of conscience" was condoned only in 1962, at the ecumenical Vatican II conference.

The Roman Church was going to have to fight to maintain the status quo, let alone to reassert its preeminence. A major sign of success would be the Jews' conversion, which would reaffirm the vitality of the *corpus mysticum*, the mystical body that was the entire Church, including its civil body, the Papal State. The ever-widening circle of those considered canonically qualified "to offer" as the eighteenth century progressed is a barometer of growing papal consternation.

There was a mythical aspect at work here as well. When, after two years of detention, Pius IX refused to return the kidnapped Edgardo Mortara in 1860, he had to have known that he was endangering his state. The French and their soldiers, who were the state's guarantors, had put him in difficult straits. If Pius remained stubborn, the soldiers would leave. But stubborn he remained. The French left, and his state fell soon after, with the Italian monarchy taking its place. It is as if the pope were restating his faith in Divine Grace, which would reward him for not yielding Edgardo and Edgardo's soul. The perennial struggle between flesh and spirit inherent in Christianity since the times of St. Paul—and which here was being realized in a conflict between confessional state and secularizing monarchy—would be decided *favore fidei,* in favor of the faith. Or as put recently by Massimo Mancini, and in the full spirit of our investigation: "The true issue at stake in the Mortara case [was] the fact that lacking the necessary distinction between religion and state power, the confessional state would consider it its prerogative to intervene in questions of conscience."[37]

4. The Confessional State

In contemporary terms, Anna's trials have the aura of the fantastic. One's Jewish identity in today's North America, and often elsewhere, rarely has public relevance.[1] We do well, therefore, to ask whether Anna's story, like that of Grazia, or of Canossa, a married woman "offered" by a paramour, as well as the stories of others, represents a specifically Roman Jewish dilemma. Was it one that could have come about only when and where it did, in the middle of the eighteenth century? Or was it a product of the much larger European Jewish past, which also embraced that of Roman Jews? It was, in fact, both. But it was also, it cannot be emphasized enough, a product of the confessional state for whose continuity the Church so greatly fought. What defined this state was its incessant pursuit of that which might be achieved "in favor of the faith," *favor fidei*.

Favor Fidei

Underlying everything that was happening in papal relations with Rome's Jews was a sharply dualistic worldview. Its core was distinguishing between acts that were said to promote the faith, *in favore fidei*, and those (said to be) committed out of hatred, *in odio fidei*. *Odio* and *favor fidei* became the gold standard for measuring correct action, and they are critical for appreciating the papacy's perception of law, but especially of legal precedence: which law or legal system was decisive when two laws (or legal systems) clashed?

Both terms had a long history. *Favor fidei* appears notably—although not for the first time—in Thomas Aquinas's (mid-thirteenth-century) discussion of forced baptism; Aquinas says that when one parent alone is a Christian (or has become one) the children are given to that parent, "to prevent the error of infidelity," and because "one must always prefer *favorem fidei*."[2] No wonder that in critical papal pronouncements of Benedict XIV, the differentiating of *favor* from *odium* comes to the fore. In both, *A quo primum* of 1751, excoriating Jews in Poland and, even more, in *Beatus Andreas* of four years later, beatifying one Andreas of Rinn, a supposed victim of ritual murder, the need to repel *odium fidei* by enhancing *favor* is unmistakable. *Beatus Andreas* applies *odium* repeatedly to characterize the motivation behind ritual murder, including that of Andreas of Rinn himself.

Benedict XIV was clearly taken by this dualistic vision. He resolved every question raised with respect to baptism and its administration, including whether to remove "offered" children from their parents, by asking if restraint created contempt for the faith (*odium*), as opposed to the "favor of the faith" that would be baptism's direct product.[3] He was not alone. Did not even the moderate legist Giuseppe Sessa say that victims of Jews were killed in *odio fidei?*

The balance of *favor* and *odium* is evident in the first comprehensive tract of law concerning Jews, the *De Iudaeis et aliis infidelibus* of Marquardus de Susannis, published in 1558, and subsequently reissued four more times. A doctor *utriusque iuris*, of both civil and canon law, not only a canonist, and someone whom Benedict cites directly, de Susannis wrote that the limitation on the number of synagogues allowed in a city was instituted *ad favorem et decorum*, for the benefit and enhancement, of the faith.[4] More pertinent, de Susannis said that a child even forcibly baptized is not to be returned to its parents *propter favorem fidei Christianae*, in deference to the Christian faith. The noted Venetian ecclesiastic and critic of the papacy Paolo Sarpi said the same thing early in the seventeenth century.[5] *Favor fidei* appears also in the extensive segments on Jews in the work of the canonists Antonio Ricciulli and Giacobo Pignatelli (1686), where it is used to justify the prohibition initiated by the late Ancient (Christianized) Roman Law Codes of Theodosian and Justinian on Jews holding public office.[6] *Favor fidei* justified closing down what was left of Jewish banking in Rome in 1682.[7]

Tradition assigned *favor fidei* true legal, if not a binding supralegal— in modern terms, constitutional—force. The [secular] laws and canons rise up before each other, says the 1169 *Summa Coloniensis*. But the canons take precedence because of the *bone ratione fidei*. "Did not the Roman *pontifex* say that the laws of princes are neither sacred nor to be venerated? . . . [Likewise] human law is not above the law of God, but beneath it. . . . Nor is it licit for the Emperor or for whatever guardian [of justice] to presume anything against piety or the law of God."[8] More directly, as put by the early-sixteenth-century Cardinal Gasparo Calderini, citing a noted text in Gratian's twelfth-century *Decretum*, the laws always cede to *favor fidei*, since there is no higher value than faith.[9] The good of the faith trumped human law always,[10] which reminds us sharply that in this "age of faith," law, which was perceived as the concrete and detailed expression of *Caritas*, the primal justice on which the order of the world rests, must never be read in isolation from its theological import. In elaborating and enforcing law, canonists and popes were verbalizing the foundations of their beliefs, which helps explain the sometimes excessively resolute quality of legal, especially canonical, interpretation.

Benedict XIV, in his 1751 bull *Probe te meminisse*, hastened to acknowledge the historical roots of *favor fidei*, citing its mention in the canon *Ex litteris* (in the title *de conversione infidelium* of the definitive 1234 *Decretales* of Gregory IX) and the commentary on that canon by Innocent IV, a canonist of great repute. Pope Innocent was sustained by late-thirteenth-century Bernard of Campostella the Younger, who said:[11] *In favorem maxime fidei Christianae respondemus patri eundem puerum assignandum*, to the very great benefit of the Christian faith, we respond that the boy (whose mother remained a Jew) should be assigned to the (converted) father. Much later, Rutilio Benzoni, in his 1595 *Speculum Episcoporum*, defended *favor fidei* much as did Calderini, saying: *fortior est lex divina et naturalis quam omnis lex humana*, Divine and Natural law is stronger, more binding, than all of human law.[12] Most informative is the fifteenth-century Domenico de S. Geminiano, who wrote: *nota quod propter favorem fidei multa statuuntur contra iura communia*, for the sake of *favor fidei* many laws have been issued nullifying those of *ius commune*.[13]

It was this standard that Benedict XIV used in 1747 to determine the legitimacy of "offerings" made by relatives other than mothers and fathers, and it was again his guide in interpreting the concept of *patria potestas*, the great power first Roman and then other law conferred upon parents over their children. Jews normally exercise this power, Benedict admitted, but the source is civil, not Divine or Natural law, or even the law of the nations.[14] Accordingly, as the product of "written human law" codified by the Romans, *patria potestas* fell as a reed before the power of Divine law—as expressed, of course, through *favor fidei*. As Giuseppe Sessa had said three decades earlier, in 1716, *per conversionem fidelis est quaesitum ius ecclesiae quod favore fidei absorbet ius infidelis,* when it comes to questions of conversion, the law of the Church overrides that of the infidel for the sake, the favor, of the faith.[15]

It was, then, anything but whim or disingenuous manipulation, and certainly not legal disregard that led to the great concern for the "favor of the faith" that papal and other texts exhibit. This overpowering concept was going to become ever more decisive in matters involving conversions, especially those which were arguably illegal. However difficult the notion may be for us today to absorb, for churchmen (and others) in the eighteenth century, zealously to sustain *favor fidei* was cardinal. Jews, like Anna del Monte, dragged into the House of Converts would pay the price.

Anxieties to defend *favor fidei* concerned more than Jews. Eighteenth-century popes had recoiled in the face of the novelties of their time. They were challenged to their roots by the ideas of rationalism and its accompanying demands for freedom of conscience and expression that went hand in hand with efforts by secular monarchs to end ecclesiastical prerogatives. These fears were the background to Pius VI's highly restrictive bull *Fra le pastorali sollecitudini,* sometimes known as his *Editto sopra gli ebrei,* of 1775. The bull stresses removing already illegal blasphemous rabbinic texts from Jewish hands. But its thrust is also consonant with *Inscrutabile,* a bull the same Pius VI issued on Christmas Day of the same year, in which (with no reference to Jews), he flails out against "plots [that] are laid against orthodox religion, when the safe [read, papal] guidance of the sacred canons is rashly despised?" It jibes, too, with Benedict XIV's fulminations of 1751 against Freemasonry, repeating those of Clement XII in *Providas* of 1738, accusing the Masonic Order of inflicting "injury on the purity of the Catholic Religion."[16]

The Church was ever on its guard against expressions of such injury, which it denominated *odium. Odium* might be found even in the annulment of a marriage, an idea that lasted from the Middle Ages through the twentieth century. The *odium* was compounded should a spouse who refused to convert depart, which, in effect, was also to mock the sacramental nature of (Catholic) marriage as that rite signified the unbreakable unity of Christ and the Church. By contrast, a spouse who converted was acting *in favore fidei.*[17]

Jews, Prime Repository of Odium

It was only to be expected that the anger of the eighteenth-century Church would focus on that classical protagonist of *odium fidei,* the Jews. It was as though controlling Jews was integral to, as well as exemplary of, the Church's attempt to rescue itself from an existential predicament. Jewish *odium,* the quintessence of "opposition," would not be allowed to vanquish or pollute the Holy Church. To the contrary, anticipatory of ultimate(ly hoped for) victory by way of an ever increasing number of baptisms *in favore fidei,* the Church would vanquish the Jews and restate its mission to the world. The Church was a ship that no storm could overturn, precisely as the classic image found in the second-century *Dialogue of Trypho with Justin Martyr* frames it. Indeed, if *in odio fidei,* Jews martyred Christians and held back those of their own who desired baptism, so, for reasons of *favor fidei,* should not as many Jews as possible be fished from the deep seas of infidelity to be reborn and saved at the baptismal font?[18] By implication Protestants and wayward Catholics, too, might be cleansed.[19]

This dualistic view of *favor* and *odium* did not end with the eighteenth century. As late as 1946, Pius XII was calling for privileging *favor fidei* and to reassert the preeminence—as he perceived it—of divine law. Addressing the judiciary of the Rota, the Church's highest court, on the subject of divorce, the pope was still battling claims made in the time of the Habsburg emperor Joseph II, about 1782, insisting that marriage be controlled by the state.[20] "Some rights and benefits are so particular to ecclesiastical jurisdiction," the pope said, "that by their very nature, they may not be objects under the control of the state judiciary."[21] It was as though Pius XII was echoing the words of Leo XIII in the encyclical *Immortale dei* of 1885, in which Pope Leo (speaking like one of his thirteenth-century predecessors) insisted that all power (citing Romans 13) came from God, whose will was expressed through the true (Catholic) faith and to whom all men and governments must be subservient. There should be no separation of church and state, no freedom to profess the faith of one's choice, nor, in matters of jurisdiction, should the Church be subject to the state.[22]

Leo XIII was refusing to look modernity in the eye. For him, whose perception of the relationship between church and state was based exclusively on the supremacy of divine order and rule, the doctrine of *favor fidei* was alive and well. His was a fictitious world-vision that chose to ignore—to be precise, openly rejected—the reality of the Church having lost all tangible political power after the formation of the unified Italian monarchy in 1870. It was only consequential that Pope Leo refused to republish texts rejecting the charge of ritual murder like that of Cardinal Ganganelli from 1758, before Ganganelli became Pope Clement XIV, or earlier bulls to this effect issued by Innocent IV.[23] Leo, moreover, was speaking for all the popes who ruled in the eighteenth, nineteenth, and the earlier twentieth centuries, who, without reservation, pursued conversionary success.

It was in the lifeblood of the papacy to demand that the precedence of divine over human law be maintained. Establishing this legal hierarchy was cardinal for the Church. The success or failure to retain ecclesiastical legal superiority, alongside the political sway it brought in its wake, was the hinge on which turned the transition from pre-modern to modern in the life of the state. Moreover, these principles, more than to protect the ecclesiastical body, were intended ideally to unify the body of the faithful and embrace all mankind in a single commonwealth in which arbitrary distinctions between individuals are odious. This ideal dates to Christianity's founding. It also resonates with the words of St. Paul in Corinthians, *unus panis multi sumus*, we are one loaf, regardless that we are many, a unity created, again according to Paul, when the members of the body of the faithful share the Eucharist. This act, as though by itself, brought into being the mystical, spiritual *Corpus Christi*, which was synonymous with the Church (1 Cor. 10:16–18). As put by the sixteenth-century theologian John Colet, "All men, nourished by the One [God himself], may be one in that by which they are [individually] nourished."[24]

How distant is this conceptual framework from that of today's democratic societies, ones in which the publicly declared bonding cement of the unified commonwealth is neither religious creed nor action, but the principle, however well observed in practice, that all members of the commonwealth are legally equal and enjoy identical civil rights! Distinctions of faith, physical appearance, and personal viewpoint are theoretically irrelevant. By definition, today's political bodies are obligated to shun religious components and sustain the position taken by the sixteenth-century Jewish physician David de Pomis, who anticipated every modern thinker on the subject by saying, "There is nothing so much a matter of the individual will as religious belief."

Ironically, de Pomis was not being original. He was citing the ancient

Church Father Lactantius (*Divinae Institutiones*, 5, 20), which shows how integrated into outside culture some Jews could be; more precisely, how knowledgeable they were about Christian literature. De Pomis's choice of Lactantius was also astute. Lactantius's message, just as that of de Pomis, spoke to the nature of the state itself. If religion was a matter of free choice, then the state should have no official religion, which the late ancient Roman state—still pagan in Lactantius's time—did, leading it to persecute those who rejected it: in this instance, early Christians. De Pomis was turning the message around: the Christian state must not persecute Jews. Nor, for that matter, he is implying, should religion be a criterion for membership in the civic body.

However, in papal Rome of the eighteenth century, nobody was listening. Rather than through legal equality, it was Paul's pithy apothegm of the one loaf that undergirded union and commonality. As in the medieval past, the civic body was to be an indisputably Christian one, the (religio-political) body of Christ—*to* which, and no less important, *in* which, only Christians might fully belong. This body was also one that shunned dissidence. As none other than St. Paul first put it, a "little leaven might sour the entire lump of dough"; and that leaven, however irrationally, was identified with the continued presence of Jews.

Anna on a Narrow Beam

Viewed in this context, which literally determined her fate and animated her story, Anna del Monte may be seen as signifying the Roman Jewish predicament. She was a figure standing on a narrow beam that could tilt one way or the other, which in Rome it did toward the defense of union within a confessional (Christian) body. Until Rome's Jews, too, joined this union, they would live in a limbo, "expelled" *into* the ghetto—albeit when mostly unwanted "opportunity" knocked, as in the case of a denunciation or an "offering," individual Jews might be pressured into joining that union by way of the *Casa dei catecumeni* and baptism.

Should, however, the beam tilt in the opposite direction, the results would be different. The union Jews would be invited to join would be a composite, whose membership, as de Pomis seems to be signaling, would be determined by humanity and civic loyalty. Nor was this structure alien to the late eighteenth century. It was, in its essence, identical to the one framed

by the American Founding Fathers and seconded in principle by the protagonists of the French Revolution. As put by George Washington, writing
in 1790 to the Jews of Newport, Rhode Island, hence, barely three years
before Anna's diary was circulated: "All [in the United States] possess alike
liberty of conscience and immunities of citizenship, [whose] government . . .
requires only that they . . . demean themselves as good [law-abiding] citizens."
Thomas Jefferson was more outspoken, saying that "all men shall be free to
profess . . . their opinion in matters of religion, and that the same shall in no wise
diminish . . . or affect their civil capacities."[25] James Madison was blunter yet,
arguing that religious multiplicity was *necessary* to safeguard the rights of all.[26]
The ideal American experience was the contra-positive of Anna's. This was a
distinction contemporaries grasped, including the leaders of the Church.[27]

The Church Resists

The forces of stasis in the Roman Church were prepared to do battle. One need
think only of the light-years separating the thought of Leo XIII on both the state
and democratic rule from the words of Washington, Jefferson, and Madison.
Nor, since Anna's day, have the most militant of these forces retreated, whose
motivation is the same anxiety for the unity and purity of the confessional Christian body as defined originally, if perhaps more generously, by St. Paul.[28]

To complicate matters, Paul may also be read backward, to say that to
attack the individual believer is to attack the whole—with which, according to Paul's notion of collective unity, the individual is interchangeable.
Thus, far more potent than an unmitigated hatred of Judaism or a desire for
revenge on the Jews for having allegedly crucified Jesus is the fear that left
unchecked, Jews will act out their (supposed) *odium* of Christianity, which
they will destroy by attacking its individual members. The Jews' very existence is a perennial threat. The later-nineteenth-century bishop Antonio de
Pol said this in just so many words in 1889, referring to Lorenzo of Marostica, a purported fifteenth-century victim of ritual murder. "The Jews," Pol
wrote, "were trying to kill not only little Lorenzino, but Christianity itself
(*lo stesso Cristianesimo*)." The (ritual) murder of one, or an offense of any
kind, is perilous for all. Such anxiety was, and, sometimes, still is linked to
charges of treachery from within. The scurrilous *Holywar.org* fuses stories
of ritual murder, fury at the reputed heresies of "liberalism" in the Catholic
hierarchy, and anti-Zionism, and then calls the three one and the same.[29]

The fear that Jews were threatening Catholic unity both directly and symbolically stiffened papal determination. The popes would entrench their conversionary drive by widening the circle of permissible "offerings." Warnings by jurists like Sessa were disregarded, although the initiative to take this assertive path was not wholly the popes' own. Objections were blocked time and again, first and foremost by converts. The will of converts, who were increasingly allowed "to offer" a relative to the faith, particularly children or a spouse, became a fiery issue that no pope could ignore. The ever more aggressive innovations of the Rector of the *Casa dei catecumeni,* who, along with his staff of mostly converts, was out to secure conversions at any price, also generated papal concessions. The pressure was unrelenting. In 1770, with what appears to have been only flimsy legal justification, Cardinal Alessandro Albani, the protector of the *Casa,* was able to persuade the new Pope Clement XIV Ganganelli to go against his inner feelings and prolong the detention of one Mazaldò, who had been "offered" to the Church by her converted husband.[30]

Ganganelli's approach to conversion was the traditional one of passive expectancy. In an irenic private letter to a Protestant divine composed very shortly before he became pope in 1769, on the subject of ecclesiastical union and burying the hatchet, the still Cardinal Ganganelli wrote that "*the time will arrive* (emphasis added) when there will be one and the same faith. Even the Jews will enter into the bosom of the Church. And it is in this firm persuasion, founded on the Holy Scriptures (John 10:16, to be precise), that they are allowed the full exercise of their religion in the heart of Rome."[31] Ganganelli's readiness to await the Jews' "entrance" was the same as that expressed at Christianity's birth by St. Paul in Romans chapter 11, and it goes a long way toward explaining why in 1758, Ganganelli willingly restated Pope Innocent IV's thirteenth-century denial of the charge of ritual murder.[32] Yet despite these apparently sincere feelings—admittedly, the phrase "full exercise" needs some qualification—as pope, Ganganelli acceded to Cardinal Albani's importuning. The popes were giving heed to radical voices.

Enlightenment Anxiety

Radical attitudes were stirred up by more than Jewish resistance. Anna del Monte's ordeal occurred at the historical crossroads where the policies of the Catholic Church toward Jews ran into the cross-traffic of the eighteenth-century revolutions in law and politics, as well as the intellectual ferment, that gave direction to the modern world.[33] The eighteenth-century Church was facing a crisis of confidence even greater than that caused by Martin Luther's early sixteenth-century revolt. Luther had impugned the sacramentalism at the core of Catholicism, the doctrine that the sacraments dispensed by ordained priests, especially baptism and the Eucharist, alone grant salvation. New thinking coming out of what is commonly termed Enlightenment rationalism challenged the efficacy of faith itself. In response, the Church set out to retard novelty in society as a whole.

The resistance of a censured and, in its own sight, suffering Church is transparent as it reacted to novelties. The popes did everything they could to counter the assertion by Emperor Joseph II of Austria in the 1780s, the French Revolution a decade later, and, eventually, Napoleon of authority over marriage. Earlier in the eighteenth century, similar assertiveness had come from Piedmont and the House of Savoy, the dynasty that ultimately would unite Italy and deprive the pope of his temporal possessions.[34] For a millennium and more, control over matrimony had furnished the Church with perhaps its most effective tool to dominate society, which it did not shirk to use.[35] The Church was no less disturbed by the reforms of the House of (Habsburg) Lorraine, which had succeeded the Medici as Grand Dukes of Tuscany in 1737, literally next door to the Papal State. Previously, Tuscany had accepted papal demands. Now, it throttled the Papal Inquisition, allowed the reading of forbidden books, removed clerical powers of civil jurisdiction, and, most of all, protected the Jews of Livorno against attempts by Church authorities to prosecute them for alleged offenses such as "atheism."[36]

All of these innovations the Church stigmatized, as it did also the much-feared Freemasons. At the time of the French Revolution, Pius VI rejected in consternation proposed reforms in France that entailed the selling of church possessions, the closure of religious orders, and the suppression of dioceses, as well as, and most objectionable of all, a reorganization of the clergy under civil rule. *I cardinali della congregazione,* the pope said, *sono concordamente d'avviso che la costituzione civile, così com è, non può essere approvata senza ricare alla chiesa un colpo mortale,* the Cardinals as a body [he said] are of the unanimous opinion that the civil constitution, as proposed, cannot be approved without striking a mortal blow against the Church. The pope spoke out again, together with other bishops, in *Caritas quae docente Paulo* of April 13, 1791, abandoning the more politic path and threatening to anathematize proponents of French reform.

Beyond matters once known as "ecclesiastical liberties," Pius and other popes feared movements that had sprung up in both Europe and the American colonies to sanction religious liberty and the exercise of "freedom of conscience."[37] Revolutions in state and legal structures that took place during the last decades of the eighteenth century on both shores of the Atlantic mirrored each other when it came to the status (and rights) of individuals. Membership and rights in the body politic were made contingent on legal observance and equality, no longer on sharing a single faith. The previously decisive association of individuals within a specific collective body, whether guild, community, or one defined by status, such as the nobility or the clergy, also became irrelevant; "nullified" might be a better way of putting it.[38] Citizenship no longer entailed espousing Christian principles, let alone a Christian identity.

Wholesale revisions like these took a heavy toll on the Church, and the resulting clash of ideologies is perceptible in Anna's diary. A threatened Church needed reassurance, and this it hoped to achieve through conversions, which for the Church represented redemption from its sufferings. Awareness of the Church's anxieties, and of how it sought to dominate them, allows us to fathom the vehemence with which Anna's conversion was pursued. It also makes it possible to grasp a special phenomenon: the numerous legal briefs written to defend other Jews—all women—in the same straits as Anna. These briefs, to be visited below, question the place of religion in the state and, in particular, the proper weight to be accorded civil law when it clashed with the canons of the Church. Portentously, this was also to debate the proper nature of the modern state.

Anna's ordeal would have been unthinkable in places like the non-confessional United States or post-revolutionary France. By contrast, the legally reinforced formal structures of religion in pre-revolutionary "confessional" states, states with official, usually obligatory, religious identities, favored, if they did not encourage, torments like those Anna suffered.[39] Far more, therefore, than illuminating Jewish issues alone, cases like Anna's illustrate crises which European society as a whole had to overcome. They supply us with tools to understand the successful, or failed, transition of Western states to a post-revolutionary, post-confessional, legal and political modernity.[40] When Tranquillo placed Anna's diary before the public eye, regardless of how limited that public was, he knew he was making a political statement. He was retelling a complex story, behind which lay a broad spectrum of contemporary concerns.

The Primacy of Law: The Changing State

The emphasis was on law. The loosening and, even more, the breaking of the bond between state and religion that was taking place in Anna's day is often portrayed as a product of the reforms and new directions mapped out by proponents of the Enlightenment; and the Enlightenment's role in encouraging new ways of thinking must not be diminished. Yet of itself, Enlightenment thought did not guarantee a one-way street to better things. Enlightenment ideas could be a trap. Those ideas tested Jews, in particular, with the covert demand that they shed their identity—as Jews—as the price to acquire citizenship.[41] Even viewed positively, Enlightenment enthusiasm might have reached a fruitless dead end—including at the decisive debates about Jewish emancipation held between 1789 and 1791 at the French National Assembly—had these debates *not* been *preceded* by a drive toward universal legal uniformity, a drive that, in turn, led to the reevaluation and eventual elimination of the bonds between religion and state.[42]

Law itself was transformed. Old codes were abrogated, most especially *ius commune*, the common law based on ancient Roman law that was in widespread use on the Continent, whether in practice or as influentially studied in the schools, and which Napoleon replaced in 1804 with the *Code civil*.[43] The result, *theoretically*, was full legal equality for all citizens and a stymying of the ecclesiastical insistence that civil law cede unfailingly to canonical demands. The achievement of legal equality had been touted as far back as the fourteenth century by the celebrated Bartolus of Saxoferato, but it was consistently blocked by the prerogatives of religion and related corporate structures, the legally established and specially privileged collectives that were so decisive under the pre-revolutionary *ancien régime*. Anna del Monte's story is a striking example of how the superannuated structures, above all the corporate Church, were fighting to hold on against such massive change.[44]

5. Conversion and the State

Let us leave for the moment themes of statecraft and ecclesiastical reaction and return to the matter of conversion, whose investigation will allow us to appreciate so much more fully the developing struggle between the confessional and the modern secular state. Over the question of conversion, the conundrum of a necessary religious unity was being fought out and resolved.

In the 250 or so years between its founding in 1542/3 and the early nineteenth century, over 2,500 Jews converted under the aegis of the Roman *Casa dei catecumeni* where Anna was taken; two out of three converts were men.[1] The institution was a living threat to Roman Jewry, whose ghetto was about fifteen minutes or so distant by foot. The church of the converts, S. Maria dei Monti, next door to the *Casa*, is still operational (for those who know Rome, the location is just a few yards from S. Pietro in Vincoli, which houses Michelangelo's Moses). Even today, a visitor quickly notes the portraits with mottos in Hebrew bearing Christological teachings that hang on the walls. These portraits made of the place what it was, a church for converts, but also what it was *not*, a church by normal standards. The ambiguity inherent in using Hebrew—not that there have been no brilliant Christian Hebraists—so well typified the convert's state.[2] "Neither in one world nor another."[3]

Everything was done to persuade those who entered the *Casa* to accept the Catholic faith, including those who had not entered of their own volition, but whom a relative or spouse had "offered." Others were "denounced" as having expressed a will to convert, most often by a man who claimed to be the betrothed, usually a convert, as well as poor, hoping to make a match to which he could otherwise never aspire. The claim of one such convert, Sabato Coen, sealed Anna del Monte's fate.[4]

"To offer" was shorthand for a powerful tool. The law gave parents power over their offspring, which, it was commonly accepted, included the power to demand that their children be taken to the *Casa* to test their religious will. The procedure operated much in the same way as when a father dedicated, or "oblated," a young son to a monastery or a daughter to a convent. The same rules applied to a spouse. The pressures exerted on those who were "offered" were great, almost guaranteeing success. Few of those who entered the *Casa* left, as did Anna, unbaptized and still Jews; the most optimistic estimate is that barely one out of four "escaped."

The term "parent" also began to be defined more loosely. Eventually it embraced almost any relative or person with a claim to guardianship over the person offered. This included unborn children, whose expectant mothers would be taken into the *Casa*, where their newborns would be removed and baptized at birth. Judging from the uniformly small size of most Jewish families, Roman Jews, who were all too familiar with this practice, may often have had second thoughts about procreating, certainly those who had converts in the family, which is to say nearly everybody.[5] For their part, some Christian clergy charged that dread of having their newborns taken away led prospective Jewish parents to have the mother abort. Jews might even kill infants at birth.

Thwarting Baptism

Jews knew this accusation well, whose origins very possibly lie in a myth, which, by the time of Anna del Monte, was thirteen hundred years old and the source of a great deal of the fierceness of eighteenth-century papal conversionary policy, a fierceness readers of the diary would have sensed on every page. The idea that Jews would cause the death of potential converts—as all "offered" fetuses were deemed—appears already in the chronicle of Gregory of Tours from the later sixth century. Gregory recounts that a father was so incensed at his son for desiring the Eucharist that he threw the boy into a furnace (from which the boy was saved and, then, transfigured by the Virgin).[6] This myth was vivified—and seemingly verified—during the First Crusade of 1096, when many Jews did slaughter their offspring to prevent their forced conversion, which Jews saw as pollution and contamination. The myth itself of the boy in the furnace was also repeated, and often—for instance, in the poetic retelling of The Miracles of the Virgin by Gonzalo de Berceo in later thirteenth-century Spain. Berceo is a small village in La Rioja, in central Spain; the myth had spread everywhere. The claim of the leading thirteenth-century theologian Duns Scotus that Jews would kill their offspring to prevent conversion was made as though the act were both frequent and a matter of common knowledge.

The perception of Jewish destructiveness—whether of Jewish children or Christian ones—was reinforced in early modern times by the idea that Jews were social miscreants, beside being religious deviants.[7] This charge is acutely present, although hardly for the first time, in the early eighteenth-century writings of Giuseppe Sessa, who was not only a theoretician of law but also the jurist in charge of Jewish affairs in Turin. It is present, too, in the work of the noble and reformer Giovanni D'Arco, in the 1780s. Both men speak of the ghetto as a locus of economic collusion.[8] The preoccupation with supposed Jewish nefariousness no doubt strengthened the belief in Jewish infanticide and contributed to accelerating its transformation into a direct accusation. At Prague, in 1694, the father of the youth Shimon Abeles was blamed for causing his son's death upon learning that Shimon was planning to convert.[9]

No similar charge of Jews murdering their own was ever pressed at Rome. But suspicion was constant, which was sometimes fanned in the writings of converts, such as Paolo Medici's translation of the Jesuit Johan Eder's account of Shimon Abeles's death, which was widely read. Even somebody as informed as Giuseppe Sessa, who, apart from his judicial duties, produced a full-length tract on the legal status of the Jews in 1716, believed that Abeles had been ritually murdered; more or less everybody else did, too. According to Sessa, the murderer was the grandfather, rather than the father.[10] So popular was the tale that it had spawned alternative versions.

Earlier myth had been reified, and the imputed murder of Shimon Abeles likely served as a catalyst in 1755, when Benedict XIV—the man who was pope at the time of Anna del Monte's kidnapping—issued the bull Beatus Andreas, in which he beatified, if he did not actually canonize, both the fifteenth-century Andreas of Rinn (near Innsbruck) and Simonino of Trent, the most famous of ritual murder victims, allegedly martyred in 1475.[11] The Jews, the bull says, killed Andreas to reenact the crucifixion. This was a charge no pope had ever before approved openly. The act, moreover, had been committed *in odio fidei*, hatred of the faith. The bull uses this term repeatedly with respect to a list of other so-called martyrdoms at Jewish hands.[12] *Odium fidei* also appears in accounts of Shimon Abeles; odium, it was said, motivated Shimon's father to kill the boy. That terms traditionally associated with martyrdom were invoked to tell Shimon's tale should be no surprise.[13]

Pope Benedict was especially firm in his convictions. When the future Clement XIV, Cardinal Ganganelli, was asked by Benedict to collect information about ritual murder in the wake of another such charge in Sandomierz, Poland, the Cardinal felt he had no choice but to temper his judgment. Jews neither murdered Christians nor used Christian blood, he wrote—except in the instances of Simonino and Andreas.[14] However, the origin of Benedict XIV's fury at supposed Jewish behavior did not lie in *Beatus Andreas*. Already in the bull *A quo primum* of 1751, Benedict raged at what he deemed Jewish incitation. Polish bishops were operating like a modern central bank, lending money to Jews at interest (the bull only alludes to this practice), who then lent the money (a second time) for their own profit (and to pay back the bishops). Were not the bishops implicitly mocking centuries of Church teachings about the evils of lending, sullying both themselves and the Church? Yet, surely, it was the Jews who had pressed the bishops to make loans in the first place. The Jews' actions were so egregious that perhaps, Benedict concluded, it would be better to do without them altogether.

Benedict made his point by heavy-handed allusion. *A quo primum* refers to Rudolph the monk, who preached killing Jews during the Second Crusade of 1146. What would Rudolph think, Benedict queried, about the sordid events of this later day? Prudently, Benedict added that Jews should not be killed and that St. Bernard had censured Rudolph for suggesting that they should be. Even so, Benedict's unprecedented imaginings are transparent. He fooled nobody, least of all Rome's Jews. They must have easily intuited that this pope viewed all Jews as murderous corruptors of the Christian faith, vicious criminals, whom he would control severely. Had he not already begun to do this in 1751, when he renewed a series of forty-four decrees even more repressive than those under which Roman Jews had labored for nearly two centuries?

Benedict's sentiments extended to harboring (unfounded) anxieties about abortion and infanticide. In the 1747 *Postremo mense*, and with the Abeles episode likely in mind, Benedict wove venerable myth and current fears into a coherent policy legitimizing the confinement of "offered" children and pregnant women in the House of Converts. If Jews would kill one, they would kill all, and they must be stopped. Benedict worried, too, about Jews hurrying pregnant Jewish women out of Rome to elude the Church and prevent the baptism of an offered fetus at birth. Such attempts to flee did occur; and those involved were prosecuted. In 1702, the *Fattori* were threatened not to assist such flight. The threat was reiterated in *Postremo mense*, as well as in the complementary *Probe te meminisse* that Benedict XIV published in 1751. The diary of Anna del Monte reports that the *Fattori* were admonished at gunpoint not to obstruct her abduction. Other texts tell of *Fattori* being jailed for similar offenses.[15]

The Church would brook no interference when it came to conversion. The concept of punishing those who thwarted baptism was not new. Papal actions, it cannot be sufficiently stressed, were rooted in canonical precedent. Legislation enabling the prosecution of those who prevented a baptism or who helped the already baptized return to Judaism dates to the year 1267. However, it had been applied sparingly. From the sixteenth century onward, the rules would be enforced strictly. In 1686, (the otherwise unknown) Benvenuta ran out of the Quattro Capi gate of the ghetto, shouting she wished to become a Christian. Overheard by Abraham Sacerdote, as Abraham's lawyer Scipio Caranza tells it, Benvenuta was spirited by Sacerdote over the Quattro Capi bridge into the Transtiber and then back into the ghetto. But the pair was caught. Fortunately, Caranza's defense of Abraham, arguing that the latter had dissuaded nobody from converting, was convincing. Abraham was released. Benvenuta, though, was held for a full quarantine (forty days) in the *Casa dei catecumeni*. But she refused to convert, insisting the whole episode was a ploy. As a rabbinical deposition describing her release relates, what she really wanted was to break an engagement to a "brute" named Procaccia.[16]

Scipio Caranza's intervention informs us that Roman Jews were not passive. Provocation by papal authorities evoked clever responses, including by seeking advantage in papal letters, even *Postremo mense* and *Probe te meminisse*. Correctly, Jews understood these bulls as setting legal limits, whose violation they would, and did, protest.[17] However, "legal," as decisions of the early-twenty-first-century Supreme Court of the United States attest, is a term that bends to commentary. When it came to furthering baptism, Benedict XIV seems to have believed that the children of nonbelievers brought to the baptismal font needed special protection.

For Benedict, the baptism of these children was akin to their undergoing a "virtual martyrdom." Visions and arguments about martyrdom had characterized Catholic responses to the sixteenth-century Reformation. Two hundred years later, these arguments resurfaced in more subtle, yet still identifiable, terms. In particular, martyrdom was traditionally pictured in Eucharistic terms, with martyrs themselves, and their blood, viewed as the Eucharist's embodiment. Hence, child baptisms, especially anxiety-producing ones of the children of nonbelievers, where the outcome was often disputed or in doubt, were seen—we need not let the apparent irrationality of this perception deflect us—as potential martyrdoms of the *innocenti*, the innocent children butchered by King Herod who were considered "baptized in blood," reinforcing Eucharistic purity.[18] Martyrs and potential martyrs also needed shielding, even from their own worst urgings, for instance, those of an Anna del Monte and others like her who spurned baptismal salvation when opportunity came knocking. The law would have to be placed on baptism's side, even when the Church had to struggle to convince itself it was acting justly—and legally—and even though, in doing so, it was compromising centuries-old Jewish rights.

Fear of Jewish Pollution

The popes and so many others were convinced that Jews were bent on polluting the holy Christian body, the *Corpus Christi*. This is the barely hidden subtext of bulls like Benedict XIV's *A quo primum*, and the unbending positions of Pius VI, followed by Pius IX and Leo XIII. The fear of pollution is equally present in Clement XIII's attacks on the Freemasons. The threat was to the *Corpus Christi*, in its varying—and intimately intertwined—emanations, whether these be Christ's human body or the *corpus verum* of the Eucharist, the true body and blood of Jesus, whose partaking unites all Christians in the *corpus mysticum*, the fellowship of all believers, the mystical body that is also Paul's *unus panis*. During the Middle Ages, the name *Corpus Christi* applied as well to the body politic, especially that of the city. Moreover, all of these bodily forms substitute for one another easily. In 1287, the alleged victim Werner of Oberwesel was pictured as the *corpus verum*, the *corpus mysticum*, and the human, physical body of Christ united,[19] a union revisited in Mel Gibson's film *The Passion of the Christ*. Gibson's suffering, yet saving, Christ-figure is patently modeled on stories of the tortured and bloodied victims of ritual murder, between whom and Christ himself there is no visible difference. Until the later nineteenth century, these victims were also invariably male.[20] Only then did young girls begin to appear, perhaps reflecting the laicization and partial secularization of the myth of the destructive Jew, couched now in economic and racial language, but still depicting dangers faced by society as a whole.[21]

Paul himself had seen a danger of another kind, from Christians who emulated Jewish acts, principally circumcision, polluting themselves, he said, and diluting the purity of Christian belief. Paul, though, was scolding believers in Jesus as the Messiah, not Jews. Later writers, basing their thinking on a passage from Matthew 15:26 identified with the Eucharist, saw the danger in emulating Jews themselves. The passage tells of a woman who begged Christ to feed her sick daughter and to whom Christ replied that he had brought the bread for the children; it should not be thrown to the (polluting) dogs. About the year 387, the bishop of Antioch in Syria, John Chrysostom, interpreted this verse by saying, We Christians were once the dogs. Those dogs are now the Jews, whose role as God's chosen has been transferred to us. This teaching, called supersession, remains very much alive. Moreover, Chrysostom continued, Jews forever seduce Christians, beckoning them to participate in Jewish rituals and contaminate themselves, much as they would do through participation in idolatrous sacrifice and as enunciated in the Levitical doctrine of *im*purity produced by unlawful contact. Later Christian writers said that to dine with a Jew or to have sexual intercourse with one polluted absolutely.

Nowhere is this doctrine of Jewish pollution through proximity more forcefully stated than in Pius VI's 1775 *Fra le pastorali sollecitudini,* the collection of forty-four restrictions, originally formulated in 1733, that Benedict XIV (re)published in 1751 and Pius VI renewed again, in 1775, this time with teeth, thus making Jewish life miserable.[22] A series of complaints found in the archive of the Roman Jewish Community leaves no doubt about the enormous discomfort these decrees created.[23]

There was still room for deterioration. In 1871, with the ghetto eliminated by the heads of the new Italian state, Pope Pius IX surveyed what was once *literally* his city and said, continuing the metaphor, We see the Jews *per le vie latrare,* barking through the streets. For him, the ghetto had been a kennel, retaining within its bounds Jewish filth. That in earlier decades the Jews of Rome had struggled to keep the ghetto clean, ensure their homes had sanitary facilities, and constructed sewage lines did nothing to improve their image. To the contrary, in 1751, Roman Jews complained that the legislation of that year endangered the city's health by discontinuing garbage removal. They singled out its novel prohibition forbidding Christian laundry women to enter the ghetto, remove soiled linens, and wash them outside. This prohibition, the Jews said, would result in illness and epidemic, first in the ghetto and then throughout Rome. The ghetto lacked the space to hang laundered clothes out to dry, not to mention sufficient running water and cisterns for washing. Their complaints fell on deaf ears. The refusal to collect refuse was repeated in Pius VI's bull of 1775. Ghetto filth would be left to molder.[24]

However, the "filth" that really mattered was the dirt of their religion, in which the Jews were immersed. The floods of the Tiber, it was said, could not cleanse the offal from Jewish souls.[25] "Who stole the bread from the oven?" asks a Chilean school song—much in the spirit of Pius IX—one that, I am told, is still being sung. The answer, of course, is "the Jewish dog," the Jewish thief, who if left unchecked, would steal and mutilate the Eucharist—no other bread is intended—wreaking havoc on Christian society. Yet in early modern Rome that dog, no matter how dangerous it was considered, could be neither sent away nor put down. To control potential damage and protect the Christian corpus, pursuing conversion was indispensable. It is here that the story of Anna del Monte comes to the fore. By renouncing Judaism, Anna as a convert would not only affirm supersession; she would preempt the contamination of Rome's very streets. She would protect the city's Christian civic integrity, safeguarding the *corpus mysticum*, if not the *corpus verum*, preventing the Eucharist itself from being befouled. Through conversion, the Jewish threat to the at once real, true, mystical, and even civil body of Christ would be removed.

The proselytizing of Anna del Monte thus signals the pursuit of an energized attempt to eliminate Jewish danger, not through the failed medieval expedients of assault or expulsion, neither of which, in the event, were open to the Church with its canonical and doctrinal teachings of Jewish protection, but through the absorption of all Jews into the Christian flock, the very solution Paul himself had augured. What was needed was for Jews to join together with the rest of mankind in the *unus panis*. Should this unification be achieved, with the conversion of the Jews leading the way, the dangers of the modern, confessionless state and society would be dealt a fatal blow. The convert, in his or her struggle to leave behind a damning past, was like a martyr tested by the dissuading forces of evil, yet, like the Church itself, left in the end unscathed by the "enemy," guaranteeing salvation for all.

The Creation of Converts

Yet had not conversion always been the policy of the Church? The answer is a qualified no. Though desired, hoped for, and occasionally the subject of full campaigns, especially in Iberia and in later thirteenth-century France and England, the pursuit of conversion in the Middle Ages, sometimes peaceful, sometimes violent, and sometimes viewed pessimistically as fruitless, is best described as phlegmatic.

We start with the first Crusade, in the year 1096, a time of Jewish calamity and slaughter, but also of forced and voluntary conversions. Jewish troubles did not start with the papally sponsored crusading army, composed principally of nobles and led by an archbishop, whose discipline held until it took Jerusalem, when the once obedient crusaders murdered all the city's Muslims and Jews.[26] Jews in Europe, specifically, the Rhineland, fell prey to crusaders of a different stripe, men—and women, too—who formed an army of rowdies, vagabonds, and the poor, all hoping to better their status. Nobles also joined the ranks, not the greatest of their class, but still men of repute. But when this army set out for the Holy Land, it was leaderless, which in part explains why—camped on the outskirts of the city of Mainz on the Rhine River and waiting to depart and eventually float down the Danube to the Black Sea—this motley crew suddenly attacked, no doubt inebriated and likely worked up by a wandering preacher. The names of over seven hundred murdered Jews have been preserved for Mainz alone. Equally deadly rioting continued in other Rhenish cities.[27]

In subsequent decades, the devastated Jewish communities revived, but the memory of the havoc lingered among both Jews and Christians. Both were appalled at the carnage. Yet as one Latin chronicle after the other explains, more than by the murders themselves, Christians were perturbed by the behavior of the nobles, who had acted rashly and without the leadership of the clergy. Worse, their rampage had resulted in a large number of dubious converts.

Hebrew chroniclers created an ethos of the martyrdom of the valiant who took their own lives rather than be killed at Christian hands. Yet *some* Jews had converted, at times impelled by conviction but mostly by fear, many of whom—after the events, and to the ire of Churchmen—returned to Judaism, thus to create an insoluble dilemma. Were these returnees to be considered Jews, or were they, as Christian authorities saw it, renegades and apostates? Even those converts who continued to profess Christianity were suspect, the sincerity of their conversion perennially doubted. Christian chroniclers also report laity incensed upon hearing that Jews had dissuaded a prospective convert from approaching the baptismal font. This was the consummate insult. In 1241, in Frankfurt am Main, one instance of dissuasion ended in a murderous riot. Long before the Crusades, the sixth-century Gregory of Tours and the eleventh-century Ahimaaz ben Paltiel reported similar events that had ended badly. That their narratives are fictions suggests we are dealing with tropes, which, in turn, indicate a recurring drama. Dating from about a century after 1096, the most famous account is that of Rabbi Amnon of Mainz, whose prevarication—as the tale's Jewish author warned his fellows—resulted in tragedy.[28]

People wanted clean lines. Converts were to have no contact with former Jews. In fact, *all* contact with *all* Jews, for whatever reason, was being increasingly censured.[29] How much the more was the conduct of possible prevaricators closely to be watched? People like these were said to participate with Jews in dire acts like the killing of Christian children or the stealing and abusing of the Host (the Eucharistic wafer). It was also being claimed that Jewish religious observance was being perverted by Talmudic teachings, which Christian law and theology had traditionally condoned as putative precursors of Christian truth.[30] This charge was amplified by the further argument that Jews rejected philosophical reason, making them less than human. For were not reason, humanity, and Christianity—none of which the Jews were said to possess, and how much the more backsliding converts—synonymous? One writer said that Jewish mothers were animals, worse than dogs, since even dogs quenched the thirst of their young by nursing; Jewish mothers held back nourishment. Likely, this was an oblique reference to (reports of) Jewish mothers slaughtering their children during the Crusades, preventing their baptism, and denying them Eucharistic succor.[31]

The myth of the Jewish Boy, found in the chronicle of Gregory of Tours, was being elaborated upon and generalized. Not only in a miracle tale praising the Virgin, but in real fact Jews were said to slaughter their offspring in order to prevent their baptism. For Catholics, this was perverse; it was to destroy with one blow both body and soul. And although the myth was never the subject of a true, specific accusation until the case of Shimon Abeles in 1694, there was always the apprehension that Jews would commit this "crime," as well as, relatedly, they might abort "offered" fetuses.

In this schema, the Eucharist, the very Eucharist that was made obligatory in 1215 for all Catholics at Eastertime, but that then became even more central during the Counter-Reformation, played a central role. The purity of the Eucharist could not be compromised, meaning that the communicant him- or herself had to be pure, a purity that proximity to Jews was said to endanger. Originally, about the third century (and following Paul's warning in 1 Corinthians 10 not to share in pagan sacrifice), Cyprian of Carthage argued that priests who became impure by serving at pagan altars should not be allowed to return and transfer their impurity—by touch—to the Christian sanctuary. By no later than the ninth century, bishops like Agobard of Lyons, in southern France, were applying this notion to Christians who frequented Jews. Not only did these Christians become contaminated and receive no benefit from the Eucharist, they were said to infect with impurity everyone with whom they came into contact. Sexual intercourse with Jews was particularly feared as was dining at a common table. One scholar said that "Jews deceive between courses." Jews might not have Christians, especially women, serving them in the home, where the possibilities for sexual mingling and other violations were many.[32] Anxiety did not abate. As late as 1592, in his *Dialogos*, the Carmelite Amador Arrais discussed the forced conversions of 1497 in Portugal and asked whether these baptisms "did not give occasion to profane the holy religion of the Son of God . . . when these [baptized, but perfidious] Jews unworthily receive the sacrament . . . and violate the mysteries and sanctity of our faith with false and simulated devotion." Worse, Arrais begins to cross the border from spiritual pollution to the endangerment of the Christian physical body—and bodies—denounced by the likes of Giovanni D'Arco, as he lamented Jewish economic deviousness. "The prosperity of the Christian Republic," Arrais wrote, "is in decline. . . . A Jew from Constantinople, we have heard, wrote to those in our kingdom, that they should ensure their sons become priests and physicians, so that they become the lords of our souls and our bodies."[33]

To prevent horrors like these, beginning in the seventh century, the Church developed a series of restrictive laws, which, however, began to be applied rigorously only from the later twelfth. The Fourth Lateran Council of 1215, which was also the locus of the decree mandating annual consumption of the Eucharist, ordered Jews to wear special, identifying clothing. Papal letters (administrative orders known as bulls from the leaden seal attached to them) never tired of repeating this decree. The clothing was symbolic—for did not most people know who was a Jew?—a reminder to keep a safe distance.[34]

Admittedly, maintaining distance calmed nerves and sustained an equilibrium enabling Jews and Christians to coexist. Nonetheless, this equilibrium was constantly threatened, most notably by the reaction to converts returning to Judaism or not having their children baptized as required. There was also no clarity about which Jews—but especially their descendants—had been baptized in 1096 and, later, had "slid back." When one came into contact with a Jew, it might instead be with an apostate, whose essential impurity mortally endangered Christianity's social order. Had not the Christian Roman law *Christianorum ad aras* made it clear that participation of any kind in Jewish rites was polluting?[35] It was best to avoid Jews altogether, most efficiently, by expulsion. Apostates, too, would disappear, and those converts who willingly professed Christianity would be isolated from pernicious Jewish influence.[36]

In England and in France, this idea was taken literally. Jews were expelled from the former in 1290 and the latter in 1306. The kings of France, pious as they were, may also have been frustrated that their designs to convert Jews had failed.[37] Some Churchmen applauded the expulsions. The popes remained silent. They had little excuse to intervene. The laws of the Church forbade harming Jews or forcibly converting them, but popes could not offer a guarantee of residence. That was theirs to give only in their own domains, where a Jewish presence *was* continuous.

Elsewhere, Jewish life became increasingly precarious. Fourteenth-century Germany was an arena for attacks, accusations, and limited, local expulsions. The only large Jewish community left was that in Spain. As early as the seventh century, in Visigothic Spain, an attempt to force all Spain's Jews to become Christians resulted in the first laws regulating apostasy. These laws, which, over the centuries, were renewed and incorporated in canonical collections and commentaries, were aimed at forbidding converts to return to Judaism except under the most extraordinary circumstance known as having been baptized through "absolute force," which almost never occurred.[38] Canonically, "absolute force" was defined as a person renouncing baptism even with a sword held at the throat, followed by a consistent refusal to participate in Christian rites, should baptism have been administered. The children of converts, or of only one converted parent, were, without exception, to be reared as Christians.

The Visigothic conversionary campaign was cut off abruptly when Arab invaders overran Iberia in the year 711. By the mid-thirteenth century, Christian armies had taken most of the peninsula, and the theme of conversion reemerged. King James I of Aragon demanded Jews attend missionary sermons, disputations were held, orders were given to censor the Talmud, and conversionary literature was composed. A steady stream of converts eventually became a flood in the wake of peninsula-wide riots in 1391. Thousands more converted in the second decade of the fifteenth century. Exceedingly repressive new laws, large-scale preaching, and a renewed attack on the Talmud, alongside the sight of the many who had already converted, led to widespread Jewish despair.[39]

By the time of the expulsion in 1492, a large portion of Spain's Jews had become Christians. Jews held fast in Portugal until 1497, when they, too, were converted, brutally, en masse, and by what in 1535, Cardinal Pier Paolo Pariseo, a professor of canon law, echoing Popes Clement VII and Paul III themselves, called "absolute force."[40] None of these people, possibly not even their children, he said, had been properly converted. Their return to Judaism could not be punished.[41] By the time of Anna del Monte, two centuries later, nobody would have dared suggest this course.

An indeterminate number of Iberian converts, however, did return to Judaism or began to practice Jewish rituals. In the past, such "backsliding" had led to intervention by ecclesiastical courts known as inquisitions, after the methods they employed, actually similar to today's state prosecutions: the court (the state) presses the charge, investigates, and tries—although without the (highly regulated legal) torture the medieval tribunals used to extract confessions. The popes had first established a Papal Inquisition in the thirteenth century. Its target was *Christian* heretics. An increase in the number of backsliding *Jewish* converts required the Inquisition to shift its focus. By 1267, the Inquisition was empowered to try *both* backsliders *and* the Jews who helped them. Few records of these trials have survived. One of a certain Baruch ended in a light sentence, when Baruch accepted that he had no choice but to live as a Christian, or so the surviving transcript of his trial reports. This was in southern France in the early fourteenth century.[42]

In Spain, the proposed solution was the Inquisition founded in the late fifteenth century to ensure that converts from Judaism did not stray. This was an ecclesiastical court, whose head, the Chief Inquisitor, was responsible to the king, not the pope. Regardless, the Inquisition failed to stop what it saw as Jewish plotting and attempts to bring converts back. That, as Tomás de Torquemada persuaded Spain's joint monarchs Ferdinand and Isabella in 1492, would be achieved only through a total separation of Jews and Christians. Literally overnight, it was decided to expel Iberia's remaining Jews.[43]

The Incipient Modern State

The decree of expulsion speaks of the Jews as a danger to the *res publica,* a term portending our present day "republic." Originally, in the Middle Ages, *res publica* signified the social or political body of Christ, also known as the *Corpus Christi,* which the Church identified with itself, claiming that *it* was the *respublica vera,* the true republic of all, just as it incorporated the entire body of faithful into the *Corpus Christi mysticum.* However, by about 1300, thinkers, notably Dante, began wondering whether *res publica* did not apply better to the Empire (and, by extension, to the various kingdoms). With the term's inclusion in the 1492 decree of expulsion, it is clear that Dante's message had been heard. The early modern state was taking on attributes once associated exclusively with the Church, seeing itself independently as an inclusive spiritual body.

The emphasis is on the word *spiritual,* so that at the most we may see here a tentative, if equally opaque, step toward the state's eventual laicization and secularization, turning the state into a secular, yet still spiritualized body. This step was as yet so tentative, however, that those who took it were most likely unaware they had done so. The process toward secularization would be painfully slow. It would be completed—and even then mostly in theory, with practice lagging behind—only three hundred years later at the time of the French and American Revolutions, not in early modern Spain. Only in the new French and American states was the mold that had endured since the late ancient Roman Empire broken and the theological aspect of the *corpus politicum* discarded to bring the ideas of Dante to their logical climax.

Instructively, it was not radical innovation, but mutations of older ideas that were making it possible to turn the corner and reverse the momentum that had sustained confessionalism and led to the near destruction of medieval European Jewry. Both France and the United States would cut the knot tying state to church, formally to become nonconfessional *corpus reipublicae politicum*, political bodies of the republic. And in doing so, they paved the way for the Jewish emancipation that in the previously confessional political entities of Europe could not, and never would, have occurred.

Viewed from this perspective, the expulsion from Spain was decreed precisely because, however greatly (and arguably) the now united kingdom of Castile and Aragon under Ferdinand and Isabella had embarked on the road to political modernity, the religious dimension remained supreme. When the 1492 decree of expulsion identifies as a motive protecting the *res publica*, it assumes that the "common good" requires the union of both political and spiritual factors, making them one (an identity that would remain intact in Spain until 1965 when Francisco Franco formally admitted Jews).

By contrast, England and France, first de facto, then de iure, respectively put religion into a minor political key or divorced the state from religion entirely.[44] Central Europe, Germany, and the Hapsburg Empire wavered, which explains much about the progress and forms, but especially the ambivalence that accompanied emancipation there.[45] Put in the abstract: in nonconfessional states, Jews achieved emancipation; in confessional, or even residually, or clandestinely, confessional ones, they were granted, at the most, only a partial improvement of rights. As for the seeming exception of England, here, as often elsewhere, it was a special case. From the moment in the earlier sixteenth century when King Henry VIII created a specifically English brand of confessionalism by declaring himself the head of the Church of England with full rights to determine matters "fully ecclesiastic," doctrine could, and did, give way to pragmatic need. Even so, only in 1858, Lionel de Rothschild was able to cross the ultimate barrier to full emancipation, that of holding public office, in his case, as a member of Parliament, when he was allowed to swear the oath of office with the words "so help me Jehovah," rather than, as was the rule, on a New Testament and invoking the name of Christ.[46] In a word, with respect to Jews and civil rights, the attitude the early modern state adopted vis-à-vis religion was decisive.

Confessionalism Restated

The critical period for these changes began in the latter half of the eighteenth century, which, importantly for us, is precisely the time between Anna's se-

questering in 1749 and her brother Tranquillo's revelation of her diary in
1793. This was also the period when, beginning with *In Eminenti* of Clement XII in 1738 (repeated by Benedict XIV as *Providas* in 1551) and extend-
ing to Leo XIII in the early twentieth century, if not beyond, the Church
responded to revolution by condemning any attempt to sunder state from
Church or, worse, to make the Church subservient to the latter: To recall the
words of Leo XIII in *Immortale dei,* "To wish the Church to be subject to
the civil power in the exercise of her duty is a great folly and a sheer injustice."[47] That "folly" was becoming ever more widespread. Western Europe's
path to modernization was as distant as imaginable from the road on which
the Catholic Church was moving. European states went forward, following
the lead of France in 1789; the Church entrenched itself in the past.[48]

Paradoxically, though, it had been the popes who had taken the lead in
the seventeenth century in modernizing their state, which they had done by
gaining control over, and centralizing, its bureaucratic institutions, including the courts.[49] Nonetheless, the nature of the papal state as theocratic and
confessional permitted modernization to go only so far. For the Church, the
concept of the body politic remained static: everything must be aimed at
glorifying the *Corpus Christi* as the *patria communis,* the homeland of all, even
where lip service was paid to civil institutions, for instance, in the opening
paragraphs of *Immortale dei.*

By contrast, the states of Europe, some, anyway, were bent on establishing a *respublica* free from religious preference, which was not easy. Popular opinion often rejected the nonconfessional state, despite its laws having become officially those of a secular body. The failure was greater the
more one moved east.[50] In the Habsburg Empire, jurists insisted that state
and religion must be one.[51] Even so forward looking a thinker as Siegmund
Jacob Baumgarten, who argued for complete freedom of conscience, could
not imagine a state without a formal religion.[52] This is the same Baumgarten
who in 1753, as if thumbing his nose at Benedict XIV and, for that matter,
the entire Catholic tradition, insisted that when a Jewish husband converted,
the authorities were to ensure that this man gave his wife a proper *Jewish*
divorce, while their offspring were to be free to choose Judaism or Christianity, both being acts the Church anathematized.[53]

Prejudices also held fast. Old religious accusations were remolded into
civil ones; the idea of a great break in attitudes toward Jews in the mod-

ern period is illusory. The real change was a laicization, secularization, and, in the case of racial doctrines, the transformation of older, religiously expressed perceptions. Ultimately, the racialized predator is but a version of the polluted Jew attacking the purity of the *Corpus Christi*. When Giovanni D'Arco in the 1780s spoke of the ghetto as a hotbed of economic crime and collusion, he was developing the fifteenth-century Franciscan idea that Jews by lending money at interest were sucking the blood (of Christ) from the town.[54] It is this same link of economic factors with the idea of ensuring the flow of society's *Eucharistic* "economic" blood that historians would do well to search out, especially when suggesting that economic competition, by itself, spurred on nineteenth-century accusations of ritual murder in Central and Eastern Europe.[55]

Regardless of prejudices, the words of the mid-eighteenth-century J. H. Merchant are telling. Jews born in England, he said, may be considered citizens, but Jewish immigrants from abroad should not be naturalized, contrary to what the Jew Bill of 1753 was just then proposing. Merchant did not object to Jews enjoying nearly full civic rights, but naturalization should be the preserve of Christians alone. The same posture held in German lands, where the *ius commune* tract of G. H. Ayrer calls Jews *incoli*, denizens, but not citizens.[56] Eastern Europe, namely Poland, then about to be dismembered, was mired legally, and conceptually, in a medieval matrix.

Challenges to Confessionalism

Where ideas truly changed was in the fledgling United States. "Freedom [of conscience]," wrote James Madison, "arises from the multiplicity of sects which pervade America and which is the best and only security for religious liberty in any society; for where there is such a variety of sects, there cannot be a majority of any one to oppress or persecute the rest."[57] The popes were saying the precise opposite.

Yet it was not the winds of tolerance, whether specifically of Jews, or others, or even those of legal toleration, which blew in this new thinking. Its origins lie in the thought of the dissenters of New England, who bridled at Congregationalism, the religion of the Puritans and their descendants, which had become legally binding in Massachusetts and Connecticut. These dissenters included people like Roger Williams, who said that only God knew the true religion, but since nobody could possibly question God directly, nobody could declare he or she possessed the truth. Religion must be disestablished.

Religious pluralism was complemented by the insistence in the Colonies on the liberty of the individual, which demanded an appropriate framework for its achievement. As Bernard Bailyn has observed: "Not that power [as perceived by those in the Colonies] was in itself—in some metaphysical sense—evil. It was natural in its origins, and necessary. It had legitimate foundations 'in compact and mutual consent'—in those covenants among men by which, as a result of restrictions voluntarily accepted by all for the good of all, society emerges from a state of nature and creates government to serve as trustee and custodian of the mass of surrendered individual powers."[58] Bailyn was reflecting on people like Samuel Adams, who wrote that a constitution of government is a "frame, a scheme, a system, a combination of powers for a certain end, namely, the good of the whole community." There had to be a balance, whose goal was liberty. As put by John Dickinson: "The natural absolute personal rights of individuals are . . . the very basis of all municipal laws of any great value."[59] Law, I myself would put it, is the key to liberty, but if so, the *cives* must achieve his or her identity—or to use the term preferred by legists, must be "regenerated"—through a governmental structure in which the law is equal for all.

The choice of words is important. The later-sixteenth-century jurist Marquardus de Susannis, writing to support the regulations imposed by Pope Paul IV, had pronounced that one became a full citizen through baptismal "regeneration."[60] But de Susannis's citizen inhabited a confessional state; de Susannis could have conceived of no other. In Dickinson's state, law, equal for all, with no religious connotation or even leaning, had replaced baptism as regeneration's instrument, and the call of Thomas Jefferson for citizens to take an oath to the law may be construed as a substitute for the baptismal font.[61] This perception was clarified in 1790 when George Washington said that "[the government] requires only that they who live under its protection should demean themselves as good [law-abiding] citizens." Did not (again) Thomas Jefferson write, "We hold these truths to be self-evident . . ."?[62] And did not John Adams write into the 1780 Constitution of Massachusetts the idea that "this is a government of laws, and not of men"?

To be sure, the law in question in the United States was a product of the British legal tradition, not the Continental *ius commune*. Even so, *ius commune* and its commentators were not foreign to American jurists, who may also have noted the debate many European jurists were pursuing over whether, and how, to free civil law from canonical restraints. John Adams, for one, along with many others, was reading the influential works on capital punishment by Cesare Beccaria, translated into English.[63] Possibly, too, attention was being paid to the writings of British jurists like the sixteenth-century Stephan St. Germain, who, writing in the shadow of King Henry VIII's assumption of the headship of the Church of England in 1533, insisted, already then, on the precedence of British common law over all other legal forms, including, of course, the canons.[64]

In the event, and regardless of which "common law" was in use, underlying the Washingtonian, Jeffersonian, and Adamsonian view is the idea, so important in European thinking, of a social contract.[65] By agreeing to obey the law, citizens vouchsafe power in an authority, which, in return, is obligated to uphold the law and guarantee individual rights, the touchstone being a single, uniform body of law. The regeneration of Jews and others, as the term was used repeatedly during the French Revolution, thus meant a social and civic rebirth through the medium of a thoroughly restructured and egalitarian legal system, a drama, indeed a sacred drama in the life of the *corpus reipublicae*, in which religion—much to papal dismay—played no role.[66]

Napoleon

The normally much maligned behavior of Napoleon Bonaparte toward Jews reveals this transvaluation of meanings with singular clarity, which is especially evident in Napoleon's actions at the Paris Sanhedrin of 1807, when he gathered Jews from France and Italy and virtually demanded they pledge allegiance to a program integrating Jews into post-Revolutionary France.[67]

There are many reasons why Jews in Napoleon's day should have felt he treated them badly, especially in the region of Alsace, where he nearly destroyed Jewish economic life.[68] Indeed, the gap between revolutionary ideals and their consistent application, certainly in France, but also in the United States, was often great. Jewish equality in practice was not achieved without forward and backward lurches. With respect to Napoleon, it is doubtful he nurtured positive sentiments toward Jews. Yet the goals he set forth at the Sanhedrin are better evaluated outside a purely Jewish context and appraised within the ambit of Napoleon's legal revolution that replaced the old matrices of *ius commune* with the new (and lasting) *Code civil* that he viewed as his greatest achievement. This is so even with respect to Napoleon's one apparently true challenge to Jews, his query whether they would accept interfaith marriages.[69] The answer in Jewish hearts had to have been no, and it is easy to accuse Napoleon of disingenuousness. Did he not know that he was asking Jews whether they would accept complete assimilation, carrying to its logical conclusion the analogy of rebirth through law to rebirth through baptism? Was he not aware that he was pressing the Jew, enfolded within the robes of the *Code civil*, to take his or her new civil identity to the extreme and dismiss any and all Jewish individuality, much as the true convert would fully discard his or her Jewish past, and certainly the Jewish identity of his or her offspring?

Yet was not secular, interfaith marriage wholly illegal, and impossible, before the French Revolution? Before 1791, marriage was a sacrament, never a civil institution that might entertain a match between members of competing (Christian) sects, let alone with a Jew.[70] Napoleon and the Revolution had insisted not only that there be civil marriage, but that it also precede any religious vows, a sequence that is now the law in most, if not all, of the United States, as well as in nearly all countries in Europe and South America. Napoleon's was a major step toward modernity. Even more, it was an attack on the *ancien régime*'s so-called corporate structure.[71] In calling for Jews to accept civil, and possibly mixed, marriages, Napoleon was insisting that Jews, whose rights as citizens he did guarantee, also participate in the nation civilly (if not socially) on the same plane as all others.[72] He was forwarding the goal announced at the National Assembly by Clermont-Tonnere, as David Sorkin has so well explained, that the Revolution do away with the corporate society that so characterized the *ancien régime*, where privileges depended on corporate identity. Furthermore, these were privileges that, in the words of the seventeenth-century Cardinal de Luca, took precedence over other legal determinations.[73]

When, therefore, Napoleon required Jews to place the law of the state above religious law, he was demanding of the Jews what he had already demanded of others.[74] Instructively, it was precisely this intention of Napoleon that the Italian economist, philosopher, and patriot Carlo Cattaneo singled out in 1836. Napoleon's goal, said Cattaneo, was to have the Jews legally "fit in," which, as Cattaneo also recognized, they themselves sought to do by agreeing to accept the validity of civil marriages between Jews and non-Jews. If, he went on, they refused to sanction these matches spiritually, they did so in order to maintain Jewish integrity in other spheres.[75] Like Cattaneo, the contemporary Jewish leader Baruch Cerf Beer, too, correctly understood Napoleon's vision. Napoleon's "wish," said Beer, "is to unite us more closely with the greatest nation on earth, so as to form but one people . . . [and that we enjoy] all the rights of French citizens." This is under a regime where "Catholics and Lutherans, Jews and Calvinists, are considered by His Majesty as children of the same father; he leaves to the Supreme Being the right of calling them to account for their opinions."[76] In this context, we should recognize how telling are the words of the historian Jacques Revel: "It was Napoleon who began the true resolution of the matter of Jewish *citizenship* by regularizing Jewish life along the same lines as *other French religious groups*, making them [by way of his legal innovations into] *Israelites-francaises*."[77] James Madison could not have said it better.

Ecclesiastic Anger

The Church was livid about the French reforms. Cerf Beer's arresting phrase "to form but one people" alludes to the *corpus ecclesiae mysticum*, the mystical body of the Church being replaced with the *corpus reipublicae mysticum*, the mystical body of the state. The state had assumed for itself the mantle of the *unus panis, multi sumus*, the "single loaf no matter how many we are" that was St. Paul's signature definition of unity within the one holy church. The ideological revolution begun by Martin Luther had been completed beyond the scope of Luther's imagination. Ideology apart, on a practical, materially painful, level, French reforms, especially those concerning marriage, compromised the Church's base of political power. Perhaps more importantly, they furnished ammunition to those scholars of *ius commune* (and their successors, expert in the ways of the *Code civil*) who had been struggling for nearly two centuries to achieve a balance between canon and civil law and to ensure that the former not invariably overwhelm the latter, as it normally did in the old regime.

Yet even these scholars had taken generations to free themselves from confessionalism and the belief that Church and state must complement each other both formally and legally. Canonists like Giacobo Pignatelli, despite a genuine concern for Jewish rights, including a vociferous opposition to (false) denunciations, nonetheless insisted that the Jews' right to live by *ius commune* extended only so far as the canons not be infringed.[78] Besides, did not *ius commune* by virtue of its very nature inherited from the late—read Christian—Roman Empire concede canon law validity in civil spheres? Not incorrectly, therefore—and with no reference to Jews, but to society as a whole —modern scholars have deemed the need to free citizens from the ties that bound together the rule of civil and canon law the principal motive for over-turning the system of *ius commune* and replacing it with the secular *Code civil*.[79]

6. Under Papal Rule

The legal revolution discussed in the preceding chapter and the accompanying drive to reinforce civil institutions were well known to Roman Jews, and that much the more to educated leaders like Tranquillo del Monte. Tranquillo was highly aware that the Jewish reality of his contemporary Rome had virtually no resemblance to that in places like France and the United States, nor could it have escaped him that policies in the Papal State especially conversionary ones, were *sui generis.* The discipline intended to break Roman Jews that had begun with Paul IV and peaked under Pius VI, precisely in the years when Tranquillo was serving as a *fattore,* was having its effects. The communal minute books cry out. Disorder had broken out. There was no money to pay the 800 scudi owed the baker in Piazza Giudia for the ever decreasing daily ration supplied to the poor, while Jews who received, as many did, licenses to travel beyond Rome for trade could see the chasm distinguishing Jewish life in Rome from that in other places.

Communal Transformation

A variety of means was being used to bring Roman Jewry to capitulate. None was more effective than an intentional weakening of their communal apparatus. From no later than the mid-seventeenth century, if not earlier, powers of internal self-discipline and governance were attacked. Lacking authorization for a formal rabbinic court with distinct powers as in Frankfurt in Germany or Metz in France, the Jews of Rome had cultivated self-governance by emphasizing and expanding the traditional practice of consensual arbitration and by adopting standardized forms of documentation created by Jewish notaries and used throughout the community; early modern, like medieval, notaries in many ways resembled lawyers, drawing contracts and other agreements.[1] These Jewish notaries had not existed until about 1536; in the fifteenth century, Roman Jews were dictating wills before Christian notaries. From the early sixteenth century onward, Christian notaries were replaced by Jews, who drew their acts in Hebrew, although it is clear these notaries were thinking in Italian and doing their utmost to preserve Italian legal forms to ensure the validity of their efforts.[2]

Papal officials, sensing that the notarial system was a major factor in preserving the integrity of the Roman Jewish Community, especially after 1555, bit by bit curtailed notarial functions, until, by 1640, they forced the institution to close. Within a few years, civil or papal tribunals were dealing with the kind of dispute that would naturally have been handled by arbiters within the Jewish *universitas* (as it was called, even though it had never exercised even a semblance of the primary jurisdiction normally possessed by corporations, which obligated litigants to resort first to corporate courts). Jews were no longer sovereign even in minor matters that properly pertained to Jewish (*halakhic*) law and usage, such as whether an engagement pact might be broken off.[3] One text suggests that Jews could not marry without the Vicar's license, and about 1708, Rabbi Tranquillo Corcos was forced to write a lengthy brief explaining why Jews were entitled to make a will of their own rather than being obligated to follow biblical ordinances alone on succession.[4]

The Jews did not take being deprived of self-governance lying down. They replied by seeking advantage in the civil courts, petitioning papal authorities, and taking advantage, where possible, of their powers of taxation, which the papacy hesitated to cancel, lest the Community become a financial burden on the state.[5] At the same time, Jewish protests sometimes took on the air of what seems proper to call tacit acquiescence, for instance, in the appeal made, sometime after 1702, by the heirs of one David Fermi to the court of the Papal Vicar, the pope's principal adjutant in Rome. Fermi had moved to Rome and then decamped to Ancona. The Jewish *Università* had tried for years, actually decades, to collect taxes on Fermi's estate. There was a failed attempt at internal arbitration, a remnant of the old system, but one that was hardly recognizable. The arbiters for the Community were rabbis, who, in the past, had rarely appeared in this role; and if they had, it was as individuals, not in their rabbinic capacity. The rabbis also appear as representatives of the Community, not its heads. To brace their authority, therefore, the rabbis cite Jewish *halakhic* codes (their only legitimate way to cite banned Talmudic materials and perhaps the only way they knew them), whereas the majority of sixteenth-century arbitrations had rested solely on what "seemed" right, without invoking the formality of law.[6] Going a step further, the rabbis cite cases from the Roman Rota and texts from Christian legal experts, and they also insist that everything they say conforms to privileges, edicts, and other rules established by pontifical authorities. Arbitration, once normally accepted by litigating parties as decisive, seems to have become but a preliminary to litigating in a civic court, according to civil procedure.[7]

Juridical limitations were complemented by economic pressure, which culminated in the 1682 closing of the so-called Jewish banks. None of these "banks" was dramatically important to the general banking system. That was reserved for Christian institutions. However, the small Jewish "loan shops," as they were called in Hebrew, had kept capital afloat within the community. Even more, they offered employment to numbers of Jews. When the Jewish banks were closed in 1682, the reaction was close to catastrophic: unprecedentedly, entire families converted, and the number of conversions was the greatest during the entire ghetto period. The grand debate held among Christian authorities and savants prior to 1682 about whether to close the Jewish banks featured the argument of the sixteenth-century Jesuit Francisco de Torres that choking the Jews off economically would forward conversion. The thirteenth-century argument that lending at interest was delaying the advent of the Second Coming and the Messianic era also returned to life.[8]

The Roman Inquisition

A difficult-to-peg element in the conversionary chain was the papal Roman Inquisition. The Inquisition did not interfere with Jews with respect to their being Jewish; Jews and Judaism were by their intrinsic nature neither heretics, heretical, nor heresy, the Inquisition's normal spheres of inquiry.[9] Carlo Luti, whom we will soon meet, said it most forcefully, treating the understanding that Judaism was not a heresy as *comunemente abbracciata*, common knowledge. Debating whether Justinian's *Novel 118* applied to Jews, which disqualifies heretics as guardians, he said, of course not: "Who does not know that Jews and heretics are not the same?"[10] Luti's "everybody" included the battery of legists and canonists (many from earlier centuries) cited in his text.

Still, while it did not pursue Jews for heresy, the Roman Inquisition did try them for violations that had been defined hundreds of years earlier, among which were blasphemy, especially that allegedly contained in (condemned) Jewish books, but also including irreverent cursing and general disrespect to Christianity.[11] More serious was aiding people to return to Judaism or preventing others from being baptized, including one's own children.[12] A notable case was that of Benvenuta, in 1686, who ran out of the ghetto crying she wanted to convert, but was quickly dragged back in by Jewish compatriots.[13] In reaction, and as on other occasions, the *Fattori* were threatened with severe punishment.[14]

Instructively, the Inquisition was most active in the city of Modena, where, until 1638, no ghetto existed. The bulk of its prosecutions ended in fines, which went to maintain the material fabric of the tribunal, but the principal aim was control. In Venice, prosecutions centered on those who had relapsed into Judaism and on their abettors. This was largely a result of the heavy Sephardi component of the Venetian Jewish community. The worst incident occurred in Ancona, when in 1556 Paul IV had twenty-four one time New Christians burned at the stake. But this event was unique.[15]

The Inquisition also prosecuted Jews for magic. Tales linking Jews and magic go back to the early Middle Ages, notably that about the Jew Theophilo, who worked a spell to secure a bishopric for a "sinner" who later repented and was saved by the Virgin. Jews were also said to use magic to promote sexual debauchery like that ascribed to an eleventh-century Count of Soissons, as reported by Guibert de Nogent.[16] Magical incantations feature in the temporary expulsion from Avignon in 1322,[17] and again in a reference to a book on which Paul IV, while still Cardinal Caraffa, wanted to get his hands.[18] Magic is noted specifically as a justification for expelling the Jews from most of the Papal State in 1569.[19] And magic became entwined with issues related to Kabbalah, although here caution is advised. Kabbalah was a discipline with a bad name, which Jewish leaders strove to keep out of popular hands. Kabbalistic beliefs like the transmigration of the soul never became standard.[20]

In short, the Inquisition and its contacts with Jews must be viewed circumspectly. When it came to conversion, its involvement was tangential, and sometimes surprising. As the studies of Adriano Prosperi have shown, the Inquisition was a legally precise organization, maddeningly so, and although it might prosecute those who prevented conversion, it was also a body that felt empowered to reject demands for improperly sequestering "offered" Jewish children and women, as it sometimes did.[21]

More one-sided initiatives were those that originated in the *Casa dei catecumeni*. Like all institutions, the *Casa* was highly invested in preserving itself, and, of course, in expansion. The *Casa* was founded in the early six-teenth century following the conversionary urgings of tracts like the *Libellus ad Leonem Decem*. Its chief protagonist was Ignatius Loyola, who peti-tioned and was granted the *Casa's* formal establishment in 1542/3.[22] Staffed mostly by converts anxious to demonstrate their loyalty, but also in order to justify its continued operation, the *Casa*—especially when headed, as it was in the late eighteenth century, by arch-conservatives like Francesco Ro-vira Bonet—could be a font of emotional violence.[23] The diary of Anna del Monte proves the point.

The Limits of Weakening

However, just how effective were the efforts to diminish the possibilities of Jewish self-discipline and destabilize the Jewish economy? How thor-oughly did they weaken Roman Jews and bring them, as Paul IV believed they would, to their knees?[24] The bull *Cum nimis absurdum* of 1555 brought together the brunt of past legislation. Nearly all of its restrictions date to the early Middle Ages and were perfected in the eleventh and twelfth centuries, as were the vast majority of canons dealing with Jews, if not earlier. Very few of these laws are not already to be found in Gratian's magisterial *Decre-tum* of about 1140. This legislation was strengthened by the imposition of distinctive clothing at the Fourth Lateran Council of 1215, with the goal of avoiding Jewish superiority and preventing the impurity created through un-desirable contact; this council, despite the common opinion to the contrary, was a culmination, not a turning point.[25]

Nonetheless, *Cum nimis absurdum* also innovated. In a costly new theme inserted into the centuries-old litany of restrictions forbidding Jews and Christians to dine together to avoid pollution and "over-familiarity," the bull forbade Jewish commerce in foodstuffs and their handling. This was a field in which, previous to 1555, Roman Jews had been highly active, for one, in the wholesaling of artichokes. There was also added insult. To ensure the prevention of Jewish superiority, Christians were prohibited from addressing Jews with respectful titles. More dangerously, the on-again-off-again assault on Jewish, rabbinic literature, which had begun in the thirteenth century, was resumed without respite.[26]

Yet what may have hurt most was a new exploitation of *ius commune* following a decision by the high papal court of the Rota made seven decades after *Cum nimis*, but in its spirit. After 1621, Jews were *obligated* to air even internal disputes both before civil courts and on the basis of *ius commune*. To be sure, Jews had always been subject to *ius commune* in matters where Jewish and civil laws clashed, just as they had always been free to turn to civil rather than rabbinic courts. But this is precisely why the notarially driven system of consensual arbitration closed off by 1640 had been so important: it kept strife *within* the community.

The Counter-Intuitive: Jewish Benefit

At the same time, and perhaps typical of the entire papal judicial system, universally judged an irremediable mess,[27] the Jews also benefited. The loss of internally controlled *halakhic* decision was a blow, but *ius commune* also afforded Jews rights, and aware of them, Jews, as we have said, did not hesitate to protest when they felt these rights were violated. Subjection to *ius commune* might be a two-way street. Rather than solely weakening Jewish strength and resolve, as had been anticipated, depriving the Jews of the refuge of internal self-governance had the sometimes beneficial effect of fostering greater Jewish integration into the system of public law, such as it was in early eighteenth-century Rome—along with the benefits this law conferred.

This process was confusing. Simultaneous deprivation and integration were creating a Jewish civil status that was deteriorating and improving at one and the same time. And it is from observing the tension between improvement and deterioration and the way it worked itself out in the drama of her kidnapping that the most important lesson from studying the diary of Anna del Monte derives. Seeing the frustrations generated by a system that moved in two ways at once, yet was never empowered sufficiently to reach the end of the road in either direction, we may properly comprehend the nature, the untenability, and even the absurdity of the confessionally driven legal divide that distinguished the *ancien régime* from the modern state. This, I believe, is precisely what Tranquillo wished readers of the diary to grasp. Tranquillo himself had understood perfectly that at one end of the road was the elimination of Judaism through total absorption, legally, socially, *and* religiously. At the other end was the acquisition by Jews of the liberty for which the Anna of the diary plainly yearns as she demands repeatedly in the diary: do not deny me my Jewish essence (*rubare l'anima*). Tranquillo himself yearned for the rights religious liberty would bring in its wake.

Two-headed Confessionalism

Here was a "stunted bifurcation," whose crux was the unresolved relationship we began to examine in the previous chapter between law, civil status, and religious doctrine. The inability to draw a firm line distinguishing between state and confessionalism, whether in the Papal State or elsewhere, impeded the creation of the kind of state the American Founding Fathers desired. As long, that is, as confessional states continued to exist, granting legal advantage to one religious group over another, the Jews could not be made fully equal.

A very important distinction must be maintained in order correctly to grasp the sticking point confessionalism created. Jews in the later eighteenth century were achieving wider rights in all the Italian states, although sometimes what seemed like rights could be deceptive. For example, the Code of Law inaugurated in 1723 under the name of Duke Vittorio Emanuele of Savoy, which was issued as a law of the state, purportedly independent of the Church, and with traditional cross-references to *ius commune* and the canons omitted, nonetheless incorporated fully traditional canonical restrictions. Real reforms were those mentioned above of Emperor Joseph II, or the special privileges, which we have not discussed, that were enjoyed by Jews in Bordeaux, Livorno, and eventually Florence, as well as in Holland and England.

However, all of these improvements went only so far, which Roman Jews themselves may well have realized as they read and assembled in a special folder in their communal archive copies of privileges from Genova (1752), Parma and Piacenza (1773), Senigaglia and Mantova (1787), Trieste (1781), Modena (1780), Livorno (1787), and Tuscany as a whole, as well as for Bordeaux (1782) and the Empire (1782, in a copy made in 1792). They could see clearly that however important were the signs of forward progress, these were, nevertheless, not the same as emancipation itself. Jews in Holland, for example, may have for decades registered their marriages civilly, as Dutch law required of all citizens, and their ability to carry on commerce and meet openly in prayer were unchallenged, but real equality in Dutch law came only in 1795, under the influence of Napoleon.[28]

True and complete emancipation, therefore, hinged neither on privilege, changes in Jewish behavior (that were demanded), nor a formula prescribing that as Jews became more westernized, European states would allow them to enter more fully into the life of the state. Instead, it hinged on the Jews' amalgamation into the revamped legal structures of fully deconfessionalized states, structures that also canceled limitations based on religion or even those rooted in *ius commune*, to wit, the prohibition on Jews holding public office or serving as judges. Jews also had to stop being classified, as they technically were in *ius commune*, as *personae odiosae*, civilly disenfranchised felons. In other words, without thorough legal revision, full civil rights (at least in theory and regardless of de facto privilege) were beyond the Jews' grasp.[29] Or, for that matter, the grasp of any other European "minority," for instance, Catholics in England or Protestants in France. It is with the Jews, however, the perennial "odd man out," that the need for a legal revision becomes so clearly distinct, a revision that would destroy old, or even residual, barriers, and regardless of earlier privileges, whether these were privileges Jews enjoyed alone or in common with other minorities. Superfluous to add, this revolution in Jewish status (or that of other minorities) did not pass from theoretical, legal revision to full implementation overnight. Even in the United States, it was decades into the nineteenth century before all states removed the barriers to Jews possessing full rights.

Legal revision also demanded reciprocity. As much as state law might eventually accommodate Jews, so Jewish law had to be accommodated to the law of the state. This process is especially visible in pre-Revolutionary Alsace.[30] However, even there, it could not properly benefit Jews prior to full legal emancipation and complete liberation from canonical restriction. As we are about to observe for Rome, without both of those changes, accommodation to civil law might be no more than a prelude to new discriminations. Indeed, as the reader may have already grasped, the insistence in Rome on Jewish legal amalgamation—namely, the extension to Jews of the rule of *ius commune* at the expense of Jewish litigation according to Jewish law—was a source of destabilization and conflict.[31] Together with the priority given the canons, law had the potential for creating havoc, and especially as the popes strove to prolong the confessional status quo, which they believed would keep their state from disintegrating before their very eyes. The prescient observation of Tom Paine, commenting on developments in France in 1791 and papal behavior, seems to fit here very well: "Persecution is not an original feature in any religion; but it is always the strongly marked feature of all law-religions, or religions established by law. Take away the law-establishment, and every religion re-assumes its original benignity." Or as Tranquillo might have commented, at least it loses its power to destroy others, their lives and well-being.[32]

7. Legal Obstacles

Control over Marriage

As put by the Torinese jurist Giuseppe Sessa, writing on the subject of Jews (and citing Cardinal Gian Battista de Luca), the law confers privileges on the Jews as *cives*, . . . except in the spiritual forum.[1] Jews had tried to live with this formulation. They had even tried to make it work to their advantage.[2] Nonetheless, while in the Papal State, the former, the privileges of being *cives*, were never entirely erased—which may have been what saved the Jews in the long run—it was the latter, the burdens (imposed by restrictive canons, together with the confessional aspects of ancient Roman Law that were absorbed into *ius commune*), that came ever more to the fore. To these burdens were added evolving legal interpretations that facilitated the "offerings" and denunciations that upended the life of Anna del Monte and many others. These interpretations and their evolution claim attention.

Jews were not the only ones affected. The demands of the burgeoning modern state (whether the papal one or any other) fell ever more heavily, and in new ways, on all residents. Using the tools of *ius commune* to augment centralized authority, the state began to interfere unprecedentedly in the personal life of its residents, in particular, in the life of the family. The freedom to contract marriage was limited, and rights were claimed over children and their education.[3] For the Church, oversight in these matters was critical, granting it greater control over the fortunes (double entendre intentional) of Christian souls. This control was solidified by the decision at the Council of Trent in 1563 to make the presence of a priest at nuptials obligatory, emphasizing marriage's sacramental essence.[4] In marriage, the unity of the Church was represented, as was the union of Christ and the Church, along with the hope for universal salvation through the baptism of offspring as close to birth as possible.[5]

One might imagine the Jews were immune from this kind of interference. Normally, Jews were not hindered in marrying according to Jewish law, which Sessa, in approving its use, had called *ceremonalia*. Yet with the exception of marriage, and to some extent inheritance, by the later seventeenth century, the growing prohibition of Jewish resort to Jewish law and the greater amalgamation of Jews into *ius commune* were being exploited as a tool to limit traditional Jewish privilege. This included the right of Jewish widows to handle money, accorded to them by the *halakhah*, but denied by *ius commune*, a predicament that led to creative solutions in order to relieve the widows' plight.[6]

The Church was troubled because, correctly, it perceived how greatly its understanding of marriage differed from that of the Jews. Sessa went so far as to call Jewish marriage a civil institution, and for precisely this reason, he said, Jews might divorce. One senses that Sessa himself favored, and perhaps even anticipated, civil marriage as a universal institution, which is exactly what the French Revolution instituted, and so, too, or almost so, did the Habsburg Catholic emperor Joseph II after about 1780. The Church would not abide this kind of marriage. Moreover, although the Church was not going to stand in the way of marriages between two Jews, when conversion, or potential conversion, was involved, it did intervene, determining what constituted a valid Jewish marriage. When the offspring of converts were at stake, it was implacable.[7]

The Offspring of Converts

This last problem was ancient. Since the seventh century, in Visigothic Spain, the canons of the Toledan Councils obligated children to follow a converted parent. This precedent was still binding a thousand years later. Benedict XIV cited it in his 1747 letter *Postremo mense*, in which the question of offspring is central. This letter, or bull, he said, was composed in response to a request for clarification on the part of the Jews of Rome themselves. They were distressed by unwarranted irruptions into the ghetto; wholly unauthorized people had snatched Jewish children from their parental homes, or even the streets, and *inalterably* (as the Church saw it) baptized them. This request, however, has led Benedict to revisit wider questions of baptism in their historical context, about which there has never been the full consensus he now wishes to achieve. To understand the motives driving the papal response, our discussion must become technical.

Benedict gave special weight to rulings by Gregory IX and Gregory XIII, as well as to Visigothic legislation. What troubled the pope most was the chain of authority in Jewish families: who in the Jewish family was the *pater familias* and who held the *patria potestas* that was crucial in establishing and maintaining the structure of a family unit. The answer to this question determined who possessed the right "to offer" children for baptism—or to refuse to have them offered. It also determined how conversion affected the pecking order of family authority. For centuries, complications deriving from these questions had created tensions, including those arising from the parallel question of who could "dedicate" to the Church, or simply denounce as having expressed a desire to convert, a person he (it was never she) called his spouse.

All legists, the theoreticians of law, agreed that Jews possessed *patria potestas*.[8] However, variable circumstances might cast doubt on the normal pecking order that vouchsafed *patria potestas* to the father.[9] Past precedent, said Benedict, had established the rule that conversion was always decisive, a principle he would make his guide as he brought to a climax the centuries-long process to install *favor fidei* as pivotal in moments of conversionary conflict.

The matter of this pope's historical consciousness and his drawing on the past is not open to debate. Benedict himself provides us with this history and the chain of interpretative authorities in the footnotes—the cross-references—that he inserted into *Postremo mense* and, four years later, *Probe te meminisse*. To suggest, as has been done, that his methods were inventively deceptive, that he was branching off on a route of his own, and that he was ignoring legal precedent is to misconstrue, if not overlook, the words, intention, and structure of the text.[10]

Perhaps the most important of these precedents occurred between 1572 and 1585, when, after great legal discussion, accompanied by strong arguments on both sides, Pope Gregory XIII acceded to the wishes of a *neofito* grandfather and allowed the latter "to offer" his grandson to the Christian faith. The child was baptized on the day of Dionysius the Areopagite in the Church of S. Celso. The child's father had died; the mother was still living.

A full discussion of this episode and its legality is found in (the already noted) 1595 *Speculum Episcoporum* of Rutilio Benzoni, a text Benedict XIV's *Probe te meminisse* cites more than once.[11] It does so, however, through the notable intermediacy of the *Tractatus de Iudaeis* of Giuseppe Sessa.[12] The rule, says Benzoni, was established by the thirteenth-century Gregory IX in the bull—and eventual canon—*ex litteris,* which says that *in favorem maxime fidei christianae respondemus, patri eumdem puerum assignandum,* because of the favor of the faith, the child is assigned to the father. Yet the head of the family line is not always the father. Should the paternal grandfather, the *Avo,* be alive, Benzoni continues, and especially should he convert, the child is assigned to him. Moreover, following *ex litteris,* the *unconverted* mother loses custody, for she might lead the child to unbelief (*infidelitatis errorem*); the reverse is true should the convert be the mother. *Ex litteris* says this openly and is seconded by the fifteenth-century canonist Panormitanus, referring to Thomas Aquinas: "The practice is always to give the child to the convert [whether the father or the mother]."[13] Justification is provided by the sixteenth-century Juan Azor in his *Institutionem Moralium.* When the good of the common faith, *communi fidei bono,* is at stake, Azor writes, considerations of *patria potestas,* sanctioned as they are by the laws (*ius commune*) and Roman law, do not hold [precisely].[14] Hence, Azor—whom Benedict XIV cites more than once in *Postremo mense*—continues by saying that the *mater fidelis,* who does not exercise *patriam potestam* according to the *ius civile,* still may offer her child for baptism.[15] A venerable policy thus existed, which the eighteenth-century popes invoked, and on which they elaborated.

There is a further ramification, one we touched on earlier. The question arose as to when might a pregnant woman whose child had been "offered" be taken into the *Casa dei catecumeni,* where, it was said, the fetus would be protected from abortion or infanticide by its parents, thus to be saved physically and, then, spiritually through baptism at birth. As put in one instance by the *Vicegerente* of Rome, the person who was ultimately responsible for the *Casa de catecumeni:* the mother must be confined until she gives birth, *per assicurare il Feto, e preservarlo dalle fraudi che possono commetter gl'Ebrei per privarlo del Battesimo,* to guarantee [the life of] the fetus and to protect it from the frauds the Jews might commit to prevent its baptism.[16]

Yet was such a radical step necessary? Had not Duns Scotus said that in the case of infanticide (equated with abortion in 1769), the infant, like the *innocenti* slaughtered by Herod, would be "baptized in blood"?[17] And Benedict XIV, who cited Scotus directly, paid him heed. Nonetheless, the concept of "baptized in blood" appears to have exercised Benedict independently of Scotus, and it is this concept that explains, I believe, the otherwise opaque clause in *Postremo mense* of 1747 in which the pope asked: *demum quomodo probari possit, eosdem aquis salutaribus iam lustratos fuisse,* how can it be proved that *those children* have already been baptized? Which children? At first blush, the context seems to point to children baptized by servants without the knowledge of parents, baptisms called illicit, yet nonetheless valid. Or, possibly, the subject is abandoned children, whom clerics had taken in and baptized. Yet, a closer look at the wording of *Postremo mense* indicates that Benedict has already discussed each of these possibilities when speaking about "[abandoned] children [who] are brought to be baptized," or when he says, "when it is discovered that they have been admitted to sacred baptism [through the action of servants or others who have entered the ghetto]." Thus, the question "how can it be proved that these same children have already been purified?" must refer to some other category of child.

But nowhere in *Postremo mense*'s more than forty pages do we learn which children Benedict means; the antecedent to "these same children," specifying their identity, is never revealed. Readers of the letter are left to their imagination, knowing, however, from the wording, that these children are ones whom Benedict is convinced have been baptized, yet for whom the very act of baptism remains to be proved. As I see it, the only kind of child who could fit this description is one still unborn, a fetus that had been offered and that, irrespective of whether it was later born live, Benedict considered baptized *in utero,* which is to say, "in blood."

It was these fetuses that Jews in Benedict's day were more than once accused of murdering, or of plotting to murder, including by legists like Giuseppe Sessa or Nicolà Rodriguez Fermosino.[18] It is my suspicion that through an elusive logic, Benedict perceived all those baptized or potentially baptized, or even offered or denounced, as somehow reenacting the drama of the *innocenti*. And it is in this sense that I suggested above that all those who passed through the *Casa dei catecumeni*, whatever the circumstances of their having arrived there, were seen as protagonists of a martyrological struggle, in which, as in all martyrdoms, the victim is perceived Eucharistically. Conversion and its struggles, therefore, like martyrdom, reaffirmed the ultimate Eucharistic truth of the Church.[19] Moreover, although their souls would be considered baptized and saved regardless of whether they lived or died, these "*innocenti*" still merited having their physical, as well as spiritual, lives protected; accordingly, their mothers were to be sequestered (in the *Casa*) until they gave birth.

There is also something more, which even resort to Scotus and theories of the *innocenti* alone will not resolve. This is the question of when life begins. As Adriano Prosperi has so well explained, notions of the origin of life with the entrance of the soul underwent great changes toward the end of the seventeenth century. Medieval lawyers debating the question of life's inception had decided that the soul enters the body about ninety days into the pregnancy and that it was at this moment that life began.[20] An alternative discussion spoke of quickening, which was at about sixteen weeks (or 112 days). This latter time was discussed in the Supreme Court decision on abortion, *Roe v. Wade*; and it is precisely here that we are heading. To guarantee that no woman carrying "an offered fetus" eluded their grasp, papal lawyers in the eighteenth century pushed back the time of life's inception to almost immediately following conception. Complementarily, they also changed the traditional teaching, which, as phrased by the jurist Antonio de Becchettis, taught that the child is like an apple hanging from a tree, part of its mother's body. It was inseparable from her and could not be baptized without baptizing the mother herself.[21]

The new thinking said the opposite. Considered alive and with a soul of its own from the instant of conception, the fetus/child was deemed an independent entity from the start, subject to even intrauterine baptism—a doctrine that was not expounded solely in the classroom or limited to expression as a theological tenet like that of the "*innocenti*," "existing in the mind of the beholder." It was a teaching acted out in real life in places as far away as Peru,[22] and a principle that, I believe, moved Benedict XIV to ordain that mothers lose all rights over their fetuses (read: their bodies); abortion is to be considered homicide; and Jewish women in Rome whose fetuses had been offered to the Church were automatically to be sequestrated in the *Casa dei catecumeni*. This teaching and the associated principle are still alive, and the context is most instructive: in 2002, the Dominican Aidan Nichols, together with the Benedictine Philippe Jobert, framed a discussion of abortion in explicit terms of "*innocenti*," "baptism of blood," and, ominously, "*odium fidei*."[23]

Innovation did not stop here. We have seen that should a mother convert while expecting or after giving birth, but not the father, the child was to be baptized and given over to her custody. The way to this end, following the opinion of the sixteenth-century Juan Azor, was to transfer parental rights to the mother—or, equally, to a female deemed in a position to act *in loco parentis* or even to possess parental rights herself, most particularly, and as it was eventually decided, to the *Ava*, the paternal grandmother, or to a person as distant as a paternal aunt, the *Amita*. The will of the Jewish father was summarily overruled. Ironically, when it came to baptism, women became the legal equals of men, but in no other respect. In other spheres, women's legal parity remained a dead letter.

The Conundrum of Divorce

There were additional wrinkles related to Jewish divorce,[24] whose rules furnish important background in cases of denunciation like Anna's. Decisive was the question of whether Anna had been married to Sabato Coen, or even betrothed with a ring (or other object of value). If the latter, Sabato could have "offered" her outright, which was far more dangerous than a denunciation. For her part, a married Jewish woman who refused to follow her husband into Christianity would no doubt seek a *get*, the formal Jewish decree of divorce. But how? This question engaged Jews and Christians equally. Papal letters over the centuries affirmed that conversion by one spouse meant that the bond between the convert and his or her Jewish spouse *had* to be dissolved. However, compounding the issue, Jewish leaders insisted that a converted husband issue a writ of Jewish divorce, whose actual issuance, till today, remains an exclusively male prerogative. Additionally, the authoritative twelfth-century Rabbi Jacob Tam had demanded that the converted husband use his Hebrew name in making out the writ.[25]

Church officials objected. But without this document—in Latin, a *libellum ripudii*—the convert's wife remained an *agunah*, an "anchored woman" who could never remarry. Papal officials may have viewed these constraints as an inducement to persuade the wife to convert.[26] They also objected that by releasing his wife through a *get*, the *neofito* husband would be Judaizing, engaging in the kind of Jewish ritual act Benedict XIV had prohibited absolutely in *Apostolici ministerii munus* of September 16, 1747. This could not be.

The famous *neofito* Samuel Nahmias-Giulio Morosini magnified negative sentiments when he complained about his own divorce in later seventeenth-century Venice, which he said cost him dearly and dragged on over many years. Morosini was one of those converts who despised his past. His tract on Jewish customs, part accurate and part deliberate distortion, emphasizes what Morosini deemed perverse.[27] Beyond his imaginative fancies, however, Morosini's ambivalences reveal the delicacy of the moment. Regardless of his lengthy struggles in coming to an understanding about the division of property with his wife, who remained Jewish, he agreed that it is improper to leave a wife with nothing, although not for humanitarian reasons. Rather, it would be an act of violence, virtually forcing the wife to convert, in disregard of the canons. Morosini might have added the warning of the thirteenth-century Johannes Teutonicus, who said that sexual relations with a nonbeliever would corrupt the believing Christian and vitiate the Eucharist's effects.[28]

Morosini notes the development of the canons. Speaking about dismissing a wife who refused to follow her husband into faith in Christ, St. Paul had apparently said both yes and no at different moments. But the matter had been settled by the time of the Visigothic Toledan Councils, which firmly prohibited continuing the relationship, a decision made canonical in Gratian's *Decretum* on the grounds of avoiding *contumelia del Creatore*. For all that, a *neofito* was allowed to leave a wife who refused to convert only thanks to the so-called Pauline exception of 1 Corinthians 7, a *privilegium concessum favore Christianae fidei*.[29] Paul's original ambivalence lingered on.

When it came to the actual *get*, Morosini warns against the Judaizing that expresses itself in "Jewish ceremonies," especially in the use of the Hebrew name, on which Jews insisted, just as they required the observance of all the Jewish laws of divorce. The *get*, says Morosini, must be written in Hebrew with "square (style)" letters and in twelve lines. In fact, the normal language of a *get* is a mix of Hebrew and Aramaic, with the operative and necessary clause "You are hereby permitted to all men" in Hebrew. The *get* may be written on any kind of paper, even by the wife herself who is to receive it—in other words, by anyone.

Morosini was influential and widely read, and his presentation may have contributed, as I am about to detail, to the popes eventually stopping the Jews from circumventing the prohibitions of Judaizing. On the other hand, these prohibitions may have aided one neophyte in his attempt to get away with a serious deception. *Neofiti*, after all, had a reason to give a *get*. It finalized their break with the past, while it also freed them from any civil claims a Jewish wife might make; and Jews used civil courts freely.[30]

One neophyte, therefore, may have been exploiting Morosini's vague reference to "Jewish ceremonies," *cerimonie ebraiche,* when he swore that he gave a *get* without putting on his prayer shawl, the *tallit,* and praying. This protest, taken seriously by one modern author, was a sham, perpetrated to ensure the *neofito*'s peace and freedom from inquisitional meddling.[31] No religious ceremony like that the *neofito*'s text describes has *ever* accompanied the delivery (*mesirah*) of a *get.* By its very nature, a *get* is a civil, notarial text, which, apparently, even the Vice Regent and his court failed to understand. Any possible agreement, as has been suggested, to enable the delivery of *gittin* by converting them into notarial documents would have been the Jews pulling the wool over papal eyes. The wording in these texts is identical to that of the standard Hebrew *get,* with the language now Italian (something the *halakhah* would accept) and the notary (also not problematic) a Christian.

The absence of a rabbi, who at the most oversees the procedure, was no impediment. Most notably, however, in the five or six documents of this sort that I have seen, the man giving the *get,* notwithstanding he was now a *neofito,* is identified *both* by his new name as a Christian and by his old name as a Jew, his precise identification—in Hebrew, according to the instructions of Rabbi Jacob Tam—being one of a *get*'s sine qua nons (along with noting the place of issue).[32] At the same time, sensitive to potential charges of Judaizing, the Hebrew name was invoked not straightforwardly, but by appending a clause saying "known [before conversion and] as a Jew as . . ."—a tactic legitimated by none other than the imposing eighteenth-century Rabbi Isaac Lampronti of Ferrara. Tradition was maintained. Jewish women otherwise forced to remain maritally forbidden were freed *halakhically* to remarry.[33]

Jews adopted other tactics, too. On one occasion, in 1710, they tried to prevent an "offered" young woman from being sequestered in the *Casa* by submitting an appeal that cites both the *halakhah* and *ius commune,* hoping to prove the validity of a debated marriage by showing that the bride— whose father had converted in Genoa and then "offered" her while *she* was in Pesaro—had been married before his conversion.[34] A legitimate marriage, for which, it was claimed, her paternal grandfather had given his consent, would have disqualified the "offering."[35] We have no idea how this appeal turned out, but this claim was not one of a kind. Others like it were frequent enough for Benedict XIV to have mentioned them disdainfully in *Postremo mense* and then to have proceeded to warn the *Fattori* against marrying off a girl whose fiancé, or pretended fiancé, for instance, Sabato Coen, was about to convert (or had converted).[36]

Conflicting Legal Systems

Canonical exigencies thus intervened at every turn in Jewish life. I am not speaking of draconian restriction or of anti-Judaism, a term I prefer to avoid for its catch-all connotations. Rather, and I cannot emphasize this enough, I mean the exigencies of law, here, canon law as it demanded primacy over any other. Only in these terms can it be understood how Jews could live under the protection of *ius commune,* yet still be denied full rights. The canonically based confessionalism that allowed popes and legists to justify their actions deracinated the canons' counterparts in civil law, precluding progress toward emancipation, let alone the achievement of emancipation itself.

The problem stemmed from more than the canons alone. Did not *ius commune* from the time of the first Christian emperors in Rome forbid Jews to hold public office, which would confer upon them the "civic honor" that was reserved for Christians alone and, worse, allow them "to rule over Christians"? This prohibition, along with its confessionalized bias, was immovably rooted in Christian mentalities. The universally believed transfer of power from Jews to Christians, as embodied in the Christological interpretation of the verse Genesis 49:10, "the scepter of power will not be removed from Judah [the Jews] until Shiloh [read as Christ] comes," moved even C. W. Dohm. Hailed as a reformer in the later eighteenth century, who spoke of improving the status of the Jews as citizens (meaning the granting of civic rights balanced by Jewish social reform), Dohm, nevertheless, counseled distancing Jews from public office during the first generations of emancipation. Most demonstrative, the tolerant William Penn, in his 1682 charter for Pennsylvania, welcomed all worshippers to settle, but reserved public office for Christians.[37] This same argument was being made in various American states well into the nineteenth century. As I said earlier, the question of holding public office was the true litmus test for determining whether the late-eighteenth-century revolution in law and legal conceptuality had sunk in and brought confessionalism, in fact, as well as theory, to a full stop.

The prohibition on Jews holding office and enjoying any position of power over Christians was rooted in canon law, too. That Jews were supposedly ruling over Christians in Poland was a prime motivation for Benedict

XIV to issue *A Quo primum*.[38] Yet it was in the (Christianized) Roman civil law of the fifth-century Theodosian Code and the sixth-century Code of Justinian that this prohibition appeared first. It is for reasons of faith, too, that the eventual *ius commune* denies Jewish communities the legal status of a corporation, which meant the community, as a unit, could not receive bequests or, more important, enjoy the modicum of internal judicial control permitted even to guilds (which were legal corporations).[39] To wit: in 1733, Giuseppe Malatesta, the President of the Rione S. Angelo, where the ghetto was located, objected that a proposed census of the ghetto could not be left in Jewish hands. "Unlike parish priests," he said, "who are authorized legally [as heads of the parish corporation] to prepare the status of souls (roughly, a census) of their flocks, the heads of the Jews enjoy authority only through the *consent* of their coreligionists."[40]

This prohibition also gave teeth to that more important decision of the papal high court in Rome, the Rota, enunciated in 1621, which said that since Jews were *cives*, they must litigate exclusively in state courts and on the basis of *ius commune*. By putting this decision, whose roots are found in Justinian's Code, into actual practice, papal authorities successfully exhausted Roman Jewish communal power.[41] Nowhere previously had Jews been *forced* to prefer civil *ius commune* over Jewish law. It was thought that demonstrating to the Jews that they had lost all political and civil power, as Christians understood the "prophecy" of Genesis 49, would encourage conversion.

However, the insistence on (an exclusivity, or near exclusivity of) *ius commune* created a conundrum, a problem for which there was no resolution. On the one hand, the limitation to *ius commune* made Jews relinquish centuries-old legal habits of internal arbitration. Or if there was arbitration, as in the Fermi case reviewed earlier, it was carried on under strict Vicarial supervision, or placed in the hands of Christian legal advocates.[42] In one instance, the eminent canonist and eventual cardinal G. B. De Luca represented one of two Jews litigating over whether to end an engagement to marry,[43] a kind of dispute that in the sixteenth century would have been handled internally.

At the same time, the new legal reality—by default—was increasingly integrating Jews into the civil processes of the state, whence I have said their status was simultaneously ascending and descending. Were it not for the brakes operated by the religiously and confessionally biased laws found in the canons and *ius commune,* the Jews—even in the Papal State, and as odd as this sounds—would, by osmosis, have eventually achieved full legal equality.[44]

New Interpretations and Jewish Response

This was a drama whose intricacies I believe Tranquillo del Monte understood, just as he understood that the Papal State's embrace of confessionalism was the source of his sister's misfortune. Tranquillo also had to have had intimate knowledge of the briefs Christian lawyers in Jewish employ had composed to defend Jews taken into the *Casa dei catecumeni* or whose children had been kidnapped; he knew that others, indeed, non-Jews, had joined him in his protests. These Christian advocates spoke their mind outright, compellingly protesting legal confessionalism, and challenging interpretations that invariably favored the canons over civil laws, unsettling Jewish lives. Their writings are vital to our narrative. Properly to appreciate them, however, it is necessary to turn once more to the issue of *patria potestas,* that staple of Roman (civil) law that we have seen interpreted over time to forward canonical interests and whose limits were always in flux.

In the thirteenth century, Thomas Aquinas cited *patria potestas* to sustain the Jews' right, stated explicitly in the twelfth-century bull *Sicut iudaeis non*—itself built on a letter of the sixth-century Gregory the Great—to protect their children from being seized and baptized against their parents' wishes.[45] Nonetheless, did not Thomas know, cite, and honor Gregory IX's decision in *ex litteris?* And just as the vast majority, if not the unanimity, of canonists, he, too, would have opted for awarding a child to a converted relative. By contrast, by the mid- and late eighteenth century, *patria potestas* was being interpreted broadly and applied to a circle of relatives wider than the limited one of father and mother.[46] Confoundingly, the base principle was constantly restated: there should be no baptism *invitis parentibus,* over parental protest. But what were the limits of *invitis* and who were the *parentes,* a question whose solution most often hinged on interpretations of *favor fidei*—which, by this time, went hand in hand with attempts to limit severely the use of Jewish law in favor of (the Christianized) *ius commune?*[47] Already by the late seventeenth century, Giacobo Pignatelli was asking whether, in the case of two competing relatives—any two relatives—one of whom was a Christian, the Christian was not to gain control of the child.[48]

The increased drive for conversion made interpretations like this one virtually foregone conclusions, although it was neither manipulative nor a product of nefarious papal design. It had also advanced in stages. The first was Gregory XIII's extension of *patria potestas* to a converted grandfather in 1583, to which there was considerable resistance. Pope Gregory himself had initial doubts.[49] However, the significant extensions *in practice* to paternal grandmothers and, ultimately, to any relative or affine (a relative by marriage) who had converted—even while both parents were still alive and although similar cases had not provoked change in the past—came only after the middle of the eighteenth century (1751 and 1783, respectively). These extensions were no doubt accelerated by the Church's growing anxieties and need for reassurance. In addition, these extensions, as the bulls of 1747 and 1751 state explicitly, and as must not be forgotten, were also responses to circumstances that required immediate adjudication. That the discussion in the bulls centers on *paternal* grandparents alone and claims to follow the line of descent prescribed by Roman law and *ius commune* is a signal that a serious attempt was made *not* to violate the law.

In the event, the *idea* to extend parental rights to others beyond the father and the mother was *not* originated by the papacy, but by Rutilio Benzoni in his justification of Gregory XIII's granting this right to the *Avo*. The possible extension to the *Ava*, the paternal grandmother, appears first in discussions by Stephano Graziano in 1625, over a century before Benedict XIV composed his two bulls. Graziano wrote that the grandchild is to be baptized even if the (Jewish) father dissents. This applies, he says, also to the grandmother, who "is to be considered a parent in place of the mother."[50] Giuseppe Sessa, building on Pignatelli's conjectures, went further to say that Graziano's decision applied *not only* when one parent was dead and the other objected, *but even* when both were alive.[51] Eager to resolve the Falconeria case of 1751, concerning a grandmother who had offered a child, Benedict XIV happily cited both of these legists, just as he intensively mined and cited Chapter 51 of Sessa's 300-page *Tractatus de iudaeis* of 1716, often using the same or words similar to those of the author.[52] It was Sessa, writing a full thirty years before *Postremo mense*, who translated Graziano's concept into the wider principle that Benedict and later popes would put into practice, furnishing them with the legal theory and weight needed unprecedentedly to accept the *Ava*'s "offering." Indeed, without the theoretical precedents of Sessa, as well as Graziano, Benedict, as he himself admits, was in a quandary—regardless of his desire to find in favor of the grandmother.

Sessa, not content with having granted the power of "offering" to both paternal grandparents, states definitively that if there are two relatives of the same grade (for example, two second cousins), then the will of the Christian relative prevails.[53] Sessa also determines that in the case of legally constituted guardians—such as in a will that vouchsafes joint guardianship in a mother along with important communal leaders, as did happen—their powers are superseded in the presence of an "offering" convert.[54] Indeed, Sessa, who was not only an academician, but also the Jews' appointed judge in Turin, a secular official, and normally respectful of Jewish rights, seems to throw off all restraints. His expansive rulings sanction offerings even by an affine, and this holds, it appears, even when there are Jewish relatives higher in the line of ascendants. A converted uncle, according to Sessa, takes precedence over a real Jewish father or grandfather. Here Sessa is anticipating Pius VI, not only Benedict XIV, who, in 1783, allowed uncles to oblate, although the child's parents were alive. Sessa further seems to be suggesting that almost any Jewish child is fair game: "regardless if *all* the Jewish relatives are vociferously opposed." It was sufficient for the child to have a converted relative, regardless of the relationship. Here was an opening to baptize all Jews indiscriminately. And Sessa, I repeat, was no ecclesiastic devoted heart and soul to promoting the cause of the Church. Confessionalism was hard to leave behind, even for one who seems tacitly to approve of what he calls the Jews' civil mode of marriage.

Beyond that, Sessa had apparently forgotten that he himself had said that many things are legally possible; but, with respect to baptism, not all are binding.[55] He had also spoken strongly against baptism *invitis parentibus* in principle, although just about everybody else had, too. Nonetheless, in the end, he succumbed to the zeal for promoting *favor fidei*, not to mention to Thomas Aquinas's call to honor this principle based on Gregory IX's *ex litteris*, which Sessa cites. The too frequently stated notion that Thomas rejected baptizing *invitis parentibus*, as opposed to Duns Scotus who promoted it, turns out to be imprecise.[56]

All of this was known to Benedict XIV, who also had to have seen Sessa's qualification about restraint in accepting offerings. However, Benedict had to make a real decision in real time, which was difficult even for him, and which likely explains why he so vividly put the "precedents" on display in the sources he cites "to footnote" *Postremo mense* and *Probe te meminisse*.[57] His arguments must be taken seriously when he says in the latter, in 1751, that despite a strong majority opinion by the Inquisition and others, he had almost given up and denied the petition of the *Ava* Giuliana Falconeria to offer her grandchildren over their living mother's objections. He was cautious, too, lest his decision in favor of the converted *Ava* be interpreted as resting on *favor fidei* alone, whence it might be interpreted as giving permission to unauthorized people to enter the ghetto and baptize children indiscriminately. This was the offense the 1747 *Postremo mense* addressed and claimed it was trying to eliminate. Benedict confessed, therefore, that *riconosciamo però con tutta buona fede esservi bisogno di qualche altra cosa di più per arrivare a stabilire esser valida lecita e doversi accettare l'offerta* [of the paternal grandmother], we acknowledge, too, with *bona fide*, that there is a need for something extra to allow us to accept the validity of the "offering."[58] That "extra," the *cosa di più*, was to take Stefano Graziano's argument as cited by Sessa and assert that the paternal grandmother could be viewed as a parent.

Yet how was this chain of reinterpretations to be justified? By the mid-fourteenth century, Antonio de Butrio, followed two centuries later by Juan Azor,[59] had said that *patria potestas* might pass to the mother through nature, regardless of civil law, which assigns this right to the father. It might also devolve upon the paternal grandfather, should the father be absent. Both of these legists, in turn, were following the thirteenth-century precedent of that most eminent Decretalist Innocent IV, who says, commenting on *ex litteris*, that just as the right of the father to decide his children's baptism is preferred should the mother dissent, so, to the contrary, is the right of the converted mother to be preferred over the will of the Jewish father. The passage from here to empowering the paternal grandmother was a short one.

For all that, just as Innocent IV's commentary relies explicitly on the legal doctrine of *favor fidei: ratio in favore fidei posita est*, so, despite his demurrer, did the decision of Benedict XIV. Even when discussing purely civil law, or laws found in the Justinianic corpus, issues of belief and confession shaped Benedict's outlook, much as Juan Azor had spoken of *communi fidei bono*, the benefit of our common faith. Thus Benedict took his stance in interpreting Justinian's legal edict, *Novella 118*, which admits women as legitimate heirs—provided they are Catholics and not heretics. The latter's exclusion, Benedict says, extends to Jewish women as well,[60] for as he saw it, *Novella 118* was issued to benefit only Christians. Should a last will and testament appoint a Jewish women as a guardian, therefore, her custodial right was in doubt and not immune to an "offering" of her children by a converted relative.

As we are about to see, not everyone agreed, whether about the correct reading of *Novella 118* or the general principle.

8. The Jews' Defenders

Benedict XIV's reading of *Novella 118* displeased Carlo Luti. Luti, whom we met briefly above, was blunt. The *Novella*'s limitation to Catholics, he said, concerns succession, inheritance. It does not, as Pope Benedict tries to make it do, address the question of who is legally fit to be a guardian. The pope has also exaggerated in putting Jews in the same class as heretics, for (and it is here that Luti makes his mocking remark) "who does not know that Jews and heretics are not the same."

The remark was an aside. The essence of Luti's message was the gauntlet he threw down before the vaunted supremacy of *favor fidei*. It was not *favor fidei*, but civil law that Luti considered inviolable, a claim that Benedict XIV was not hearing for the first time. Luti was far from alone. Innocent IV could invoke *favor fidei* in the thirteenth century with no objection. In his day, it was an idea considered self-evident, as the *Summa Coloniensis* shortly before had made clear. Objectors queried who was to supervise the faith; they did not doubt the primacy of faith itself or the invincibility of its law. By the eighteenth century, as is so clear from the words of Tom Paine cited earlier, the idea of faith's legal superiority, along with the corollary that divine laws should invariably trump civil ones, was being widely questioned. That a pope as educated in law and theology as was Benedict XIV was unaware of these objections is more than doubtful.

In addition, regardless of whether Benedict knew that already in the sixteenth century barristers of the British Common Law were asserting the necessity of that law's dominance for the sake of the commonweal, he could not ignore Henry VIII's assertion of supremacy over the Church and its clergy—and not only jurisdictionally, which had long been a bone of royal-papal contention. Henry had asserted his right to preside over matters that were purely ecclesiastical (*mere ecclesiasticum*), a claim that Pope Clement VII had rejected, and which he repeated explicitly in letters to the Portuguese king Joao III. Demands made by those like Carlo Luti to recognize the superiority of *ius commune* or by later eighteenth-century rulers to supervise marriage must have seemed to Pope Benedict and his curia like an ominous replay of the English drama of the sixteenth century—which, from the papal viewpoint, had been a knockout.[1] Like the depths of his legal acumen, Benedict's historical consciousness must not be placed in doubt.

This was the same Benedict who erected the majestic Fontana di Trevi in Rome and who also, despite his strict policies, was surprisingly open to intellectual debate. At one point, he had corresponded with figures like Montesquieu, just as he had read and cited Protestants like Buxtorf and Selden on the nature of Jewish marriage. Benedict was also a prolific writer with notable intellectual powers.[2] Accordingly, his rationale for putting into practice the novel—and heretofore theoretical—interpretations of Graziano and Sessa concerning *patria potestas* must be judged as carefully considered. He wrote, *haec trutinae pars alteri praevalet propter illud ponderis quod ex favore religionis eidem accedit*, one arm of the scale bends the other, thanks to the extra weight accorded religious favor. The Italian translation of the 1751 letter that bears this explanation is found in a column parallel to the Latin in the *Magnum Bullarium Romanum* and is even more effusive: *prevale questa parte della bilancia all'altra per sopraccarico che se le aggiunge, che è il favore della religione, motivo ben considerato e molto come dovevasi valutato dagli antichi peritissimi commentatori* [namely, Innocent IV, Antonio de Butrio, and Juan Azor], what tips the scale is an extra weight (*sopraccarico*), that of *favor fidei*, a valued justification promoted by the most venerable of legal experts.[3] It is as though Pope Benedict were anticipating an attack, one that in fact did not take long to come.

What right did the pope have, Carlo Luti responded sharply, to rest his case on the notion of a *sopraccarico*, treating the canons—signified by *favor fidei*—as inviolable and supreme? Admittedly in Jewish employ, as were a number of other lawyers, Luti and his contemporaries advanced arguments that suggest full sincerity in protecting their clients. These arguments were the only refuge for Jews, whom experience had taught that direct appeal resulted all too often in vague—and ultimately empty—papal promises that traditional Jewish privileges would not be violated. Still, Luti and the other lawyers who represented Jews had wider visions, demonstrably preoccupied as they often were with the proper balance between civil law and the canons in general. Their concerns extended far beyond the laws governing conversion to other complex and subtle issues. These, too, rested on the legal "balance" they considered decisive in shaping the way an entire society looked and operated.

Luti and his ilk, one must imagine, could no longer make peace with absurdities like the following: that in a dispute between a married Jewish couple, if the wife were to become a Christian, she might sue her husband in court, where the case would be decided by strict legal rigor, benefiting her as a Christian. Were both spouses Jews—or Christians—the decision would be based on "written equity," which generally prohibits summoning a spouse to court, leaving neither party with an advantage.[4] In plain English, in litigations with a Jew, *favor fidei*, or something close to it, always advantaged the Christian party.

Moreover, did not reliance on the prop of a *sopraccarico*, an "extra weight," to justify legal outcomes like this tacitly acknowledge that the balance between justice under civil as opposed to canon law had gotten out of kilter? One imagines that Luti was also thinking of *sopraccarico*'s Latin twin, *supraccarico*, in its technical meaning as a person entrusted with full authority, usually over maritime commerce, but in effect over any undertaking.[5] Attributing such power to this concept, said Luti, would open the floodgates of justice, and one could follow the logic of extension *ad infinitum: per offerire lecitamente non solo l'avola ma tutti quanti i congionti sino al decimo grado sarebbero in libertà di offerire al battesimo, perché di tutti questo può dirsi che totalmente estranei non sono*, justifying "offerings" down to the *decimo grado*, the tenth grade of relations (Luti, I suspect, knew that Sessa's theorizing had permitted just this kind of extension).[6] This is also to say—especially in the tight-knit ghetto, where virtually everybody was related in some degree—that just about anybody could "offer" anybody else. Benedict's legal reasoning may have been logically sound, but its implications were horrific.[7]

Luti protested that Benedict's resort in 1751 to *favor fidei* to justify the paternal grandmother Juliana Falconeria's offering of her grandchildren while their mother was still alive (the father had died) should be a one-time event. *Favor fidei* must as a rule respect the body of accepted law and interpretation, which Benedict's arguments violate.[8] True, Luti proceeds, a prince may remove a child from a parent for abusing parental power, but that means for doing such criminal things as teaching a child to rob or kill or for prostituting a daughter.[9] In issues governed by supernatural law, the prince has no power to intervene, certainly not in affairs that pertain to a higher power; a prince cannot force subjects to accept baptism. Even if the pope had this power, he did not have it over Jews, since it is universally conceded they have a right to their own religion. Besides, in spiritual matters, Jews are *de foris*, outside the Church and beyond its jurisdiction,[10] while, in civil affairs, Jews *tanquam habeant omnia quae competent Romanis, quorum iure utuntur*, Jews enjoy the same civil rights as other Romans.[11]

Should one parent convert, Luti continues, the matter would be different, and, following the decision of the (universally cited) Toledan Councils enshrined in the canons, that parent may decide that his or her child should be baptized. But such clear-cut options, where *favor fidei* can openly be applied, are not the norm. This is why caution is needed, lest *favor fidei* be too freely invoked, making of it (citing and questioning Benedict's invocation of *ex litteris*) indeed a *supraccarico*, but in a pejorative sense. In terms of (his own day's) legal discourse, Luti is implying that *favor fidei*, though sometimes a legitimate motive, can also be artificial. Old medieval lines of argumentation no longer work despite their firm foundations, and when papal legal discourse resorts to them, it is sadly detached from contemporary legal trends. Put otherwise, in Luti's estimation, the appeal to a *supraccarico* and *favor fidei* was one of pitiable desperation.[12] And judging from their sharp, emotional reaction to so much going on around them, the popes were well aware of what was being said. For that matter, and as we have argued, so were Roman Jews.

Luti was not finished. He brings his attack to a head, writing that when Benedict XIV claimed that *favor fidei* allowed him to extend, and emend, the laws of *patria potestas*, his real intention was to assert a *potestas suprema*, the supremacy of papal power, putting the pope above the law.[13] It was this that invoking a *supraccarico* really meant, with the pope trying to play the absolute monarch at a time when absolutism elsewhere was on the wane.[14] Luti may have also intuited—but here we must hesitate—that the by now cumbersome system of *ius commune* was itself on the ropes; its Catholic bias and support of corporate privilege troubled both Enlightenment and revolutionary figures.[15]

It would certainly be overreaching to suggest Luti could foresee the legal revolution worked by the replacement of *ius commune* by Napoleon's *Code civil*, just as it would be going too far to ponder whether he could have imagined the complete end to corporate privilege that would occur in France in 1791—only decades after he was writing—and its substitution by legislated legal equality and, even more, by the institution of the kind of direct relationship between the individual citizen and the state that, paradoxically, had been the position Jews had held vis-à-vis their rulers since the Middle Ages.[16] Indeed, it was not that Jews would become like everyone else in the wake of the French Revolution and emancipation. Rather, *legally* speaking, in terms of the tie binding individuals to rulers, everyone else would become like the Jews. No wonder the reaction to Jewish emancipation was so sharp. No wonder the Church resisted it so greatly.

Luti's argument, moreover, though framed as a response to Benedict's letter of 1751, was in actual fact directed toward Clement XIV, Benedict's successor, who had carried matters to an extreme in 1762–63 by sanctioning an offering by a grandmother even though *both* parents were alive.[17] Here, as Luti saw it, the pope was blatantly exercising *potestas suprema*, and he spoke with outright disdain. *Favor fidei*, he said, is not served by snatching and baptizing young children against parental will; it seems that the need of the authorities to increase the number of baptisms is so great that they are willing to rest their case on the thinnest of strands.[18] Their desperation, Luti speaks out in his peroration, is counterproductive. Among other things, it leads the Jews to hate the Church.[19] The heads of the Church, he says, would best give heed to the distinguished Austrian Franciscan and theologian Benjamin Elbel (1690–1756), who writes in his *Moral and Sacramental Theology* that ". . . baptism *invitis parentibus* gives rise to anxiety about a great number of serious ills, in that parents in these straits might cause harm to their children, or even murder them; they will become more averse to the Christian religion (and themselves never convert). The Scotists—the followers of Duns Scotus, who support taking children *invitis parentibus*—should be more thoughtful and recognize that it is damaging to promote baptism at all costs.[20] This is what I, Carlo Luti, think should be said about Pope Benedict's [1751] letter."

Perhaps Luti's indirect reference to Jewish child-murder was a lawyer's tactic, playing on commonly held beliefs, including—as has been inferred from the bull *Beatus Andreas* and the reception given to the story of Shimon Abeles—on the part of the popes themselves. The charge was so commonplace that it appears as though indisputable in the writings of the later sixteenth-century jurist Marco Antonio Natta.[21] Or maybe, like even Sessa, in the back of his mind, Luti, too, wondered whether Jews were capable of this extreme? More probably, and as the structure of his argument suggests, he may have sympathized with the Jews as they faced such charges. Luti, after all, defended Jews in 1751, 1762, and, in a drawn-out case, between 1764 and 1774. We must imagine that between Luti and the Jewish Community a relationship of mutual trust had grown; he had gotten to know them, and they him.[22] Regardless, with people like Luti supporting them, Roman Jews were not swimming in a stormy sea with no hope of rescue.

Luti, we have said, was also not the first or the only person—or institution—to advocate subordinating *favor fidei* to civil power. Nor was the subject only Jews. Luti must have known about the debates going on in Austria in his day and the positions being taken by people like the jurist Joseph Eybel, who advocated placing the prince above the Church.[23] He must have also known that others had defended Jews, such as Domenico Fiorello and Antonio de Becchettis, or Carlo Trenca, seconded by Gian Maria Cipriano, both of whom warned of allowing *favor fidei* to overwhelm civil law. Carlo Trenca took his stance in 1781 (and onward) while defending Regina del Borgo, the Jewish maternal grandmother and guardian of her son Moise Terracina's children, whom a distant neophyte uncle had "offered" to the Church. To accept this offering, wrote Trenca, would be "to impugn the majesty of the law."[24]

Others who defended Jews were Scipio Caranza, who, in 1686, represented the men accused of dragging Benvenuta back to the ghetto after she ran out of the *Quattro Capi* gate saying she wished to become a Christian.[25] Nicolò Pignatelli (not to be confused with the canonist of the same family name) defended David Nizza, who reneged on his promise to convert and baptize his children. To baptize these children, said Pignatelli, was to exert indirect force on the father, which was illegal. Pignatelli also defended Ercole Servi in 1678, whose children had somehow been "offered" by a *neofito* named Sabato. Instructively, it was the Inquisition, following the law, which restored the children. Pignatelli's honorarium of 3 sc. 40 was paid by the Jewish Community of Rome, which, here, as in other instances, assumed responsibility for its individual members.[26]

In 1713, Francesco Spannochio defended the pregnant Chiara, already held in the *Casa dei catecumeni* for forty days. She should, he said, have been taken to a neutral place, as the law warranted, and held a much shorter time.[27] In 1737, this time in Ferrara, also part of the Papal State, Giacomo Magnani protested that the will of Ventura Caricioli was violated when his widow, Ester Zarfati, voluntarily entered the House of Converts in that city and "offered" her two small daughters, ages four and five.[28] Finally, with an interesting twist, an unnamed advocate in the Veneto, who insisted (in 1753), as had De Luca and Sessa before him, that Jews were part of the civil body, warned that seizing children against parental wishes placed the state in danger. There might be reprisals initiated by Jews under Turkish rule, which would damage the Venetian economy.[29] Nor was this the only time the welfare of the state was brought into the debate about the advisability of pursuing doubtful conversions.

These legal challenges to the Catholic status quo had little chance of success. Nonetheless, ecclesiastical authorities viewed them as threats. Some may have also seen in them the "writing on the wall," foreshadowing new defenses based on newer argumentation. Following the forced cessation of Jewish lending in 1682, a number of the lenders hoped to use their remaining capital to enter the retail trade outside of Rome. This, they said, was the only way they could extract themselves from heavy debt, the same debt that, as we have noted, may have brought entire families to the baptismal font. Allowing Jews to recoup their fortunes—and possibly reverse this trend—likely aroused clerical resistance. It certainly agitated some Roman merchants, who, fearful of competition, went to court, leading the Jewish ex-banker/merchants, together with the Community, to employ four advocates to plead their case, which they did in 1689, seeking precedent in a bull of Clement VIII from 1593 that allowed Jewish commercial enterprise beyond the city. All four resorted to one version or other of the traditional theme for sustaining Jews, *caritas*, which they tempered by saying that to permit Jewish commerce would serve the "public good."

One of the four, however, Antonio di Filippo, tried another tack. Citing Cardinal de Luca, di Filippo argued that it was the Jews' right as *cives* to carry on their trade. Jews were "not *personae odiosae*, and in human (everyday, civil) matters, they should be treated like other citizens." He was aware, of course, that denominating Jews as *personae odiosae*, roughly, outlaws or just unacceptable, was sometimes the justification adduced to explain why the Jews as a community lacked rights. By protesting this categorization, di Filippo was challenging the entire legal structure that limited Jewish civil rights,[30] including the privileging of religiously over civilly based authority, a line that would be continued by Giuseppe Sessa, who wrote in his comprehensive tract of 1716 that in litigations involving Jews the competent authority to pass judgment is the civil, not the ecclesiastical one. As he had emphasized many times over in his 300-page composition, Jews live under *ius commune*. This is the same Sessa who seems to have implied that the civil marriage of the Jews would be well implemented for all.[31]

Establishment Response

The Church could not let such defiance of the primacy of the canons (and the limits of Jewish "citizenship") pass unanswered. The response to Carlo Luti's questioning of papal (and Catholic) power, accordingly, was brusque. The counselor of the Papal Inquisition and papal Vice Regent Bishop Domenico Giordani dressed Luti down, taking a perch on traditional ground to demand to know what justified Luti's insolence. No lesser a pope than the thirteenth-century Innocent III, said Giordani, had established in law that the pope held the place of God on earth, *vicem eius*, whose declaration to this effect Pier Paul Pariseo had cited in 1535 to argue that "what he [the pope] does is as though done by God Himself." Giordani's retort to Luti that the pope was the arbiter of divine law on earth was anything but original. Luti and Giordani (not to mention the papacy) were operating in two different worlds, and the gap between them was not about to close, if it did not become wider yet.[32] As we saw earlier, by 1789, arguments of Christian lawyers to end onerous restriction had taken a step backward, resorting primarily to canons like *Dispar nimirum est* and only secondarily to civil laws.

The stiffness of papal authorities comes again to the fore in discussing "denunciations," about which there was also some agreement. Denunciations, we recall, were declarations that a particular person (including children) had expressed a will to be baptized—but many of them were false. One intuits that the always suspect (in the view of both sides, in fact) staff of the *Casa* was highly involved in pushing *neofiti* to act or in goading poor Jewish men to convert, promising to make them a "good match" with a Jewish girl otherwise beyond their reach: for instance, the poor Sabato Coen and the well-to-do Anna del Monte.

Everyone agreed that maneuvers like these boded trouble. In the words of Giacobo Pignatelli, the same Pignatelli who pondered whether any Christian relative suffices for an offering, false denunciations led to cursing and lewd teachings about Christianity, as well as sham conversions, followed by

Judaizing, and sometimes apostasy. They also hampered efforts to increase the number of converts. Pignatelli understood that young women who had been denounced feared to go back to the ghetto, where they would be perennially under suspicion of treachery (to Judaism); and as a result, he said, some converted *ficto animo*, insincerely, and were prone to relapse.[33]

Benedict XIV, too, was bothered by denunciations. He knew that as opposed to "offerings" made by virtue of *patria potestas* and other legal precedents, many spousal offerings and denunciations were fraudulent, made with an eye to personal advantage.[34] What bothered the pope most, I believe, were possible violations of canonical marital procedures as they had been established at the Council of Trent in 1563—and potential Judaizing. Hence, just as he had put brakes on mentioning a Hebrew name in the *gittin*, the bills of divorce *neofiti* sent their Jewish wives, so he insisted that any claim of marriage by a convert be judged by whether the match was valid according to Catholic standards, which are based more on verbal declarations than on the contractual procedures and formulae Jewish law requires.[35] Had the convert Sabato Coen been able to demonstrate that his relationship with Anna del Monte met these Catholic criteria, he would have been able "to offer" her outright. As it is, the diary treats Anna as denounced, suggesting the only relationship between the two was the one created by Sabato's attempted fraud.[36]

Following a denunciation, young women (or men, but especially women) were to be held and their wills tested for twelve days. This time limit was established in 1641, which, as the *Memoriale* about Grazia di Iacchetto reveals, the Jews themselves knew very well. However, as Giacobo Pignatelli explains, the place of detention was intended to be elsewhere than the *Casa dei catecumeni*.[37] Domenico Fiorello, writing at the start of the eighteenth century, began his defense of denounced women by cleverly citing Pignatelli's words. But Fiorello was a consultant of the Inquisition, bent on encouraging conversion, not a paid advocate in Jewish employ. Thus for all its apparent sympathy for women trapped into spending days in the *Casa dei catecumeni*, Fiorello's tract, composed in September 1720, and thus well before *Postremo mense* of 1747, is titled "How to facilitate approaching the baptismal font on the part of those who desire baptism, but have hesitated to request it."

But often the person denounced had not expressed a desire to convert.

There was also the question of by what authority had the denouncer the right to speak out. Were this person legally a spouse, the denunciation would have become a more binding "offer." There had been more than one complaint about tomfoolery in cases like these—and violence. In the later seventeenth century, Crescenzio de Benedictis accused the Rector of the Madonna dei Monti Church of barging into his house with *sbirri* and making off with his fourteen-year-old daughter, whom Salomon Francesi *cathecumeno* had named as his bride.[38] This was impossible, said Crescenzio: there was no record of *sponsali* (*tenayyim*, signed agreements), no contact (*ketubah*), no *kiddushin*, or betrothal. The two were not married, and Francesi had no right to oblate his daughter, not to mention that the girl had been crying out continuously she did not want to be a Christian.[39]

Equally troubling was the dubiously observed rule limiting to twelve days the detention of those *merely* denounced. The promise of the Papal Vice Regent near the end of the diary that nobody again will suffer as did Anna must indeed be queried. In the spirit of Ibn Verga's sympathetic prelates, it reveals most about what did *not* happen. A truer scenario may be the one exposed by the threats the denizens of the *Casa* make to Anna that they can keep her as long as they want, for two or even three quarantines.[40] There were also systematic violations of the rule that young women "denounced" by their supposed fiancés were to be taken to a neutral house, regardless of the time limit enforced—not to the *Casa*, as was Anna, the inside of which she should never have seen. Furthermore, the Vicar or Vice Regent was supposed to evaluate denunciations for their reliability before any action was taken. In Anna's case, he had not.[41] Domenico Fiorello's recommendation that girls like Anna be held for only a few hours was a dream.

By contrast, proof that Anna and Sabato Coen had merely *spoken* of marriage would have sealed her fate. In *Postremo mense*, Benedict XIV wrote that he had examined the rules of Jewish marriage intently, relying on Selden and Buxtorf, two Protestants, and (the Rabbi) Leon Modena. Not satisfied, he turned to Paolo Medici, even though he acknowledged that this convert was prejudiced.[42] Finally, he called "a Jewish expert" whom he had known when he, Benedict, had been the Bishop of Ancona. Jewish betrothal, Benedict concluded, required a *giuramento*, an oath, taken by both bride and groom.

He erred.[43] After all his elaborate investigations, the pope had confused the act of *kiddushin*—during which the groom makes a formal declaration, which the bride accepts by allowing the groom to place a ring on her finger—with the handshake that might seal a written pre-engagement pact (the *kiddushin* being true betrothal or, in contemporary Italian terms the *matrimonium*, after which a formal repudiation, the *get*, is required).[44] All of this, however, was irrelevant. What determined the outcome, said Benedict, was some indication, even simple oral testimony, that the now Christian spouse had spoken in a way to comply with the marital rites of the Church. Should it turn out that the two parties, man and woman, had made what amounts to a promise *de futuro*, creating a first step toward the *verbum de presenti*, or true *matrimonium*, then the one who refused to convert (to be sure, the woman) would be taken to a neutral place and queried. Or as happened to Anna—and most others—she would be taken straightaway to the *Casa dei catecumeni*.

For all that, it was necessary to avoid the chicanery that had a negative effect, including, as Piatelli put it, conversion *ficto animo*. To accept baptism falsely, said Fiorello, is a mockery, the worst of all possible misdeeds. The untoward interference stemming from the *Casa* and its inhabitants leading to such travesties must be stopped. The "chastity" of the girls brought to the *Casa* under doubtful circumstances is also impugned.[45] So it was with Anna del Monte herself, whose sexual propriety was indirectly questioned by the Vice Regent, when he asked her about contacts with men. During *her* twenty-two-day reclusion in the *Casa*, Olimpia Pippi, too, was accused of having had dealings with a Christian in the Pescaria, the fish market located just outside the ghetto wall, leading to her denunciation.[46] No wonder that Fiorello, in order to avoid the suspicions of future infidelity to Judaism that hounded young women released from the *Casa* as Jews and made them unmarriageable, called for respecting the decree of 1641.[47] These girls should be taken to a neutral place and quizzed for a few hours only, which was sufficient time to uncover their intentions.[48]

Surprising Overlap

The opposing tilting points were well defined. Pignatelli and Benedict XIV concentrated on the welfare of the Church. Fiorello, too, wished to promote conversion, but he also had at heart the welfare of the young women who had been denounced. Both agreed about avoiding fraud, but one was taken with safeguarding *favor fidei*, the other with not damaging individual legal rights. In the same way, *Postremo mense* refers to both the decree of 1641 and the edict fixing twelve days of detention, while Pope Benedict still directed his efforts toward preventing these rules from derailing a possible conversion.[49]

The divisions on denunciations and the questions of when baptism is legal thus seem neat—but they are not. On some points, stances overlapped. All sides saw the necessity of justifying their respective positions as beneficial to the state, as a state. They also agreed that the state, whatever its nature, must vindicate itself and its policies by appealing to law. How, they asked, did religion, law, and the state best interact to benefit both the individual and the state? Accordingly, in *Postremo mense* and *Probe te meminisse*, Benedict XIV insisted that he was adhering to legal precedent, not simply the idea of *favor fidei*, aware, as he had to have been, that in his day old verities were being contested. Moreover, just as Luti had partners in rejecting Benedict's arguments, so the pope, too, had his helpers, legists seeking to perform a balancing act and out to show that law and *favor fidei*, even in the context of the emerging modern state, did not, as Luti was claiming, collide discordantly. To the contrary, law and *favor fidei* complemented each other and stimulated political, alongside individual, well-being.[50]

This position was not new. Much as the concept of equal and identical rights for all citizens may be traced (with many qualifications) to the towering legist Bartolus in the fourteenth century, historical roots also underlie the notion that law and *favor fidei* were mutually supportive in their promotion of the state's "highest good."[51] When Carlo Luti insisted that at times *favor fidei* cede priority to civil law, he was, I conjecture, possibly responding indirectly to the arguments of Giuseppe Sessa, not only to those of Benedict XIV. But Luti's real target was the advocate G. B. Riganti, who had argued in favor of the *Ava* Giuliana Falconeria's "offering" of her grandchildren.

Riganti made a complex case for *favor fidei*, one from which Benedict XIV himself may have borrowed in constructing his final decision, including his determination that Justinian's *Novella 118* did not apply to Jews.[52] Are not Jews "worse than heretics?" Riganti wrote, citing the canon *peiores* in the *Decretum* of Gratian and reading as hard fact what in Gratian is metaphor. Even more than Benedict, Riganti emphasized the precedent of Gregory IX in *ex litteris*. He also seems to suggest that already in the fifteenth century, Martin V had allowed the paternal grandfather "to offer."

But Riganti, as had Benedict, needed to go beyond canonical principle to ground his argument, and, therefore, he followed Sessa, to say that the state, as a state, and through its law, had the powers to order Falconeria's orphaned grandchildren (they had a mother, but their father had died) baptized. It could do so even over the adamant objections of the children's living mother. Just as princes draft soldiers, Riganti wrote, repeating Sessa, so they may override parental authority in order to press baptism on their subjects. If need be, princes may even invalidate rights to achieve this end, for they are doing so to promote the *summum bonum* of the individual, which, collectively, and by implication, is identical with the highest good of the state, as well as with the moral and religious well-being that rulers are obligated to protect.

For Riganti, the *summum bonum* of the state and *favor fidei* were transparently synonymous, much as Sessa had said *conversionem Judaeorum ad fidem causam esse concernentem bonum publicum*—conversion is a matter of the public good.[53] However, Sessa had qualified himself and concluded his exposition by saying that what is possible is one thing, what is advisable another. He no doubt recognized that by suggesting rulers might baptize Jewish children (and even adults) at will, his words bordered on violating venerable Jewish rights. He was also pushing to the limits, if not beyond, concepts like the Jews' special relationship to their rulers, in which, uniquely, no true corporate status stood between the Jews and the state, leaving rulers free to make special demands.[54]

Regardless, the state Sessa was touting was a confessional one, whose citizens, too, if not even more than the state itself, were defined confessionally. As Marquardus de Susannis had explained two hundred years earlier, the citizen gained his or her civic rights through baptismal regeneration. Riganti agreed, but he also ignored Sessa's reservations, and this allowed him to rebut the kind of argument Luti would make. The challenge, Riganti said, was not the confrontation between civil law and the canons and *favor fidei*. It was to ensure that even in the modern centralized state, civil law continued, as in the past, to complement confessional needs.[55] To guarantee the achievement of the *summum bonum* with which the state's highest aspirations were equated, law must advance canonical aims.[56] With respect to children and their best interests, their removal from their parents and subsequent baptism, *velint nolint parentes,* the parents willing or unwilling, was a foregone conclusion.

Ulrich Zasius

None of this was Riganti's invention, nor, apart from the example of drafting soldiers, was it Sessa's. Riganti's ideas derived from the thinking of the eminent, late-fifteenth-century Swiss jurist Ulrich Zasius, whose own point of departure was the determinations of the thirteenth-century pope Innocent III. Pope Innocent had encapsulated the status of the Jews with respect to the Church and the canons by saying the Jews' guilt (for killing Christ) had consigned them to "perpetual servitude." This definition was strictly theological. It had nothing to do with real servitude, as Innocent himself clarified more than once. However, in Innocent's day, Jews were also being called *servi Regis* or *servi camerae nostrae*. The meaning of the first term, used in Iberia, is easy to guess. The Jews were "the king's (metaphorical) servants," which well describes their heavy dependence on medieval Spanish rulers; they, and even more Spain's Muslims, were called "the royal treasure."[57] The second term, "Serf of the Royal Chamber," is more daunting. It was coined to define the Jews' civil status in the Empire (German lands). In the absence there of *ius commune*, which allowed calling them *cives*,[58] they lacked a properly defined civic (constitutional) niche.[59] The Imperial term "Servants of the Royal Chamber" was created to fill the gap, the "chamber" being the treasury, which unlike the king's mortal body, was said "never to die."[60] The problem was the term's artificiality, which, rather than promoting a stable, ongoing status, opened the door to exploitation, as well as dangerous legal theorizing.[61] Some legists began to fuse the Jews' two "serfdoms," the theological and the civil, turning Jews into true serfs, if not rightless slaves.[62]

This was not mainline legal opinion. The great majority of legists said that Jews are not *servi* in the strict sense.[63] Benedict XIV, for one, insisted that Jews receive justice, because they "cannot war on us now." He was restating a canon discussed earlier, Alexander II's *Dispar nimirum est* from 1063, forbidding attacks and forced baptism, since Jews *semper parati servire sunt*, that is, they obey Christian authority; obey, not "are in slavery to [Christians]."[64] He meant the same when he said the Jews are in "civil servitude," a unique term introduced by Thomas Aquinas and adopted commonly by legists to signify the direct link between Jews and their rulers.[65]

Nonetheless, regardless of how Jewish "civil servitude" was conceived, in a confessional state, unrestrained government-to-citizen rule could be dangerous.[66] Accepting that the state drafts soldiers into the army or sets the rules of marriage and custody is a far cry from applying force in matters of conscience, speech, or belief. This latter is precisely what Riganti desired—as did Zasius before him, whom Benedict XIV's *Postremo mense* cites. Zasius agreed with the bulk of legal authorities that Jews possessed *patria potestas,* a right normally belonging to freemen alone, which should have prevented seizing Jewish children. However, said Zasius, this right was limited, for ultimately Jews *were* real slaves, and the state might intervene for its citizens' good, including by baptizing Jewish children without parental consent.[67] The cardinal Jewish privilege prohibiting forced baptism, which had existed for centuries, might be ignored. So constructed, moreover, Zasius's argument made even the device of "offerings" theoretically superfluous.

Zasius's thought had a second vector, which was even more innovative, and surely more dangerous. The state, he argued—verging on the concept of royal absolutism that would crystallize by the eighteenth century—had the right, as a state, to act as a super-guardian, authorized to intervene when parents failed to promote the best interests of their offspring. Should it judge it appropriate, neither parental will nor *patria potestas* should hold back the state from baptizing Jewish children. "Official kidnappings" organized by papal officials were thus fully legalized, the highly censured kidnapping of Edgardo Mortara in 1858 and its aftermath being the best-known case.[68]

At the same time, because of the way it empowers the state, Zasius's view has correctly been said to anticipate modernity. The same applies to Riganti. In the long run, by equating *favor fidei* with *favor reipublicae,* as, in fact, he was doing, Riganti was playing on the same pitch as Luti. Both were determined to create the ideal state. It was their ideals and the means toward their achievement that so sharply clashed.

The Persistency of the Confessional State

In the Papal State, Riganti's model was going to hold the upper hand. What should have been a transparent, open-and-shut, *civil* argument (made in 1702) about vesting the custody of five children in their mother Grazia's hands, as established by the will of the late Joseph Anticoli and supported by a bevy of laws, was by itself insufficient to carry the day. The Jews' status as "*veri cives,* whether in civil, municipal, or even customary law," granted the mother *patria potestas,* said Grazia's advocate, Antonio Maria de Becchettis,[69] not to mention that civil law, which regulated *patria potestas*, never assigned that right to a paternal uncle, nor did it ever remove it from a parent who was alive. And with this strong argument, based on civil law, the case should have been closed. Yet to win, de Becchettis had to go further, much as we saw happen in the opinions from 1789 urging the end to legal limitations; he had to cite copious canons, to remind the judges of the custom of the Church that the weight of canonical opinion reserved only to those possessing *patria potestas* the decision whether to baptize their young.[70] He was making first and foremost a case *in favore canonum*, much as it is unquestionable that he would have preferred to stress the force of civil laws. The Inquisition agreed; and, as Giovanni Riganti tells us, it ordered the children restored to their mother, even though, as may be imagined, he would have turned cartwheels to ensure the opposite.

The precedent would also stand. Fifteen years later, this time in Florence, Domenico Fiorello began by framing the case of Dolce Piazza (identical to that of Grazia Anticoli) purely in terms of civil law. Baptism, he said, was a religious issue, while oblation, "offering," was a civil matter. But Fiorello also knew that his valiant effort to give primacy to civil laws would convince the very few. More decisive was the Anticoli precedent; and thus he hastened to cite Grazia's case.[71] To Fiorello, however much he was also an advocate of promoting baptisms, it was obvious that ever more zealous ecclesiastical officers were becoming ever more willing to subordinate the Jews' status as *veri cives* to canonical priorities, in other words, to the confessionalism of the state.

To Fiorello and the lawyers who defended Jews, especially ones like Antonio di Filippo, who, we saw, grounded the petition of the Jews to carry on trade outside of Rome and the ghetto on their status as *cives*, the justifications of the canonist Antonio Ricciuli must have sounded hollow. Ricciuli had said that Jews are bound to the same laws as all other subjects, however, not because they are *cives romani*, but because with Christ, their own law ended.[72] Nonetheless, it was not Fiorello or those like him with their appeal to civil laws who were setting the tone. That, rather, was being set by advocates of a strong canonical position, including by conservative extremists like Francesco Rovira Bonet, the rector of the *Casa dei catecumeni* in the final decades of the eighteenth century, who composed a tract condemning the Jews for "ritually murdering" Simon of Trent. It was with people like Rovira Bonet that the popes were ever more readily falling into step.[73]

The greater the affront to confessionalism, and the sharper the protest, the more the popes advocated, or undertook, radical action. Listen to the words of an unnamed advocate in 1783, lamenting what amounted to the total breach of the gates when Pius VI accepted an offering made by an uncle. In *Probe te meminisse*, this advocate noted, Benedict XIV had said we must not rely solely on *ratio fidei*, [for the truth is that] *quando tutto il sistema unicamente si appoggiasse al favore della fede, ne seguirebbe che facendosi da qualsivoglia persona, benche estreanea, l'offerta* [would be accepted], *il che è contrario alla dottrina di San Tommasso, a cui l'altri teologi communemente aderiscono,* should the whole structure rest on *favor fidei*, it would be possible for anybody to make an "offering," even one from outside [the family], which is wholly out of step with the teaching of St. Thomas, with whom [all] other theologians are in agreement; [there is also no ground for saying Jews are *servi*, or that they do not exercise *patria potestas*].[74] Pius VI, however, paid no heed to the advice of his papal predecessors. Unlike them, he did not hesitate to stretch the law to allow this most dubious avuncular offering. That he chose this path reveals the crux that clarifies the whole.

The essence of the drama we have been viewing or, better, the match—to return to the metaphor of playing on the same pitch—was a tug of war. On one side were arrayed the forces promoting integration of the Jews into the laws of the state and the reciprocal commitment of the state to a unified regime of law equal for all—otherwise known as (or, at least, as the preamble to) emancipation. Opposing them were the champions of the same integration, however, an integration directed toward preserving the state's confessional unity, even at the price of odious legal distinctions and possibly forced conversions.[75] Ideally, the irreconcilable contradictions of a state seeking legal uniformity, as was the papal one, yet still following its confessional drives to the point of legalizing kidnappings in the name of the faith, should have risen to the surface, as they did elsewhere, and propelled the Papal State to perceive the untenability of its position. In Rome, however, ideals that conflicted with the good of the Church were spurned. Legal uniformity in the civil sphere, yet without equality in all spheres, would persevere, breeding, for the city's Jews, only frustration. The *aequitas* for which David de Pomis had called would not be achieved. Burdened by the inertia of ecclesiastical traditions, the Papal State's overtures to modernity fell short, and the state itself kept marching in place, if not backward.[76]

The Perils of Tenacity

It is precisely this dilemma of forward legal progress stymied by confessional priorities that becomes ever more apparent from studying the case of Anna del Monte. Fixated as they were on "enlightening" those still living in what they considered "darkness," the Churchmen of eighteenth-century Rome were consumed with fulfilling the promise of John 10:16 that one day there would be one [sole] flock and one [divine] pastor, whose place was being held for the time being by God's Vicar on earth, the pope. Reassurance that the process was already in motion came from each individual conversion. It mattered little that the conversions were the product of dubious (at the best) free choice or that these excesses stood in stark contrast to the firm civil observance that was being promoted elsewhere. It was conversion and only conversion, it seems, that counted. Conversion, the Church's leadership was apparently convinced, and as we have already observed, would prove more than anything else that the ship of the Church had not foundered. No wonder that the same policies pursued with Jews were also being used to bring Protestants, too, back to the fold, including kidnappings and deceptions. Children were urged to sign themselves with a cross, which was called a pledge of Catholicism.[77] This was the same kind of deviousness that was tried during Anna's stay in the *Casa dei catecumeni*, and failed.

9. Jewish and Christian Awareness

The Jews of Rome were perfectly aware of the forces that governed their existence. Accordingly, when legal, spiritual, cultural, and social distinctions of persons were summarily removed under Napoleonic rule, in the Roman Republic of 1797 (albeit for less than two years), the Jews hastened to respond optimistically. The inimitable words of Antonio Pacifici are clear. Standing under the *Albero della Libertà* in the Piazza delle Scuole del Ghetto in Rome on 18 February 1798, Pacifici addressed fellow Jews and other Romans: "From here on, if you [Jews and Christians] are good citizens . . . [a single] law will judge us both; in civil life, all that will distinguish us one from another is virtue, and not religious belief."[1] Pacifici was effectively elaborating on the dictum first spoken by Baldo degli Ubaldi in the fourteenth century: *quia mundus est omnibus communis patria,* the world is a *communis patria* for everybody.[2] By implication, all people merit equal treatment.

However, the Jews did not need to await Napoleonic liberation to appreciate how contradictory and absurd had been their condition. In 1720, as we saw, they made the point with indomitable irony as they petitioned the pope to ask why authorities should not halt the oft-repeated insult of importing bad wheat into the ghetto, wheat that could be sold nowhere else, and demanding that it be purchased by the Jews?[3] "Were Jews not considered by the popes subjects no different from others embraced by civic statutes that are the same for all, and only in spiritual [matters different]?" This protest was gallows humor, in which, nevertheless, there was truth. Unless *ius commune* was stripped of its religious face—that aspect of it, which, united with discriminatory canons, consigned Jews to mere toleration as a religious group and made room for insults like this one—legal equality would be impossible.

Yet was not confessionalism innate to the Papal State's structure, as well as to *ius commune* itself?[4] Legal equality, emancipation in its full sense, could be achieved in Papal Rome, therefore, not only when the canonical invasiveness of papal rule came to an end, but when *ius commune*, too, was eliminated root and branch, to be replaced by a body of law much like Napoleon's *Code civil*. This great leap, though, was anticipated in ideas like those put forward decades earlier by Giovanni Battista de Luca, Carlo Luti, and even Giuseppe Sessa. All three openly questioned, or were at least uneasy about, the paradox of Jews being simultaneously *cives* yet still denied full civic rights. It is to the thinking of these forerunners of the kind of thought we see in Washington, Jefferson, and Madison that the stories of Anna and Grazia point. The persona of Anna del Monte as Tranquillo fashioned it is indeed that of "a figure on the seam." Anna's story, Anna's fate, encapsulates the winds of the past, but it was no less a prologue to a sometimes precarious future. What would happen when the confessional state passed from the scene?

ɔℵɛ

It was against the abuses of this kind of state and the legal institutions sustaining it that Tranquillo made Anna del Monte's diary cry out. He focused on Anna's travails, but he wrote with the confidence that readers would fill in the rest on their own, acknowledging that papal and canonical structures, the legal system in the Papal State, were strangling Rome's Jews.

For the Jews of Rome, their troubles would be resolved only with the Papal State's fall. The emancipation they tasted under Napoleon at the end of the eighteenth century and the start of the nineteenth quickly faded away. There would be a second breath of air during the great revolt of 1848–49, when the Roman constitution of 1848 realized the eighteenth-century papacy's greatest fears, placing the church under secular supervision. "The exercise of civil and political rights," the constitution states, "does not depend upon religious belief; the Head of the Catholic Church will obtain from the Republic all the guarantees necessary for the independent exercise of his spiritual power." The pope's rule would pertain solely to spiritual matters; he would no longer act as Rome's civil head. However, the revolution of 1848–49 collapsed. Its principles would triumph only in 1860, reaching their culmination when the walls of Rome were breached on September 20, 1870.

In the later nineteenth century, Luigi Luzzatti—a Jew and for a brief moment Italian Prime Minister—declared that the submission of religious to civil power is the desired state. We must laud, he writes, American political structures and praise the desire of the American founding fathers to protect freedom of religion, which they did by ensuring religious multiplicity and demanding as emancipation's facilitator no more than that citizens observe the law. Free access for all religions, without specifying which faiths are permitted, more than precluding discrimination, guarantees that state and religion stay distinct. Was Luzzatti thinking of George Washington's letter to the Jews of Newport or the words of James Madison with which our study opened, who said: "Our laws have applied the only antidote to this vice, protecting our religious, *as they do our civil rights*, by putting all on an equal footing"?

The key is disestablishment, in which, says Luzzatti, only trustees, not the Church itself, own its property, as is the law in many places in America, although, lamentably not in Italy. Even after unification, the Roman Church was preferred as a state religion, and only Judaism and Waldensianism (Italian Protestantism) were sanctioned as alternatives. The laws also favored the Church.[5] Under these circumstances, the state's, let alone the Jews', emancipation was incomplete.

Here, then, were the Italian inheritors of the eighteenth century affirming the main lines of what has been said in the last hundred or so pages. Until civil law—now the *Code civil,* and its parallels, no longer *ius—commune—* gained primacy, the old would not go away, and the new would lack perfection.[6] Luzzatti, moreover, had hindsight. The philosopher and economist Carlo Cattaneo—later a political activist during the revolution of 1848— was making these same points in the 1830s, in terms almost identical to those this present study has offered.

The Jews, Cattaneo writes, have become disproportionately wealthy (so he is persuaded), but this is *not* to be attributed, as medieval and early modern commentators have done, to their evil nature, their hatred of Christianity, or any other behavioral trait. Rather, it is a function of discriminatory, confessional legislation. It is discriminatory laws that have kept Jews from universities, the professions, and the ownership of land, the last in particular, since *"dominio"* was always equated with the *"signoria"* that was forbidden the Jews.

Cattaneo has inverted the image found in D'Arco and Sessa that laicizes medieval charges of plotting to destroy the political *Corpus Christi* of the town through usury. Discriminatory confessional legislation is the culprit, not Jewish malice, or even persecution.[7] Bad law, Cattaneo continues, has made the Jews reproduce faster (he claims) and grow in numbers out of proportion to others.[8] The modern state augurs an end to this unwanted condition. The French Revolution and that of the United States (the example of the American republic was not lost on Cattaneo) shut down corporate society. Once, for lack of more stable institutions, all peoples had to meld into a corporate structure, with its built-in competition and inequalities. Now the *Code civil* has been "promulgated in the name of an absolute prince, deviating neither from its (the Code's) nor from his (Napoleon's) principles, nor from those of the antique Roman legislation [which had united all mankind in the once vast and diverse Empire]. The result was that popular and absolute power concorded [on the need] to dissolve [special, corporate] privileges and to equalize opportunity and usefulness. In turn, all members of the state became equal before the law and in the enjoyment of civil rights.

"Where there was a single faith, this fusion [and equality] was more easily achieved. But where this union did not exist, the multitude reserved the idea of juridical equality to itself. . . . [However] the Constitutional Assembly [of France] destroyed all the civil interdictions among Christians with one quick blow. [It took, though, another] two years, [while] it hesitated, to dissolve the restrictions inflicted upon the Jews. The civil and economic unification of dissident sects with the majority communion is the last and most difficult triumph of social equity; for men give up advantage more easily and rapidly than they do opinion."[9]

Yet, when this unification occurred, no harm ensued. Anyone who feared this change would lead to a Judaization of society, Cattaneo goes on, should ask how many Christians has he heard of who have recently become Jews?

The Jews themselves, Cattaneo continues, have cooperated. He summarizes the events in France—the Assembly of Notables held in 1806, followed by the Sanhedrin of 1807—which he understands correctly. The Jews in their responses to Napoleon, he says, stressed their submission to the law of the state, even in the matter of marriage, where they accept that there is to be no marriage or divorce before a civil license or decree is executed.[10] It is the unity of law married to the demise of confessionalism that makes the modern state possible, and it is this new equality that perforce will bring changes into the world of the Jew. Cattaneo's goal may sound the same as that of the Enlighteners—to "improve" the Jew—and he surely knew that even under Napoleon, the achievement of real emancipation and equality was anything but an unimpeded uphill passage. But his method says the true goal is something else. It is not the Jew who must better and prove him- or herself. It is the state that must "change its spots." Civil law and society must come to take precedence over the canons and confessional opinion.

Plus ça change . . .

Here was the kind of society of which Tranquillo could only dream as, in 1793, he witnessed the events taking place beyond the borders of the Papal State and was reminded of his sister; regrettably, although he continued to serve the community, he falls silent after this date. But in the meantime, he had a message for his fellow Jews, which contains the diary's final lesson. There was something they could do, even as they waited and hoped. As much as the Jews might lament their political morass, they should look inward and judge themselves. In sharing the diary with others, Tranquillo was determined to remind his fellows that they, too, were acting poorly. Blaming the forces of the Church alone for the fate of denounced girls was to shirk responsibility. Why, Tranquillo was asking, should women "burnt" by a brush with conversion remain alone, unmarried, and distrusted? Why should they be shunned by fellow Jews and "anchored," as was very likely his own sister Anna, in an unspoken social ostracism from which they were powerless to escape all the days of their lives? Anna had suffered not once, Tranquillo was saying, but twice.

This was the real tragedy. The outdated confessional society from without, in clinging to its principle of faith above all, was corrupting the society of the Jews from within. The traditions of mercy and compassion that lay at Judaism's core, as, in the event, Tranquillo imagined them, were being worn down, imperiling Roman Jewry and its continuity. Perhaps Anna's troubles properly told would hold back this process, if not do more, and it was in this spirit, that at the end of the introduction, Tranquillo penned the following optimistic lines:

I am faithfully transcribing [the diary and the poem of Moisè Mieli] and adding the account of the great happiness of the people, of the Jews of the ghetto [at the end of Anna's ordeal], in order to conclude the account with joy, as everyone would wish, which serves to lift morale and to enable us to suffer reverses in peace. [It also instills] faith in God, who protects the innocent. But most of all, it reminds us that innocence is like hot oil. When poured rapidly into other liquids, it splatters, but when added in tiny doses, it stays on the surface and triumphs gloriously.

Bit by bit, perseverance would win the day. Maybe even the world of the Papal State would change. There was always the Higher Power in whom to trust, who—with the help of his faithful—defends innocence; and so Tranquillo let others read his sister's tale.

There was, though, little reason to share Tranquillo's hopes or to be optimistic. The ghetto itself was in a shambles. From the mid-eighteenth century, Jews repeatedly called for relief from mounting piles of garbage and even human refuse. The old system of daily carting away and of a fixed carter, a *mondezzaro*, had been abandoned or even disallowed. Lines carrying refuse to the river were in need of repair; the river itself was becoming irreparably foul. The population, as the Jews perceived it, was growing denser, crowded into narrow streets filthied by the passage of carriages and horses. The sense of density must have been especially oppressive, for the ghetto's population was in fact shrinking. The 4,036 souls of the 1733 census had been reduced to about 3,600 by 1796; a census made in 1817 reveals that after the ghetto was restored with Napoleon's departure, another 600 fled, leaving only 2,997 in 778 families, for the low family average of 3.85 souls each.[11]

As the Jews saw it, the ghetto was being let to go to seed, and deliberately. Would not more and more Jews raise their hands in despair, seeking a permanent way out, whether by emigration—or conversion? Their sense of intentional abandonment stands out even more strongly in protests against the restrictions promulgated anew by Pius VI in 1775. Beyond forbidding the entrance of laundry women and refuse sweepers into the ghetto, these edicts put an end to the licenses traditionally granted Jews to employ Christian wet nurses. Jews, their appeal argued, lacked both the *teoria* and the *prattica* to engage in this profession. Were Jewish infants to be left hungry and die?[12]

There was also the comportment of Rome's citizenry and that of Christians outside of Rome, where Jews had been permitted to carry on commerce on a "temporary" basis. The moment the Roman Republic under the French in the closing years of the eighteenth century declared Jews equal citizens—freed, among other things, from the obligation to wear a distinguishing hat—disturbances, even riots, broke out. Whatever relations Jews had had with Christians, it was clear that amicability was possible only so long as clear lines of demarcation remained in place.[13]

In these circumstances it is doubtful that Tranquillo's hopes would soon be fulfilled or that anybody in the ghetto would believe they might be. Besides, conversionary intrigues had only heightened. On September 13, 1823, Pellegrino Toscano presented himself to the "*Catecumeni*." Four days later, his wife Flaminia, pregnant with child, was taken there against her will. But by mid-October, Pellegrino had changed his mind and returned to the ghetto. At first blush, it appears that the kind of terrible anguish experienced by Anna and those like her, the endless chain of "quarantine until submission," was no more. Pressures had decreased. Or had they? For the text goes on to say that three days later, at about 9:00 p.m., Flaminia, too, "returned—however, on condition that the deputies of the Congrega of Sixty guarantee that the fetus be handed over [to the *Casa*, to be baptized] the minute it sees the light of day."[14]

The maneuvering had become more insidious than ever. The resistance to change, as it had revealed itself in so many places during the previous half century, was growing. It would climax, beginning in the mid-nineteenth century, in a great battle within the Church itself, between so-called modernists and anti-modernists, known also as integralists or ultramontanists, and it would be exacerbated by the fall of the Papal State in 1870. The pope would be declared doctrinally infallible; and all stops would be pulled out when it came to the Jews. Did not Pius IX lament in 1871, that with the ghetto torn down and Jews free to live wherever they wished, they were going about *per le vie latrare*, barking in the streets? The "Jewish Dog" was polluting the pope's now lost domain.[15]

Read against this background, of an old world striving to maintain itself at all costs as it ran up against the forces of a new one straining to overthrow the old beyond recognition, the story of Anna del Monte stands out in its true colors as one that represents far more than the fate of one young woman alone. Anna herself may have been but a dot on a broad historical canvas, but her experience marks the swan song of a waning world-order. Or as her brother Tranquillo chose to recount it, it was a protest against injustice and a plaint against that which, in memorials sent to King Vittorio Emanuel I in 1870, the Jews of Rome would name "the many difficulties and the bitterness brought about by the legal, economic, moral, and intellectual, . . . [indeed,] the exceptionally sad state . . . of the Jewish Community . . ."

As of September 20 of that year, everything had changed. The Jews of Rome, indeed, the Jews of all united Italy, had passed from "legal inter-diction to a regime of civil equality." No longer were they "barely more than strangers." Rather, as they wrote the king a brief five days after September 20, and again on October 7, they were, as they sincerely believed, now, and at once, Italians, Romans, and Jews,[16] titles and statuses the papacy had labored never to concede them. Tranquillo would have rejoiced. Yet the euphoria—the illusion—was short lived. The 1929 Concordat between the Catholic Church and the Fascist state breathed new life into a once rejected confessionalism, and in 1938, a brief sixty-eight years after Italian unity and emancipation, the bond between Hitler and Mussolini and the subsequent racial laws of 1938 brought the newfound "equality" of Roman Jews to an abrupt and tragic end.[17]

Appendix I: Leo XIII
The Encyclical Immortale Dei of 1885

*Leo was pope between 1878 and 1903. http://www.vatican.va/holy_father/leo_*
xiii/encyclicals/documents/hf_l-xiii_enc_01111885_immortale-dei_en.html

The following segments of the bull display the kind of thinking that underlies the
papal thought discussed in this study.

27. Now, when the State rests on foundations like those just named—and for the time being they are greatly in favor—it readily appears into what and how unrightful a position the Church is driven. For, when the management of public business is in harmony with doctrines of such a kind, the Catholic religion is allowed a standing in civil society equal only, or inferior, to societies alien from it; no regard is paid to the laws of the Church, and she who, by the order and commission of Jesus Christ, has the duty of teaching all nations, finds herself forbidden to take any part in the instruction of the people. With reference to matters that are of twofold jurisdiction, they who administer the civil power lay down the law at their own will, and in matters that appertain to religion defiantly put aside the most sacred decrees of the Church. They claim jurisdiction over the marriages of Catholics, even over the bond as well as the unity and the indissolubility of matrimony. They lay hands on the goods of the clergy, contending that the Church cannot possess property. Lastly, they treat the Church with such arrogance that, rejecting entirely her title to the nature and rights of a perfect society, they hold that she differs in no respect from other societies in the State, and for this reason possesses no right nor any legal power of action, save that which she holds by the concession and favor of the government. If in any State the Church retains her own agreement publicly entered into by the two powers,

men forthwith begin to cry out that matters affecting the Church must be separated from those of the State.

30. Accordingly, it has become the practice and determination under this condition of public polity (now so much admired by many) either to forbid the action of the Church altogether, or to keep her in check and bondage to the State. Public enactments are in great measure framed with this design. The drawing up of laws, the administration of State affairs, the godless education of youth, the spoliation and suppression of religious orders, the overthrow of the temporal power of the Roman Pontiff, all alike aim to this one end—to paralyze the action of Christian institutions, to cramp to the utmost the freedom of the Catholic Church, and to curtail her every single prerogative.

32. A well-spent life is the only way to heaven, whither all are bound, and on this account the State is acting against the laws and dictates of nature whenever it permits the license of opinion and of action to lead minds astray from truth and souls away from the practice of virtue. To exclude the Church, founded by God Himself, from life, from laws, from the education of youth, from domestic society is a grave and fatal error. A State from which religion is banished can never be well regulated; and already perhaps more than is desirable is known of the nature and tendency of the so-called civil philosophy of life and morals.

34. Thus, Gregory XVI in his encyclical letter *Mirari Vos*, dated August 15, 1832, inveighed with weighty words against the sophisms which even at his time were being publicly inculcated—namely, that no preference should be shown for any particular form of worship; that it is right for individuals to form their own personal judgments about religion; that each man's conscience is his sole and all-sufficing guide; and that it is lawful for every man to publish his own views, whatever they may be, and even to conspire against the State. On the question of the separation of Church and State the same Pontiff writes as follows: "Nor can we hope for happier results either for religion or for the civil government from the wishes of those who desire that the Church be separated from the State, and the concord between the secular and ecclesiastical authority be dissolved."

35. From these pronouncements of the Popes it is evident that the origin of public power is to be sought for in God Himself, and not in the multitude, and that it is repugnant to reason to allow free scope for sedition. Again, that it is not lawful for the State, any more than for the individual, either to disregard all religious duties or to hold in equal favor different kinds of

religion; that the unrestrained freedom of thinking and of openly making known one's thoughts is not inherent in the rights of citizens, and is by no means to be reckoned worthy of favor and support. In like manner it is to be understood that the Church no less than the State itself is a society perfect in its own nature and its own right, and that those who exercise sovereignty ought not so to act as to compel the Church to become subservient or subject to them, or to hamper her liberty in the management of her own affairs, or to despoil her in any way of the other privileges conferred upon her by Jesus Christ. In matters, however, of mixed jurisdiction, it is in the highest degree consonant to nature, as also to the designs of God, that so far from one of the powers separating itself from the other, or still less coming into conflict with it, complete harmony, such as is suited to the end for which each power exists, should be preserved between them.

Appendix II: Conversion and Innovation in Canon Law

The following summarizes legal developments and the steps taken to create papal conversionary policy over the centuries.

First, a letter of the late sixth-century Gregory the Great to Pascasius, the bishop of Naples, edited into the canon *qui sincera* (D. 45, c. 3), in Gratian's *Decretum*, laid down the principle of no forced conversions. Gregory's letters demonstrably survived, but whether they were read or used before 938 is speculative; see Amnon Linder, ed., *The Jews in the Legal Sources of the Early Middle Ages*, 622–33. The Toledan councils of Visigothic Spain, whose clerical participants may have read Gregory's writings, set the precedent forbidding return to Judaism following baptism and for insisting that children follow the converted parent. Even where the baptism was conferred without legitimacy, the Fourth Toledan insists the child be taken; Gratian, *Dist. 26, q. 1*. Should these children and others act heretically, they are to be treated as Boniface VIII prescribes in *Contra, De hereticis* (Sext. 5, 2, 13). The Toledan Councils were also the direct source of the canon *de Iudaeis* (Gratian, D. 45, c. 5), which says that persons forcibly baptized must be made to observe the Christian faith: *de iudaeis: quia iam constat eos sacramentis diuinis associatos, et baptismi gratiam suscepisse, et crismate unctos esse, et corporis Domini extitisse participes, oportet, ut fidem, quam . . . susceperint tenere cogantur, ne nomen Domini blasphemetur, et fides, quam susceperunt, uilis ac contemptibilis, habeatur.*

The critical canon *Ex litteris* (first a bull of Gregory IX) in the *Decretals* also refers to the Councils. The demise of the Visigothic kingdom following the Arab conquest of Spain in 711 made its decisions temporarily moot, but the Crusades restored them to center stage. The massacres of 1096 produced enormous confusion. So many had converted. Wibert of Ravenna, the anti-pope Clement III, protested the Imperial policy of Henry IV that allowed "backsliding." No doubt the twelfth-century bull, and then canon, *Sicut iudaeis non* (X, 5, 6, 9), known as the *Constitutio pro iudaeis,* was in part a response to Jewish protests that the kind of force Wibert championed was getting out of hand. In fact, so it was remembered as late as Pope Pius VI in the eighteenth century; JTS microfilm 4026a, Copies of Roman documents.

A letter of Innocent IV of 1245 approved conversionary initiatives of Jaime IV of Aragon, but only indirectly; see Stow, *Catholic Thought,* 20–21, in regard to Innocent's accepting all of the king's proposed actions by name, except the one concerning sermons. Here, he remained silent. Great canonist that he was, Innocent IV had to know forced attendance was illegal.

The question remained: who was validly baptized? The bull *Maiores* of Innocent III, which Benedict XIV also relied on heavily, insists that anything short of "absolute force" obligated those baptized to remain faithful to Christianity. At the same time, *Turbato corde* of 1267 prohibited return to Judaism and outlawed aiding returnees; the *Liber Sextus* (5, 2, 13) finally made these principles into law. The provisions applied even to children baptized by stealth without their parents' knowledge. To remind us, however, that there was a push and pull and that the principles announced by Gregory the Great had never been abandoned, we may recall the commentary of Panormitanus *Quartum et Quintum Decretalium Commentaria* (Lyon, 1559), cited by Sessa, *Tractatus,* 186. On the one hand, Panormitanus sustained the restrictive canonical rulings just mentioned, especially those about the assignment of children, but, on the other, in his remarks on the critical *Sicut iudaeis non,* which insists that all baptism of Jews be voluntary, he made it clear that the canonical *perpetua servitudo* of the Jews, as propounded by Innocent III in *Etsi iudaeos* (X. 5, 6, 13), demanded subservience to the canons alone, not the true servitude that would have deprived Jews of *patria potestas.* It was this right that protected Jews against having their children taken away and baptized forcibly, which, in turn, would have indirectly—and illegally—forced the parents to follow (*eorum parentes indirecte cogerentur ad fidem suscipiendum*).

(Anti-pope) Benedict XIII's *Estsi doctoris gentium* of July 23, 1415, laid out for the first time a full papal conversionary policy. Previous papal initiatives like those in the later thirteenth century were both inconsistent and tentative: for instance, the bull *Vineam sorec* urges missionary sermons, but falls short of insisting on attendance because that would have entailed direct force. Gregory XIII, the same sixteenth-century pope who allowed an *Avo* to offer a grandchild, thought otherwise, and in 1584, he authorized obligatory sermons; later, Giuseppe Sessa would explain these sermons as *persuasion*. How else, he writes, would Jews learn about Catholic truth? Gregory XIII had no doubt been following the advice of Benedict XIII, who had unprecedentedly insisted on sermons. Indeed, the true importance of Benedict XIII's policy was in setting the tone that would be repeated in the sixteenth century, when, under Paul IV, but with signs of its coming already visible three decades earlier, the papacy finally launched a long-term conversionary policy: erecting the Roman Ghetto, putting in place economic limitations, reinforcing the position of the *Casa dei catecumeni* founded in 1543, burning the Talmud, (later) instituting sermons, and applying a bevy of other strict laws—to the end (as framed in the words of Francisco de Torres) that Jews be made to suck at husks and so desire conversion (see Stow, *Catholic Thought*, 211–20, 247–48), following the advice of Querini and Giustiniani in the *Libellum ad Leonem decem*, as noted above, to apply *piis verberibus*.

Sustaining this policy theoretically was the *De Iudaeis et aliis infidelibus*, composed in 1558 by the legist Marquardus de Susannis in order, as the book's dedication states, to support Paul IV's innovations. The tract cites tens of laws and canons on the subject of conversion, including the rules on the non-return of baptized children first announced by the Toledan Council and renewed by Gregory IX. The tract became a classic, referred to by all subsequent legal experts, including Giuseppe Sessa—and Benedict XIV.

Appendix III: The Limits of Port Jewry's Achievements

Important studies of Jews involved in trading, the phenomenon referred to as that of the Port Jew, have demonstrated links between modifying attitudes and laws toward Jews as they modernized, served, and became more active participants in the life of the state. However, as significant as these newer attitudes were in promoting Jewish absorption into society (in some cases) and in allowing Jews to adapt to changing worlds, in no place did attitudinal change, or even ever-widening privilege mean—or bring, of themselves— the complete, and unequivocal, legal equality that is the essence of emancipation. To try to see a progression from the achievements of Port Jews that ends directly in actual emancipation is to pass over the crucial role played by fundamental legal change, both theoretical and practical, that occurred in Europe, not only with the decision of the National Assembly in 1791, but even more with the *Code civil* in 1804. In the United States this change, codified in the Constitution, was a product of views expressed by Washington, Jefferson, and Madison (which had to do as much, if not more, with changing the status of Protestant sects and Catholics, as they did with changing that of Jews; Madison, in Virginia, promoted multi-sectarianism among Christian denominations without taking into account Jewish interests).

These major legal innovations shortened by decades, if not generations, the process to full emancipation. In particular, they resolved (theoretically, if admittedly only much later in fact) the crux of Jews holding public office. The issue had been fundamental since the Theodosian Code formalized the Jews' status as second-rate citizens by prohibiting them from obtaining positions of civic authority, along with any and all "honors," meaning judgeships. To restore this right was the sine qua non of complete and true emancipation, the clear dividing line between additional privilege and actual full citizenship. Another less visible barrier was that *ius commune* commentators regularly categorized all Jews as *personae odiosae,* meaning notorious and civilly disenfranchised. Without fundamental reform in *ius commune* (or its elimination), emancipation was legally impossible.

Hence, regardless of the singular and undeniable importance of the Port Jew phenomenon, until there was a flawless cut that deconfessionalized not only the state but also its laws, either full emancipation was not going to occur, or it would be delayed considerably—this is the central theoretical argument of this book. This book's sub-theme is that to understand the need for this revolution in conceptions and law, one must examine Jewish life in the Papal State, where the origins (the legal-confessional foundations) of old discriminations stand out so sharply, whereas in Western Europe, the steady stream of Jewish achievement masks the real issue, which scholars like Jacques Revel have, nevertheless, so perspicaciously spotted. Anna del Monte's diary is symbolic of the confessional impasse.

It is with this perspective that we should approach the important work of David Sorkin, who has persuasively argued that a basically uniform model of the Port Jew was present and functioning in France, Holland, England, and the United States. Incrementally, in all four, Jews gained first de facto and then de iure full rights. And I would agree with him that in that sense, comparatively, American emancipation was not unique. As in Europe, at the state level (although not the federal), American Jews, too, had to petition to end discriminations, especially—and significantly—about office-holding. England as well drew lines about the nature of citizenship; see J. H. Merchant, *A review of the proposed naturalization;* naturalization, he stressed, did not mean equal rights, which even Jews born in Britain achieved only in 1858.

Yet, as I have just said, a true break required something more, which was a reevaluation of the nature of the state, the citizen, and the very nature of law, as embodied in the *Code civil* or the American Constitution. In a battle, which some might say has never ended, the state/s had to shed any and all religious attributes. Would, one must ask, individual states have caved in on office-holding in the early nineteenth century without the Constitution and without the thinking of its authors; one may point to the obvious that in the United States, questions of public religious practice are always decided, in the final instance, at the federal level, often by the Supreme Court itself. Complementary to this line of reason are the findings of Francesca Trivellato, who has shown that there is a gap which legal integration does not close, which is that between commercial and social integration, *The Familiarity of Strangers*. Francesca Bregoli has been even blunter, challenging the idea that Port Jew advances led in a direct line to emancipation; see her *Mediterranean Enlightenment*, 237–38, concerning Livorno, where the effectively corporate structure of the community was maintained rather than giving Jews full rights. See David Sorkin, "Beyond the East-West Divide: Rethinking the Narrative of the Jews' Political Status in Europe, 1600–1750," *Jewish History* 24 (2010): 247–56; and "Is American Jewry 'Exceptional'? Comparing Jewish emancipation in Europe and America," *American Jewish History* 96 (September 2010): 175–200; also Lois Dubin, *The Port Jews of Habsburg Trieste, Absolutist Politics and Enlightenment Culture* (Stanford, 1999), 64–92; on Joseph II, Dubin, 175–84. See, too, vol. 24 of *Jewish History* in its entirety, edited by Francesca Bregoli and Federica Francesconi, with their valuable introductory essay, "Tradition and transformation in eighteenth-century Europe: Jewish integration in comparative perspective," *Jewish History* 24 (2010): 235–46; Federica Francesconi, "From ghetto to emancipation: the role of Moisè Formiggini," *Jewish History* 24 (2010): 331–54; Francesca Bregoli, "'Two Jews walk into a Coffeehouse': the 'Jewish question,' utility, and political participation in late eighteenth-century Livorno," *Jewish History* 24 (2010): 309–29; and, Francesca Bregoli, *Mediterranean Enlightenment*, esp. Chapter 1. Important discussion occurs in the full issue devoted to Port Jews of the journal *Jewish Culture and History* 4.2 (2001), special issue: *Port Jews: Jewish Communities in Cosmopolitan Maritime Trading Centres, 1550–1950*. On thinkers who did see a need to revise basic structures before emancipation would be possible, see Jonathan Karp, *The Politics of Jewish Commerce, Economic Thought and Emancipation in Europe, 1638–1848* (Cambridge, 2008), 127–34.

England, to be sure, stands out, for it emancipated Jews without ceasing to be, as it still technically is, a confessional state with an official religion. The head of that religion, however, is the king, not the Archbishop of Canterbury or any other ecclesiastic. As early as 1529, Henry VIII was asserting jurisdiction in purely church matters (*mere ecclesiasticum*). Thus if England continued as a confessional entity, it was one subject to pragmatic winds, where, critically, matters of commonweal and church were decided by one and the same authority, the king, allowing for measured, gradual change. Perspicaciously, G. R. Elton, *Reform and Reformation*, 167, spoke of Thomas Starkey, a member of Cromwell's inner circle, saying that "Starkey's purpose was to defend . . . the idea of the unitary national state and Church subject to the rule of constitutional monarchy and embodying the principle of moderation, that middle way between the extremes of radical reform and conservative reaction"; or as Elton put it succinctly, ibid., 199, "the lay absorption of the Church [into the sovereign powers of the realm exercised by the 'King in Parliament']." Rephrased by J. A. Guy, "Henry VIII and the Praemunire Manoeuvres of 1530–1531," *The English Historical Review* 97 (1982): 481–503, esp. 496–97: Henry VIII made his move "by reclassifying as 'temporal' what had once been 'spiritual,'" which is to say that he had deconfessionalized the confessional, placing the "favor of the realm" above the strict "favor of the faith." In this light, compromise, as that of 1858, with Lord Rothschild taking office, was possible, a matter of maturation over time, without a revolution, whether legal or political. By contrast, though the pope, too, held sway over both spiritual and political realms, the palpable tension between civil law and the unquestioned primacy of the canons (*favor fidei*), the very primacy barristers like Christopher St. Germain in England and Carlo Luti in Rome were attacking, made an "English solution" in the Papal State impossible.

Appendix IV: Lorenzo Virgulti (1685–1735)
L'ebreo catecumeno istruito

*L'ebreo catecumeno istruito ne' principali misterj della santa fede cristiana, e
cattolica dalla legge di Mosé, e dalle scritture de' profeti. Opera utile anche a i
cristiani, che desiderano di sapere i fondamenti della loro fede . . .*
—In Roma, Per Gio. Zempel e Gio. de Meij, 1728

There are ten chapters; 1. Need for faith, time of messiah, who is Christian,
and signs of the true Church. 2. Mystery of the Trinity. 3. Mystery of the
Incarnation. 4. Mystery of the Passion. 5. Mutation of the Law (from Old to
New). 6. Circumcision. 7. Cult and Adoration. 8. Sabbath. 9. Foods. 10. Sacraments and Prayer. And a closing Chapter on *neofiti* themselves, much out of
character with the rest of the book. Virgulti is preaching to the converted.
Following are detailed summaries of the book's chapters. Material enclosed
by parentheses indicates my observations.

Chapter I. Introduction
Faith is a gift of God, but to live without it is sin, for which there is no excuse.
The sinner is condemned, especially if he or she (Virgulti himself does not
specify gender) knows there is faith. Those who do not know of faith can
do well in this life, but not the future one. To be without faith is as though
to have been outside Noah's Ark. Anything, moreover, that was true before
Christ is no longer true with respect to faith. Hence, the Jews have had no
scepter (ruling power or jurisdiction) since the time of Herod, no Temple
from the time of the signs of Christ (his chronology is a bit off), and no
redemption. The real enemies of Christ are: passions, sins, all defeated by

grace. Christ came for all, not for Jews alone. The Jews say [salvation is for them alone]. But look at Isaiah 49:6, "I will be the light for the Nations." Jews say the messiah will bring with him material goods, but this is wrong. The church is one, with one head, the universal pastor. The Church is holy in doctrine and behavior. It is catholic and universal. The verse "from Zion will come forth the Torah" refers to the preaching of the Church. The Advent was for our souls.

Chapter II. The Credo

The Trinity is a mystery known only by divine revelation. Even if we hear *Shema yisrael,* the mystery is above that. God likes the modest catechumen, unlike the other Jews "who presume to know everything because they know *Quattro parole ebraiche,* four Hebrew words." God reflects himself and produces a perfect image of Himself. The Word, the Idea, and Love. Then Wisdom is generated, which took on human nature. From Isa. 48:16 (in Hebrew, v. 17): Behold I am your Redeemer, the Holy one, *santo* of Israel, I the Lord your God; I teach you for your good; I am the guide on the right road (my translation). We see the Holy Spirit here. Jews say this interpretation is nonsense, *sciocchezze,* that the one sent is Isaiah himself (actually, it refers to Isaiah's contemporary King Hezekiah, 715–686 B.C.E., 2 Kings 18–20).

Chapter III. Incarnation

It is not that God became flesh; divinity was "transmutated." Humanity into the Divine, and vice versa. Nonetheless, both are united in a way that the humanity remains humanity and the divine all to make satisfaction for our sins. One person, two natures. Incarnation proves God's mercy. Man has evil proclivities, but God will save mankind, especially the soul. God waited so long after Adam to incarnate Himself, so that man would realize how evil he is and that he is in extreme danger. It was necessary to rein in honor, sensuality, and wealth, and to instill humility. The virgin birth—the Jews think in carnal terms, that Christ was born and conceived like all others. But if they think the virgin birth impossible, how can they nevertheless still believe in Creation? The prophets foretold how, when, and where this would take place.

Chapter IV. The Passion

It is all in the Prophets, Zacharaiah 13:6–7, Psalm 68:22, Isa. 52:13 (these references are to the Vulgate numbering). The rabbis say Isaiah in Chapter 52 is referring to the Jews in the Diaspora, but this cannot be, since the subject is singular (this is Isaiah's suffering servant, which, in proper context, is unquestionably the Jews. Christians took it as a prophecy of Jesus). Zachariah: O sword, Rouse yourself against my shepherd, the man in charge of my flock, says the Lord of Hosts. This is surely Christ. The Jews make efforts to learn the Law, but the Torah has no value for salvation, which is what Paul said about Judaizers in Galatians. (Paul actually meant Christians who behaved like Jews; Virgulti means anybody who leans on the Torah.) If Law (Torah) and the blood of circumcision are sufficient for salvation, then why did God spill Christ's blood? (The problem here is double. First, Jews speak of the righteous sitting in the Garden of Eden and studying, not, as Paul, of the soul's personal salvation. Second, circumcision is a sign of covenant, not a sacrament like baptism, which guarantees reward. Commandments are observed because they are God's will.) To achieve eternal salvation, faith alone is not enough (down with the Lutherans). Good works are also essential (this is what the Church teaches, but it is self-contradictory and comes close to Donatism, an early heresy which said that works were necessary for salvation).

These works must be understood properly. The *mitzvot*, commandments, are laws of nature, which do not cease, and there are rituals, *ceremonialia*, too, but the messiah overcomes them all, including Jewish observances (Virgulti is being vague, perhaps purposefully, suggesting residual ambivalence on his own part). With Christ, the Jews' criminal and civil laws ceased, too, since after all, the Jews live under another government, which is not their own (hence, it is just that the pope has removed their powers of self-governance). The splendor of God becoming man is also greater than Sinai. Moses spoke only to an angel (an incredible invention by Virgulti), whereas Jesus performed so many more miracles than at Sinai. For all its *strepito*, the uproar it created, Sinai did not stop idolatry. Deut. 12:9 says the Laws will change: You still have not come to the final resting place and inheritance which God is giving you. The Sabbaths, too, have been cancelled. Christ has annulled circumcision as well. In the Law, Torah, servitude ends at the Jubilee (the fiftieth year). Your servitude is perpetual (*perpetua servitudo*, meaning subservience to canon law). The Old Law does not heal from sin. It allows divorce, polygamy (*he knows he is pushing a point*), and usury taken from strangers.

The Jews have their oral Torah (rabbinic teachings and the Talmud, which, in fact, they had not had since 1553, when it was burned). It allows every form of iniquity. The rabbis invented this Torah and it is depraved. (This had been a constant argument since the thirteenth century.)

Chapter VI. Circumcision

Abraham thought his was an eternal covenant through circumcision, but the Hebrew means only "a long time." (Virgulti cites St. Thomas, who did not know Hebrew.) The concept was Judaeo-centric. Real circumcision is through Christ. Salvation is for all mankind. Had all men required circumcision, Jonah, who preaches universal repentance, would have mentioned it. If the first Christians were circumcised, this is because they lived before the Gospel was set into writing.

Chapter VII. Adoration

The Virgin, images, the Catholic cult. They are not idolatry. Images are worshipped only in thanks for the saint's intercession. The Virgin is a Mother. Images are not in place of God, as the Ten Commandments forbid. (If there was anything that mystified Jews, it was the worship of images.)

Chapter VIII. The Sabbath

That was meant to be observed only in the Desert, a remembrance of God. But the real freedom [and repose] is in Christ. So there is no need for the Jewish Sabbath. The real Sabbath is supernatural, not a collection of ceremonies. Sunday is honored because it is in memory of the Resurrection. It is good to remember the idea of Creation, not however in parochial Jewish terms about which the rabbis make a great fuss, *fracasso* (Virgulti cites Rashi and ibn Ezra).

Chapter IX. Foods

Observance of ceremony (*kashrut*, whose rules he presents correctly, but in order to mock them) denies the value of Christ and redemption. Discrimination in foods is only for temporal ends like health, but Christ says: flee from the matters of the flesh. Admittedly, some *neofiti* have problems when it comes to food. Food discrimination was also established to keep Jews from gentiles. The pig reminds us of carnal people. But once the carnal law was voided and replaced by a spiritual one (Christianity), all the significations changed. It is nature that makes animals like the pig and lamb what they are. Christ wanted men to realize God created all things, including the pig. What makes man impure is not what goes in but what comes out of the mouth. To abstain, says Paul, indicates a lack of freedom. And do not Jews eat to excess what they are permitted in order to compensate for what they are forbidden? As for not eating the sciatic nerve, the rabbis blew up a single incident (Jacob wrestling with the angel) into a general rule. They did the same with the law about not cooking a kid in its mother's milk. To carry this distinction to knives (and other utensils) is absurd. The rabbis are manipulating when they speak of cheese made only by a Jew (the problem is the animal rennet used in making the cheese). How come one can eat cheese, rinse one's mouth, and eat meat, but the other way around, one must wait 6 hours? There is no logic. (This is surprising, since Italians, like Sephardim, wait 3 hours; Ashkenazi Jews wait 6.) In their rabbinic manipulations, the rabbis want people to think the authority is from the Torah and Moses (they do, but putatively, not pejoratively as here). As for blood, the original object was so that people would hate spilling human blood. Yet "the Jews poison the blood of their enemies, especially of Christians (the blood libel), and they judge unworthy of the name of a Wise One (*haham*, a scholar and rabbi) who does not preserve hatred in his heart or the desire for revenge, just as the serpent conserves its poison." And in the Talmud it says "*Tov she-bagoyyim harog*. Kill the best of the Goim." Blood prohibitions were given to keep people away from idolatry, but the idolatry meant is truly that (not Christianity). Blood is also to expiate for sin (which now Christ does). If Paul at first allowed Jewish ritual, it was only for the Jewish Christians who could not break away from old habits. But only for them. (This is correct.)

Chapter X. Sacraments

Grace comes through the sacraments. The difference between the old law and the new is that the latter "are not the cause of Grace, they only promise it." And the promise is through Christ. The sacraments follow the order of life's course and are rational; he lists them and explains that marriage multiplies the number of faithful; baptism and its effect are indelible, which makes one who is baptized part of the Church and requires obedience. It saves us from the fires of Hell. The Eucharist unites us with Christ, and it is Christ fully and wholly. Confession is "the remedy so simple and sweet to attain pardon and to warn the conscience against relapse."

XI. Converts

(Virgulti, himself a neofito, excoriates convert behavior. What role this chapter has in the tract is perplexing, all of which Anna could easily have thrown back in his face.) There are so many bad neofiti, "who make this poor Nation [of neophytes] abominable in people's eyes." They *are* accused of *superbia*, haughtiness. The *neofiti* think people owe them everything just because they became converts. They become insupportable in the way they treat their *padrini*, godfathers, even threatening to return to the ghetto. But these "people forget that in that abominable place, even though they fatigued themselves daily like dogs (punning on the common reference to Jews as dogs), they could barely earn enough to purchase a piece of bread. . . . You (Virgulti inexplicably switches to second person) better remember, then, that to be a Christian benefits you, not us [whomever he means by "us"]. And that you were freed from Hell, to which you would have been eternally condemned were you to die a Jew. So stop thinking that we are all obligated to give you everything you ask. Hence, you had better get some skills and work hard. Becoming a Christian doesn't mean you can sit idly and wander about the city. You must also make a practice of receiving the sacraments and reading spiritual books, hearing sermons, saying the rosary. Remember what happened to the Jews in the Wilderness. Fight temptation, especially relapse.

NOTE: Virgulti's attack on Jewish rituality as fatuous or wrong-headed was very much in fashion. Rabbi Leone Modena wrote a response, the *Riti*, about 1630. Judaism, he argued, was rational, while converts like Antonio Margaritha and Paolo Medici called Jewish practices absurd; on whom, among others, see Yaacov Deutsch, *Judaism in Christian Eyes*, and also Stow, "Medieval Jews on Christianity." Apart from Virgulti, one might consult the manual of the former rabbi and convert Giov. Antonio Costanzi, *La verità della Cristiana Religione contro le vane lusinghe de' moderni ebrei* (Rome, 1749).

Notes

Introduction

1. Anna, also called Graziosa (Anna is Hannah, which is also "grace," hence, Graziosa, as is typical of Italian usage of Hebrew-Latinate name pairings), is listed as part of family n. 397 in a census of the ghetto prepared in 1733, fully transcribed by Manuela Militi, "Descriptio Hebreorum, Trascrizione," in *Gli abitanti del ghetto,* ed. Angela Groppi (Rome, 2015).

2. I refer in particular to the distinction debated in 1791 at the French National Assembly between "passive" and "active" citizens, the latter possessing special rights like office-holding.

2. Crises

1. See the reflections of lawyers like Fiorello and de Becchettis on the difficulties ascribed to young women in Anna's situation.

2. The case appears in Marina Caffiero, *Battesimi Forzati, Storia di ebrei, cristiani e convertiti nella Roma dei Papi* (Rome, 2004), on which see Kenneth Stow's review in the *Journal of Religion* 93.2 (2013): 239–42; Caffiero, *Battesimi,* 231–35. Many other cases are listed by Milano, *Il Ghetto di Roma* (Rome, 1964), 283–95.

3. On all the problems of dates and dating, as well as for a careful synopsis of the somewhat confusing language in the Introduction, see Sermoneta's *Ratto,* chapter 2, *Il manoscritto,* passim, where Sermoneta also conjectures that the diary was to serve as a tool to fight the *Casa,* a conjecture with which I agree, but on which I have also tried to elaborate.

4. The rule concerning "denunciations" was established in 1641, as mentioned by, among others, F. M. Spannochio at ASCER, b. 2Zd 10 sup. 2, fasc. 06; and see more on the fate of women dragged into the *Casa* later. The rule

was often violated, and some women, even those only "denounced" were held for forty or eighty days.

5. Sessa, *Tractatus,* chap. 51, p. 200, says it is prohibited: "nulla ipsis vis aut iniuria inferenda, neque dure aut aspere . . . tractandi"; in theory, of course.

6. Fiorello in ASCER, b. 2Zd 10 sup. 2, fasc. 06: "[these women] capiantur invitae per Satellites [and are taken to the Casa], magnam apud ipsos tamquam attentantes deferere Haebreorum Ritus. Unde periculum imminent ut praepudore non audeant redire ad suos, atque ideo ficto animo, suscipiant Baptismum, non sine magna huius Sacramenti Iniuria et blasphemantes Christum vivant inter Christianos, tamquam Hebraeae et proclives ad Judaicos Ritus. (Can. plerique 92, de consecrate., dist. 4) ad quos facile redeunt, suas doceant superstitiones in perniciem puritatis nostae fidei, ut ponderat Pignattellus in v. 4"; citing Pignatelli's *consultum* vol. 7, no. 39; *Iacobi Pignatelli in Salentinis sacrae Theologiae acI.V. Doctoris Consultationum canonicarum . . . Venice 1687, vol. 14.* A parallel text, ASCER, 1Ub 2 inf. 1, fasc. 10: "Magnum patiuntur fam(a)e et pudoris detrimentum quando semel fuerunt ducte ad domum cathecumenorum nec facile ab hebreis recipient(es) in matrimonium. Ideo . . . grave damnum quoties invite capiuntur."

7. It is difficult to say whether we may learn something significant from Anna's story about the state of women in Rome, Jewish ones in particular. Anna has been romanticized as a "heroine"; Marina Caffiero, *Rubare le anime* (Rome, 2008), 50–53. A perhaps more pertinent question would be whether there was a correlation between the ability to resist conversion of young women, who, like Anna, were well educated, even if not to the sophisticated level the diary ascribes to her, and came from comfortable families as opposed to the resistance put up by women lacking these attributes, who may have also been susceptible to the "bribery" of a better material state. Did these latter give in more easily? Apart from that, important a question as it is, the study of the diary does not increase our knowledge of issues pertaining to women per se, for instance, about arrangements concerning marriage and matches; what is reported with respect to denunciations, especially in papal letters, is almost entirely external fantasizing. The same goes for the giving of bills of divorce. For views of Jewish women in Rome, see Stow, "Marriages Are Made in Heaven," and "The Jewish Woman as Social Protagonist: Jewish Women in Sixteenth-Century Rome," in ed. Claire Honess and Verina Jones, *Le donne delle minoranze* (Turin, 1999).

8. On some of the possible legal absurdities that might arise, especially with dowries, see Kenneth Stow, "Equality under Law, the Confessional State,

and Emancipation: The Example of the Papal State," *Jewish History* 25.3–4 (2011): 319–37. See also Stow, "Jewish Pre-emancipation," and Stow, *Jewish Life in Early Modern Rome.*

9. Pignaetelli, *Consultationum canonicarum,* vol. 7, no. 39. "Secundo sit saepe ut qui nunquam de baptismo cogitarant, postquam diutius in domo cathecumenorum detenti sunt, eos pudeat redire ad suos, apud quos in tota vita male audiunt, qui aliquando religionem suam deferere cogitarunt; ideo ficto animo suscipiunt baptismum et inter christianos vivunt, tanquam hebrei, exercentes malas artes, nec rato, data occasione, fugiunt in eas partes, ubi ilis publice liceat iudaizare, id quod non semel contigit." Pignatelli as laying the ground for the novelties of the eighteenth century as propounded by Giuseppe Sessa will soon be discussed. The contradiction must give us pause.

10. Family no. 653 in the 1733 Census lists Leone son of Sabbato Coen, his wife Perla, Sarra, a three-year-old daughter, Sabato Moisè, two years old, and Tranquillo, one year old. The age fit is perfect, and the only other Sabato Coen in the census is much too old, with a twenty-two-year-old son. Naming patterns among Italian Jews are rigid. A grandson is always named after the grandfather, regardless of whether the latter is living; Ashkenazim never name after a living relative. The census shows the del Monte family was a large one, with about eighty members. The name in Hebrew, as often registered by the Community, is *min ha har,* from the mountain, as, of course, del Monte. The name appeared in southern France in the Middle Ages, suggesting the family's medieval origin was in the region of Montpellier.

11. ASCER, b. 1Ul 2 inf. 2 a series of miscellaneous gathers; here, no. 85.

12. Reactions to the Portuguese Inquisition in the sixteenth century will soon be discussed. Legal responses will appear in the full section on lawyers like Carlo Luti.

13. It is not clear precisely when the *Casa* was moved to its present location in the neighborhood of Monti. An extraordinary text, ASCER, b. 2Zd 10 sup. 2, contains the following directive from March 9, 1617: "che li hebrei quando sono catechumeni nella casa non possino passare dall'infrascritte strade, cioè da capo al palazzo de SS. Astalli per andar a campidoglio sino al palazzo del Signore Mario Fano esclusive, et per il vicolo a capo al palazzo dove è il lavatoio che si va verso la casa de cathecumeni et alla parta et parte dietro detto palazzo de Astalli et intorno et dinanzi la porta della casa de cathecumeni et della chiesa di giovanni di mercatello et la casa delle donne . . .

et quando non ci sono cathecumeni, possino passare per tutta la strade drita che va a campidoglio dalle parte di qua dalla fontana, lasciando di passare di la dalla fontana nella piazzetta et dinanzi la casa dei cathecumeni." This text places the *Casa,* until this date, close to the ghetto, somewhere along the present Via delle Botteghe Oscure, near the Palazzo degli Astalli. I thank the late Giancarlo Spizzichino for confirming my reading of the text.

14. A clear example of the control exercised over *neofiti* are the rules for those living and studying in the *Collegio* of neophytes, a separate, if related institution from the *Casa;* these *neofiti* lived under a strict regimen, including constant prayer, even during meals, and minimal contact with the outside, especially relatives, visits with whom were directly supervised. Could this have contributed to the frantic behavior of those who preached to Anna? On rules in the *Collegio,* see *Archivio Segreto Vaticano: Sacra Congregazione della visita apostolic, Urbani VIII, pars tertia, 1624–30* (vol. 4, ff. 848–52: *Visitatio Collegii Neophytorum prima Februarii 1627, rione Sant'Eustachio*); I thank Carolyn Wood for most generously sharing her notes with me.

15. See Appendix IV for a full paraphrase of this tract. Lorenzo Virgulti's (1685–1735) *L'ebreo catecumeno istruito ne' principali misterj della santa fede cristiana, e cattolica dalla legge di Mosè, e dalle scritture de' profeti. Opera utile . . . In Roma, Per Gio. Zempel e Gio. de Meij, 1728.*

16. See the texts published by Kenneth Stow, "Conversion, Christian Hebraism, and Hebrew Prayer in the Sixteenth Century," *Hebrew Union College Annual* 47 (1976): 217–36.

17. See Solomon Grayzel, *The Church and the Jews in the Thirteenth Century,* vol. 2, ed. Kenneth Stow (New York and Detroit, 1989), 2:82, 191.

18. See Stow, "*Neofiti* and Their Families."

19. See Piera Ferrara, "Lungo i percorsi della conversione: i neofiti romani nel XVIII secolo," in ed. R. Morelli and G. Fiocco, *Città e campagna: un binomio da ripensare, Annali del Dipartimento di Storia dell'Università degli studi di Roma Tor Vergata,* 4/2008 (Rome, 2009).

20. On these matters, see Dyan Elliott, *Fallen Bodies: Pollution, Sexuality, and Demonology in the Middle Ages* (Philadelphia, 1999), esp. 100–106, and 122–26. She cites Peter Damian: "What business have you [the married priest] to handle the body of Christ, when by wallowing in the allurements of the flesh you have become a member of antichrist . . . ?" (104); Elliott also speaks (122) of "active [feminine] malice," going beyond the "passive pollution" women, and priests' wives in particular, may cause. Heresy, too, was considered to contaminate (154). The parallels are obvious to the charges

made against Jews, which Elliott herself notes. See also Dale Martin, *The Corinthian Body* (New Haven, 1996), 176, on the body of the individual polluting that of Christ and the Church, but also vice versa, 177: ". . . the man's penetration of the prostitute makes Christ a penetrator of the prostitute also," a fear which is expressed, inversely, when the Jew is the perpetrator, in ritual murder libels.

21. See again Appendix IV for an approximation in Virgulti's tract.

22. See Kenneth Stow, *Jewish Dogs: An Image and Its Intepreters* (Stanford, 2006). and "Was the Ghetto Cleaner?," in *Rome, Pollution and Propriety: Dirt, Disease and Hygiene in the Eternal City from Antiquity to Modernity,* ed. Mark Bradley, with Kenneth Stow (Cambridge, 2012).

23. See above the discussion of Gen. 49:10 and Gen. 25:23.

24. See Ludovico Carrito, *Epistola ad Iudaeo* (Paris, 1554), who uses elementary Kabbalah, saying such things as: "If you see the structure of the upper world, the so-called 'primordial man,' you will see God is composite (triune)." There is also God's female aspect, the *shekinah,* which is the Holy Spirit. The Trinity appears in phrases like *el elohim adonai* (God, God, God, under three different names).

25. See Jacob Katz, "Even though a sinner, he is still of Israel" (in Hebrew), *Tarbiz* 27 (1958): 203–27.

26. See Kenneth Stow, "Jewish Approaches to the Papacy and the Papal Doctrine of Jewish Protection, 1050–1150" (in Hebrew), *Studies in the History of the Jewish People and the Land of Israel* 5 (1981): 75–90.

27. See Kenneth Stow, "The Cruel Jewish Father: From Miracle to Murder," in *Studies in Medieval Jewish Intellectual and Social History: Festschrift in Honor of Robert Chazan,* ed. D. Engel, L. H. Schiffman, and Elliot R. Wolfson (Leiden, 2012).

28. The classic and most precise study of this kind of Christian Kabbalah remains Chaim Wirszubski, *Three Studies in Christian Kabbala* (Jerusalem, 1975) and *A Christian Kabbalist Reads the Law* (Jerusalem, 1977), both in Hebrew.

29. Mystical interpretations of Judaism sometimes go beyond cleaving to God and approach union, but this is not normative.

30. On Herman, see J. C. Schmitt, *La Conversion d'Hermann le juif: Autobiographie, histoire et fiction* (Paris, 2003). On Alfonso, see Y. F. Baer, *A History of the Jews in Christian Spain,* trans. L. Schoffman, 2 vols. (Philadelphia, 1961), vol. 2. On Paolo Medici, as well as on Antonio Margaritha, see, most recently, Michael Walton, *Antonius Margaritha and the Jewish Faith* (De-

troit, 2012). On converts to Protestantism, see Elisheva Carlebach, *Divided Souls: Converts from Judaism in Germany, 1500–1700* (New Haven, 2001).

31. On Carmi, see Renata Segre, *The Jews in Piedmont, 1297–1723* (Jerusalem, 1986–88), doc. 2625, 20 August 1720. On the similar story of Hester, in Modena, see Katherine Aron-Beller, *Jews on Trial: The Papal Inquisition in Modena, 1598–1638* (Manchester, 2011), 154–60.

32. Giuseppe Sessa, *Tractatus de Iudaeis* (Turin, 1716), chap. 51, 200. This young woman had, says Sessa, promised to marry a Christian and convert. But the parents heard about the promise and spirited her away. They were caught, and the girl spent twelve days in the *Casa* in Turin, to be released on the thirteenth, to great festivity, "qui eam cum magna totius synagogae festo exceperunt, et veluti costantis perfidiae testimonium, ac exemplar pueris, puelisque Hebraeorum celebrant et propununt."

33. The report speaks of Salomon di Segni (*sic*), who was told: "'o muori, o fatti cristiano!' Disse che si saria fatto Cristiano: fu da essi [a group of Trasteverini] condotto a Catecumeni. Appena partiti i Trastevererini, si fè mettere alla stanza degli ostinati e doppo 40 giorni ritornò in Ghetto, colla solita spesa di scudi 13:35." As the story continues, Tranquillo tells us that a sum of money was needed from within the community to provide for those who suffered during the siege. But only some of it, which the *Consiglio* of Sixty tried to impose as a tax, was raised: "perchè uno de più opulenti, non volle contribuire la soma impostagli." In the case of two other aids raised by the *Fattori* themselves, it is said that "pochissimi furoni i renitenti." Of course, this may have been a way to emphasize the personal leadership of the *Fattori* as opposed to that of the organized Community as represented by its Council, whom they actually represented and by whom they were chosen. Still, the point remains. The formal community had no power to stand up to individuals. The report was published by Enzo Sereni, "L'assedeo del Ghetto di Roma del 1793 nelle memorie di un contemporaneo," *Scritti in Memoria di Enzo Sereni* (Milano and Jerusalem, 1970), 168–97. Finally, note the phrase *solita spesa*. *Solita*, customary, shows there were a number who made it out as Jews; Anna was not alone in surviving the ordeal. But "she" left us a full story. The Jewish Community, nonetheless, had to pay Salamone di Segni's upkeep, the customary 13:35 scudi.

34. The Terracina affair will soon occupy us. On the London episode, see Cecil Roth, "The Forced Baptisms of 1783 at Rome and the Community of London," *Jewish Quarterly Review*, new series, vol. 16, no. 2 (Oct. 1925): 105–16.

35. For Grazia, see ASCER, b. 2Sd 9 sup 3, fasc. 01 n. 5, October 28, 1792; with the full text as here being ASCER, b. 01Ul 2 inf 2, fasc. 03.

36. A series of small incidents involving the *Casa* may also have been instrumental in prompting Tranquillo's decision, on which see ASCER, b. 2Sd 9 sup 3, fasc. 01, 1793. These were no. 17, in fasc. 1, to pay a "facchino 20 baiocchi, per aver trasporato le robbe di Alessandro Abbina fatto cristiano in due Oraggi"; no. 84, 12 scudi are paid to the "Curato de Catecumini per il ritorno di Salomon di Segno," the same Salomon as in Tranquillo's report of the 1793 siege; and no. 5, a payment of 3:60 scudi to the rector of the *Catecumeni* for returning "disrata e la ricevuta."

37. ASCER, b. 1Ui, 2 inf. 2. "Che tutte le volte che si siano spianati nostre di grani il pane fatto da quella se sia mandato nel [totally unjustly] Ghetto e consegnato alli Fattori dell'Università . . . si debba consumare dall'ebrei [unjustly] poiche gli ebrei come corpo materiale non vengono considerati da sommi pontefici con niuna differenza dagli altri sudditi della sede apostolica leggendosi nelle loro constitutioni che gl'ebrei senza di niuna distintione da qualli [other citizens] debbano esser compresi nelli statuti delli [*sic*] città dove habbitano e solo nello spirituale essendo dalla chiesa tollerati in testimonium fidei vengono suborndinati a giudici ecclesiastici et all'ordinarii di luoghi. [This is virtually a citation of De Luca; also cited by Sessa.] Onde non pare che di raggione poss'obligarsi gl'ebrei a dover mangiare qual pane che per qulache imperfettione partricolare non si fa vendere da publici fornari di Roma a Christiani"; "Every time," they said, "that crushed, ruined grain is found in the bread [baked in the city], that bread is sent into the Ghetto and given to the *Fattori* to distribute . . . This is totally unjust. Is it not true that as a group, the popes consider the Jews no different from other subjects? Does it not appear in their constitutions that Jews are to be included in civic statutes with no distinction from others, and that only in spiritual matters (are they perhaps citing De Luca and Sessa directly?) is their status that of those tolerated by the Church in Testimony to the Faith, subordinate to ecclesiastical judges and local bishops? Hence, there is no reason to obligate Jews to eat bread so bad that Rome's bakers will not sell it to Christians."

38. *Dispar nimirum est,* as cited in *All'Illustrissima,* ASCER, b. 1Rf fasc. 13. The canon cut from a letter of Pope Alexander II is Gratian, *Decretum,* C.23, q.8, c.11; in *Corpus iuris canonici,* 2 vols., ed. E. Friedberg (Leipzig, 1879, 1881). See, too, ASCER, b. 2Zl (letter l) 10 sup. 3, texts 185 and 189; material in

square brackets is paraphrased; the legal references to jurists, of which there are many in the original, have been omitted.

"[Addressed to the] eccellenza il signore Senatore di Roma Generale della milizia civica per l'univiversità degli ebrei di Roma. [Two Jews are out to earn bread,] uno chiamato Angelo Frascati [the other Mose Aron Zarfadi]. Fu il primo invitato da due cristiani suoi amici a bere una foglietta e rimase il Zarfadi di fuori." [The soldiers walk in, approach Frascati, take the wine from his hands, and pour it on his head. Zarfadi is outside, not noticing. The soldiers exit, and it is then they bayonet him. Apart from the citations to be noted the writer asks: how can you make a person take off his hat at such great risk?] Questo modo di procedere ripugna diametralmente alli principi della legge naturale e sopra tutto la Carità, di cui esser deve ornato ogni Cristiano, in forza della quale deve amare ogni suo simile come se stesso, sia Nazionale, sia estero, sia della stessa religione, sia diversa, sia amico, sia anche nemico. Chi può ripromettersi che cio non succeda? Chi c'e' che non comprenda il tumulto, e la sollevazione? Ecco tutta la Soldatesca al Ghetto. Ecco unito alla soldatesca il Popolo. Ecco da una scintilla un' incendio. Ed ecco . . . [puntini nel testo]. [They protest. In this] stato ecclesiastico, the Jews non sono . . . schiavi, ma sudditti a paragone di tutti gli altri cittadini, [which appears in the Code and de Luca, Disc. 182, de Regali par 9 e 10, and Ferrari (under Hebreus par. 222), forbidding injury to Jews; on Ferraris, see Stow, "Expulsion." The Rota decis. 269, part 4, n. 17, says Jews] in temporalia . . . dicuntur essere de Populo et corpore Civitatis, . . . Benedict XIV in Postremo de Baptismo iudaeorum, [who says], contumelia . . . omnis asilio ipsis concesso penitus adversatur. [The act of doffing their hats is against the law of nature and all carità. Moreover, these events occurred in 1793, the same year as the disorders, indeed], fin dall'anno 1793 in cui insorse il noto amutinamento contro la . . . nazione ebrea [and the soldiers did this when Jews passed the Quartieri Civici]. A similar plea was made with respect to one Abramo Laudadio. There was a brawl, and the Jews appealed to Justinian's Code 1, 9, 7/8 (the law that declares Jews to be *cives*), and then to De Luca, at just the point that Sessa, whom the Jews cite at length, cites. (We must beware of the term *amici*. It is not clear what is really meant. Moreover, these are lower-class people; and time and again, it is among the lower classes that formal barriers set by confessional difference fall away. Places of public drinking led to various decrees of social mixing, including between members of different religions; see Bregoli, *Mediterranean Enlightenment*, chap. 6.)

39. See, here, ASCER, b. 3Cc 10 inf 2, fasc. 4 for the *Memoriale;* and also, for the commercial petition, once again ASCER, b. 2Zl (letter l) 10 sup. 3, texts 185 and 189. In the *Memoriale,* the Jews who say they are virtually bankrupt bring a long list of rights and privileges they once had. They begin, 2v: "Di più, atteso il loro genio già da troppo lungo tempo contratto di servire fedelmente i principi ne di cui stati dimoravano, come abbiamo nel Decreto par. 2, Caus. 23, q. 8, Canon dispar, ivi Hi vero ubique servire parati sunt; [they proceed to define 'servi civili' exactly as said here, rebutting the 'common crowd' that thinks they are vile slaves:] Si maraviglierà di tanta protezione del Diritto canonico per gli ebrei chi, pensando col grosso Volgo, riguarda questa nazione come un gregge di servi e di schiavi, ma chi in essi ravvisa alttettanti uomini liberi, altrettanti cittadini, si recherà più tosto a stupore come posteriormente le opinioni dell'idiota e della plebe abbiano potuto derogare al retto ed alla equo e porre in dimenticanza li più giusti e più antichi canoni, e si maraviglierà come a riscrontro delle opinioni sudette si veggano di presente trattati in Roma questi miseri sudditi. Del rimanente la chiesa che non ha risguardato per servo se non chi primi si era mostrato pubblico nemico de' Cristiani non ha potuto tenere se non in luogo di liberi li quetissimi ebrei sempre pronti non a perseguitarla ma a servirla volontariamente, come insegna [il canone dispar, again cited]."

40. ASCER, b. 1Qn parte 1, fasc. 05, "Giacche' trovandosi prima gli Ebrei in conformità del diritto commune in possesso della piena libertà," not only to practice whatever art, but to possess "stabili," immovable property, and to be free of the rule of the "università cristiane." However, Paul IV made confusion reign, and now we want matters set straight [that is, to have our proper rights].

3. The Roman Ghetto

1. That there was sudden change in the eighteenth century is the thesis of Marina Caffiero, *Forced Baptisms: Histories of Jews, Christians, and Converts in Papal Rome,* trans. Lydia Cochrane (Berkeley and Los Angeles, 2011) (original Italian: *Battesimi Forzati*).

2. Compare the thesis of Stefanie Siegmund, which detaches actions concerning Jews in the Florentine Duchy from papal initiatives; on which see Kenneth Stow, "The Medici State and the Ghetto of Florence: The Construction of an Early Modern Jewish Community by Stefanie B. Siegmund," *American Historical Review* 112 (2007): 302–303.

3. On discipline, see Paolo Prodi and Adriano Prosperi, eds., *Disciplina*

dell'anima, disciplina del corpo e disciplina della società tra medioevo ed età moderna (Bologna, 1994), and Prosperi's *Tribunali di Coscienza* (Turin, 1996), but see also William Hudon, "Religion and Society in Early Modern Italy," *American Historical Review* 101 (1996): 783–804.

4. See chapter 2 for further discussion of Paul IV. See also Kenneth Stow, *Catholic Thought,* and see the recent comments of Benjamin Ravid, "Cum nimis absurdum and the Ancona Auto-da Fé Revisited: Their Impact on Venice and Some Wider Reflections," *Jewish History* 26 (2012): 85–100. Ravid's argument is that the specific contents of Venetian and papal policies resemble each other greatly, implying that the two policies were nearly the same, which they were not because of the papacy's conversionary push, to whose analysis most of Stow's book is devoted. *Cum nimis* is, indeed, not singular for its innovations, except in its commercial clauses, which, in the event, pursue the traditional aim of avoiding contamination by contact. *Cum nimis* is singular in dealing with law as a conversionary device. The Venetians shared the papal desire to segregate, but had no serious (large-scale) conversionary aims.

5. The major reform document of Paolo Giustiniani and Pietro Querini, *Libellus ad leonem decem* (1513; reprint, Artioli, 1995), makes mission to the Jews central to its entire program, even though its underlying issue was the health of a Church in need of repair. See on this tract, Stow, *Catholic Thought,* 217–20, and Stow, *Alienated Minority: The Jews of Medieval Latin Europe* (Cambridge, MA, 1992–94), 305, whose arguments and the texts cited are repeated by Serena di Nepi, citing the pages in Stow, but without reference to the ideas and texts appropriated, omitting, furthermore, Stow's larger contextualization in both books; *"Un'anticipazione del Ghetto? Modelli di conversion e strategie di proselitismo nel Libellus del 1513,"* in *Conversos, marrani e nuove comunità ebraiche in età moderna,* ed. Myriam Silvera (Florence, 2015).

6. On de Susannis, see Stow, *Catholic Thought,* passim. De Susannis dedicated his book to Pope Paul IV, who may have commissioned its composition.

7. See above on this tract with reference to Paul IV and his conversionary program.

8. The Jewish population of Poland, so large in later centuries, was still relatively small.

9. On hesitancy about the sincerity of converts, see David Berger, "Mission to the Jews and Jewish-Christian Contacts in the Polemical Literature of the High Middle Ages," *American Historical Review* 91 (1986): 576–91.

10. See Maria Pia Donato, "Roma in rivoluzione (1789, 1848, 1870)," in *Storia*

d'Italia, Annali 16, *Roma, la città del papa: Vita civile e religiosa dal giubileo di Bonifacio VIII al giubileo di papa Wojtyla*, ed. L. Fiorani and A. Prosperi (Turin, 2000), 907–33; and related essays in in *Annali 16, Roma, città del papa*.

11. See Romans 11:24–26 on mass conversion heralding the end of days.

12. See Claudio Canonici, "Condizioni ambientali e battesimo degli ebrei romani nel seicento e nel settecento," *Ricerche per la storia religiosa di Roma* 10 (1998): 234–71, esp. 250–52.

13. Enforced Jewish quarters started to appear elsewhere toward the end of the fifteenth century, for instance, in Kazemierz, a suburb (more, a section) of Cracow, in Poland. Frankfurt am Main began closing in Jews shortly after midcentury, as did Barcelona. None of this, however, was ever achieved with the sophistication and regulation of the Italian ghettos.

14. Robert Bonfil, *Jewish Life in Renaissance Italy*, trans. Anthony Oldcorn (Los Angeles and Berkeley, 1994), 38–44.

15. See Kenneth Stow, "Sisto V, the Jews, and Their Ghet," in *Essential Papers on Jewish Culture in Renaissance and Baroque Italy*, ed. David Ruderman, (New York, 1992). This figure of divorce is not to be confused with Daniel Boyarin's various discussions of Jewish men as womanly.

16. See Kenneth Stow, "Was the Ghetto Cleaner?," on both inundations and sanitary measures.

17. See Simone Feci, "The Death of a Miller: A Trial contra Hebreos in Baroque Rome," *Jewish History* 7.2 (1993): 9–27; see, too, Kenneth Stow, "Sanctity and the Construction of Space: The Roman Ghetto as Sacred Space," in *Jewish Assimilation, Acculturation and Accommodation*, ed. Menahem Mor (Lanham, MD, 1992).

18. Kenneth Stow, *The Jews in Rome*, 2 vols. (Brill, 1995–1997), miscellaneous documents on rental and rights, passim.

19. See Stow, "Corporate Double Talk: Kehillat Kodesh and Universitas in the Roman Jewish Sixteenth-Century Environment," *Journal of Jewish Thought and Philosophy* 8 (1999): 283–301; but see also Kenneth Stow, *Taxation, Community, and State: The Jews and the Fiscal Foundations of the Early Modern Papal State, Päpste und Papsttum* (Stuttgart, 1984), chap. 2, which details how the Jewish leadership was turned into a papal tax-collector. At the same time, exercising this function faithfully was instrumental in keeping the community itself alive, counter to papal designs of fragmentation and destruction.

20. See the late Giancarlo Spizzichino, "Tra controllo e repressione: L'Università degli ebrei di Roma e il Sant'Uffizio (1731–1741)," in *Gli abitanti del ghetto*, ed. Angela Groppi (Rome, 2015).

21. See ASCER, b. 2Oe, 7 sup 2, fasc. 1, and numbers 148, 225 in this fascicle, and also ASCER, b. 2VM, 10 sup 2, on multiple *Fattori*.

22. "Ne ricavavano il modo di industriarsi tutti gli altri singoli del ghetto, chi con il vendere e comprare, e chi con il lavoro, che con la suppressione di quelli (banchi) li capitali restorono morti"; ASCER, b. 01Th, 2 inf 1, fasc. 4. The appeal may have had some success; the popes feared a Jewish bankruptcy, which would have weighed directly on their finances. Thus in 1719, although perhaps not fully until 1734, none other than Benedict XIV wrote that the Jews may "continuare tenere magazzini fuori del recinto del ghetto verso il pagamento di scudi 12 annui di tassa" (ASCER, b. 1Tc [parte 1], 2 inf 1), and in 1738 (same source) Benedict confirmed a "sentenza a favore degli ebrei contro l'università dei mercanti fondacali permettendo la vendita di robba nova." Toward the end of the eighteenth century, Jewish merchants were carrying on trade and, apparently, living in towns outside of Rome; on which see Manuela Militi, "Gli ebrei 'fuori dal Ghetto': Incontri e scontri con il Lazio durante la Repubblica romana (1798–1799)," *Archivi e Cultura* 40 (2007): 195–215.

23. See Katherine Aron-Beller, *Jews on Trial*, 163–90. With respect to the fines Jews often paid, it is important to remember that only Christian heretics like Giordano Bruno might be executed; see Anna Foa, *Giordano Bruno* (Bologna, 2011).

24. See Irina Oryshkevich, "*Roma sotterranea* and the Biogenesis of New Jerusalem," RES: *Anthropology and Aesthetics* 55/56 (2009): 174–81. See Raffaele Pittella, "Labirinti archivistici e contesti istituzionali," in *Gli abitanti del ghetto*, ed. A. Groppi, for contrasting views of a ghetto integrated into the city fabric, although one suspects these views by seventeenth-century cartographers require further study.

25. Samuela Marconcini, "The Conversion of Jewish Women in Florence (1599–1799)," *Zeitsprünge: Forschungen zur Frühen Neuzeit* 14 (2010): 532–48, has described an increasing percentage of women among converts from the later eighteenth century and into the nineteenth, ascribing the desire of mainly poor or mistreated women, the latter sometimes of means, to liberate themselves from suffocation as a possible motif. This corresponds to what is often said about men, too. Whether Tranquillo del Monte wanted to use Anna's diary to persuade women "to remain steadfast like his sister" we may only speculate. However, I tend to think not, given the diary's small circulation.

26. Kenneth Stow, "From Civil Society to the Family: Transformations in Early Modern Jewish Confraternal Structure," in *Brotherhood and Boundaries/ Fraternità e barriere*, ed. Stefania Pastore, Adriano Prosperi, and Nicholas

Terpstra (Pisa, 2011). My sense is that closeness of age in a couple indicates that the match was of their choosing, signifying mutual desire and emotional bonding. That virtually all the matches surveyed show this characteristic made me feel justified in seeing the small family as an unstated policy, or tool, of Jewish preservation. Now, see, too the precise figures for the earlier and mid-eighteenth century in Michael Gasperoni, "Note sulla popolazione del ghetto di Roma in età moderna: Lineamenti e prospettive di ricerca," in *Gli abitanti del ghetto,* ed. Groppi.

27. On the decline of Roman Jewish confraternities, see again Stow, "From Civil Society to the Family." For its part, the Community tried to keep up a pool of available partners, lest some men despairing of finding a partner convert. Gasperoni, *Note,* reports that the number of women leaving Rome was small, which may have been an effect of the heavy tax the Community put on dowries being exported. Because the pope needed these taxes to keep the Community from sinking even deeper into bankruptcy, he preserved, as we have said, the Community's power to tax, while attacking all other powers. Besides, the real power was in the hands of the Vicar and his adjutants: hence, the Jews speak of the need to give *la dovuta esecuzione alli veneratissimi commandi di Monsignor Illustrissimo e Reverendissimo Tesoriere sudetto;* see ASCER, b. 2Za 10 sup 2, fasc. 04.

28. See the discussion in ASCER, b. 1Ui 2 inf. 2, fasc. 07.

29. See Kenneth Stow, "Delitto e castigo nello Stato papale: ebrei e carceri a Roma alle fine del Cinquecento e agli inizi del Seicento. Primi sondaggi," *Italia Giudaica II* (Rome, 1986), 173–91, for examples of Jews and Christians coming together, sometimes unpleasantly, but also ASCER, b. 1Zb 2 inf. 3, fasc. 06, for a list of about sixty criminal condemnations of Jews from 1566 to 1701. These include brawls between Jews, but also with Christians, violations of rules about Jews and Christians eating at the same table and sexual liaisons of Jews with Christians (women); the former about ten times, and the latter a mere five, two of which were with prostitutes. There is no way of knowing how complete this list is, and generalizing is dangerous. Nor should we assume that the cases tried were the only violations. Doubtless many went undetected and unpunished. Yet the sparseness—sixty violations brought to trial in about one-hundred-fifty years, and with no more than a quarter involving fraternization—suggests that social interchange occurred, but was not common. A later text concerning a complaint about the Roman Civil Guard suggests otherwise, that there was nothing unusual in drinking together (Italian Jews as a matter of course

drank Christian wine, unlike Ashkenazim who refrain) and that Jews did have Christian *amici*. Yet in this same fascicle, a complaint by Jewish leaders from 1679 asks to revert to the previous status quo in the Roman prisons, where there were special rooms for Jewish prisoners. At the time, Jews and Christians were mixed, which was troubling: "ponderate [says the petition] le necessità di destinare agl'ebrei una situazione di maggiore commodo, e che questa sia separata dal commercio ed introduzzione dei cristiani con li quali non è possibile il conversare in carcere senza un quotidiano sconcerto, ossia per la diversità nell'orare e per l'altra nel vitto." In short, one must not go overboard, either way; cf. Caffiero, *Legami pericolosi*, passim.

30. These are specified in Pius VI's edict of 1775 (see above); see, too, Dana E. Katz, "'Clamber not you up to the casements': On Ghetto Views and Viewing," *Jewish History* 24 (2010): 127–53, on anger in Venice concerning what Jews might see from the ghetto looking outward.

31. ASCER, 1Ql 1 inf. 05, fasc. 07, has various texts on carnival exaggeration and complaints like that about *neofiti* entering the ghetto; see esp. 1Ub 2 inf. 1 fasc. 12.

32. On Giudiate, see Lynn Gunzberg, *Strangers at Home: Jews in the Italian Literary Imagination* (Berkeley and Los Angeles, 1992).

33. See Yaacov Deutsch, *Judaism in Christian Eyes* (New York, 1912), passim.

34. ASCER, b. 1Uh 2 inf. 2, fasc. 02.

35. See Bregoli, *Mediterranean Enlightenment*, 58–59, on Joseph Attias, who also prided himself on the knowledge of *ius commune*, local Tuscan law, and even the canons.

36. Giuseppe Sermoneta, "Jewish Culture at Rome in the XVIII Century as Seen Through New Documentation" (in Hebrew), *Italia Judaica* III (Rome, 1989): 69–96.

37. Massimo Mancini, "Pier Gaetano Feletti e l'affare Mortara," in *Dominikaner und Juden/Dominicans and Jews*, ed. Elias H. Fuellenbach and Gianfranco Miletto (Berlin, 2015), 421–37, 437: "il vero problema del caso Mortara. . . . il fatto che, senza la necessaria distinzione tra religione e potere statale, uno stato confessionale si considera legittimato ad intervenire nelle questioni di coscienza, diventando percio' una inaccettabile struttura di oppressione."

4. The Confessional State

1. See Karen Brodkin, *How the Jews Became White Folks, and What That Says about Race in America* (New Brunswick, 1998).

2. Thomas of Aquinas, 4 sen. Dist. 39, q. 1, art. 4, circa fi. "Semper enim in favorem fidei est inclinandum;" also *Summa Theologica*, II, II, 10.12. See also Antonio Ricciulli O.I.C. Roblanense, Patritiae Rhegino, in Aula Romana Advocato, *Tractatus de iure personarum extra ecclesias gremium existentium, cui propter argumenti similitudinem annexus est alter Tractactus De Neophytis, Romae, sumptibus Io. Angelo Ruffinelli et Angeli Manni*, 1622, lib. 2, cap. 32. n.3 et sequen, on no force being applied to parents. Antonio Ricciuli, advocatus, canonist, professor of law, bishop, and Vice Regent of Rome, was the person who supervised much of what happened in the city. He was an intimate of the pope on Roman matters and also supervised the Rector of the Roman House of Converts.

3. On the importance attached to the act of baptism at this time, see Prosperi, *Dare l'Anima, storia di un infanticidio* (Bari, 2005); but see also Adolfo N. Dacanáy, "Disputed Questions Concerning Those to Be Baptized: Comments on Cc. 868, 870, 871, and 913," *Diwa* 33 (2008): 36–57, discussing questions of baptism when only one spouse is a Catholic, referring also to *Postremo mense*.

4. Marquardus de Susannis, *De Iudaeis et Aliis Infidelibus* (Venice, 1558), part 1, chap. 3, pars. 8–15; and summarized in Kenneth Stow, *Catholic Thought*, passim.

5. Referred to in Benjamin Ravid, "The Forced Baptism of Jewish Minors in Early-Modern Venice," *Italia* 13–15 (2001): 259–301, 266.

6. *Iacobi Pignatelli in Salentinis sacrae Theologiae acI.V. Doctoris Consultationum canonicarum . . . Venice 1687. 14 Volumes, Tom. 7, consultatio 39:* "Tertio, an pueri ante usum rationis qui habent affines hebraeos et christianos in aequali gradu debeantur potius hebraeis cum sint quasi in possessione, an vero christianis in favorem fidei?" And 7, 192, "haec res tendit ad favorem fidei, cum nimis sit dedecens, atque absurdum redundetque in ignominiam christianae religionis, quod in officiis publicis filius liberae sujbijciatur [*sic*] filio ancillae, et maior serviat minori."

7. On this event, see Kenneth Stow, "The Good of the Church, the Good of the State." See also Pietro Regis, *De iudaeo cive* (Turin, 1793); like others at the time, Regis—beginning in 1682 (see again "The Good")—calls for Jews to work in agriculture, but calls also for all the laws limiting Jews to be sustained. The question of Jews in agriculture is an old theme that would appear again during discussions in both France and Poland at the end of the eighteenth century. Regrettably, copies of Regis are extremely rare, and I was unable to consult the book except through a summary by the highly reliable late Vittore Colorni.

8. *Summa Coloniensis,* ed. S. Kuttner and G. Fransen (New York, 1969), 19–20. "Unde et Romanus pontifex leges principum nunc sacras nunc venerandas appellat. . . . Lex humana non est supra legem Dei set subtus. Item Syxtus, 'Non licet imperatori nec cuiquam pietatem custodienti aliquid contra legem Dei presumere.'"

9. *Consilia* (Venice, 1497), no. 487.3, fol. 72v, discussing C. 2, q. 7, c. 26; cited by Aviad Kleinberg,"Depriving Parents of the Consolation of Children: Two Legal Consilia on the Baptism of Jewish Children," in *De Sion exibit lex et verbum Domini de Hierusalem: Essays on Medieval Law, Liturgy and Literature in Honour of Amnon Linder,* ed. Yitzhak Hen (Turnhout, 2001), 129–44, esp. 133–34. I thank Isabelle Poutrin for this reference.

10. One notes the review of Caffiero by Ann Jacobson Schutte, *Sixteenth Century Journal* 37/1 (2006): 282: "Let us return to *favor fidei.* Caffiero demonstrates that although inquisitors made use of the concept, they were not responsible for inventing and publicizing it. That dubious honor belongs to Benedict XIV." This is incorrect; see, in this regard, Federico Marti, *Il "favor fidei" nella Decretalistica* (Rome, 2011); and also Marcelo Fernando Parma, *El favor fidei en el Decretum Gratiani* (Roma, 2009); both titles leave no doubt about the antiquity of the term. In the event, it is clear from Benedict XIV's own words that he saw himself as building on traditions of centuries' standing. If Benedict's letter soon became the benchmark for deciding future cases, this was not because of innovation. To the contrary, as put by C. Ruch in the *Dictionnaire de théologie Catholique* under the heading of *Baptême:* "Petite somme sur le baptême des infidèles, surtout sur celui des enfants, les lettres de Benoît XIV présentaient un enseignement traditionnel, définitif et à peu près complet. Les principes sont, à la lettre, ceux qu'a posés saint Thomas. Les conclusions sont empruntées aux décisions des papes et des conciles à l'enseignement commun des théologiens. . . . Quelques cas nouveaux sont résolus; mais les réponses données s'harmonisent avec les solutions qu'avaient reçues les problèmes précédemment étudiés. [To be sure,] l'enseignement du pape a fait loi" (but this is clearly because, as Ruch says explicitly, the texts of this pope summarized so elegantly the past).

11. *Ex litteris* is *Decretales,* Book 3, Title 33, canon 4. See *Probe te* for Bernard, and also the discussion of G. M. Riganti, from whom Benedict may have been borrowing in discussing Gregory IX. What these authorities all agreed upon over the ages was the principle that a converting spouse decided a child's religious fate. Isabelle Poutrin's full-length essay examining

in the greatest detail the history of commentary on *Ex litteris,* especially that touching the concept of *favor fidei,* awaits publication.

12. Venice 1595, Book 1, Question 9, Doubt 1; Benzoni (1542–1613) was a theologian, a canonist, and, for years, the bishop of Loreto-Recanati.

13. Domenico de S. Geminiano, Commentary in the margins of *Liber Sextus,* 5, 2, 5.

14. "Compertum est patriam potestatem neque ad jus Divinum positivum, neque ad jus naturale, neque ad jus gentium pertinere, sed juris, ut aiunt, humani Romani esse (emphasis in the original), [and the Emperor Antonius bestowed this upon the Jews]." That is, the "patria potestas," which had been debated for centuries with regard to the question of baptism, "invitis parentibus," pertains, or stems, not from divine or natural law, but from human law.

15. Giuseppe Sessa, *Tractatus,* pp. 170–72, referring also to Antonio Ricciulli, *Tractatus de iure personarum extra ecclesiae gremium existentium,* bk.2, n. 32, par. 26, who in turn refers to the canon *Ex litteris* and the comments on it by various legists.

16. For a text of *Providas* of Benedict XIV, citing *In eminenti* of Clement XIII, see http://digilander.libero.it/magistero/b14provi.htm (visited Sept. 2012). On the Freemasons, see Dudley Wright, *Roman Catholicism and Free Masonry* (Kessinger, 2003), 56. *Inscrutabile* may be consulted in English at *Papal Encyclicals Online,* http://www.papalencyclicals.net/Pius06/p6inscru.htm (visited Sept. 2012): par. 2: "We have undertaken the task of guarding and protecting the Church at a time when many plots are laid against orthodox religion, when the safe guidance of the sacred canons is rashly despised, and when confusion is spread wide by men maddened by a monstrous desire of innovation, who attack the very bases of rational nature and attempt to overthrow them."

17. On *odio* in ending a marriage, see Domenico de S. Geminiano, Commentary in the margins of *Liber Sextus,* 5, 2, 5. The pairing and reciprocity of the opposites *odium* and *favor* is neither accidental nor my invention. Gratian (c. 2 C. 28, q.2.) speaks of a spouse who leaves his mate "in hatred of the faith," and a commentator speaks of "Contempt of the Creator." On the other hand, there are the *Normae pro dissolutione matrimonii* in favorem fidei *ab auctoritate supreme pontificii* (1934), based on the so-called "Pauline exception" of 1 Corinthians 7:15. To be sure, the idea of annulments (*dissolutio*) is later than Gratian and was perceived as a distinctly papal power, as John

Noonan explains; John T. Noonan, Jr., "Indissolubility of Marriage and Natural Law," 14 *American Journal of Jurisprudence* 79 (1969): 82, 92, 93; and see the *Code of Canon Law,* Canon 1143, §1: "In virtue of the Pauline privilege, a marriage entered into by two unbaptised persons is dissolved in favor of the faith of the party who received baptism, by the very fact that a new marriage is contracted by that same party, provided the unbaptised party departs." This concept does not intrinsically touch Jews, but certainly may apply to them.

18. The same reasoning applies in counterpoising ritual murder to baptism. Ritual murder, committed *in odio fidei,* or the prevention of a child from receiving baptism, attacks the purity and united body of the *Corpus Christi.* The martyred, Eucharistic victim of ritual murder promotes *favor.*

19. The logic of inversion was stated canonically in the *Liber Sextus* of Boniface 8, canon *in fidei favorem, de haereticis* (Sext. 5, 2, 5), where the gloss by Domenico di S. Geminiano (d. 1436, a student of none other than Antonio de Butrio), speaking of allowing those otherwise prohibited to testify, says: "et hoc in favorem fidei ut melius istud crimen [of heresy] possit detegi, isti infames excommunicati et participes criminis admittuntur ad testificandum"—the words of those who have behaved wickedly, to the point that they were excommunicated or deemed notorious, those who acted, therefore, *in odio fidei,* may be used in the service of the faith's *favor.*

20. Joseph II's precedent would become the norm. Increases in state power that occurred in the early modern period went hand in hand with increasing control over marriage. For similar developments elsewhere, see Lloyd Bonfield, "Developments in European Family Law," *The History of the European Family,* vol. 1: *Family Life in Early Modern Times, 1500–1789* (New Haven, 2002), 87–113, 120–24. On this same issue from another angle, see Sarah Hanley, "Engendering the State: Family Formation and State Building in Early Modern France," *French Historical Studies* 16.1 (1989): 4–27; and Hanley, "The Jurisprudence of the Arrêts: Marital Union, Civil Society, and State Formation in France, 1550–1650," *Law and History Review* 21:1 (2003): 1–40.

21. *Discorso di sua santità Pio XII al tribunale della Sacra Romana Rota:* "D'altra parte, però, vi sono diritti e beni così peculiari e propri della giurisdizione ecclesiastica, che per la loro natura non sono né possono essere oggetto del potere giudiziario dello Stato. Palazzo Pontificio di Castel Gandolfo— Domenica, 6 ottobre 1946." http://www.vatican.va/holy_father/pius_ xii/speeches/1946/documents/hf_p-xii_spe_19461006_roman-rota_

it.html#top. This three-part text also discusses the forced conversion of Orthodox Christians by Croatian Catholics in 1941, a force the pope here denies, citing Lactantius about freedom of religious choice, paradoxically, the same text we shall see David de Pomis citing later on.

22. The classic studies on medieval political theology—I find Kantorowicz persuasive and Ullmann at times exaggerated—fit the patterns dancing in the head of Leo XIII at the end of the nineteenth century; E. H. Kantorowicz, *The King's Two Bodies* (Princeton, 1957); Walter Ullmann, *The Growth of Papal Government in the Middle Ages* (London, 1962), and "Juristic Obstacles to the Emergence of the Concept of the State in the Middle Ages," *The Church and the Law in the Earlier Middle Ages* (London, 1965). The bull *Immutabile* represents the kind of thinking dominating the curia at this time. See Appendix I for citations. The bull protests, for example, par. 27: "The Catholic religion is allowed a standing in civil society equal only, or inferior, to societies alien from it; no regard is paid to the laws of the Church, and she who, by the order and commission of Jesus Christ, has the duty of teaching all nations, finds herself forbidden to take any part in the instruction of the people."

23. See Giovanni Miccoli, "Santa Sede, questione ebraica e antisemitismo fra Otto e Novecento," in ed. Corrado Vivanti, *Gli ebrei in Italia, Annali,* vol. 2 (Turin, 1997).

24. See also Odo of Cambrai, twelfth century, who said: "He feeds us with his blood and body so that . . . we are him and he is one with us," cited in Anna Sapir Abulafia, *Christians and Jews in the Twelfth-Century Renaissance* (London, 1995), 130; and John Colet, in *John Colet's Commentary on First Corinthians,* ed. Bernard O'Kelley and Catherine Jarrott (Binghamton, 1985), 213, and its direct continuation: "Nor do they transform the nourishment into themselves, but they are themselves transformed by the nourishment, as by a stronger thing, into itself. For from this comes the conformity and unity of all."

25. Washington: "Letter to the Jews of Newport," August 18, 1790, Washington Papers, 6:284–85, cited in http://www.tourosynagogue.org/index.php/history-learning/gw-letter (visited August 28, 2013); Jefferson, "1786 Virginia Act for Establishing Religious Freedom," drafted originally by Jefferson in 1779. http://religiousfreedom.lib.virginia.edu/sacred/vaact.html (visited August 15, 2013).

26. A full citation of Madison appears in n. 57 of chapter 5.

27. On subtleties of the American experience, and of Jews and Christians, es-

pecially Protestants in the early nineteenth century, mixing and living side by side, see most recently Jonathan Sarna, "God Loves an Infant's Praise: Cultural Borrowing and Cultural Resistance in Two Nineteenth-Century American Jewish Sunday-School Texts," *Jewish History* 27 (2013): 73–89.

28. For instance, on websites like mostholyfamilymonastery.com (visited March 3, 2013).

29. https://www.google.com/search?q=holywar.org&oq=holywar.org&aqs =chrome.69i58j69i57j0j5l2.20645j0&sourceid=chrome&espvd=210&es_ sm=93&ie=UTF-8. Accessed March 3, 2013.

30. Caffiero, *Forced Baptisms*, 231–35, who does not give us the name of the lawyer who composed a petition sent by the Jewish Community and to which the pope responded (in Caffiero's judgment) sharply, citing ACDF, Sant'Officio, Stanza Storica, BB1-c. And see Ravid, "Forced Baptism," 287–92, on pressure applied by the *Casa dei catecumeni* in Venice in the early eighteenth century. These tactics were centuries old. In 1546, Paul III issued a circular addressed to all clergy, indiscriminately, to assist Philip Herrera Romanus, formerly Rabbi Salomon. Salomon and his sons had converted. The clergy were to help him locate his wife Sarra and daughter Perna, who were in Mantua, and bring them to convert; Shlomo Simonsohn, *The Apostolic See and the Jews* (Toronto, 1990), 7:2535, doc. no. 2605.

31. *Interesting Letters of Pope Clement XIV, translated from the French*, vol. 2 (London, 1781). The book was originally owned by Charles Frances Adams, grandson of John Adams and son of John Quincy Adams. Nineteenth-century Americans were interested in matters Continental; they were also familiar with *ius commune*.

32. See Mario Rosa, "La Santa Sede e gli ebrei nel Settecento," in *Gli ebrei in Italia, Annali,* vol. 2, ed. Corrado Vivanti (Turin, 1997), where he points to enabling commercial legislation, which Pius VI quickly canceled, a move that jibes with the approach in this letter. Yet Rosa also points to Jansenists who at this time took the same conversionist approach. Hence, there is a link, making sense of his actions regarding Mazaldò. See Kenneth Stow, *Catholic Thought,* chap. 11, passim, on John 10:16.

33. On the popes and the Jews in the eighteenth century, especially in Rome, see, among others, Attilio Milano, "L'impari lotta della comunità di Roma contro la Casa dei catecumeni," *Rassegna Mensile di Israel* 16 (1950): 355–68 and 408–19; Giovanni Miccoli, "Santa Sede, questione ebraica e antisemitismo fra Otto e Novecento," in *Gli ebrei in Italia, Annali,* vol. 2, ed. Corrado Vivanti (Turin, 1997); Mario Rosa, "Tra tolleranza e repressione: Roma

e gli ebrei nel '700," *Italia Judaica* 3 (Rome, 1989); Cecil Roth, "Forced Baptisms in Italy: A Contribution to the History of Jewish Persecution," *Jewish Quarterly Review,* n.s., 27.2 (1925): 105–16; Laura Luzi, "Inviti non sunt baptizandi: La dinamica delle conversioni degli ebrei," *Mediterranea: Ricerche storiche* 10 (2007): 225–70; Kenneth Stow, *Jewish Dogs: An Image and Its Interpreters* (Stanford, 2006), 158, and "The Church and the Jews" (in Italian), *Atlante del Cristianesimo,* ed. Roberto Rusconi (UTET-Torino, 2005), revised English version in Stow, *Popes, Church, and Jews in the Middle Ages* (Aldershot, Hampshire, 2007).

34. Geoffrey Symcox, *Victor Amadeus II: Absolutism in the Savoyard State, 1675–1730* (London, 1983), 190–225. On France, see the reference to Ronald Schechter on infringements on the jurisdiction of church courts.

35. Even over Jews: see JTS (Jewish Theological Seminary) microfilm 4026a, Copies of Roman Documents (erroneously catalogued as documents from Finale), page 113 (pdf; there is no consecutive pagination in the documentary collection itself), which contains for August 20, 1777, the registration by Capitoline Notaries (technically notaries of the Roman municipality, but who were overseen, if not directly controlled, by papal authorities) of a *get* (a bill of divorce) that Moise Jacobo di Nepi gave to Pazienza Piazza. These same notaries had for centuries kept specific records of the contents of dowries, including items like clothing and bedding, as is frequently stipulated in premarital agreements (*tenayyim*) drawn up by Rome's Jewish notaries in the sixteenth century; for which, see Kenneth Stow, *The Jews in Rome* (Leiden, 1995 and 1997), 2 vols., passim. I thank Federica Francesconi for alerting me to the JTS collection, which may be accessed at: http://garfield.jtsa .edu:1801/view/action/singleViewer.do?dvs=1384094435671~913&lo cale=en_US&VIEWER_URL=/view/action/singleViewer.do?&DE LIVERY_RULE_ID=10&search_terms=finale&adjacency=N&applica tion=DIGITOOL-3&frameId=1&usePid1=true&usePid2=true (visited November 12, 2013).

36. See Francesca Bregoli, *Mediterranean Enlightenment,* 64.

37. Luigi Fiorani and Domenico Rocciolo, *Chiesa romana e rivoluzione francese, 1789–1799* (Rome, 2004), 178: "I cardinali della congregazione sono concordamente d'avviso che la costituzione civile, così com è, non può essere approvata senza ricare alla chiesa un colpo mortale." On the relationship of Church and state, as well as on religion and spirituality in an Enlightenment key, see David Sorkin, *The Religious Enlightenment: Protestants, Jews, and Catholics from London to Vienna* (Princeton, 2008). On Napo-

leon, see Adriano Cavanna, "Mito e destini del *Code Napoleon* in Italia," in *Excerptiones iuris: Studies in Honor of André Gouron*, ed. Bernard Durand and Laurent Mayali (Berkeley, 2000). And on attitudes toward Jews and Jewish reactions to new directions, see Kenneth Stow, "Jews and Christians, Two Different Cultures," in *Interstizi: Culture Ebraico-Cristiane a Venezia e nei suoi domini tra basso medioevo e prima epoca moderna*, ed. Uwe Israel, Robert Juette, and Reinhold Mueller (Rome, 2010), and Stow, "Jewish Pre-emancipation: *Ius commune*, the Roman *Comunità* and marriage in the early modern Papal State," in *Festschrift for Robert Bonfil* (Jerusalem, 2011), originally in Kenneth Stow, *Jewish Life in Early Modern Rome: Challenge, Conversion, and Private Life* (Aldershot, 2007). Caffiero on pp. 43 and 45 of *Forced Baptisms* (references to the English edition will be to this title, while those to the Italian original will be to *Battesimi Forzati*) makes only glancing references to the Revolution and the Enlightenment and their relationship to renewed pressure on Jews. Whereas external events were a prime factor in eighteenth-century attitudes, those of the late nineteenth and early twentieth century were shaped by conflict *within* the Church, on which see Stow, *Jewish Dogs*, passim. For a Church under Benedict XIV unprecedentedly fearful of Jewish disruption, see *Jewish Dogs*, 158.

38. On papal reaction to post-Revolutionary legal innovations, see the bull of Pope Leo XIII (1878–1903), *Immortale dei*. Protesting the new order, where no religion is preferred and men (and women) are allowed to think as they please, the pope writes (par. 27): "They claim jurisdiction over the marriages of Catholics, even over the bond as well as the unity and the indissolubility of matrimony. They lay hands on the goods of the clergy, contending that the Church cannot possess property. Lastly, they treat the Church with such arrogance that, rejecting entirely her title to the nature and rights of a perfect society, they hold that she differs in no respect from other societies in the State, and for this reason possesses no right nor any legal power of action, save that which she holds by the concession and favor of the government. If in any State the Church retains her own agreement publicly entered into by the two powers, men forthwith begin to cry out that matters affecting the Church must be separated from those of the State." http://www.vatican.va/holy_father/leo_xiii/encyclicals/documents/hf_l-xiii_enc_01111885_immortale-dei_en.html (viewed July 18, 2013).

39. On the confessional state, see Heinz Schilling, *Early Modern European Civilization and Its Political and Cultural Dynamism* (Hanover, NH, 2008), esp. 11–32.

40. Siegfried Jacob Baumgarten supported confessionalism, but opposed automatic priority being given to Church law. Baumgarten had opponents, as seen in Sorkin, *The Religious Enlightenment*. See also Henry Strakosch, *State Absolutism and the Rule of Law* (Sydney, 1967), 192–93, citing one Professor Gross of Prague: "The citizens of the state enjoy without exception liberty and equality *in accordance with their rank* (emphasis added)." This was a code for corporatism or confessional priority, an attempt, says Strakosch, "to reconcile corporate notions of the hierarchic structure of society with the current ideas of the equality of men." Gross went on, saying that "those [Jews] whose residence in these states is not permanent, because they expect the arrival of a new king (the Messiah) and pray to God for it, are not to be regarded as true patriots and subjects; they are merely tolerated cosmopolitans and do not deserve to enjoy the same rights as patriotic citizens." His view, though, was not universally shared. Hupka of Vienna, by contrast, said: "All subjects without difference of age, rank or faith should generally enjoy equal rights."

41. The argument of Shmuel Trigano, "The French Revolution and the Jews," *Modern Judaism* 10 (1990): 171–90.

42. On incipient legal uniformity, especially as it impinged on Jews in Metz, see Jay Berkovitz, *Protocols of Justice: The Pinkas of the Metz Rabbinic Court 1771–1789* (Brill, 2014), chap. 4. On the overall problem of uniformity in law, or at least a coordinated legal system, see Michael P. Breen, "Patronage, Politics, and the 'Rule of Law' in Early Modern France," *Proceedings of the Western Society for French History* 33 (2005): 95–113.

43. On the Code, see Adriano Cavanna, "Mito e destini," and Antonio Padoa-Schioppa, "La storia del diritto italiano: una identità problematica," in *Excerptiones iuris*, ed. B. Durand and L. Mayali; R. C. Van Caenegem, *An Historical Introduction to Private Law* (Cambridge, 1988), passim; Carlo Ghisalberti, *Unità nazionale e unificazione giuridica in Italia: la codificazione del diritto nel Risorgimento* (Roma/Bari, 1982); see also Ghisalberti, "Sulla condizione giuridica degli ebrei in Italia dall'emancipazione alla persecuzione; spunti per una riconsiderazione," *Italia Judaica* 4 (Roma, 1993). Antonio Padoa-Schioppa, "A Common Law of Europe, Reflections on the decline and rebirth of a model," *Towards a New European Ius Commune*, ed. A. Gambaro and A. M. Rabello (Jerusalem, 1999), 25–26, points to how "European law today has many of the pitfalls of old *ius commune*, namely, that not only was it (*ius commune*) a system so convoluted that anything could be made to seem as contradicting the other, so overlapping as to be

beyond detangling, and so unclear as to the proper source of legislation (local, *ius commune*, or of the prince), that the system was in practice one composed of many 'laws,' which resulted in confusion, for instance, about how the judiciary was to be appointed, each court having a mass of different rules." The old *ius commune* simply had to fail, as it did in an instant (by way of the *Code civil*). "[It was a problem of] obsolescence of many legal institutes and many legal rules which no longer reflected the values of eighteenth-century society. No wonder this edifice fell virtually at a single blow. So decrepit was the structure and so swift the blow that not even the attempts made during the Restoration could breathe life into the old order." For all that, Padoa-Schioppa goes on to discover that determining whether it was its flaws or, more simply, the triplex legal system (*ius commune*, ecclesiastical law, and custom) that brought about *ius commune*'s demise will require a great deal of research. Padoa-Schioppa continues that already in the later seventeenth century, jurists like Cardinal de Luca were discussing the system's failure, as did earlier Francois Hotman and later Ludovico Muratori.

44. See Carlo Cattaneo, *Ricerche economiche sulle interdizioni imposte dalla legge civile agli Israeliti, estratto dal vol. xxiii degli Annali di Giurisprudenza pratica, compilati ed editi dall'Avvocato ZINI* (Milan, 1836), who, as far back as 1836, understood these links, especially their legal aspects, and criticized them directly. We will return to Cattaneo later on.

5. Conversion and the State

1. *Case dei catecumeni* were to be found in Bologna, Pesaro, Ferrara, Ancona, and Avignon in the Papal State, and also in Florence, Modena, Venice, Mantua, Milan, and Genoa. See Luciano Allegra, *Identità in bilico* (Turin, 1996), on events in Turin; Matteo Al Kalak and Ilaria Pavan, *Un' altra fede: Le Case dei catecumeni nei territori estensi (1583–1938)* (Florence, 2013); and Samuela Marconcini, *Tesi di perfezionamento in Storia Moderna, La storia della pia Casa dei catecumeni di Firenze (1636–1799)* (Florence, 2011).

2. On this church and on the inscriptions, with plates, see Carolyn H. Wood and Peter Iver Kaufman, *"Tacito Predicatore:* The Annunciation Chapel at the Madonna Dei Monti in Rome," *Catholic Historical Review* 90.4 (2004): 634–49, esp. 637.

3. On ambivalence toward and on the part of converts, see Kim Siebenhuener, "Conversion, Mobility, and the Roman Inquisition in Italy around 1600," *Past and Present* 200 (2008): 5–35, and Brian Pullan, "A Ship with Two Rud-

ders: Righeto Marrano and the Inquisition in Venice," *Historical Journal* 20 (1977): 25–58. On theories about accepting converts, see Kenneth Stow, "The Letter of Maestro Andrea," in *Community and Culture: Essays in Jewish Studies in Honor of the Ninetieth Anniversary of the Founding of Gratz College*, ed. Nathan M. Waldman (Philadelphia, 1987); Stow, "Neofiti and Their Families: or, Perhaps, the Good of the State," *Leo Baeck Year Book* 47, no. 1 (2002): 105–13; and Stow, "Church, Conversion, and Tradition: The Problem of Jewish Conversion in Sixteenth-Century Italy," *Dimensioni e problemi della ricerca storica* 2 (1996): 25–34.

4. The diary itself says denounced, which meant Anna had voluntarily expressed a desire to convert. However, the diary's introduction says that Sabato Coen called Anna his *sposa*. This should have led to a forty-day quarantine (from *quaranta*=forty). It did not. We do best to call the use of the term a slip. No evidence or record of Anna has emerged in any of the possible archives to confirm this detail, or deny it.

5. On this, see Kenneth Stow, "From Civil Society to the Family: Transformations in Early Modern Jewish Confraternal Structure," in *Brotherhood and Boundaries/Fraternità e barriere*, ed. Stefania Pastore, Adriano Prosperi, and Nicholas Terpstra (Pisa, 2011).

6. The origins of this myth may be Byzantine; see John M. Duffy, "The Jewish Boy Legend and the Western Twist," in *Byzantine Religious Culture*, ed. D. Sullivan et al. (Leiden/Boston, 2012), 313–22; and Pamela Patton, "The Little Jewish Boy: Afterlife of a Byzantine Legend in Thirteenth-Century Spain," in *Images and Afterlife: Essays in Honor of Annemarie Weyl Carr*, ed. Lynn Jones (Aldershot, in press); and relatedly, "Constructing the Inimical Jew in the *Cantigas de Santa María*: Theophilus' Magician in Text and Image," in *Beyond the Yellow Badge: Anti-Judaism, Anti-Semitism and European Art before 1800*, ed. Mitchell Merback (Leiden, 2008). However, one wonders whether this story is not a polemic variation of the midrash of Abraham, who was thrown into a furnace by Nimrod, to escape unharmed, proving his loyalty to God. Abraham, who in the midrash is forsaking the idolatry of his father or simply impugning that of the evil Nimrod, is also the father of Christianity according to Paul in Romans. The transference from Abraham to the converting boy seems clear. Early Christians knew midrash; Jerome, as well as Eusebius, mentions the biblical Nimrod. See the legend in Midrash Rabbah, Genesis 38:13.

7. St. John Chrysostom, *Homilies against the Jews* 1.11.1–2, trans. Wayne Meeks and Robert Wilken, in *Jews and Christians in Antioch in the First Four*

Centuries of the Common Era (Missoula, Mont., 1978); and also in the *Internet Medieval Sourcebook*, ed. Paul Halsal, www.fordham.edu/halsall/source/chrysostom-jews6.html (accessed May 13, 2005).

8. Giambattista Gherardo D'Arco and his *Della influenza del Ghetto nello Stato* (1782; reprint, Bologna, 1981). See Jonathan Karp, *The Politics of Jewish Commerce in Europe, 1638–1848* (Cambridge, 2008), and Kenneth Stow, "The Good of the Church, the Good of the State: The Popes and Jewish Money" (in Hebrew), in *Economics and Religion*, ed. Menahem Ben-Sasson (Jerusalem, 1994); revised English version, in *Christianity and Judaism: Studies in Church History*, ed. Diana Wood 29 (1992): 237–52; reprint, *Jewish Life in Early Modern Rome*. Also notable, at the time of the French Revolution, was the Abbé Sieyès, who, like Dohm (Karp, p. 134) or others, such as Fichte, and even Sessa (*Tractatus de iudaeis* [Turin, 1716]), 116–22, had all assumed that the Jews' economic identity was pernicious. Sessa wonders in chap. 37, p. 122, "Unde ex iis videretur dicendum saltem presumptione iuris Judaeos esse malos, fures, et Reipublicate Christianae perniciosos, . . . Et consequenter nullatenus puniendos esse Christianos injuria verbali afficientes judaeos?" Pointedly, he cites John Chrysostom on Jewish deviousness and criminality—the link between religious attitudes and economic ones is patent—just as he cites (on the same theme) the expulsion bull of Pius V of 1569, which also calls Jews thieves.

9. The full impact of the charge lies in Abeles being the realization of a centuries-old belief; he might also be called a Jewish Simonino of Trent (1475). See, too, Kenneth Stow, "The Cruel Jewish Father: From Miracle to Murder," in *Studies in Medieval Jewish Intellectual and Social History: Festschrift in Honor of Robert Chazan*, ed. D. Engel, L. H. Schiffman, and Elliot R. Wolfson (Leiden, 2012). For a full treatment of the Abeles episode, see Elisheva Carlebach, *The Death of Shimon Abeles: Jewish-Christian Tension in Seventeenth-Century Prague*, The Berman Lecture, Queens College (New York, 2001).

Charges of Jews murdering children are found in Duns Scotus, Commentary to the Sentences of Peter Lombard, *4* Sent. Dist. 4, q. 9, n. 2. *Opera Omnia*, 26 vols. (Paris, 1891–95), 16:487–89. See, too, Thomas Aquinas on the same passage, as well, as he is most specific in *Secunda Secundae* (the Second part of the Second part), q(*uestion*) *10, 12*, of his *Summa Theologica*. Both commentaries are noted in *Postremo mense* by Benedict XIV. Thomas is conveniently found in English translation at http://www.newadvent.org/summa/3010.htm#article1 (visited August 4, 2013).

10. As already cited, and see also Thomasso Caliò, *La leggenda dell'ebreo assassino* (Roma, 2007), 108, and more widely, "Antisemitismo e culto dei santi in età contemporanea: Il caso del beato Lorenzino da Marostica," in *Il pubblico dei santi: Forme e livelli di ricezione dei messaggi agiografici*, ed. Paolo Golinelli (Rome, 2000), 421, 427, 412, in that order.

11. The literature on Simon of Trent is enormous. The charge led to the deaths of all Jewish men and the forced baptism of their wives and children in the town of Trent. Most accessible is R. Po-chia Hsia, *Trent 1475: Stories of a Ritual Murder Trial* (New Haven, 1992).

12. Nicola Cusumano, "I papi e le accuse di omicidio rituale: Benedetto XIV e la bolla Beatus Andreas," *Dimensioni e problemi della ricerca storica* 2 (2002), 9ff.

13. Giuseppe Sessa, *Tractatus de Iudaeis*, 207, 237. Sessa, who also cites Duns Scotus, went so far as to call Abeles a martyr, speaking of his *martyrium*, killed *in odio fidei*. He also says that Abeles was killed by his grandfather, and that he, Shimon, had been baptized as a young baby when ill. Abeles was to be considered an *Innocento*, baptized in his own blood, a new version of the Jewish Boy of Bourges story, and, hence, a Christian in every theological sense at—if not before—the moment of his death. This is no small matter, for what it legitimates is the notion that an unborn fetus may already be deemed a Christian awaiting the formal act of baptism after birth, should the fetus have been offered. It also legitimates the sequestering of the mother during her pregnancy to avoid the child's death; see below on Aidan Nichols and Philippe Jobert describing contemporary twenty-first-century abortion—with no reference to Jews—in identical terms.

14. Most recently on this pope, see Gaetano Greco, *Benedetto XIV: Un canone per la Chiesa* (Salerno, 2011). On Ganganelli, see Cecil Roth, *The Ritual Murder Libel and the Jew: The Report by Cardinal Lorenzo Ganganelli (Pope Clement XIV)* (London, 1934). We look forward to Magda Teter's new approach to Ganganelli soon to be published. In the meantime, see her *Sinners on Trial: Jews and Sacrilege after the Reformation* (Cambridge, MA, 2011) for numerous cases of ritual murder in eighteenth-century Poland. See also Ippolito Menniti, *Il governo del papa nell'età moderna* (Rome, 2007), esp. 98–99.

15. See the debate about turning over to the authorities women who had fled, in Isaac Lampronti, *Pahad Yitzhaq* (Lyck, 1869), 84 of vol. 8, s.v. *'alilah*, where a woman ran from a Christian who claimed she had agreed to marry him. The rabbinic debate about returning her to the authorities from whom she

had run (the place is not identified) has to do with matters of "life or death," since conversion to Christianity, even forced, was considered a horror, whose avoidance required a person to lay down his or her life. Obviously, this was highly theoretical. Nonetheless, the dilemma is one that must have recurred on various occasions; see the variation on the case of Benvenuta. For a fuller discussion of the episode in *Pahad Yitzhaq*, see David Malkiel, "Ebraismo, tradizione e società: Isaaco Lampronti e l'identità, ebraica nella Ferrara del XVIII secolo," *Zakhor* 7 (2005): 41.

16. For the texts, see ASCER, b. 1Ud 2 inf. 2, fasc. 05. The wording is interesting: "[that she was moved to say what she did to get out of a bad match] iustificata fuit per depositionem Rabbini Hebraei qui dictam Mulierem post redditum a Domo Neophitorum praevia licentia Iudicis Ecclesiastici . . . absoluit a iuramento pro rescindendis sponsalibus cum . . . Procaccia." It would seem the rabbis just made a deposition, a statement to the effect that Benvenuta had taken an oath that freed her from the engagement; the Latin *sponsalibus* may indicate confusion about Jewish marital practice, the same kind we will see in discussing *Postremo mense*. The ecclesiastical permit would refer to the justification for Benvenuta leaving the *Casa*. Or is it only that? Another more general text from 1671 seems to suggest that even Jewish marriage—something Sessa classified as *ceremonalia* and, hence, allowed to be supervised by the Jews themselves—was somehow contingent on ecclesiastical license; a petition asked, "perchè fosse inhibito alli sposi hebrei che non potessero pratticare con le loro spose se non doppo contratti il matrimonio e mediante la licenza di Monsig. Vic.?" On Tranquillo Corcos's explanation of why Jews could make a will going beyond strict biblical rules, see ASCER, b. 1Ud 2 inf. 2, fasc. 05. The will would have been deposited with a Christian notary in the absence of Jewish ones after 1640; see Carmelo Trasselli, "Un ufficio notarile per gli Ebrei di Roma," *Archivio della R. Deputazione Romana di Storia Patria* 60 (1938): 231–44.

17. See Claudio Canonici, "Condizioni ambientali," 234–71, esp. 250–52.

18. See Stow, *Jewish Dogs*, 27–28, 31–32, 60–61.

19. On Werner, see Stow, *Jewish Dogs*, 62–63.

20. The rare exception is the girl from the late fifteenth century mentioned in the bull *Beatus Andreas* of 1755.

21. In the recent issue of *Jewish History*, 26.3–4 (2012), devoted to essays on modern ritual murder accusations, one sees a groping after a modernization, but the classic motif of ritual murder as a threat to the integrity of an entire society retains its force.

22. I thank the late Giancarlo Spizzichino, who reminded me that the bull of 1775 is a copy of an edict prepared in 1733, issued, and then reissued by Benedict XIV in 1751, as indeed its first lines say explicitly; and see Caliò, *La Leggenda*, 108. Caffiero perplexingly treats the edict of 1775 and this bull as two different texts, *Forced Baptism*, 42, 194, and 314. Though the bull deals with conversion, the essence of its regulations is the avoidance of contamination through contact. See the reference to this bull in Jeffrey Collins, *Papacy and Politics in Eighteenth-Century Rome: Pius VI and the Arts* (Cambridge, 2004), 56–57. Collins stresses Pius VI's concerns with the Englightenment's challenge to Church authority.

23. ASCER, b. 1Tg 2 inf. 1, on which see more in the final chapter.

24. This issue will soon receive more complete treatment.

25. Cited in Stow, "Was the Ghetto Cleaner?"

26. As reported in Jonathan Riley-Smith, *The First Crusade and the Idea of Crusading* (Philadelphia, 1986), 50–57, esp. 54–57.

27. The literature on the subject is vast. For a reevaluation of the progress of these attacks, see Kenneth Stow, "Conversion, Apostasy, and Apprehensiveness: Emicho of Flonheim and the Fear of Jews in the Twelfth Century," *Speculum* 76 (2001): 911–33; see importantly Eva Haverkamp, "Martyrs in Rivalry: The 1096 Jewish Martyrs and the Thebean Legion," *Jewish History* 23 (2009): 319–42.

28. On R. Amnon, see Kenneth Stow, "Medieval Jews on Christianity," in *Cristiani, ebrei, musulmani nell'Occidente medievale=Rivista di storia del cristianesimo*, ed. Roberto Rusconi, 4 (2007): 73–100, esp. 79, and the literature cited there.

29. More and more historians are writing about Jewish-Christian contacts in the Middle Ages, which Stow, *Alienated Minority* (1992), takes as a basic assumption. Nonetheless, imitation, borrowing, or inversion of behavior does not testify to *social* contacts. About these, we know little except by inference from material such as laws prohibiting proximity, whose reflection of reality is never assured. I recommend, as thought provoking, the speculative fiction of Sharan Newman, *The Devil's Door* (New York, 2004), among others, and Maggie Anton's trilogy, *Rashi's Daughters* (New York, 2007–9). Could fraternization have reached in reality the heights these novels describe? We must think twice.

30. It is my opinion that the attack on the Talmud, beginning in 1236 and culminating in one or more burnings in Paris in the 1240s, an attack, moreover, that was confined in geographical scope and chronological duration, was in

some way motivated by scholars in Paris angry about the new papal *Decre-tales* issued just two years previously. The canons of the *Decretales*, mostly of papal provenance rather than biblical origin, as Parisian scholars insisted, were truly the *nova lex* that these scholars, especially the secular clergy, the majority signers of a 1248 petition, condemned, censuring the Talmud for precisely this reason. I remain unpersuaded by the arguments of Cohen that at stake in Paris was the supposedly heretical quality of Judaism. These arguments do not consider the overall policies of especially Innocent IV, nor do they query the nature of royal participation or that of the secular clergy in the condemnations. Besides, it is one thing to accuse the Talmudic text of harboring heresies, and another to say Judaism itself was heretically flawed, a distinction both Jewish and Christian contemporaries appreciated. See Stow, *Alienated Minority*, 245–58.

31. Willis Johnson, "Before the Blood Libel: Jews in Christian Exegesis after the Massacres of 1096" (MA thesis, Cambridge University, 1994 [typescript]): *"huic assimilantur filii Israel,"* the Jews, the carnal sons of Israel (Jacob); and see Tomasso Caliò, *La leggenda dell'ebreo assassino*, 89, saying the Lammia is also a witch; the tradition of a witch killing and eating children can be seen in Benjamin Klar's edition of the *Megillat Ahimaaẓ* (Jerusalem, 1974), 24.

32. Noted in Stow, *Jewish Dogs*, 21.

33. Cited and translated into Italian by Giuseppe Marcocci, *"'. . . per capillos adductos ad pillam,' Il dibattito cinquecentesco sulla validità del battesimo for-ẓato degli ebrei in Portogallo (1496–1497),"* in *Salveẓẓa delle anime, disciplina dei corpi. Un seminario sulla storia del battesimo*, ed. Adriano Prosperi (Pisa, 2006): "E non vi pare che fu sottrarre l'autorità a Dio e andare controla giu-stizia e la dolcezza del Vangelo costringere ad essa anime ribelli e impedire la libertà della volontà? Cos'altro fu questo, se non dare l'occasione perché attraverso la finzione si profanasse la santa religione del figlio di Dio e si aprisse la porta ai perfidi ebrei perché ogni giorno ricevessero in modo in-degno i sacramenti che Cristo ha ordinato a prezzo del suo sangue e violassero i misteri e la santità della nostra fede con simulata e finta devozione? Perciò declinano le nostre cose e la prosperità di una repubblica cristiana tanto fio-rente va sempre più peggiorando. Ho sentito dire che da Costantinopoli un ebreo aveva scritto a quelli della sua nazione che abitano vicini a questi regni, che facessero i loro figli medici e sacerdoti, perché fossero signori delle anime e dei corpi dei cristiani."

34. See Stow, *Alienated Minority*, 247–51. It cannot be overemphasized that the laws of this Council, except the law of special clothing, were not, as

is constantly said, a thirteenth-century novelty. Collections of law dating from the seventh and eighth centuries leave no doubt about this; see Amnon Linder, ed., *The Jews in the Legal Sources of the Early Middle Ages* (Detroit and Jerusalem, 1997), passim. Special clothing was to aid against aborting the perennial goal of social separation. On this, Innocent III is unequivocal.

35. Issued originally by Emperor Gratian in 383, to reappear in the Theodosian Code of 438 (*C.T.* 16.7.3), this law directs Christians to shun not only pagan ritual, but also that of the Jews.

36. See Stow, "Conversion, Apostasy, and Apprehensiveness."

37. William C. Jordan, *The French Monarchy and the Jews* (Philadelphia, 1989), 214–38.

38. There were five or six moments of tension that generated canonical, legal innovation with respect to conversionary policy. They were the times of Gregory the Great and Visigothic Spain, the Crusades, the mid-thirteenth century, and the fifteenth century in Iberia, but only this last set a precedent for sixteenth-century Rome and after. See Appendix II for details.

39. On Talmud burning in the sixteenth century, see Kenneth Stow, "The Burning of the Talmud."

40. P. P. Pariseo, *Consilia* (Venice, 1570), vol. 4, cons. 2: *quinimmo volentes non statim sunt baptizandi, sed per tempus expectare debent, ne facile ad vomitum perfidiae redeant;* see also [Gratian] *de cons. dist.* 4. c.93, *iudaei et cap. ne quod absit, et* C.28, q.1. c.12, *saepe, et* C.23, q.6. c.4, *iam vero.* Pierpaolo Parisio (1473–1545) was an Italian bishop and cardinal. He was a legate to the Council of Trent, at its first session in 1542. Born at Cosenza and created cardinal in 1539, he was made bishop of Anglona e Tursi, in 1528, and bishop of Nusco in 1538. The term also appears in papal letters relating to events in Portugal, e.g., *Sempiterno Regi* of Clement VII, April 7, 1533: *coacti fuerunt;* Simonsohn, *Apostolic See,* 5:1857, doc. no. 1601. See also Giuseppe Marcocci, s.v. "Pariseo, Pietropaolo," *Dizionario Biografico degli Italiani,* vol. 81 (2014); and Marcocci, *Pietro Paolo,* in *Dizionario storico dell'Inquisizione,* A. Prosperi, with Vincenzo Lavenia and John Tedeschi, III (Pisa, 2010), 1172.

41. The Portuguese Inquisition violently disagreed. On the Spanish Inquisitor Seleya, see Alexandre Herculano, *History of the Origin and Establishment of the Inquisition in Portugal,* trans. John C. Branner (Stanford, 1926; repr. New York, 1972, with a Prolegomenon by Yosef H. Yerushalmi), 293, and the comments of Salo W. Baron, *A Social and Religious History of the Jews,* 2nd ed. (Philadelphia, 1969), 13:330, n. 55. Baron writes that Selaya "insisted

that bestowal of so great a benefit as baptism upon any recipient, however unwilling, could not be regarded as absolutely forcible (and, besides, in the event, no absolute force had been applied)." It was to him and those like him that Pariseo was replying.

For a full discussion of theological views echoing or challenging Pariseo, see Giuseppe Marcocci, ". . . *per capillos adductos.*"

42. Solomon Grayzel, "The Confessions of a Medieval Convert," *Historia Judaica* 17 (1958): 89–120.

43. The Inquisition built its case by concocting a ritual murder tale known as The Holy Child of La Guardia, in which the plotters were both Jews and "new Christians" (as those who converted after 1391 were known), members of a single family; see Yitzhak Baer, *A History of the Jews in Christian Spain,* vol. 2 : 398-423.

44. England was unique, which may explain why full emancipation occurred only in 1858; see Appendix III.

45. Poland is a special case, but it is also outside our immediate realm of interest.

46. Israel Finestein, "Anglo-Jewish Opinion during the Struggle for Emancipation (1828–1858)," *Transactions (Jewish Historical Society of England)* 20 (1959–61): 113–43.

47. On modernism and integralism, see Stow, *Jewish Dogs,* 39–44.

48. See Maria Pia Donato, "Roma in rivoluzione (1789, 1848, 1870)," in ed. L. Fiorani e A. Prosperi, *Storia d'Italia,* Annali 16, *Roma, la città del papa. Vita civile e religiosa dal giubileo di Bonifacio VIII al giubileo di papa Wojtyla* (Turin, 2000), 907–33; and Donato, "Cultura dell'antico e cultura dei Lumi a Roma nel Settecento. La politicizzazione dello scambio culturale durante il pontificato di Pio VI," *Mélanges de l'École française de Rome, Italie et Méditerranée* 104 (1992): 503–48.

49. See Paolo Prodi, *The Papal Prince: One Body and Two Souls: The Papal Monarchy in Early Modern Europe* (Cambridge, 1987); and Irene Fosi, *Papal Justice: Subjects and Courts in the Papal State, 1500–1750,* trans. Thomas V. Cohen (Washington, D.C., 2011). See on courts and Jews, Simona Feci, "The Death of a Miller"; and Feci, "Tra il tribunale e il ghetto: le magistrature, la comunità e gli individui di fronte ai reati degli ebrei romani nel seicento," *Quaderni storici* 99 (1998): 575–99.

50. See Natalia Aleksium, "Jewish Students and Christian Corpses in Interwar Poland: Playing with the Language of Libel," *Jewish History* 26.3 (2012): 327–42, showing persistence of old rhetoric into the twentieth century.

51. Strakosch, *State Absolutism and the Rule of Law,* 52, saying that to the re-

formers in the Empire, the Church seemed "to be a remnant of corporate autonomy and as such incompatible with the new order and the real obstacle on the way to reform."

52. Sorkin, *The Religious Enlightenment*, 152–63.

53. See the summary and analysis of Baumgarten in Udo Arnoli, *Pro Iudaeis: Die Gutachten der hallischen Theologen im 18. Jahrhundert ʒu Fragen der Judentoleranʒ* (Berlin, 1993), 173–85; I thank Anke Koeltsch for providing me with this text. See also on ethnographies of Jews especially by Protestants, Yaacov Deutsch, *Judaism in Christian Eyes* (New York, 2012), as well as Stephen G. Burnett, "Distorted Mirrors: Antonius Margaritha, Johann Buxtorf and Christian Ethnographies of the Jews" (1994), *Faculty Publications, Classics and Religious Studies Department*, Paper 63, University of Nebraska; published in the *Sixteenth Century Journal* 25 (1994): 275–87.

54. It is commonly said is that there is a true break between what is called the anti-Judaism of premodern times and anti-Semitism starting in the early modern period. This opinion rests on the entrance of racial doctrines or the incipience of the idea that Jews were out to destroy Christian society, on which, see, for example, the otherwise excellent essay of Gabriele Rigano in Beer and Foa, *Ebrei, minoranʒe e Risorgimento*. As I have argued variously, but most recently in *Jewish Dogs*, a better framework than a clear break is that of evolution and modification. The Jew was perceived in the past as the enemy of the *Corpus Christi*, meaning the mystical body of the Christian faithful; in modern terms, this perception was transformed into enemy of (Christian) society at every level. The modern period does witness a change of context, but it is essentially of terminology, from sacred to profane, from religious to racial, both of which are a laicization of the old in secular guise. The medieval distrust of converts also foreshadows racial teachings. This said, because of the movement from sacred to lay, the structures of anti-Semitic expression are entirely different.

55. See again the recent issue of *Jewish History* 26.3–4 (2012) on modern versions of the blood or ritual murder libel.

56. J. H. Merchant, *A review of the proposed naturalization of the Jews* (London, 1753), 66 and 67. Merchant says that in consequence of their deicide, Jews may have no government, but neither may they be "incorporated" [through "naturalization"] into a Christian state (43). "Jews, I conceive, are not entitled to naturalization for two plain reasons; the first is because they are Jews, the next because they are not Christians" (57). "I believe that every nation under heaven establishes a principle by which their faith and tem-

poral government walk hand in hand. So how can we naturalize those who oppose Christ?" See also Heinrich Stephani (1761–1850), *Ueber die absolute Einheit der Kirche und des Staates* (n.p., 1802); and see Robert Liberles, "The Jews and Their Bill: Jewish Motivations in the Controversy of 1753," *Jewish History* 2 (1987): 29–36.

G. H. Ayrer, *Tractatio iuridica de iure recipiendi Iudaeos tum generatim tum speciatim in terris Brusvico Luneburgicis* (Goettingen, 1741), cap. II, par. VII, pp. 17–18, cited in Laura Luzi, "Octo sunt permissi. Controllo dei nuclei ebraici," *Mediterranea: Ricerche storiche* 12 (2008): 95–132, and Luzi, more in depth and with other sources cited in "Dallo status civitatis alla cittadinanza. La crisi del diritto comune attraverso il mutamento dello statuto dell'ebreo," *Mediterranea: Ricerche storiche* 5 (2008): 527–66; and Wilhelm Guede, *Die rechtliche Stellung der Juden in den Schriften deutschen Juristen des 16. und 17. Jahrhunderts* (Singmaringen, 1981). Johannes Beck, in his *Tractatus de Iudaeis* of 1731, speaks of accepting Jews, but maintaining old privileges. The same applies to Pietro Regis in his *De iudeo cive,* as summarized in Vittorio Colorni, *Legge ebraica, legge locale.* Regis seems to be making the counter-case to that of people like Carlo Luti.

57. See Frederic Cople Jaher, *The Jews and the Nation: Revolution, Emancipation, State Formation, and the Liberal Paradigm in America and France* (Princeton, 2002), 142–46. Jaher is citing James Madison, *Memorial and Remonstrance Against Religious Assessments* (1785): http://religiousfreedom.lib.virginia .edu/sacred/madison_m&r_1785.html. The above statement was Madison's justification for withholding all support, especially through taxation, from any Christian denomination. The separation of church and state was to be total. The website, as in the text of Jefferson already cited, is maintained by the University of Virginia. Likewise, see Madison, responding in a holograph to Mordecai Noah in 1818: "Our laws have applied the only antidote to this vice, protecting our religious, as they do our civil rights, by putting all on an equal footing." http://www.jewishvirtuallibrary.org/jsource/ loc/madison.html (visited 25 February 2011, citing Abraham J. Karp, *From the Ends of the Earth: Judaic Treasures of the Library of Congress* [Washington, D.C.: Library of Congress, 1991]).

58. Bernard Bailyn, *The Ideological Origins of the American Revolution* (Cambridge, MA, 1992), 55–69.

59. Bailyn, *Origins,* 78, for Dickinson and Adams; note that the idea is not libertarianism, but rights balanced by governmental supervision, as Bailyn puts it in the long citation here.

60. The French reinvented—secularized, or at least laicized—the meaning of *régénération;* see again, Stow, "Equality under law," at notes 27–28, and Jay R. Berkovitz, "Acculturation and Integration in Eighteenth-Century Metz," *Jewish History* 24 (2010): 271–94.

61. Jaher, *The Jews and the Nation,* 142–46. The link between an end to legal corporatism and religious freedom is as transparent as it is explicit. Jefferson notes that the ideal, even in the United States, had yet to be fully realized, referring most likely to various state constitutions, which would be emended within decades. "A Bill for Licensing Counsel, Attorneys at Law, and Proctors, 18 June 1779 [Main Series 2:589]," *The Papers of Thomas Jefferson Digital Edition,* ed. Barbara B. Oberg and J. Jefferson Looney (Charlottesville, 2008).

62. It would be amiss not to point out that Bartolus of Sassoferrato held that the rights of all those recognized fully as *cives* in the *civitas* (the city) must be equal, whatever the source of their status as *cives,* be it birth, naturalization, or some other criterion; see Julius Kirshner, "'*Civitas Sibi Faciat Civem.*'"

63. See Alfred Iacuzzi, *John Adams, Scholar* (Ragusa, 1952), 40–55.

64. On St. Germain, see Appendix III.

65. Giuseppe Duso, *Il contratto sociale nella filosofia politica moderna,* 2nd ed. (Bologna, 1998), 9; and Aldo Mazzacane, "Diritto e giuristi nella formazione dello Stato moderno in Italia," in *Origini dello Stato,* ed. Giorgio Chittolini, Anthony Molho, and Pierangelo Schiera (Bologna, 1993), 331–49; original (briefer) version: "Law and Jurists in the Formation of the Modern State in Italy," in *Origins of the State in Italy, 1300–1600,* ed. Julius Kirshner (Chicago, 1966).

66. Once more on *régénération,* see Ronald Schechter, *Obstinate Hebrews: Representations of Jews in France, 1715–1815* (Berkeley and Los Angeles, 2003), 86; on Thiery, as well as other discussions, where Schechter argues that the idea of *régénération* did not imply full equality. He points to Thiery and Gregoire, who see the Jew as imperfect, almost by nature, and thus hesitate to award Jews complete rights, most notably, political ones and the holding of public office. The key, though, is in understanding the term's prehistory as it is presented by de Susannis. C. W. Dohm's famous stricture in his tract *Concerning the Amerlioration of the Civil Status of the Jews,* trans. H. Lederer (Cincinnati, 1957), 65–66, that Jews must wait a few generations before achieving office is also indicative of the true underlying issue. Those who wished to hold back on full rights had failed to divorce the state entirely from the notion that it is a Christian, or spiritual, entity, "the mystical body

of the republic"—as opposed to "the mystical body of the Church," the classic expression, in which the Jews could never be full members. It was originally Roman Christian Law that had blocked Jewish entry into public office, so that Jews would not rule over Christians, a principle the popes reiterated literally tens of times. It was Christian messianism that underlay arguments that Jews must return to the soil, which can be clearly seen in debates as to whether Jewish banks in Rome should be closed in 1682; see Stow, "The Good," but even more, James Harrington, *The Commonwealth of Oceana and A System of Politics*, ed. J. G. A. Pocock (Cambridge, 1992), 6, 86–90. It is imperative that those studying Revolutionary phenomena be fully acquainted with the legal past to understand the terminology and the frame of reference within which thinkers at the time were expressing themselves.

67. See Jaher's summary in *The Jews and the Nation*.

68. See Jay Berkovitz, "The French Revolution and the Jews, Assessing the Cultural Impact," *AJS Review* 20 (1995): 25–86. See the discussion of the decrees of 1806 and 1808 in particular.

69. See the classic translation into English by M. Diogene Tama, *Transactions of the Parisian Sanhedrim, or Acts of the Assembly of Israelitish Deputies of France and Italy convoked at Paris by an Imperial and Royal Decree, Dated May 30, 1806* (London, 1807), Second Question, 152–54.

70. The primacy of the state over marriage was asserted on November 9, 1791, by the Constituent Assembly. Ronald Schechter has shown in an oral presentation at the Center for Jewish History on October 6, 2013, that well before the Revolution, the Parlement of Metz was interfering in Church affairs, no doubt at royal behest, even regarding decisions by church courts to suspend priests. This was, to adopt the terminology of basketball, a full-court press.

71. In France, *ius commune* was formally disallowed after the establishment of the *Code civil* (although large segments of the former were embodied in the *Code*). When, therefore, Napoleon demanded in 1802 that Jews submit to civil marriage, he was not challenging their ancient usages as much as he was making them accept changes in marital law to which the general population had been subject since 1791, and to which Napoleon himself had given his full support, much to the ire of the Church.

Lloyd Bonfield, "Developments in European Family Law," *The History of the European Family*, vol. 1: *Family Life in Early Modern Times 1500–1789* (New Haven, 2001), 128–29, 137–42.

72. See again Berkovitz, "The French Revolution" and *Protocols of Justice,* which argues clearly that just as the Jews, in the language of the Metz rabbinic court, were accepting the need to approach and reach a rapprochement with the law of the kingdom, so royalty—for instance, in the translation of Jewish civil law under the name *Receuil des lois, coutumes et usages observés par les juifs de Metz,* completed in 1743 by the French legist Nicholas Lançon—was seeking to subsume Jewish law into that of the state, much, however, as the king was doing with the clergy, as Schechter's classification of the decrees of the Metz Parlement has shown. This development may be construed as the French parallel to the refusal in the Papal State to allow Jews to use Jewish law at all. Nor should we forget that the pre-Revolutionary French state, as absolutist as it was, was also a confessional one, and that law privileged Christians. Otherwise, there would never have been a need for the debates on Jewish citizenship of 1789–91 at the National Assembly. Moreover, even though in the north of France, the prevailing law was "customary law," *ius commune* still exercised much influence, and *ius commune* was confessionally based.

73. Despite his title, de Luca accepted employment by Jews, more than once, and he was most effective as their advocate. And see David J. Sorkin, *The Count Stanislas de Clermont-Tonnerre's "To the Jews as a nation . . ." : The Career of a Quotation* (Jerusalem, 2012).

74. Compare ASCER, b. 2Zm 10 sup. 3. This is a complex text from 1842 to the Vice Regent. The Jews say they should have control over *denuncie* made concerning matters like births (or so it seems). Here we have the other side of the coin. The Jews are saying, yes, we are citizens (*cittadini*), but there are things we want to have in our own power, in effect, to retain a measure of (Jewish) confessionalism. Yet by implication they are intimating that if the state were fully to secularize as Napoleon intended, they could accept the changes.

75. Cattaneo, *Ricerche Economiche,* to which we shall return; Schechter, *Obstinate Hebrews,* 98, attributes to Mirabeau the idea that Jews could not be expected to be virtuous considering the regime of restrictive laws under which they lived. Cattaneo takes this idea a large step further.

76. Tama, *Transactions,* 158. Schechter emphasizes the Jews' necessary submission to a body of law in which the Emperor was, in Schechter's opinion, the centerpiece, an interpretation that ignores the nature of legal structures prior to Napoleon and Napoleon's need, accordingly, to find a way to persuade, or convince, or even pressure all into accepting his *Code.* Most

legists welcomed the revolution in law, but that is not the same as popular acceptance. Oddly, Schechter never addresses the Sanhedrin's discussion of intermarriage. This discussion is the key to what was going on and the real prompt for Cerf Beer's remarks; this is not to say Jews were happy about the change, but they seem to have understood it. A final point: Schechter rests heavily on distinguishing "subjects" from citizens. However, caution is needed. The Jews make a case for themselves by arguing that they are *sudditi a paragone di tutti gli altri* [equal to all other] *cittadini,* which reveals the term's flexibility. A real difference is in distinguishing *cittadini* from *incoli* (denizens).

77. Jacques Revel, *"Juifs et citoyens: Les incertitudes de la Révolution française,"* in *From Florence to the Mediterranean and Beyond,* ed. Diogo Ramada Curto, et al. (Florence, 2009), 543–44. Revel does not mention the *Code civil* and the subsequent Jewish Assembly and Sanhedrin in 1806 and 1807, but he clearly views law as the engine of change; on the *Code* itself, see esp. Adriano Cavanna, "Mito e destini del Code Napoleon."

78. Once more, Pignatelli, *Consultationum canonicarum,* vol. 7, no. 39.

79. The *Code* was slowly adopted throughout Europe, except in England with its Common Law tradition; British Common Law is not to be confused with Roman law–based *ius commune.*

6. Under Papal Rule

1. See Kenneth Stow, *Theater of Acculturation* (Seattle, 2001), passim.

2. Anna Esposito, "Sefarditi a Roma all'inizio del '500, una nota dai testamenti," in *Studi sul mondo sefardito in memoria di Aron Leoni,* ed. Pier Cesare Ioly-Zorattini, Michele Luzzati, and Michele Zarfati (Florence, 2012).

3. The assault on Jewish law took many forms, beginning with direct limitation of its usage. The Jewish Community's ability to act as an administrative, let alone judicial, unit was also under siege (legally, *ius commune* would not recognize Jewish communities as true corporations, based on Justinianic Code 1, 9, 1). The Venetian Geronimo Barbarigo in 1618 called the Jewish threat to excommunicate those who would bypass Jewish communal organs of arbitration an attempt to erect a "state within the state"; see David Malkiel, *A Separate Republic* (Jerusalem, 2009). With greater detail, and as late as 1782, Giovanni D'Arco, writing, instructively, to support the recently issued *Tolleranzpatent* of Joseph II, bemoaned that in the "rabbini [one finds] consolidata un autorita' politica e civile, independente dall'autorita' di che

regge lo stato . . . [an authority established] sotto la denominazione modesta di arbitrimento . . . [maintained, and kept distant from appeal to the state] dalla minaccia delle scomuniche [through the threat of excommunication]." The remedy, he said, was to suppress Jewish self-governance through the "suggezione delle leggi stesse cui ubbidisce la natione in mezzo alle quale esiste," namely, by enforcing *ius commune*, which, D'Arco went on—somewhat cynically (at least as I read it)—would promote "le massime di fraternità ed ugualianza." The thinking of both D'Arco and Sessa was in line with the early modern German school of *Judenrechtswissenschaft* (whose Latin writings were known in Italy), which was saying the same: "Atque coram Christiano Judice agere et conveniri debent . . . ut iudaei legibus propriis uti prohibentur . . . legisbusque Romanis vivere compellantur." *Ius commune* was also to be decisive regarding Jewish marriage: *sed secundum jura et leges Romanas matrimonia contrahant.* Sessa directly indicated that successive charters in Turin between 1603 and 1667 moved internal Jewish arbitration in that city from obligatory (*cogerentur*) to voluntary, with appeal solely to the Jews' *Conservatore,* that is, in this case, to Sessa himself. See Giambattista Gherardo D'Arco, *Della influenza del Ghetto;* and Wilhelm Guede, *Die rechtliche Stellung der Juden.*

4. Corcos's text is in ASCER, b. 1Ud 2 inf. 2, fasc. 05. The 1686 case of Benvenuta mentioned earlier may have been the last of its kind. See the cases cited in Stow, "Jewish Pre-emancipation." Cardinal de Luca himself represented Jews in cases involving dowries, which never would have happened earlier, when Jews handled such cases internally. See also ASCER, b. 2ZD 10 sup. 2, fasc. 02, also 2Va 10 sup. 2; and ASCER, b. 1Ul 2 inf. 2, page 519, 1756. A man has a child out of wedlock and wants to divorce his wife and marry the lover-mother. He becomes violent, and the rabbis get a permit for a *scommunica,* first in June 1755 and then May 1756. The *scommunica,* strictly a decree that all agree to either testify to a violation or refrain from action, prohibits giving the *get* (the written decree of divorce); the violence was against the wife, when she refused the divorce. The rabbis are not sure that if she does agree to accept the *get* a year later, she is acting willingly, and they want to prevent "scandal." However, in the *Foro Civile del Governo,* Angelo, the husband, had already been fined, and this was after the so-called agreement, which was reached in June 1755, with an addendum in Latin by [the Vice Regent] allowing the Jews—in this specific case—to use the *scommunica.* Now, a year later, they have come back with a new complaint. What is clear from all this is that Jews cannot move without assent from the Vice

Regent or some papal official, although the authorities must allow rabbis to write a *get,* since there is no divorce in either canon law or *ius commune.*

5. For examples of protest, see the discussions of forced purchase of bad wheat and on inappropriate treatment by the papal gendarmerie, ASCER, b. 2Zl 10 sup. 03. To be sure, even much earlier, Jews had turned to civil courts in civil matters, especially monetary ones, when they thought this was to their advantage. The point is that now they were being left with no choice. See Bregoli, *Mediterranean Enlightenment,* 58–59.

6. Papal activity may have given impetus to rabbinic moral authority, especially as any residual halakhic powers Roman rabbis exercised were stripped, and the Community from the end of the sixteenth century was weakened; see Robert Bonfil, *Rabbis and Jewish Communities in Renaissance Italy* (London, 1993), 177–86, on the lack of an official rabbinate in sixteenth-century Rome, indicating, too, that rabbis never dominated as communal leaders. Recent claims to the contrary have a weak documentary basis; see Serena di Nepi, *Sopravvivere in Ghetto* (Rome, 2014). The files of Rome's Jewish notaries reveal the rabbis as strictly minor figures in litigations, participating in no more than 15 percent of them, often as only one of two arbiters, while formal *batei din* (rabbinic courts) were unexceptionally appointed and supervised by the *Fattori.*

7. This is an ongoing issue, on which see Suzanne Last Stone, "The Intervention of American Law in Jewish Divorce: A Pluralist Analysis," 34 *Israel Law Review* 170 (2000); likewise, Zvi Jonathan Kaplan, "A marital dilemma: French courts, foreign Jews and the secularization of marriage," *Journal of Jewish Studies* 64 (2013): 365–82; and see the parallels in Stow, "Jewish Pre-emancipation." See also ASCER, b. 2ZD 10 sup 2. Fasc 02, Jan. 23, 1708, where Tranquillo Corcos appears before the Vicar to restructure the terms of the 1645 will of Raphael de Rossi, who had left everything to the *Ozer Dalim,* Talmud Torah, and similar confraternities, but now, following, indicatively, the bank closures of 1682, there was less income. Corcos's arguments are taken down by a Christian notary in Italian, with some Latin cited for good measure. There were heavy challenges Corcos needed to rebut, in particular, the claims of Gioachino Stefani in his *de iurisditione iudaeorum* that all Jewish inheritance must follow biblical rules, which Corcos refutes; and see Corcos again in ASCER, b. 2VH 10 sup 2. fasc. 01. In the litigation here, the rabbis cite a "Constantin" among Christian sources, whom I have been unable to identify further.

8. See Claudio Canonici, "Condizioni ambientali," 250–52; and again Stow,

"The Good." See, too, Domenico Rocciolo, "Catecumeni e neofiti a Roma tra '500 e '800: provenienze, condizioni sociale e 'padrini' ilustri," in *Popolazione e società a Roma nel Medioevo all età contemporanea*, ed. E. Sonnino (Rome, 1998). On Gregory the Great, see the canon *iam vero, Decretum* C. 23, q. 6, c. 4, with the comment of Guido de Baysio, d. 1313, in his *Rosarium*.

9. Copies of the great bulk of the Roman Inquisition's documentation touching matters of conversion in Rome are housed in the ASCER. ASCER documentation, on which this study relies, is much broader and, hence, my preference for ASCER over the Inquisitional Archive, the ACDF. For a broad investigation into the holdings of this latter archive, see Stephan Wendehorst, "The Roman Inquisition, the Index and the Jews: Sources and Perspectives for Research," *Jewish History* 17 (2003): 55–76.

10. Luti, ASCER, b. 1Ul, 2 inf. 2, fasc. 07, is arguing why Justinian's *Novel 118* does not exclude Jews; nor does it include them under the rubric of heretics, saying: "Item in quantum ibi Text. Dicit catholicae fidei non intelligit excludere judaeas aut Judaeos sed intelligit excludere haereticos dum istud est expressum in illo Text. in Haereticis (the law by this name). [Further, the text is explicit, not to mention that] niuno ignora che non è lo stesso eretico ed ebreo. Sono tanto tra loro diversi quanto è diverso un christiano da un infedele. Eppero ella è sentenza comunemente abbracciata che sotto nome di eretico non restino mai compresi gli ebrei, come osservano Theodor. Balsain in collect. Ecclesiastic. Constit. ex cod. et novell. justinian. Graece edit. et a Joann. Ieunclav. Latine reddit apud Justell. in Bibliotec. Jur. Canonic. Tom 2, pag. Mihi 1295 col 2 in fin." See also Farinacci, *De haeres. Quest.* 178 *par* 6 n. 128.

11. Recent discussions by Marina Caffiero, *Legami Pericolosi* (Turin, 2012), and Jeremy Cohen, *Living Letters of the Law* (Berkeley and Los Angeles, 1999), esp. 157–59, 321–43, have tried to press the idea that Judaism itself could be adjudged a heresy, as well as the Jews in their essence. They have used expressions like the "insanities" of the Talmud or expressions that Jews are not *eretici proprie* to shore up their case, or the grouping of Jews along with other nonbelievers, ignoring that a reading of early medieval texts reveals that the process worked the other way around, whereby heretics are depicted as Jews; see Stow, *Alienated Minority*, esp. 31. In the event, accusations of blasphemy (insanity) and acting like heretics (*proprie*, which, in legal terms, means they do not fall into the category of heresy as it is precisely, technically, defined) do not prove the assertions. Laura Luzi's expression of the matter is clear. "Iudaei (. . .) licet non possint esse haeretici, quia non ad-

mittitur in eis separatio (αιϱεομαι), 'cum sint extra nos,' spiega il Toschi. Concordano anche il Deciani, il Farinacci e Baldo, per il quale: 'Iudaei non sunt haeretici proprie (. . .) quia Iudaei habuerunt principium veritatis.'" Laura Luzi, "'Tanquam capsari nostri': Il ruolo del giurista di diritto comune nei confronti degli ebrei," *Mediterranea: Ricerche storiche* 9 (2012): 111–42. In a word: Jews maintain the essence of the "truth," regardless of their (occasionally aberrant) behavior or thought. Centuries earlier, Nicholas Eymeric, too, had made it clear that Jews could be accused of heresy only for such acts as denying God's existence; see Kenneth Stow, "Ebrei e inquisitori," in *L'Inquisizione e gli ebrei in Italia,* ed. M. Luzzati (Bari, 1994), 6. An anonymous author, writing sometime in the later eighteenth century, argues that Jews should have confiscated books returned, because, he insists, Judaism is legitimate: ASCER, b. 2Zm 10 sup. 3, no. 324. People like this author and the legist Carlo Luti knew where to draw critical lines. This is not an academic or rhetorical distinction. As heretics truly said (*proprie*), Jews could have been deprived of everything, including their lives. No one in the hierarchy suggested that. See also Thomas Brechenmacher, *Das Ende der Doppelten Schutzherrschaft.* Päpste und Papsttum 32 (Stuttgart, 2004), 145, who makes it clear Jews are not heretics. I leave the last word, however, to Thomas Aquinas, whose distinction in the *Summa Theologica,* IIa, IIae, 10, 6, could not be clearer: "In this way, the unbelief of heretics, who confess their belief in the Gospel and resist that faith by corrupting it, is a more grievous sin than that of the Jews, who have never accepted the Gospel faith. Since, however, they accepted the figure of that faith in the Old Law, which they corrupt by their false interpretations, their unbelief is a more grievous sin than that of the heathens, because the latter have not accepted the Gospel faith in any way at all." Heathens, heretics, Jews: each distinct.

12. See Katherine Aron-Beller, "*Buon Purim:* Proselytizing, Professing Jews and the Papal Inquisition in Modena," *Jewish History* 26 (2012): 161–77; see also Kenneth Stow, "Papal Mendicants or Mendicant Popes: Continuity and Change in Papal Policies toward the Jews at the End of the Fifteenth Century," in *Friars and Jews in the Middle Ages and Renaissance,* ed. S. McMichael (Leiden, 2004), 255–73; and also Cusumano, "I papi e le accuse."

13. As reported by Scipio Caranza, who was hired by the Jews to defend Benvenuta, ASCER, b. 1Ud 2 inf. 2, fasc. 05; see also Francesco Maria Spannocchio, ASCER, b. 2Zd 10 sup. 2, fasc. 06.

14. ASCER, b. 1Ul 2 inf. 2, repeating a text of Innocent XI from October 14, 1659.

15. On Modena, see Katherine Aron-Beller, *Jews on Trial*. For Venice, see Pier Cesare Ioly-Zorratini, *Processi del S. Uffizio contro ebrei e giudaizzanti* (Florence, 1982–92), 16 volumes. It should be stressed that a great deal of the Modenese Inquisitorial records have survived, unlike elsewhere, which explains in part the number of studies on this Inquisition, on which see the literature cited by Beller. The number of Jews burned in Ancona is sometimes given as twenty-five; see Isaiah Sonne, *Mi-Pavolo ha-Revi'i 'ad Pius ha-hamishi* (Jerusalem, 1954). I have conjectured that Paul IV was reacting to the policy enunciated by Pier Paolo Pariseo and supported by Clement VII and Paul III, which viewed these "Portuguese" as forced converts, not at all as Christians.

16. Valerie Flint, *The Rise of Magic in Early Medieval Europe* (Princeton, 1991), 344–47; Guibert in J. F. Benton, *Self and Society in Medieval France* (New York, 1970), 134–37, 209–11.

17. See Stow, "Papal Mendicants."

18. Archivio di Stato, Roma, *Tribunale del Governatore, Criminali, Constituti*, vol. 38, fols. 11–13, and see Stow, *Theater of Acculturation*, 45, 155.

19. Pius V, *Hebraeorum gens, Bullarium Diplomatum et Privilegiorum Taurensis editio* (Turin, 1857–72), 7:740–42; and Stow, *Theater*, 45, with the literature cited there.

20. See Robert Bonfil, *Jewish Life in Renaissance Italy*, trans. Anthony Oldcorn (Los Angeles and Berkeley, 1994), 170–71.

21. Adriano Prosperi, *Tribunale della coscienza*, passim.

22. The bull *Illius qui* of February 19, 1543, in *Bullarium Romanum*, 6:353–58.

23. On *neofiti* associated with the *Casa*, see ASCER, b. 1Ui 2 inf. 2, fasc. 03, a text from October 27, 1766: "Chirografo della santità di nostro signore Papa Clemente XIII, con cui si costituisce Monsig. Viceregente di Roma giudice privativo di tutte le cause passive de'neofiti, e si confermano i loro privilegi." These privileges for the *Nazione dei Neofiti*, dating to 1692, are reported in this text as follows: mostly poor, the *neofiti* are exempt from minor taxes on opening barber/surgeon shops, street payments, and the like. They are also said to need support against the Jews, who constantly give them problems. If they become bankrupt, they do not have to wear the "green hat" of debtors (*capello verde*). Without these privileges, it was clear neophytes would be unable to pay taxes to support their *Università* (the confraternity of converts) and the *Chiesa dei neofiti*. They are also obligated to frequent their *Oratorio* and *Università*. The privileges are good for the *neofiti* him- or herself, *mariti*, and children in the first degree.

24. See again, Ravid, *"Cum nimis absurdum."*
25. Traditionally, historians say this legislation is a product of the Fourth Lateran Council of 1215. But see John Gilchrist, "The Perception of Jews in the Canon Law in the Period of the First Two Crusades," *Jewish History* 3.1 (1988): 9–24, which corrects this faulty impression. On *Dispar nimirum est* and the precursors of the text of *Sicut iudaeis non,* see John Gilchrist, ed., *Diversorum patrum sententiae sive Collectio in LXXIV titulos digesta* (Vatican City, 1973), no. 310.
26. On this decision, see the discussion of Ricciuli, *Tractatus de iure personarum extra ecclesias gremium.*
27. Fosi, *Papal Justice,* and Laurie Nussdorfer, *Civic Politics in the Rome of Urban VIII* (Princeton, 1992).
28. For Savoy, see Allegra, *Identità in bilico,* chap. 1.
29. For a fuller discussion of these critical issues, especially as reflected in the work of David Sorkin and recently questioned by Francesca Bregoli, with whose critique my own readings agree, see Appendix III, along with full bibliographical references.
30. See again Berkovitz, "Acculturation and Integration in Eighteenth-Century Metz," and now *Protocols of Justice: The Pinkas of the Metz Rabbinic Court, 1771–1789,* 2 vols. (Leiden, 2014). The Jewish notaries of Rome (Stow, *Theater of Acculturation,* esp. chap. 3) were being pushed into legal obsolescence already in the later sixteenth century. The problem of accommodation still pops up in matters such as the recognized modes of granting a Jewish divorce in the presence, or absence, of a civil decree; see again, Stone, "The Intervention of American Law."
31. See esp. Ricciuli, *Tractatus de iure personarum extra ecclesias gremium.*
32. The Rights of Man, 1791 (visited July 8, 2015), http://presspubs.uchicago .edu/founders/documents/amendI_religions57.html

7. Legal Obstacles

1. "Hebraeos dici in omnibus Cives, tam in odiosis et onerosis, quam etiam in favorabilibus et privilegiativis . . . exceptis iis quae concernunt forum spirituale, seu internum"; Sessa, *Tractatus,* 4.
2. For instance, in the demand of 1720 concerning bad wheat.
3. On these issues, see John Bossy, *Christianity in the West 1400–1700* (Oxford, 1985), 22–26; Sarah Hanley, "The Jurisprudence of the Arrêts"; Michael Mann, "The Autonomous Power of the State: Its Origins, Mechanisms and

Results," *Archives européennes de sociologie* 25 (1984): 185–213; James Collins, *The State in Early Modern France* (Cambridge, U.K., 1995), 77–156; and David Parker, "Sovereignty, Absolutism and the Function of the Law in Seventeenth-Century France," *Past and Present* 122 (1989): 36–74. I thank Jay Berkovitz for these references.

4. See Kenneth Stow, "Marriages Are Made in Heaven," *Renaissance Quarterly* 48 (1995): 450, citing Christiane Klapisch-Zuber, "Zacharias, Or the Ousted Father," in *Women, Family, and Ritual in Renaissance Italy*, trans. L. Cochrane (Chicago, 1985), 187–89, 194–95.

5. And sometimes even before birth. On the Franciscan Francesco Cangiamila, see Adriano Prosperi, *Dare l'Anima*, 129–49; as well as José G. Rigau-Pérez, "Surgery at the Service of Theology: Postmortem: Cesarean Sections in Puerto Rico and the Royal Cedula of 1804," *Hispanic American Historical Review* 75 (1995): 377–404; and Anne S. Blum, Tamera Marko, Alexandra Puerto, and Adam Warren, "Women, Ethnicity, and Medical Authority: Historical Perspectives on Reproductive Health in Latin America," *Latin American Studies CILAS Working Papers* (University of California, San Diego), Year 2004, Paper 21.

6. See Angelina Arrù, "Donare non è perdere: I vantaggi della reciprocità a Roma tra Settecento e Ottocento," *Quaderni Storici* 98 (1998): 361–82; Kenneth Stow, "Marriages Are Made in Heaven: Marriage and the individual in the Roman Jewish Ghetto," *Renaissance Quarterly* 48 (1995): 452–91.

7. Civil marriage was instituted in Italy only in 1865–66. There was initial confusion, with some marrying only religiously and then finding their children declared illegitimate. See Giacomo Martina, "Roma, dal 20 settembre 1870 all'11 febbraio 1929," in *Roma città del papa*, ed. Luigi Fiorani and Adriano Prosperi, 1067. For the Empire, see Strakosch, *State Absolutism*, 157.

8. See especially Philippo Pascal, *De iuribus patriae potestatis* (Cosenza, 1669), part 1, chap. 7 (pp. 96–99), who makes it clear Jews possess this right and also discusses when it passes to the paternal grandfather, the *Avus*. Note, too, the annotations, there, of one F. M. Pratis, *avvocatus*, in Naples.

9. On the question of who has the right to baptize Jewish children, see Steven W. Rowan, "Ulrich Zasius and the Baptism of Jewish Children," *Sixteenth Century Journal* 6.2 (1975): 3–25. Rowan was among the first to examine this question. See, too, the anonymous opinion of a Ferrarese lawyer trying to show that Benedict's decision, especially of 1751, rested on civil law, beyond solely the canons embodied by "favor fidei: le leggi non solo sottopongono alla potesta paterna il figlio ma anche il figlio del figlio. Per il che non fu

il solo favore della Religione quello che mosse l'istesso Illmo Pontefice in questa istessa Lettera Decretale a dichiarare che ancora all'Ava materna competta il diritto di offerire il Nipote infante, oppure impubere alla santa Cristiana Religione, ancorchè dissentano o il padre, o la madre, oppure ambidue restati nell'ebraismo"; ASCER, b. 1Ui 2 inf. 2, fasc. 07.

10. This is Caffiero's repeated argument in *Battesimi Forzati;* see again the review of Kenneth Stow of the English translation in the *Journal of Religion,* April 2013.

11. Venice 1595, Book 1, Question 9, Doubt 1; Benzoni (1542–1613) was a theologian, canonist, and for years the bishop of Loreto-Recanati. See Adriano Prosperi, "L'Inquisizione romana e gli ebrei," in *L'inquisizione e gli ebrei in Italia,* ed. M. Luzzatti, 90.

12. Understanding this chain of legal borrowings is vital to perceiving the nature of the texts being discussed here. The authors are all legal scholars and professionals, most often known as *doctores utriusque iuris,* specialists in both canon law and *ius commune.* These experts cited, agreed, and disagreed with each other, seeing themselves as participants in an ongoing debate that continued over the centuries. They were so familiar with each other that citations (found always in the body of a discussion, not in the modern footnote form) were terse, often just a name (and often abbreviated), with a vague reference to a book's title, if that, and to a page or paragraph. Laws were cited even more tersely. We are writing about a club in a manner of speaking, although the analogy should not be pushed too far. Still, it must be clear that citations of early writers were no mere formality. The citation or application in the eighteenth century of ideas first voiced in the twelfth reveals a continuity of both thought and developing legal application.

13. Panormitanus, *Quartum et Quintum Decretalium Commentaria* (Lyon, 1559), cited by Sessa, *Tractatus,* 186. In *Ex litteris,* Pope Gregory cited the seventh-century Visigothic precedent. Citations of decisions of the Toledan Councils are ubiquitous. Parents were also compelled to give converted children their inheritance portion at once. See, for instance, Prospero Farinaccio, *De haeres. Quest.* 178: "Iudaei conversi hoc gratificantur; quia compelluntur parentes ad consignandum illis legitimam portionem, licet non debeatur filio viventibus parentibus. (. . .) Statutum excludens foeminas propter masculos, licetbhabeat locum in Iudaeis. Secus est, si foeminae sunt conversae ad fidem, et masculi Iudaei. (. . .) Quod dicitur de favore filiorum conversorum ad fidem contra parentes Iudaeos idem sit dicendum ad favorem parentum conversorum contra filios Iudaeos & infideles, ut conversio habeat

privilegium, et favorem maius. (. . .) Iudaei effecti Christiani possunt re-
tinere bona sua, quae non sunt quaesita ex usuris, quaesita autem ex usuris
tenentur erogare in usus pios." See also Domenico Toschi, *Practicarum . . .* ,
cit., *Iudaei conversi habent multa privilegia, Concl.* 376. On this problem, see
Kenneth Stow, "*Neofiti* and Their Families: or, Perhaps, the Good of the
State," *Leo Baeck Year Book* 47, no. 1 (2002): 105–13.

14. *Institutionem Moralium* (Milan, 1608), part 1, lib 8, cap 25, q. 9.

15. "Ubi de communi fidei bono agitur, nulla habenda est ratio patriae potestatis, quam leges et jura Romana sanxerunt; et propterea mater fidelis, quamvis ei ius civile patriam potestatem non tribuat, jus habet ad baptismum filium offerendi; Greg IX in cap. ex litteris, de conversione infidelium [saying
that the Christian convert father has precedence] in favorem maxime fidei
christianae respondemus, patri eumdem puerum assignandum." Azor was
also taking a page from Innocent IV and Antonio de Butrio as both commented on *Ex litteris:* Pope Innocent IV, that erudite canonist, wrote that
just as the right of the father to decide his children's baptism is preferred
should the mother dissent, so, to the contrary, is the right of the mother preferred; "ratio in favorem fidei posita est"—the reasoning is in favor of religion. The mid-fourteenth-century Antonio de Butrio backed up Pope Innocent, saying: "ob favorem fidei potest quod mulier vir evaserit et ex matre
pater effectus sit"—because of *favor fidei,* the woman becomes a man, the
mother a father. More startling yet is the idea that a "parentum spiritua-
lium" may offer a child, superseding all other forms of *patria potestas,* an
idea taken from St. Antonio of Florence, which is repeated in the *Consilium*
of Pier Paolo Pariseo, who otherwise strictly opposed forced baptism.

16. Cited in Caffiero, *Battesimi,* p. 172. An example of pulling a pregnant
woman into the *Catecumeni* comes from as early as 1542; see Simonsohn,
Apostolic See, vol. 6:2319, doc. no. 2197.

17. See most recently John Christopoulos, "Abortion and the Confessional in
Counter-Reformation Italy," *Renaissance Quarterly* 65 (2012): 443–84, who
argues that it was Sixtus V, at the end of the sixteenth century, who first
condemned abortion as homicide, but whose view was shelved for decades.
For Scotus, see *In 4 Sent. D.4, q.9, Opera Omnia,* 26 vols. (Paris, 1891–95),
16:487–89, on the *innocenti;* and on Shimon Abeles, see Kenneth Stow,
"The Cruel Jewish Father." See also Nicolas Rodriguez Fermosinus, *Tractatus Secundus Criminalium* (Lyon, 1670), 41, n. 9, cited in Luzi, "Inviti non
sunt baptizandi: La dinamica delle conversioni degli ebrei," *Mediterranea:
Ricerche storiche* 4 (2007): 225–70, esp. 250, who points out Fermosino's po-

sition, derived from Scotus, that a parent who does not save a child baptis-
mally has murdered him/her. This would be a vicarious ritual murder. Such
thinking is still current.

18. Sessa, *Tractatus*, 207, 237; Fermosino, *Tractatus Secundus Criminalium*, 41, n.
9; cited in Luzi, "Inviti non sunt baptizandis," 250.

19. See Stow, *Jewish Dogs*, 60–66.

20. Prosperi, *Dare l'Anima*, 129–49; Prosperi already raised the subject in his
"L'Inquisizione romana."

21. ASCER, 1Un 01 2 inf. 2, *Ferrarien. Oblationis Puerorum ad Fidem.*

22. The practices Cangiamila advocated (1749) were put into effect in some
places almost immediately.

23. Nichols and Jobert link the idea of the innocents to all abortion, which the
following selection written as recently as 2002 describes in terms identical
to those seen for ritual murder: *Innocenti,* children baptized in blood, and
killed *in odio fidei,* even the Marianic intervention that capped the story of
the Boy of Bourges, all with the purpose of preventing salvation. This is,
regardless, I must emphasize, of whether the authors of the two selections
here, which were published together, had any awareness of the implications
of the terms they chose with respect to charges made against Jews. Nonetheless, these two selections can be read to say "all abortion is a nefarious act
of ritual murder by Jews." What is more, considering the identity of supposed victims like Werner of Oberwessel with the Eucharist and Christ, in
this description, the Jews are still guilty of the crucifixion, as though *Nostra
Aetate* of 1962, denying the Jews' guilt, had never been written.

Abortion and Martyrdom, ed. Aidan Nichols, O.P. (Herefordshire,
U.K., 2002). "The special status of aborted children as at one and the same
time personal innocents and defenseless victims has to be theologically
significant. Perhaps, unknown to the present writer, theologians here and
there are already turning their minds to the question of the soteriological
particularity of such children—the special niche they may inhabit in the
divine plan of salvation for the world. Could Catholicism, which already
venerates as blood-witnesses to revelation the Jewish babes of Bethlehem,
massacred in place of Christ, affirm of these children that they too died in
silent testimony to a truth greater than themselves—in their case, the truth
of the divine command, 'Thou shalt not kill': thou shalt not destroy innocent life? . . . In the late summer of 1999, Dom Philippe Dupont, the Abbot
of Solesmes graciously hosted a modest 'Consultation.' . . . The Consultation, chaired by the editor of this study, consisted, it may be said, of max-

imalists and minimalists: those who wished theology, and the Church, to acknowledge the largest possible number of the aborted (perhaps all) as recipients of the 'Baptism of blood', and those who considered this thesis temerarious, and were willing to consider as candidates for such recognition only a tiny minority of cases. . . . [Then, Philippe Jobert O.S.B. writes:] It is a commonplace of Catholic theology that infants, even in the womb, who are killed from *odium fidei*, 'hatred of the faith', may be regarded as having undergone a 'Baptism of blood'. [Moreover] *odium fidei* is at work not only in human intentions originated so as deliberately to express such hatred, but at the transcendent level of angelic causality ('the Dragon' of the Apocalypse). In such a context, aborted infants are brought to their deaths by the same 'rulers of this age' (I Cor. 2:8), who crucified Jesus, and constitute, indeed, icons of his 'crucified Innocence'. . . . And of all the needy, those about to be aborted—already potential members of the Church—are the weakest and most abandoned. It is through her wounded Motherhood that Mary is united in a particular mode to these children. http://www.christen dom-awake.org/pages/anichols/abortion&martyrdom1.htm (visited August 3, 2013).

24. See again Suzanne Stone, "The Intervention of American Law."

25. On the prohibition of a couple to remain married in which one partner was a convert, see de Susannis, *De Iudaeis,* part III, par. 7. For Rabbi Tam, see *Sefer Ha-yashar* (attributed to R. Tam), ed. S. Rosenthal (1898), 45, cited in Jacob Katz, "Even though a sinner, he is still of Israel" (in Hebrew), *Tarbiz* 27 (1958): 203–27 (in Hebrew).

26. In reality, as Giulio Morosini explains it, the resolution of this problem was not simple. See Benjamin Ravid, "'Contra Judaeos' in Seventeenth-Century Italy: Two Responses to the 'Discorso' of Simone Luzzatto by Melchiore Palontrotti and Giulio Morosini," *AJS Review* 7 (1982): 301–51.

27. Giulio Morosini, *Via della Fede,* part 2 (Rome, 1683). See also Cecil Roth, "The Jews of Malta," Paper read before the Jewish Historical Society of England, March 28, 1928. Roth's note 26 speaks of Letizia Nahmias, who refused to follow her husband into Christianity. http://www.jhse.org/book/export/article/14560 (visited March 29, 2013). Morosini argues the following: If one does not return the dowry, leaving the wife penniless, she "verrebbe violentata ad abbracciare la legge di Chriso contro la dispositione de' sacri canoni, Bald. Novel. diss. 21, n. 47," she would be forced into baptism, in effect, against canonical disposition, as indicated in the works of Baldus Novello. Further (page 1013), "[In the event,] the one converted should re-

fuse to lie with the unconverted, for this [lying together] would generate "contumelia del Creatore." However, here a problem is created (1006). The Jews talk of human substance, and therefore the woman needs a *get*. However, they want that *get* to be "cascer. Onde si dichiarano gli ebrei, che non possono ricever il libelo del ripudio dal convertito, che non sa conforme alla Legge Mosaica (1043)." But it is Judaizing to have to use the Hebrew name or to participate in the act at all, and he asks: since the *mumar* is considered civilly dead, is not the wife a widow, who does not need a divorce, therefore (pp. 1034–36, 1044), there should be no permission to give a *get*, "alle mogli con cerimonie ebraiche, dove non era solo il pericolo di giudaizare, ma l'istesso giudaizare era."

28. Stow, *Jewish Dogs*, 21, 23, 51.

29. See Noonan, "Indissolubility of Marriage."

30. Morosini's problems stemmed from his inability to give a *get*.

31. Caffiero, "Forced Baptisms," 230–34.

32. ASCER, b. 2Zd 10 sup. 2, loose gathers, no. 80.

33. For the view of R. Tam, see Kenneth Stow, "A Tale of Uncertainties: Converts in the Roman Ghetto," *Shelomo Simonsohn Jubilee Volume*, ed. D. Carpi et al. (Tel Aviv, 1993), 257–81. For Lampronti, see *Pahad Yitzhaq* (most recently, Jerusalem, 1962–86), s.v. *"mumar megaresh."*

34. The text in question is ASCER, b. 2Zd 10 sup. 2; other texts by Rabbi Tranquillo Corcos make it clear Jews understood *ius commune* well. See, too, the Pallarella case, also here, in which Corcos cites Thomas Aquinas using correct legal and theological abbreviations. He cites, too, a tract on marriage by de Luca, *De Matrimonium*, alongside *halakhot, specific Jewish laws*. Corcos is clearly at home in both laws.

35. ASCER, b. 2Zi 10 super. 3, no. 81. This text cites Maimonides, Joseph Karo, Bartolocci, Pignatelli, *Consultationes*, cons. 50, nos. 7.8 in tom. 5, and also cons. 79, n. 19, and tom. 6, cons. 16, n. 8, on dissolving marriages, and Matt. 5:19, and even Budé, all trying to explain that a real Jewish marriage is legally binding, just as canon law binds.

36. For a similar case in 1773, in Rome itself, see that of Dolce di Isaaco Abodram; JTS microfilm 4026a, pdf 173. For some reason, Isaaco wished to break off Dolce's engagement to Angelo da Cori. Furious, the latter goes to the *Catecumeni*. It is feared he will offer Dolce, so Isaaco takes her to Livorno, where he makes a match and the marriage is celebrated and consummated, obviating any attempt "to offer" her. The groom is Sabato di Nola, a typical Roman name. Had Isaaco brought Sabato along with him? An ear-

lier case is reported in Urbino, in Isaac Lampronti, *Pahad Yitzhaq*, s.v. *safeq qiddushin* (Lyck, 1866), 75, *volume samakh:* here, however, the girl's fiancé had become mentally unstable and promised to (or actually did) convert, and the girl, fearing that priests would come running after her, was taken in by her uncle, betrothed (*qiddushin*)—with her full consent, as the text emphasizes—and married. It should be noted, however, that the text goes on to say that the original fiancé recovered and claimed there had been a betrothal. The *halakhic* question then became to whom was she betrothed, which is the text's real interest. My deduction is that such events as here and the one in Pesaro were not totally unknown and could be used for what I believe to have been a theoretical discussion. See also David Malkiel, *"Ebraismo, tradizione e società,"* 36–38, citing columns 569–617 of Lampronti, s.v. *'ishah 'einah mitqadeshet,* where a groom threatened to convert if he was not allowed to marry his pregnant fiancé within a short time. This, to me, seems too theoretical. They are speaking, in fact, in veiled terms of the fate of both the fiancé and the child, perhaps more the child. Moreover, what may really be worrying them, apart from this preposterous dilemma (of course, everything is possible) is the fate of children of Jewish prostitutes, of which, there were a few, like Rachel Carmi and Hester, as discussed by Beller in *Jews on Trial.*

37. See again Pietro Regis, *de iudaeo cive;* Penn's 1682 "Frame of Government" is at http://www.constitution.org/bcp/frampenn.htm (visited August 8, 2013).

38. See also Iacobi Pignatelli in Salentinis sacrae Theologiae acI.V. Doctoris *Consultationum canonicarum . . . Venice 1687. Tom. 7, consult. 192,* "haec res tendit ad favorem fidei, cum nimis sit dedecens, atque absurdum redundetque in ignominiam christianae religionis, quod in officiis publicis filius liberae sujbijciatur (*sic*) filio ancillae, et maior serviat minori, an vero in favorem fidei semper praeferendi sint christiani hebraeis?" This is a reference to the parallel (to Gen. 49:10), "the elder shall serve the younger." Gen. 25:23, Romans 9:10–12.

39. Notably, in the case of the *Massari* of Livorno, it appears Jews did enjoy certain autonomies, but these were at the rulers' pleasure; see Bregoli, *Mediterranean Enlightenment.* On the theoretical issues, see again Stow, "Corporate Double Talk."

40. Emphasis added. See Groppi, "Numerare e descrivere gli ebrei del ghetto di Roma," in *Gli abitanti,* ed. Groppi. Consent as the sole motor of authority in the ghetto argues that no formal corporate association existed.

41. Justinianic Code, *Corpus iuris civilis,* ed. Paul Krueger and Theodor Mommsen (Berlin, 1888), Code, 1, 9, 8, together with C. 1, 9, 1.

42. ASCER, 2Zd 10 sup. 2.

43. See De Luca cited in Stow, "Equality under Law."

44. Again, this is the argument, with citations, in Stow, "Equality."

45. Gregory the Great, in Gratian's *Decretum, qui sincera,* D 45 (c.3). And see the interpretation of Martin de Azpilcueta, a.k.a., Navarro, *Opera Omnia* (Venice, 1601), *Consilium* 434, n. 14, tom. 3.

46. Recently on *patria potestas,* see Cesarina Casanova, "Patria potestas. Due nuovi contributi alla storia del diritto di famiglia," *Storicamente* 3 (2007), http://www.storicamente.org/04_comunicare/casanova.htm (visited May 29, 2013).

47. See comments by Philippo Marchino, *de Bello divino* 1, chap. 2, who recounts that in 1624, the protector of the *neofiti,* Cardinal Vetalli, decided "in favorem Mosis Avi de Bononia against Abramae . . . patris," and he notes a similar decision taken during the reign of Clement VIII some years earlier; Stefano Graziano in his *Disceptationes forenses,* n. 977.

48. See Pignatelli, *Tom.* 7, *consult.* 39: "Tertio, an pueri ante usum rationis qui habent affines hebraeos et christianos in aequali gradu debeantur potius hebraeis cum sint quasi in possessione, an vero christianis in favorem fidei? Item pueri qui habent plures affines hebraeos, unum tantum christianum in aequali gradu, an debeantur hebraeis? Item utrum pueri in aequali gradu debeantur potius affini qui est tutor, aut curator, an vero Christianis? Quarto an credendum sit uni dicenti puerum aliquem esse sibi affinem vel filium et ideo sub sua potestate an vero exploranda sit veritas antequam pueri capiantur? Quinto an praeferendi sint caeteris paribus viri mulieribus affines ex parte patris iis, qui sunt exparte matris, quando plures sunt, qui pueros ad se pertinere dicunt, an vero in favorem fidei semper praeferendi sint christiani hebraeis?" Pignatelli warns, as ultimately does Sessa himself, against the use of force, especially kidnappings, which he says result in hatred of Christianity and discourage conversions. Importantly, he has set out the possible categories of those eligible to make an "offering." His position is complex. The law, he says, must be observed on both sides. However, a child is always given to the Christian when there are competing *parentes* or guardians at the same relational grade. For the *Avo* to exercise control, the father must be dead. It must be proved *juridice* who has the *potestas* over the child. One witness is not sufficient. A problem is that the Jews tend to hide the child when they suspect there might be a claim. "In omnibus ergo

casibus relatis [in my third question] pueri debentur potius christianis quam hebreis favore fidei." Essentially, the only step missing in Pignatelli, despite his great caution about denunciations, is that of the parents being alive, the innovation of Graziano and Sessa. There is nothing at all arbitrary in his *consilium*. And see the text of Pignatelli that Sessa also cites, which is even more direct.

49. Discussed by Benzoni.

50. Stefanus Gratianus, *Disceptationes forenses* (Rome, 1625), decision 977: "avo paternus consentiens nepotem baptiszari praefertur contradictioni patris. Contrarium concludi Navarra, sed contra eum fuit iudicatum. . . . Appellatione parentum venit avo etiam ex propria significatione. Avia venit appellatione matris."

51. Tractatus, chap. 51: "Infertur quinto eandem rationem militare pro Avia paterna, si ad fidem conversa petit sibi assignari nepotes infantes ut baptismo donentur, eius quippe consensus favore animae et religionis praevalabit dissensui sive alterius sive etiam utriusque parentis immediati prout dictum est de Avo cum et Avia veniat appellatione matris. . . . favor fidei amplissimus est. [What is more, when we realize that the *Ava* has the same status as a mother who had converted] ex his constitui potest regula generalis quoad omnes consanguineos in lineam transversali ut in pari gradu, favore fidei preferenda sit semprer conditio fidelium, nullam habitam sexus vel numeri ratione, quam tradit ex resolutionibus Sanctae Inquisitionis, Pignatelli, tom 5, cons. 14, n. 221, idest in affinibus sive ex parte Patris sive ex parte Matris, et etiamsi Hebraeus affinus et contradicens tutor sit, aut curator, quia nihilominus Christianus praeferetur. . . . Quod vero dicendum sit in casu quo deficientibus omnibus consanguineis ascendentibus, et ius patria potestatis habentibus concurret fidelis et infidelis, sed in gradu inequali. Vel fidelis tantum affinus est, infidelis consanguineus? Censeo et hoc casu potiorem esse conditionem fidelis non obstante quasi possessione infidelis forte in gradu proximioris vel consanguinei quia illa quasi possessio non debet tanti esse momenti ut fidei favori et spirituali infantium saluto praevaleat, maxime fidelis consensu. Adde quod sicut possent infantes ex casu absoluti baptizare [even if] omnibus Judaeis etiamsi consanguineis reclamantibus . . . Nec obstat si forte aliquis ex Judaeis contradicentibus sit tutor etiam a patre constitutus." Note that the discussion of "equal grade" comes from Pignatelli. Note, too Graziano: *disceptationes,* who recounts a case in 1624 where at the behest of an *Avus,* a child was baptized even though both parents were alive.

52. Sessa, *Tractatus,* 169–73, esp. chap. 51, par. 73, reinforcing the idea of a chain

of transmission. Sessa himself cites Graziano, in whose words, with respect to the *Avo* and *Ava:* "veniunt appellation parentum ubi quod eodem modo appellatione matris venit avia (par. 28)." See also the text of Pignatelli. Sessa cites many other legists who confirm his opinion.

53. Here, the mother and father were both alive; in the Falconeria case of 1751, the mother alone was living, with the *Ava* offering, which was going to serve Clement XIII in the Serena case of 1762.

54. See here *Thomae Sanchez Cordubensis ex societate jesu de Sancto Matrimonii sacramento disputationum* (Venice, 1712), vol. VII, p. 73, and vol. X, p. 1, on Jewish divorce and problems with children of converts.

55. Sessa, *Tractatus,* 177, chap 51, nn. 131–32, says clearly we cannot baptize indiscriminately. That statement, along with others that Jews are entitled to justice, seems blurred by the statements just cited, which follow closely his warning against indiscriminate baptisms. "Adstringat obligatio illos baptizandi? Respondeo . . . dicto obligatio non adstringat . . . extra casum necessitatae extremae."

56. Ravid, "Forced Baptisms," 285, mentions two cases in Padua, 1673, and Cividale, 1646, where children were seized with their parents alive. One would like some more detail before confirming that what appears to be a novelty in the mid-eighteenth century was actually practiced in the mid-seventeenth. If it was, why the complex fighting in the eighteenth?

57. The sources, as we have noted was common, are incorporated into the text, in a mode similar to today's social science citation style.

58. *Probe te meminisse,* par. 21.

59. Gregory XIII, cited in the letter of 1747, had said outright that according to Roman Law, *patria potestas*—along with the right "to offer" a child—could be exercised by the paternal grandfather.

60. Justinian, *Novel 118,* cap. VI: "We desire that everything which We have enacted with reference to intestate successions shall be applicable to those who acknowledge the Catholic faith, for We order that the laws already promulgated by Us with reference to heretics shall continue to be valid, . . ." http://webu2.upmf-grenoble.fr/DroitRomain/Anglica/N118_Scott.htm, (visited May 5, 2013). This text also says the following. Although it does not touch the subject of this book, many readers will find it most interesting: "We prohibit all women, except mothers and grandmothers, from acting as guardians. We only permit the latter to be the guardians of their children in the order of succession, and where they, by means of written instruments, renounce the right to contract other marriages, and the benefit of

the Velleian Decree of the Senate." Hence, the Florentine cruel mother as described by Christianne Klapisch-Zuber has a solid grounding in Roman Law. Jews, I note, and have written about, seem not to have observed any such prohibition. A mother could remarry and still be the guardian.

8. The Jews' Defenders

1. Most notable of the barristers was St. Germain, who was, moreover, representative of a large group that wished to keep in check not only canon law, but also recent inroads made by the "civilians" (protagonists of *ius commune*). St. Germain argued that only with British Common Law at the helm could the realm, under royal secular and spiritual tutelage, be united for the good of the commonweal; on which see Diarmaid MacCulloch, "Henry VIII and the Reform of the Church," in *The Reign of Henry VIII: Politics, Policy and Piety,* ed. Diarmaid MacCulloch (London, 1995), 167. For Clement VII's responses to Joao III, unquestionably conditioned by Clement's contemporary struggle with Henry, see the bulls in Shlomo Simonsohn, *The Apostlic See and the Jews,* esp. no. 1653. See also G. R. Elton, *Reform and Reformation, England, 1509–1558* (Cambridge, MA, 1977), esp. 124–25, but elsewhere, too, on the statute of *praemunire;* and pp. 150–55, on earlier clashes with the Commons and lawyers especially. See, too, G. W. Bernard, *The King's Reformation: Henry VIII and the Remaking of the English Church* (New Haven, 2007), passim, and 49–50.
2. See again Greco, *Benedetto XIV.*
3. Rome, 1756, vol. 3 of four volumes of the letters of Benedict XIV, 433, par. 19. On maintaining power over minorities by means of removing political rights, see Gal Ariely, "Exploring citizenship spheres of inclusion/exclusion: rights as 'potential for power,'" *Patterns of Prejudice* 45 (2011): 241–58.
4. Ricciulo, *de personarum,* chap. 20: "Limitatur iste casus ne procedat quando simul cum aequitate scripta ad favorem Hebraei concurret rigor scriptus, qui, assisteret Christiano, tunc non essent iudaei iudicandi secundum rigorem. Unde licet de aequitate scripta vir non possit conveniri ab uxore, nisi in quantum facere potest, l. maritum ff. soluto matr., hoc tamen non procedit quando maritus est iudaeus et mulier est effecta christiana, quia tunc aequitas concurrit cum rigore scripta quae assistit Christianae, Bald. novell. de dote."
5. See *Supraccarico, de luca teatrum, Jo. Baptistae De Luca Venusini . . . Theatrum veritatis et justitiae. . . .* (19 volumes, 1669–77; 12 volumes, Cologne, 1689–

99). De Luca is speaking of risks of maritime insurance: *de crédito e debito*, 106, par 33. The *supraccarico* is the person appointed as overseer; for instance, when the owners of a shipment do not trust the captain, they appoint a *supraccarico*, whom the insurance firm would hold, in addition, responsible in case of loss, which is the subject de Luca is directly discussing here.

6. Luti would have been referring to Sessa, *Tractatus de Iudaeis*, p. 169, p. 173, "Favor fidei amplissimus est," and he cites a Card Vetalli from 1624. "[What is more, he says, from when we realize that the *Ava* is like a mother, in particular, one who had converted] ex his constitui potest regula generalis quoad omnes consanguineos in lineam transversali ut in pari gradu, favore fidei preferenda sit semper conditio fidelium, nullam habitam sexus vel numeri ratione, quam tradit ex resolutionibus Sanctae Inquisitionis, Pignatelli tom 5, cons. 14, n. 221, idest in affinibus sive ex parte Patris sive ex parte Matris, et etiamsi Hebraeus affinus et contradicens tutor sit, aut curator, quia nihilominus Christianus praeferetur." Pignatelli himself goes on even more forcefully: "Denique illud generaliter servandam eft ut in gradu favore fidei nulla habita sexus ratione potior conditio consanguineorum fidelium quam infidelium. Ita ut verbi gratia amita vel matettera chriftiana patruo aut avunculo Judeo aut alterius sectae infedeli semper praeferatur."

7. *ASCER*, b. 1Ul. 2 inf. 2, fasc. 07, "Rem enim penitus inauditam ipse etiam a se proferri cognovit Avum maternum posse baptizare nepotes etiam vivente et reluctante eorum patre. Suspende amice Lector judicium donec assertum rationibus probetur. . . . suspendimus libentissime et invictissimum argumenti genus expectamus."

8. Luti, *ASCER*, b. 1Ul 2 inf. 2, fasc. 07, argues that *patria potestas* is limited to biological parents and that ancient Roman law never intended it to be exercised by women, especially in the presence of a male; Luti is arguing the Serena case of 1762/3, where *both* parents are alive. That law, he goes on, does not allow a grandparent to enjoy *patria potestas* when a true parent, of either sex, is alive. Luti is brushing aside the arguments of Azor et al. to the contrary. His position is that they, too, were overusing *favor fidei*. He supports his argument by citing natural law, a touchy issue for the Church: "Quanto alla potesta naturale, questa pure è totalmente aliena dall'avola. Le leggi della natura gelose all'estremo della umana libertà non stabilirono in questo punto altra soggezione che per i propri genitori." He cites Grotius, de iur. bel. et pac. lib. 2, cap 5, par. 1; Puffendorf, de iur natur et gent. Vol 1, lib 6, cap 2 de potest. Patr. Henning (likely Justus Henning Boehmer).

9. Luti may be alluding to the Jews' so-called civil servitude, a term that the

common legal opinion accepted, derived as it was directly from Thomas Aquinas, *Summa Theologica* IIa IIae, 10, 12. "Ad tertium dicendum quod Iudaei sunt servi principum servitute civili, quae non excludit ordinem iuris naturalis vel divini." This term must be understood correctly, as a way of saying and understanding that Jews, unlike anyone else, were citizens linked directly to their rulers, an idea that would emerge in full flower—and be applied *to all citizens*—during the French Revolution. The term has nothing to do with "penal slavery" or even notions like "perpetual servitude" (the theological term); Sessa, *Tract. de iudaeis,* chap. 21, is most direct, saying: "[Jews not true *servi* as some say] per passionem D.N.I.Christi [which] factos esse servos Principum, *c. etsi Judaeos, de Iud.,* unde filios Iudaeorum in potestate parentum minime esse tenendum sit. [Rather Jews are subservient to princes] quae sunt civium Romanorum; Marq. III, 4, 10." "*Servi camerae nostrae,*" invented by Frederick II, is close to "civil servitude" but carries undesirable undertones, although when Aquinas said Jews "are in civil servitude to the princes," he may indeed have been thinking of Frederick's term, which, given Aquinas's clear definition, becomes, as interpreted in Stow, *Alienated Minority,* 273–77, a way of defining Jewish legal status, not a mode of "enslaving" Jews or anything close to that. Aquinas may also have been thinking of the French *Tanquam servi,* but that term always had pejorative overtones.

10. Luti is correct; see B. Z. Kedar, "Canon Law and the Burning of the Talmud," *Bulletin of Medieval Canon Law* 9 (1979): 79–82, which lists the categories of direct power the canonist Sinibaldo Fieschi (Pope Innocent IV) asserted the pope exercises over Jews; it does not include the power to force them to convert.

11. This is De Luca cited by many like Sessa. One notes that unease with what was perceived as canonical distortion did not necessarily lead to arguments as forceful as Luti's. Ravid, "Forced Baptism," 287–92, reports a priest named Celso in Venice (1708), who argues in favor of Jewish *patria potestas,* but otherwise relies on canonical interpretation to argue the need to restrain the acts of the *Casa dei catecumeni* in that city.

12. It was not a drama of subterfuge and dissimulation (*escamotages*); see Caffiero, *Battesimi Forzati* (the Italian original of *Forced Baptisms*), passim for the use of this term.

13. *ASCER,* b. 1Ul. 2 inf. 2, fasc. 07, par. 51: "At nos ne id ipsum quidem sine suprema potestate fieri potuisse contendimus." The text originates after 1761. Luti argues that the 1751 letter of Benedict XIV is limited in its ap-

plication and potential effect, lacking in "consequence," since it is contrary to *ratio iuris*. He cites the arguments of de Becchettis and a case from 1763, in which the Inquisition invalidated an offering by an *Avia*. Moreover, if the qualifications do not square with the rules of oblation of a child to a monastery, how can one rely on the argument of *favor fidei?* In short, he is calling the use of *favor fidei* weak and out of place. At par. 35, he goes on boldly, saying that since it is clear—by every possible legal standard—that it is forbidden to take the child from the refusing mother, what remains to justify the act of taking it? Nothing but *favor fidei*, which is insufficient. In n. 37, he argues that even when Benedict XIV brings up the argument of slaves, that does not work because Jews do not fall into this category, nor are they subservient to the power of a master. To say that power is taken away from a legitimate guardian based on the "suspectus" that the tutor may rear the child in Judaism is "indaudita" (par. 41). There must be some way to show that the person offering has legal *potestas*. Even cardinals have said that one cannot use *favor fidei* when it means violating natural law. Hence, the only justification for taking the child is (the invalid one of) the "potestas suprema" of the pope. Nor does the axiom work which says that it is better in a case of doubt to favor faith rather than do nothing. The whole structure [of the papal argument] offends the faith.

14. ASCER, b. 1Ul. 2 inf. 2, fasc. 07, "Rem enim penitus inauditam ipse etiam a se proferri cognovit Avum maternum posse baptizare nepotes etiam vivente et reluctante eorum patre. Suspende amice Lector judicium donec assertum rationibus probetur. . . . (suspendimus libentissime et invictissimum argumenti genus expectamus)."

15. A. Padoa-Schioppa has said that *ius commune* and its failure were already being noted in the later seventeenth century by Cardinal de Luca, and others like François Hotman and afterward by Ludovico Muratori. Why not by Luti as well?

16. See Sessa citing de Susannis on this point.

17. See on this, the Serena case, ASCER, 1Ub 2 inf. 1, fasc. 07 and 08.

18. Luti, pars. 55—60.

19. This is a stock theme in other briefs. See Thomas Aquinas in the *Summa*, IIa IIae 10.3. Also Fiorello.

20. Benjamin Elbel, *Theologiae moralis sacramentalis, per modum conferentiarum casibus practicis applicatae, & illustratae . . . Editio tertia / ab autore revisa & correcta. (Augustae Vindel;* Graecii : Sumptibus Philippi, Martini, & Joannis Veith, 1733–), vol. 3, conference 6, par. 53., cited by Carlo Luti, *Romana*

Oblationis Puerorum ad Fidem super Epistola Benedicti XIV edita Anno 1751
(handwritten copy, ASCER), paragraph 60 (the year 1751 refers to the year
of the epistle, not Luti's response).

21. Marc. Aton. Natta Astensis, *Consiliorum seu responsorum,* 2, Lyons 1566, and
    3, in Monte Regali ex officina Torrentiniana, 1566 (cons. 434, fol. 393, vol.
    2, Lyons). The context is whether a girl who is eight or nine years old can
    ask for baptism and receive it. He says she should be restored to the parents,
    because Pope Paul III said twelve is the age of consent, and it is generally
    nine and a half for a girl and ten for a boy. This is not the frequently stated
    rule of seven. He says this is not the custom of the Church and one cannot
    innovate here. But then he says: "nam si abstraherentur a iudaeis eorum filii
    ad fidem ipsis nolentibus, occiderent eos iudaei et ita homicidia commiter-
    entur." Like Sessa, Natta is no "enemy." He inserts Jews into the scheme of
    law; he is clear they enjoy *patria potestas;* and he calls arguments about real
    servitude false: "tamen ipsi utuntur falsis rationibus." The age of discretion
    for seeking baptism, note, is not related to the age of possible manumission
    from *patria potestas,* which, in the event, does not occur, if at all, at a fixed
    age.

22. On the question of close relationships between Jews and others at this time,
    see Daniel Jutte, "Interfaith Encounters between Jews and Christians in the
    Early Modern Period and Beyond: Toward a Framework," *American His-
    torical Review* 118 (2013): 378–400. The question is whether Jutte's riveting
    case is the rule or an exception under special circumstances. Francesca Tri-
    vellato's *The Familiarity of Strangers* would suggest extreme caution; also
    Bregoli, *Mediterranean Englightenment.*

23. See again Strakosch, *State Absolutism,* 50–60.

24. ASCER, b. 1Ui 02 inf. 2, fasc. 07. Carlo Trenca, seconded by Gius. Mar-
    silio Cipriano, "avvocato nella Romana curia [writing in 1783]: mi eccitò
    primieramente l'esempio di moltissimi dotti e riguardevoli teologi, cano-
    nisti, e giureconsulti, i quali non ebbero in casi simili la menoma difficoltà
    di propalare il loro sentimento in favore delli stessi ebrei; Sarebbe lo stesso
    che impugnare e sconvolgere le prime idee del giusto, e ricalcitrare contro
    la maestà delle leggi le più sagrosante . . . [it would be also] contro li dettami
    della raggione che esigge una qulache annuenza." In the event, the children
    should have been placed in the custody of the *Fattori,* which is the *prat-
    tica antichissima,* who would have had to follow the Vice Regent's orders
    precisely. This is the practice that was followed in 1751, which led to the
    letter of Pope Benedict XIV. He brings other cases . . . including that of the

children of a mother held in the *Casa* for forty days, but then released, who returned to the ghetto and received her children. Now these two children have been held in the *Casa* for fifteen days, and he wants them released. They should have been held only twelve. In decrees of the Inquisition and the popes, "li stessi denunziati, vale a dire quelli che sono si una volta dichiarati volontariamente di voler abbracciare" have been held no longer than this.

25. ASCER, b. 1UD 2 inf. 2, fasc. 05. [She was so moved because she did not want to marry Procaccia], "quae causa iustificata fuit per Depositionem Rabbini Hebraei, qui dictam mulierem post redditum a domo Neophitorum praevia licentia iudicis ecclesiastici tribunalis eminentissimi D. Cardinalis Vicarii absolvit a iuramento pro rescindendis sponsalibus cum praenominato Procaccia."

26. Nicolò Pignatelli, ASCER, b. 1Ud 2 inf. 2, fasc. 08. This is the case of Ercole Servi in 1676–78. The *sbirri* came in violently and with force and took his children, oblated by a Sabato Cathecumen. The Inquisition issues a decree in favor of Ercole (apparently restoring the children). There is a receipt from a lawyer for his honorarium of 3 sc. 40, which is paid by the *Università*, a sum that is neither large nor particularly small. See also Pignatelli in the case of Davide Nizza, ASCER, b. 1UB fasc 04 02 inf. 1.

27. *Central Archive of the Jewish People, Jerusalem* (CAJP) HM 4837A. This is the site of his argument that the fetus is part of the mother, "accessorium ad semetipsam, . . . velut pomum immaturum pendet ab arbore, et velut accessorium separate non posit a principali." (These documents are copies of materials held in ASCER, but which were read in the CAJP, Jerusalem. Regrettably, the CAJP did not list the ASCER *segnatura*, in part because at the time of the photography, the Roman Archive had yet to be properly ordered.)

28. CAJP 4837B. Found here are the following: 1. Ventura Caricioli leaves two girls and a boy and names as *tutores* Amex Ambron and Leon Livoli (no mother mentioned). 2. In 1775, Malcha Sonatore, wife of Benedetto di Castro, and the daughters Rachel, Bella Stella, and son Isacco are ordered interned. 3. An order by the Vice Regent for the *Fattori* to consign to the *Casa* Grazia Ascarelli *consorte di* Samuel Leone Ascarelli in 1775. 4. *Marinari* enter the ghetto on a Sabbath and seize a fifteen-year-old girl and there is a brawl. 5. Brief orders to the *Fattori* ordering the consignment of various persons to the *Casa*.

29. Noted in Ravid, "Forced Baptism," 292.

30. The four lawyers appear in briefs titled *Illustrissimo Domino Thesaurario Romana Mercaturae pro universitate et mercatoribus Hebraeorum contra DD. Mercatores Fundaci et fundacales urbis*, Rome, *Typis Rev Cam. apost. 1689*, printed documents found in the Rare Book Collection, Lillian Goldman Law Library, Yale Law School. The authors are di Filippo, Maximillo Scipioni, Cyriaco Lancetti, and Pellegrino Maseri. Di Filippo explains that "ditioribus Hebraeis qui olim usuaras exercebant et hodie in huiusmodi mercimonia se implicant eorum gravissima onera potissimum substineantur," while Scipioni adds that "summa pietate sunt substinendi pro bono publico . . . hac necessitate subveniendi miserabilibus hebraeis ne fame pereant." Lancetti and Maserio more or less repeat Scipioni. Di Filippo cites Card. de Luca, *de servit. disc. 70, n. 3, de Regalib. disc. 182, n. 9*, and on *Rota decis. 269, n. 3 et seq. par. 4. tom. 2. recent.* He says Jews "non debent iudicari personae odiosae sed debent in humanis actibus uti caeteri Christiani cives tractari." Further, Jews are to have what all have by nature, which is "modum vivendi seu se alendi." Jews themselves appealed to natural law, as in the case of the hat not doffed. The bull of Clement VIII is *Cum superioribus mensibus* of July 2, 1593, to be found in Moritz Stern, *Urkundliche Beitraege*, 164, n. 157.

31. Ravid, "Forced Baptisms," 300, emphasizes that Venice, too, was wary of ceding jurisdictional rights to the Church—rights the Republic had jealously guarded over for centuries—which it would have done by not returning doubtfully baptized children to their parents. That is, until the later eighteenth century when the tendency grew to give in to demands to keep children from their parents. Ravid quotes Pier Cesare Ioly-Zorattini, who argues that when a baptism had actually taken place, the *Serenissima* normally gave in, but refused to do so when no baptism had taken place following the sequestering of a child. The Republic also seems to have fixed fourteen as the age for consent. This meant that it had pulled the rug out from under the feet of much ecclesiastical pressure, which, as did Benedict XIV, set the early age of seven as the moment when a child might be deemed to have reason and could therefore legally elect to be baptized. Ravid, 297, gives an example of cession to the Church, foiled by the flight of the Coen family, whose daughter had been returned to them.

32. Carlo Luti, *Romana Oblationis Puerorum ad Fidem*, and the response of Giordani to Luti in Marina Caffiero, *Forced Baptisms*, 123. The canon of Innocent III is *c. quanto, de translatione episcopi* (X [*Decretales*]. 1, 7, 3), cited by Pier Paolo Pariseo, *Consilia*, 1570: "Et factum ab ipso reputetur factum a deo." Innocent's original text is slightly different, as is the name of the Title

(7), perhaps because Pariseo was writing before the definitive edition of the *Decretals* of 1584: "Romanus pontifex qui non puri hominis sed veri Dei vicem gerit in terris . . . [and who acts] divina potius auctoritate." Tracing the evolution of the formula between the thirteenth and sixteenth centuries, as the papacy lost power, might prove informative. The weaker the popes, the stronger the claims, something that has not gone unnoted in histories of the papacy.

33. *Consultationes,* cons. 7, n. 39 "Secundo sit saepe ut qui nunquam de baptismo cogitarant, postquam diutius in domo cathecumenorum detenti sunt, eos pudeat redire ad suos, apud quos in tota vita male audiunt, qui aliquando religionem suam deferere cogitarunt; ideo ficto animo suscipiunt baptismum et inter christianos vivunt, tanquam hebrei, exercentes malas artes, nec rato, data occasione, fugiunt in eas partes, ubi ilis publice liceat iudaizare, id quod non semel contigit."

34. Benedetto XIV, *De Baptismo,* 231–32, cited by Luzi, *"Inviti,"* at n. 143: "non essendo la prima volta (. . .), che qualche Ebreo di rango vile, innamorato d'Ebrea civile e comoda, disperato di conseguirla nell'Ebraismo, ha tentato d'averla per questa strada, cioè supponendo falsamente gli sponsali contratti." This idea appears also in *Postremo mense.*

35. In *Postremo mense,* Benedict says he consulted Selden and Buxtorf about Jewish marriage, but then finishes with the above solution. It can be seen as hair splitting, even manipulation, but it is also perfectly consistent with what one should expect of an exponent of canon law and a Catholic clergyman. The Jews' lawyers would see it differently, but, of course, *they* were the *Jews'* lawyers.

36. See again Fiorello. See also ASCER b. 1Ue 2 inf. 2, fasc. 03. Abramo Sonnino asks for his son Salomone, held since July 21, to be returned; he was denounced as saying he wanted to become a Christian. Fiorello produces the 1641 text that says denounced Jews are to be not to be taken straight to the *Domus,* but to a neutral place for examination. However, since a third neutral place was not always possible, a rescript issued by Benedict XIII to the House of Converts in 1727 said: "Tunc denunciati ad Domum Cathecumenorum duei (*sic*) et collocari in loco separato, ad hunc effectum destinato, in eoque PER DUODECIM DIES (u.c. in original) detineri possint, ut super veritate et Constantia declarationis eorum voluntatis suscipiendi baptismum explorentur . . . Solamente quelli I quali s'offrono alla Fede Christiana si ritenghino nella Casa de catecumeni per giorni quaranti prattticata fin'ora." [Examples are then adduced of those held only twelve days, who are Rachel

figli di Santoro Anau, Olimpia Pepi/Pippi (who, in fact, was held for twenty-two days), "Sara Gabai due volte e Allegrezza Carciola." The text date is 1736. For a parallel text, see ASCER, b. 1Ub 2 inf. 1, fasc. 10: "Magnum patiuntur fam(a)e et pudoris detrimentum quando semel fuerunt ducte ad domum cathecumenorum nec facile ab hebreis recipient(es) in matrimonium. Ideo . . . grave damnum quoties invite capiuntur."

37. Pignatelli, 7, 39: "apud aliquam mulierem nobilem . . . examinari . . . ipsaque nolente fidem amplecti, fuit parentibus restituta 26 Mail 1615 and 29 Octob. eiusdem anni." And see CAJP 3835D, 1713 case of Angelo who wants his wife Clara restored to him. She is pregnant, has been in the *Casa* for 40 days, and does not want to convert. The lawyer is Francesco Maria de Spannochis, who argues that the decree of 1641 speaks of a neutral place, not the *Casa*. Hence, this woman's rights were violated. Furthermore, if this practice continues, soon all Jewish women will be taken in and the Jews will hate the Catholic faith; and why assume all children are going to die?

38. Variations on this theme included the Rector of the *Casa dei catecumeni* arriving with a band of armed *neofiti*, who, when they did not find the children offered, randomly took infants (*lactanti*) hostage. This kind of action put the whole ghetto on edge. ASCER, b. 1Ud 2 inf. 2, fasc 03. When, as in 1783, the *Fattori* warned of disturbances in the ghetto following Pius VI's ruling allowing offerings from almost any source, this was no idle threat. It was a reminder of what had happened more than once in the past. And with the *Fattori* deprived of most of their powers, the message was also that this was a predicament the papal authorities themselves would have to resolve.

39. See ASCER, b. 1Ue 2 inf. 2, fasc. 07.

40. Sessa, 38, says that they can lengthen the twelve days; cf. Attilio Milano, *Il Ghetto di Roma* (Rome, 1964), 292–93.

41. ASCER, b. 1Ui 2 inf. 2, fasc. 03, Carlo Trenca, seconded by Giuseppe Marsilio Cipriano, produces a decree of the Inquisition from 1641 that two witnesses are necessary before taking a person to the *domus*, and that their probity as witnesses must, moreover, be demonstrated. The person denounced is to be examined outside the *Domus*. Benedict XIII approved this arrangement in 1727. The Vice Regent is supposed to examine the person to ensure the denunciation's propriety.

42. See ASCER, b. 1Ql 1 inf. 5, a printed memorial of 1697 by Tranquillo Corcos saying (19), "Il detto neofito non ha altra intentione (*sic*) che di caluniar questa natione [the Jews]."

43. One wonders whether Benedict XIV's so-called expert from Ancona men-

tioned in *Postremo mense* was the converted preacher Anna meets in the *Casa*; see the diary. Or it might have been Giulio Morosini; or the "expert" was somebody who had read Morosini on Jewish marriage. In chap. 60, p. 985, of his *Via della fede*, speaking of *sposalitio* (his word), Morosini uses *Irusin* rather than the correct *kiddushin* for what takes place under the *baldachino-huppah*. He should properly have referred to the "birkat 'erusin: meqadesh . . . al ydei huppah ve-qiddushin." He says also "chiamano la funtione dello sposalitio קידושין." This would have been enough for Benedict to confuse *erusin*, an engagement, merely promissory, with no formal *halakhic* standing, with *kiddushin*, a true and binding *verbum de presente*. Morosini then obscures matters further when he says they proceed to a "giuramento," which is the "kinyan sudar" that goes along with the signing of the "patto dotale=tenayyim," which now seems confused with the *ketubah*, the actual wedding contract. Hence, *Postremo mense*'s utter confusion about what constitutes Jewish marriage.

44. Caffiero, *Forced Baptism*, 153, is unaware of Benedict's confusion, calling him an expert in Jewish matrimonial law.

45. Fiorello, ASCER, b. 1Ue 2 inf. 2, fasc. 03. There is also the problem "ut fraudes et collusiones praesertim Neophitorum evitentur." Future research may one day tell the story of the *neofiti* adepts of the *Casa* themselves and what they were doing to keep the institution alive.

46. Olimpia had been in the *Casa*, not the required neutral place, for twenty-two days. No one knows, or says, who denounced her. Moreover, although there is a window looking out on the *Pescaria*, the fish market, nonetheless, it is too high for conversation. Her father thinks the problem has been compounded, since he himself was a *Fattore* at this time, and it could be a fraud against him. Then he points out: "nel tempo della sua detenzione in detta casa de cathecumeni ha patito suggestioni tali e è stata soggetta ad attioni e condotte così improprie che col Padre non essendosi stato presente, ma havendole solo udite dalla Figlia, non si vole avanzare di rappresentarle in particolare ma unicamente expone cio' in generale all'Eccellenze Vostre per che potranno con la loro autorità rincontrarne il vero." Not to mention, in closing, that the neutral house was not meant as a locale to catechize, as it has been used, but to discover whether the denunciation was true. The replication of the case of Anna seems perfect. See CAJP 3835D. The text seems to continue in CAJP 3833C.

47. ASCER, b. 2Zd 10 sup. 2, fasc. 06. *Dominicus Caesar Florellus A.C. in criminalibus Locumtenens Generalis, S. Officii Consultor, et Reorum Advocatus.*

*Consultation super dubio an et quomodo sit procedendum com infidelibus denun-
ciatis, quod velint, sed per se nequeant comparere et petere Baptismum, ex quo
praepeditur eis aditus, ne fidem Christi amplectantur.* Monaldi, 1721. This is a
very measured text that begins by speaking of no force and attempting to
expound on the decree of 1641 about neutral places. It notes that the Church
has no power over infidels, since Paul in 1 Cor. 5 said what do we have to
do with those? "quod mihi de eis; de foris sunt. Nam eos Deus iudicabit."
There is also the problem "ut fraudes et collusiones praesertim Neophitorum evitentur." The problem is *neofiti,* whom Fiorello does not trust; and he
tells of women converting out of despair, fearing to go back to the ghetto.
He notes Gregory the Great's teaching that a *rusticus* may be forced to convert by placing heavy financial burdens on him. Nonetheless, Fiorello asks,
what is the legitimate level of force?, a question he answers based on Innocent III's bull (and then canon) *maiores.* Among other things, he adds, Jews
are *sui iuris* and rules applying elsewhere do not apply to them. He derives
his conclusions mostly from Pignatelli, *cons.* 39, who is most circumspect.
Fiorelli's text is from 1721 (date of printing, but composed shortly before,
after Sept. 1720). He says that in denunciations, one witness is insufficient,
which goes back to the Moreno defense by Spannochio. The recipe is to take
them to a third place, and keep them for a full day, till their anger at being
taken subsides, and then facillimum est quod post paucas horas, si quae concitatio in eius animo facta fuit per passam capturam, statim pacatus quiescat, et lux consultricis potentiae in eo reviviscat. Demum explorata dicto
tempore habili voluntate denunciatorum et comperta eorum obstinatione,
illos dimitterem, quae iniusta eo casu esset ulterior detentio. Shortly after,
Fiorello takes up a case in Florence of Angelo Piazza, with the mother a
joint *tutrice, insolidum* with others, even after a second marriage (and he
offers opinions that a second marriage does not cancel *tutela*). The father's
brother wants to oblate her child. Fiorello says no. This is against the rules
of force (as Thomas on the canon *qui sincera,* D. 45, c. 3, even the Fourth
Toledan, and one could argue against Pignatelli and Navarro [Azpulqueta],
even Graziano). He cites a case of 1702 where, again, an uncle is not allowed to offer under similar circumstances.

48. ASCER, b. 2Zd 10 sup. 2: "[Who could predict that following marriage
    they might not one day convert, or, worse, that arbitrarily they would be
    returned to the House of Converts, especially if they were mothers or
    carrying a child?] Quod certo certius admitti debet in subiecta materia in
    qua nulla praecedit ira, nullusque iustus dolor infedelis denunciati si vere

animum habuit amplectendi fidem christi. Unde facillimum est quod post paucas horas si quae concitatio in eius animo facta fuit per passam capturam statim pacatus quiescat et lux consultricis potentiae in eo reviviscat." See here Malkiel, *"Ebraismo, tradizione,"* 40, the opinion of one Shabbetai del Vecchio, who argues that these women and others are easily returned by the Church, which, perforce, waits forty days before baptism. It is hard to say from where Del Vecchio derived his ideas. Did he mean the statutory forty days before baptism that was never observed in practice? And on what basis was he thinking of return? A case from Venice is cited, but Venice, as Ravid's argument reveals, is no criterion for Rome.

49. The bull does not mention Fiorello by name, but doing so would have been unnecessary, since the principles Fiorello stresses are mentioned: a neutral place and twelve days.

50. See De Luca, *Theatrum, De iudiciis disc. XXXV,* who says that in the Papal State, the canons are the supreme law, meaning that civil law, in a conflict, must cede to the former. This is a quasi-civilian codification of the principles of the *Summa Coloniensis.* Feudal law is something special. De Luca mentions Lombardy in particular, and moves to *ius particulare, seu municipale,* which is temporal, and which, he explains, are the common laws in the various principalities and other jurisdictions. They are the primary laws in these places, and he notes especially Venice. However, "ideoque est potius ius subsidiarium juxta illam comparationem quam habemus in foro eclesiastico, sive in terris ecclesiae inter ius canonicum et istud civile quod scilicet civile attendendum est in subsidium illis casibus in quibus per canones non fuerit aliter provisum ob eorundem canonum hordinationem; ac properea istud particulare ius principatus vere et proprie in eo est commune." Further, the canons treat as subsidiary to even *ius commune* the "particular laws" of the other jurisdictions.

51. See again Kirshner, *"Sibi Faciat Civem";* Strakosch, *State Absolutism and the Rule of Law,* 192–93; Sorkin, *The Religious Enlightenment,* 152–63; and Schilling, *Early Modern European Civilization,* passim.

52. ASCER, b. 1Ul 2 inf. 2, and see also b.1UB 2 inf. 1, fasc 04. *Io. Baptista Riganti Adv. Pro Juliana Falconeria, Josepho Ercolani et litis Neophitis, Contro Perlam Vid. Rel. Salomonis Narni et litis etc. Hebreos* (Rome, 1751).

53. This argument opened the way to the claim, strongly contested, that one can privilege one guardian over another, to the extent that almost any relative would have the right to oblate a child. Sessa appealed directly to the "the good of the State": as *cives,* Jews were to enjoy the benefits but also

bear the burdens of this status; yet as *cives,* he said, they "are born [to serve] the State, then, just as the state conscripts soldiers, it may also invade Jewish parental privilege." Sessa, *Tractatus,* 172, 182, 207, 225, 237; "causam . . . bonum publicum. And see esp. *Io. Baptista Riganti Adv. Pro Juliana Falconeria:* certum est Pontificem aliosque principes supremos rite et iuste demandare posse ut infantes iudaei baptizentur quamvis parentes reluctentur eam ob rationem quia de iure ad baptismi validitaem sufficit consensus offerentium una cum materia, forma, et intentione baptizantis . . . Accedit quod in lege evangelica Christus praecepit parvulos omnes per Baptismum sibi consecrari; unde princeps qui est in Terra minister iustitiae et iudeos habet subditos potest profecto eorum infantes auferre ac Deo per baptismum consacrare, velint nolint parentes, qui sunt domini particulares, Maxime quia de iure princeps privare valet subditos iuribus temporalibus si aliud non superest medium consulendi saluti animarum . . . [the custom—*usus*— of the Church opposes this, nonetheless] contra enim urget quod usus et consuetudo coarctans potestatem competentem de iure ac etiam restringens favorem religionis simulque praepediens animarum salute ut in casu nostro in quo sine baptismo nemo summum bonum consequitur, hic, inquam, usus ita intelligi et interpretari debet ut minus quam possibile est, officiat, in tantum ut si urgens ratio suadeat aut potissima aliqua subsit causa tunc vel ab eodem usu omnino recede debet."

54. Once more on the Jewish Community's lack of corporate standing, see Stow, "Corporate Double Talk," and Kenneth Stow, "Jews in the Middle Ages," in *A Companion to the Medieval World,* ed. Carol Lansing and Edward English (Oxford, 2009), commenting on Baron's noted "Ghetto and Emancipation: Shall We Revise the Traditional View," *Menorah Journal* 14 (1938): 515–26, which may be more applicable to Poland than Western Europe. Objections to this argument usually stem from a lack of appreciating the details of *ius commune,* which is akin to trying to understand the American governmental system without attending to the Constitution. See Ricciuli, *de personarum,* chap. 45, on testaments; Ricciuli writes that nothing can be left to a Jewish *collegium* (Community), although it is permissible to individual Jews, and this is because their *universitas* is not "approved," or legitimate, not to mention worse than a sect of heretics (making a metaphor in Gratian's *Decretum, c. peiores* into hard law, and who would be followed by Riganti). "Moventur, qui collegium iudaeorum (ut ipsi dicunt) non est reprobatum ratione sectae, prout sunt collegia haereticorum et paganorum l. cognovimus, C. de haeret. Et l. prima C. de pagan. Et sacrific. eorum, sed

est reprobatum quia non est a iure approbatum, cum in reliquis vedeamus iudaeorum sectam tolerari, tum de iure canonico ut in cap. Sicut iudaei et in cap qui sincera dist. 45. Tum etiam de iure civili ut in l.spadonem par. iam autem. ff. de excuss. Tut. Et in l. circumcidere ff. ad leg. Cornel. De Sicar. Ubi autem collegium non est reprobatum ratione sectae, tunc licet non posit legari collegio, tamen potest legari singulis, quia personae singulares non sunt incapaces, d. l. cum Senatus, ff. de reb dub. Sed hoc argumentum in eius maiori propositione plusquam falsissimum est, si enim est reprobate secta paganorum utique multo magis est reprobate secta iudaeorum, quos constat esse peirores . . . Nec refert quod iura Canonica et civilia tolerant iudaeos quia ut infra dicam, ista tolerantia non facit ne dicantur reprobata, nam tolerantur in eis etiam ritus, quos constat esse impletos et consequenter quo ad usum reprobatos, contrarium proinde opinionem." On the concept of the *collegium illicitum*, see P. W. Duff, *Personality in Roman Private Law* (repr. New York, 1971), 116–18, 172, 234–35; and F. M. de Robertis, *Storia delle corporazioni e del regime associativo nel mondo Romano* (Bari, 1973), where in simple terms such a *collegium* is one without the approval of the Roman Senate, hence, one that is not allowed to convene, *convenire*, transact business as a corporate body, and whose membership might be classed as *odioso*, a term Ricciuli hints at but does not use, preferring Gratian's comparing Jews to pagans. Sessa uses *odioso* explicitly, meaning reprobate, even felonious.

55. Riganti certainly knew that reality was becoming ever more the opposite of this ideal as he witnessed the kind of reform that was taking place in Tuscany under the Habsburg duke Peter Leopold (afterward Emperor Leopold II). We must read Riganti's argument as potentially touching far more than the Jews and knowingly currying favor by promoting a worldview and status dear to the Church, but which was also slipping out of its grasp. See Francesca Bregoli, "'Two Jews Walk into a Coffeehouse.'"

56. Following Sessa, Riganti states that as *cives* (not "as Jews," suggesting servitude), Jews "are born [to serve] the State; hence, just as the state conscripts soldiers, it may also invade Jewish parental privilege." Sessa, *Tractatus*, 172, 182, 207, 225, 237; "causam . . . bonum publicum."

57. John Boswell, *The Royal Treasure* (New Haven, 1977), deals principally with Muslims, but uses this term also to apply to Jews, who were more often called *"servi regis."* See, too, the following from *El Fuero de Teruel*, ed. Max Gorosch (Stockholm, 1950), par. 568: "Mas a saber es que el judío no a part en su calonia, o sea de ferida o de omjçilio, que del sennor Rey es toda. Qual

los judíos sieruos son del sennor Rey et sienpre a la real bolsa son co[n] tados. (Of a Jew, who has no share in his compensation for injury *[caloña]*:" But it should be known that the Jew does not have any part of his *caloña*, whether for injury or death, for it is entirely the Lord King's. For the Jews are siervos [serfs or slaves] of the Lord King and always assigned to the royal treasury); translated by the late Elka Klein. The key, usually unnoted in discussing this term, is belonging (assigned) to the fisc or treasury. This is the same quality justifying legally the Jews' presence in a kingdom with respect to the Imperially coined "servi camerae nostrae." Compare Ilan Shoval, "'Servi Regis' Re-examined: On the significance of the earliest appearance of the term in Aragon, 1176," *Hispania Judaica Bulletin* 4 (2004): 22–69.

58. See Stow, "Equality," and Osvaldo Cavallar and Julius Kirshner, "Jews as Citizens in Late Medieval and Renaissance Italy: The Case of Isacco da Pisa," *Jewish History* 25.3–4 (2011): 269–318, to understand this term as applied to Jews in the thirteenth century.

59. For instance, they could not be called feudal vassals, since that would have required taking a religious oath. Nor could they occupy an integral niche in the medieval city, which identified itself as the political "body of Christ."

60. See again Kantorowicz, *The King's Two Bodies*, 164–91.

61. On the dangers of this status, see Stow, *Alienated Minority*, 277–80, as well as on the term's evolution beginning in charters from 1157 by Frederick I, who said that Jews: *ad cameram nostrum attineant*, virtually the same as in the text from 1176 in Teruel, which says *"real bolsa."*

62. For example, Guido de Baysio in the early fourteenth century, commenting on Gratian, as cited by Oldradus de Ponte, consilium n. 87 found in Norman Zacour, *Jews and Saracens in the Consilia of Oldradus de Ponte* (Toronto, 1990), 83. The contemporary theologian and canonist William of Rennes was explicit: Jewish children might be seized, since, as *servi*, Jews did not enjoy *patria potestas;* I thank Maurice Kriegel for this reference; see Wikipedia under William of Rennes for the citations.

63. See again Philippo Pascal, *De iuribus*, and the sources he cites in 1669, summarizing the argument over time. Also see Marc. Aton. Natta Astensis, *Consiliorum seu responsorum*, vol. 2, cons. 434, fol. 2.

64. See again the *Memoriale*, as mentioned in n. 39 of chapter 2.

65. Aquinas, *Summa Theologica*, IIa IIae 10, 12. *Ad tertium dicendum quod Iudaei sunt servi principum servitute civili.*

66. See once more, Ravid, "Forced Baptisms," 292, bringing the opinion of an

unnamed advocate, who seems to be copying Luti, perhaps directly, saying Jews are not slaves, but in civil servitude, and part of the civil body (as say Sessa and de Luca). The advocate is arguing the case of the three-year-old Graziosa, which he lost.

67. Rowan, "Ulrich Zasius," and also Prosperi, "L'Inquisizione romana," 90.

68. See again Kertzer, *The Kidnapping*.

69. Benedict XIV's subsequent attempt in 1751 to discover the line of descent in Jewish law seems odd. It is not a question, as Caffiero reports, of an uncle taking precedence over a wife (mother). The law is clear in Maimonides's *Mishneh Torah;* one does not, as she does, use the Bible directly to derive *halakhah*. Descent is through the sons, including, however, female heirs (sisters). Wives collect their marriage portion and dowry, often large enough to justify appointing them guardians over the entire estate. On the other hand, as lawyers like Sessa, and even de Susannis, had discussed regarding questions of Jewish inheritance, it was not clear to legists whether Jews were to observe the *halakhah* or civil law. It seemed, though, the latter. And there, a mother certainly did inherit and exercise *patria potestas*. One could try to exclude her by saying Jews were *servi*, but, as even Benedict makes clear, nobody took this argument seriously.

70. Antonio Maria de Becchettis, *Sacra Congregatione Sanctissimae Inquisitionis, Romana Tutelae pro Davide de Castro Novo et Gratia Vidua Relicta q. Iosephi de Anticulo Hebraei contra D. Ioannem Baptistam Pauli Neophitum*, Rome, 1702, in ASCER, 1Un 01 2 inf. 2, 1702: "Iudaei in locis in quibus degunt vivunt sub iure civile romanorum, illiusque privilegiis utuntur, prout et omnibus aiis privilegiis et statutis et beneficiis quibus caeteri cives potiuntur . . . sunt veri cives loci ubi existent et ubi sunt domiciliarii habent usum activum et passivum legum sive communium sive municipalium ac consuetudinum in materiis termporalibus et prophanis." But he proceeds, citing canons prohibiting forced baptism, especially *Qui sincera* from the Fourth Toledan Council of 633 (D. 45, c. 5), which is the same text discussed by Kenneth Stow, "Conversion, Apostasy, and Apprehensiveness: Emicho of Flonheim," at n. 39, and which had become the basis for making converts, even unwilling ones, remain Catholics. De Becchettis, it appears, is intentionally turning the text on its head, assigning it the role of prohibiting all force. His arguments were also cited more than once by Luti.

71. Fiorello, in *ASCER*, 1Ub 2 inf. 1, fasc. 10.

72. Antonio Ricciuli, *de iure personarum*, Lib. II, cap.14 (p. 59); on di Filippo.

Ricciuli admits Jews are *cives*, but according to his narrow understanding of the term.

73. Canonici, "Condizioni ambientali," 250–52, stresses the actions of Francesco Rovira Bonet, the author of heavy-handed polemic materials, including about Simon of Trent, but who, most importantly, was Rector of the *Casa dei catecumeni* during the enormous stretch between 1760 and 1798. Rovira Bonet's schemes remind us that not all conversionary initiatives were papal, nor should all episodes of conversionary excess be ascribed to the popes. See also Stow, "Papal Mendicants," on curial strife forceful enough to shape papal Jewry policy in the late fifteenth century.

74. *Probe te meminisse*, par. 15, and ASCER, b. 1Ui 2 inf. 2, fasc. 03; he is actually citing Luti; the lawyers ignore Thomas's actual ambivalence when one parent converts, changing the rules of the game.

75. The comments of Ricciulo, *de iure personarum*, Lib. II, cap.14 (p. 59), point out the contradiction—while at the same time limiting, if not prohibiting, *halakhic* observance—saying Jews are bound to the same laws as all other subjects, moreover, not because they are "cives romani," but because with Christ, their own law ended. Thus they are also bound to local statutes. Jews are of "the people of the city," although they are not of the people of the Church. Consequently the Prince or the City [through its authorities] is always presumed to have taken counsel to treat the Jews as citizens "[insofar as legal observance is concerned], de populo civitatis quamvis non sint de populo Ecclesiae (Baldus, Hostiensis, de Butrio, Panormitanus) Et consequenter sive Princeps, sive Civitas constitutat, semper praesumitur voluisse consulere iudaeis, in illa parte, in qua uti cives considerantur (Baldus). [The Church] tolerat iudaeos in ritibus, et ceremoniis non autem in iudicialibus"—tolerates the Jews in the rites and ceremonies (ceremonial law, like marriage, derived from the Bible) but not in judicial matters (civil, let alone criminal, law). [The question then is what happens when the Jews want to observe something that is not in] "lege Mosaica, sed introducto ex consuetudine vel ordinationibus inter eos [as in the Mantua senate] ubi quod iura omnia dicentia ius Hebraeorum esse servandum inter Hebraeos, sunt intelligenda de lege Moysi, non autem de ordinationibus rabbinarum et hanc eandem opinionem Rota probavit in causa Romana praelationi 20 nov. 1609 coram R.P.D. Ottembergo, ubi hac ratione fuit resolutum super iure inquilinatus quod ipsi vocant gazaka esse servandam ius nostrum, non autem interpraetationes rabbinorum [the Mantua Senate's decision in 1609,

that Jews could follow their own interpretation of *ius ca*ʒ*agà*, was nullified by a decision of the Roman Rota]."

76. Test oaths of a confessional nature for holding public office were nonetheless residual in many states beyond that of the popes, even in the United States (Maryland until 1828, and New Hampshire until 1877), in Canada through 1831, and in England through the 1850s.

77. See Benjamin Kaplan, *Divided by Faith: Religious Conflict and the Practice of Toleration in Early Modern Europe* (Cambridge, 2010). Kaplan notes that in the late seventeenth century, there was a Catholic program throughout northern Europe virtually to kidnap the offspring of "mixed" marriages, Catholic-Protestant unions, when the Protestant parent died. They would persuade a child to make the sign of the cross, claiming this was an expression of Catholic will. Kidnapping of Jewish children thus becomes part of a much wider politic.

9. Jewish and Christian Awareness

1. ASCER, 1Th, 2 inf. 2: "Di qui innanzi se voi siete buoni cittadini, siete pure nostri fratelli, nostri eguali: una stessa Legge giudicherà noi e voi. Nella vita Civile non il culto diverso, ma la sola virtù dintingue ciascuno." Pacifici had no way of knowing, of course, that Napoleon's first rule in Rome would end within a year of his speech, made, for that matter, in an air of giddiness. The reality, as the references to Napoleon earlier make clear, was far more complex and far less optimistic; on which, see Jay R. Berkovitz, "The French Revolution and the Jews."

2. *Consiliorum sive Responsorum D. Ioan Petri Surdi Casalensis J.C. Praeclariss. et Monti. sferrati Senatus praesidis Dignissimi, Liber Secundus Venice 1600* (Venice, 1584), vol. 2, n. 174, where Sordi is talking about a statute of Montiscalvi (Moncalvo) limiting residence, which says a "forensis cannot come and live there nisi quibusdam servatis." About this, says Sordi, there is something wrong, since it is said, "quia mundus est omnibus communis patria, Bal. c.1, par. 1 de forma fidelit . . . et servus potest ubi vult habitare dummodo solvat tributum domino . . . et non est alicui denegandum quod ab humana societate conceditur . . . proinde non etiam expellendi sunt Iudaei, ut probat Oldr. in cons. 264,1 (even though in cons. 87 Oldradus wanted to say the opposite)."

3. ASCER, b. 1Ui, 2 inf. 2.

4. On attitudes at this time in the Papal States, which sought to maintain the

old confessional matrix, see Mario Tosti, "Force of Arms, Force of Opinions: Counterrevolution in the Papal States, 1790–1799," in *Republics at War, 1776–1840: Revolutions, Conflicts, and Geopolitics in Europe and the Atlantic World,* ed. Pierre Serna, Antonino De Francesco, and Judith A. Miller (Houndsmills, 2013).

5. Luigi Luzzatti, *God in Freedom* (New York, 1930), 168, esp. 176–88.

6. Regardless of systemic renewal, the argument is that the law as practiced was still that of *ius commune*. On possible conflicts, see Vincenzo Gioberti, *Rinnovamento civile d'Italia* (Paris and Turin, 1850), esp. bk. 2, chap. 3.

7. Note the difference: Law, not persecution (a topic not at all raised), repression, or violence is the cause of Jewish actions judged undesirable. Nor has the culprit inborn or inculcated traits. These more general terms are what one finds in writers like Dohm or Gregoire, from whom Cattaneo differs in his direction of approach.

8. He may be referring to Poland (in his time dismembered).

9. Cattaneo, *Ricerche,* 135–36: "È un fenomeno curioso che il Codice civile di Francia intrapreso dai tribuni fu compiuto e promulgato a nome di un principe assoluto, senza alcuna deviazione né da' suoi prinicipi né da quelli della antica legislazione romana. Tanto il poter popolare come il poter asoluto convennero nella dissoluzione dei privilege e nell'adeguamento delle utilità. L'effetto si fu di pareggiare i membri dello Stato nel cospetto della legge e nel godimento dei diritti civili. Dov'era l'unità della fede, questa fusione riescì più agevole. Ma dov'essa non esisteva, la moltitudine preponerante riserbò l'idea dell'eguaglianza giuridica a sè stessa. Chi era fuori della comunione religiosa, si trovò fuori della comunione civile. E qui giova richiamare uno dei fatti da cui prendemmo già le mosse. L'Assemblea Costituente distrusse d'un precipitoso colpo tutte le interdizioni civili tra cristiani, ma per più di due anni esitò a sciogliere le interdizioni inflitte agli ebrei. L'unificatzione civile ed economica delle sette dissidenti colla comunione predominante è l'ultimo e più difficile trionfo dell'equità sociale; perché gli uomini cedono più docilmente i loro interessi che le loro opinioni."

10. See Tama, *Transactions of the Parisian Sanhedrim.*

11. See Groppi, *Abitanti,* for the figure of 4,036; for 3,600, see *ASR, Camerale II, Ebrei,* b.1, fols. 71–120; and for 2,997, same source, fols. 312–32.

12. ASCER, b. 1Tf, 2 inf. 1, fasc. 03, 1751. Apparently, the 1733 decrees were not fully observed, since the Jews treat the 1751 version as a novelty. The complaint went as follows. To stop Jews from selling meat to Christians—a restriction that was centuries old, but apparently now about to be applied

rigorously—would mean they could eat no meat at all. The cost would be too high to discard the parts of the cow or other animals that the laws of kosher dining prohibit (on which see Riccardo Shmuel di Segni, "L'attacco alla shechità nell'Europa di oggi," *Rassegna Mensile di Israel* 78 [2012]: 157–165, esp. 159, where he estimates that only 30 percent of meat slaughtered as kosher is ultimately designated kosher, and that without being able to sell the remaining 70 percent, mostly the hind-quarters, which are never kosher, through non-kosher outlets, the price of kosher meat, even today, would be prohibitive). Worse, and fascinating, to cancel the ability, long possessed, to have a license allowing for a Christian wet nurse spelled death for many infants: "riconoscendo il medesimo Cardinale che non vi sono nel ghetto donne capace di tal mestiere come sono le mammane cristiane, che hanno teoria e prattica" in this profession. With respect to the prohibition on Christian laundry women entering the ghetto, they wrote: it is known that "non vi sono in ghetto commodi di lavatori né siti capaci da per fisare né chi sia capace di tal esercitio, onde venendoli vietato tal permesso potrebbe apportare un'infezzione universale con qualche grandissima epedemia, lo che recarebbe non poco disordine attraversola città intiera, [and a text of Sixtus V would seem to allow this activity]." See also ASCER, b. 2Zm 10 sup. 3, petition of 1736—preceded by many similar ones over the previous twenty years, seeking the "riedeficatione d'un mondezzaro in un sito congrauo sopre il fiume, come sempre è stato in d'o ghetto."

13. See Manuela Militi, "Gli ebrei 'fuori dal Ghetto,'" and Militi, "Il costo della Repubblica 'sorella' per gli ebrei di Roma (febbraio 1798-settembre 1799)," *EuroStudium,* on-line journal, La Sapienza, Rome. April–June 2012, http://www.eurostudium.uniroma1.it/ (viewed August 7, 2014).

14. ASCER, b. 41Tf 2 inf. 1, fasc. 04, *Congrega dei Sessanta.* Entry for: 1823, sett. 13, "Pellegrino Toscano si portò a Catecumeni," whose representatives then appear and remand his wife, Flaminia, despite a protest by her *zio paterno* Lazzaro. A bit over a month later, on October 24, at 3 1/2 hours of the night (about 9:30 p.m.), *ritornò Pellegrino Toscano;* and on the 27th, "fu supplicata Monse VG il ritorno di Flaminia consorte." This indeed happens three days later, on the 30th: "La sera ad ore 3 circa è ritornata colla condizione che i deputati garantiscono per il feto che appena uscito all'aria del mondo debbesi consegnare."

15. On De Pol, see Thomasso Caliò, "Antisemitismo e culto dei santi."

16. Jewish Theological Seminary microfilm 4026a, 25 sett. 1870:

Sire: Ora che un valoroso esercito nazionale e' venuta restituire Roma nel
uso della sua libertta' ed ella salute insieme coll'Italia, . . . questi Israeliti
sentono il bisogno d'offrire alla Maesta' vostre l'omaggio della loro im-
mensa gratitudine, come Italiani, come romani, come Israeliti.

Come Italiani noi godiamo . . . il glorioso Regno della M.V. . . . a con-
seguire con Roma la sua integrita' ed una stabilita' sempre più grande.

Come Romani noi esultiamo vedendo la nostra città natale liberata
correre con effusione . . . [con il] affetto all'amplesso della città sorelle ed al
godimento . . . del vostro governo costituzionale.

Come Israeliti sottoposti finora ad una condizione eccezionalmente
dolorosa, noi entriamo anelanti di gioia nel diritto commune, e salutiamo il
giorno auspicatissimo in cui esso trionfa finalmente anche nella città che ci
diede la luce. Noi ricordiamo qui ora il nome d'israeliti per l'ultima volta
nel momento che passiamo da uno stato d'interdetto legale al tanto regime
dell'uguaglianza civili, perchè un dovere speciale ce lo impone. Ma retti dal
vostro decreto costituzionale, noi fuori di nostri templi non ci ricorderemo
d'essere (Israeliti), e non saremo che Italiani e Romani.

7 ottobre 1870

passando or noi dallo stato giuridico dell'eccezione all'uguaglianza civile e
politica sotto il regime di libere istitutzioni [we now pass to the rights given
us in our congregation. . . . we have to get rid of the old amarezze, but we
also need to educate, inculcate religious values, and take care of the poor].
ma la religione e la carità non vennero mai meno in questi Israeliti, ma la
gioja di essere cittadini nella patria tanta amata, ove fin qui erasi meno che
stranieri lievi le abnegazioni e i sacrifizi richiesti per innalzare all'altezza del
nostro stato novello, (?) ma l'aiuto di Dio non e' per mancare alle opere
della virtù e dell'onore.

17. Stefano Caviglia, *L'identità salvata* (Bari, 1995), shows that after World War
     I there were already problems. Gadi Luzzatto Voghera, *Il prezzo dell'egua-
     glianza. Il dibattito sull'emancipazione degli ebrei in Italia (1781–1848)* (Milan,
     1998). For Jewish self-fashioning in the nineteenth century, see Carlotta
     Ferrara degli Uberti, *Fare gli ebrei italiani, Autorappresentazioni di una mino-
     ranza (1861–1918)* (Bologna, 2011).

Glossary

British Common Law, the law still used in England. Centuries old, it is not to be confused with the Continental *ius commune*.

Canon law, the law of the Catholic Church, which developed incrementally from the early Middle Ages. The principal sources were edited papal letters. Legal scholars cited laws and precedents from centuries before their time, turning canon law and its interpretations into a timeless, uninterrupted chain.

Casa dei catecumeni, or the *Catecumeni*, the place where Anna del Monte was taken, established in Rome in 1542 to promote conversion. Other houses appeared afterward in various Italian cities. A predecessor existed in thirteenth-century England.

Cinque scole, the five synagogues of the Roman Jewish Community, within the ghetto, all housed in one building, which burned down in the early twentieth century.

Cives, literally citizen. Citizenship entitled a person, including an Italian Jew, to benefit from *ius commune*, except when religion intervened to apply strict limitations.

Code civil, the law code established by Napoleon in 1804, nullifying *ius commune*. Today, it is the foundation of most European legal systems.

Confessional state, a state with an official religion to which all must either adhere or, at least, profess in order to qualify for full civil status and holding public office. In the Middle Ages and early modern times, confessional uniformity was policed.

Corpus mysticum, Corpus Christi, the body or "society of the faithful," which the Catholic Church strove to unite, insisting that all belong to one faith. Jews were the exception, but highly regulated.

Enlightenment, the broad name given to eighteenth-century rationalist thinking in Western Europe, often at loggerheads with Catholic thought.

Fattori, the three revolving heads of the Roman Jewish Community.

Favor fidei and *odium fidei,* supralegal, or constitutional, principles guiding the Church since the Middle Ages. *Favor* refers to actions advancing the faith; *odium,* to those which detract.

Freemasonry, secretive society, perceived by the Church as an existential threat. Members have included Samuel Adams, Benjamin Franklin, and Wolfgang Amadeus Mozart.

Ghetto, originally, an island in Venice, turned, in 1516, into an enclosed place of Jewish residence. Rome followed with one in 1555, and other cities did so later.

Ius commune, the medieval and early modern reworking of ancient Roman Law, still applied in eighteenth-century Italy and influential in universities throughout Europe until 1804.

Nostro ghet, the term Roman Jews used to refer to the ghetto, punning on the Hebrew *get,* a bill of divorce, as the term appears, written in Hebrew letters, twice in Anna del Monte's diary, expressing ghetto Jewry's sense of divorce from Roman society.

Novella 118, a new law of the late Roman Empire. *Novella* number 118 named those who did not possess "paternal power."

"To offer" (denounce), or more properly, "to oblate," the act of offering a person to the Church. Originally, this referred to parents offering children as monks or nuns; later, it applied to the "offering" of Jewish children or adults by those deemed parents or spouses.

Papal letters, or bulls. Letter is the proper term for papal commands or responses to questions. Appended is a lead seal, the bull. Letters are named by their *incipit,* or first words, which are sometimes revealing, as in *Cum nimis absurdum,* or "how absurd it is"—in the view of the letter's issuer, Pope Paul IV, in 1555—that Jews could freely circulate in Rome. Other *incipits* are opaque, for instance: *Postremo mense,* "in the coming month."

Patria potestas, the Roman Law principle of "parental power," entitling a parent to make decisions for offspring. In ancient times, this included decisions over life and death. Commentators agreed that Jews possessed this right. Interpreters like Pope Benedict XIV debated who the true "parents" were.

Piis verberibus, "pious lashes," suggested in 1513 as a means to prompt Jewish conversion. The term was originated by Pope Gregory the Great (590–604).

Regeneration, taken from canon law, referring to the effects of baptism, but eventually applied by the French Revolution to civic *régénération,* or rebirth, on the part of citizens, particularly Jews.

Res publica, the modern "Republic," not be used anachronistically, applied to the Middle Ages, when it meant the body of the faithful.

Ritual murder, or blood libel, the charge that Jews killed Christians out of *odium* or to acquire blood for ritual purposes.

Roman Inquisition, established by the pope in the thirteenth century and revived in the sixteenth century to combat (Lutheran) heresy, but then charged with policing Jewish behavior; not to be confused with the Spanish or Portuguese Inquisitions, which pursued "Judaizing" by converts from Judaism and their offspring.

Supersession, meaning the asserted replacement of the Synagogue, Jews, and Judaism by the Church and Christians as the divinely chosen people.

Bibliography

Archivio di Stato, Roma, Tribunale del Governatore, Criminali, Constituti, vol. 38, fols. 11–13; Camerale II, Ebrei, b.1.

Archivio medievale e moderno, fondo AMM, Università degli ebrei di Roma, Archivio Storico della Comunità Ebraica di Roma, henceforth, ASCER, b. 1Qn parte 1, fasc. 05; b. 1Tf, fasc. 03; b. 1Tf, 2 inf. 1, fasc. 04; b. 1Th, 2 inf. 2; b. 1Ub 2 inf. 1, fasc. 07, 08, 10; b. 1Ud, 2 inf. 2, fasc. 05; b. 1Ue, 2 inf. 2, fasc. 03; b. 1Ul, 2 inf. 2, fasc. 07; b.1Zb, 2 inf. 3, fasc. 06; n. 2Zd, 10 sup. 2; b. 2Zd, 10 sup. 2, no. 80; b. 2Zi, 10 super. 3, no. 81; b. 2Zl, 10 sup. 3, texts 185 and 189. See also references to ASCER under specific authors, e.g., Carlo Luti.

Central Archive for the History of the Jewish People, Jerusalem. CAJP 3835D, HM 4837 A, and CAJP 4837B F.

Jewish Theological Seminary, microfilm 4026a, copies of Roman documents listed erroneously as from Finale in the index. http://garfield.jtsa.edu:1801/view/action/singleViewer.do?dvs=1384094435671~913&locale=en_US&VIEWER_URL=/view/action/singleViewer.do?&DELIVERY_RULE_ID=10&search_terms=finale&adjacency=N&application=DIGITOOL-3&frameId=1&usePid1=true&usePid2=true

Ariely, Gal. "Exploring Citizenship Spheres of Inclusion/Exclusion: Rights as 'Potential for Power,'" *Patterns of Prejudice* 45 (2011): 241–58.

Arnoli, Udo. *Pro Iudaeis: Die Gutachten der hallischen Theologen im 18. Jahrhundert zu Fragen der Judentoleranz*. Berlin, 1993.

Aron-Beller, Katherine. *Jews on Trial: The Papal Inquisition in Modena, 1598–1638*. Manchester, 2011.

———. "*Buon Purim:* Proselytizing, Professing Jews and the Papal Inquisition in Modena," *Jewish History* 26 (2012): 161–77.

Arrù, Angelina. "Donare non è perdere: I vantaggi della reciprocità a Roma tra Settecento e Ottocento," *Quaderni Storici* 98 (1998): 361–82.

Augustinus Aurelius, *Adversus Judaeos,* trans. Fathers of the Church, vol. 27: 391–416. Washington, D.C., 1965.

Ayrer, G. H. *Tractatio iuridica de iure recipiendi Iudaeos tum generatim tum speciatim in terris Brusvico-Luneburgicis.* Göttingen, 1741.

Azor, Juan. *Institutionem Moralium.* Milan, 1608.

Azpilcueta, Martin de, a.k.a., Navarro. *Opera Omnia.* Venice, 1601.

Baer, Y. F. *A History of the Jews in Christian Spain,* trans. L. Schoffman, 2 vols. Philadelphia, 1961.

Bailyn, Bernard. *The Ideological Origins of the American Revolution.* Cambridge, MA, 1992.

Baron, Salo W. "Ghetto and Emancipation: Shall We Revise the Traditional View," *Menorah Journal* 14 (1938): 515–26.

———. *A Social and Religious History of the Jews,* vol. 13. 2nd ed. Philadelphia, 1969.

Beck. Johannes. *Tractatus de Iudaeis.* 1731.

Beer, Marina, and Anna Foa, eds. *Ebrei, minoranze e Risorgimento: Storia, cultura e letteratura.* Rome, 2013.

Benedict XI. *De Baptismo,* cited by Luzi, "Inviti." (See below.)

Benedict XIV. *Bullarium . . . in quo continentur Constitutiones epistolae,* vol. 3. Rome, 1756.

———. *Providas.* http://digilander.libero.it/magistero/b14provi.htm, visited Sept. 10, 2012.

Benton, J. F. *Self and Society in Medieval France.* New York, 1970.

Benzoni, Rutilio. *Speculum Episcoporum.* Venice, 1595.

Berger, David. "Mission to the Jews and Jewish-Christian Contacts in the Polemical Literature of the High Middle Ages," *American Historical Review,* 91 (1986): 576–91.

Bernard, G. W. *The King's Reformation: Henry VIII and the Remaking of the English Church.* New Haven, 2007.

Berkovitz, Jay R. "The French Revolution and the Jews: Assessing the Cultural Impact," *AJS Review* 20 (1995): 25–86.

———. "Acculturation and Integration in Eighteenth-Century Metz," *Jewish History* 24 (2010): 271–94.

———. *Protocols of Justice: The Pinkas of the Metz Rabbinic Court 1771–1789.* Leiden, 2014.

Blum, Anne S., Tamera Marko, Alexandra Puerto, and Adam Warren. "Women,

Ethnicity, and Medical Authority: Historical Perspectives on Reproductive Health in Latin America." Latin American Studies CILAS Working Papers University of California, San Diego. Year 2004. Paper 21.

Bonfield, Lloyd. "Developments in European Family Law." *The History of the European Family,* vol. 1: *Family Life in Early Modern Times 1500–1789.* New Haven, 2002.

Bonfil, Robert. *Rabbis and Jewish Communities in Renaissance Italy.* London, 1993.

———. *Jewish Life in Renaissance Italy,* trans. Anthony Oldcorn. Los Angeles and Berkeley, 1994.

Bossy, John. *Christianity in the West, 1400–1700.* Oxford, 1985.

Boswell, John. *The Royal Treasure.* New Haven, 1977.

Brechenmacher, Thomas. *Das Ende der doppelten Schutzherrschaft.* Päpste und Papsttum, 32. Stuttgart, 2004.

Bregoli, Francesca. "'Two Jews Walk into a Coffeehouse': The 'Jewish Question,' Utility, and Political Participation in Late Eighteenth-Century Livorno," *Jewish History* 24 (2010): 309–29.

———. *Mediterranean Enlightenment: Livornese Jews, Tuscan Culture, and Eighteenth-Century Reform* (Stanford, 2014).

Bregoli, Francesca, and Federica Francesconi. "Tradition and Transformation in Eighteenth-Century Europe: Jewish Integration in Comparative Perspective," *Jewish History* 24 (2010): 235–46.

Burnett, Stephen G. "Distorted Mirrors: Antonius Margaritha, Johann Buxtorf and Christian Ethnographies of the Jews," 1994. Faculty Publications, Classics and Religious Studies Department, University of Nebraska. Paper 63; revised version in the *Sixteenth Century Journal* 25 (1994): 275–87.

Caffiero, Marina. *Forced Baptisms: Histories of Jews, Christians, and Converts in Papal Rome,* trans. Lydia Cochrane. Berkeley and Los Angeles, 2011. Original Italian, *Battesimi Forzati.* Rome, 2004.

———. *Legami Pericolosi.* Turin, 2012.

———. *Rubare le anime.* Rome, 2008.

Calderini, Gasparo. *Consilia.* Venice, 1497.

Caliò, Thomasso. "Antisemitismo e culto dei santi in età contemporanea: Il caso del beato Lorenzino da Marostica," in *Il pubblico dei santi: Forme e livelli di ricezione dei messaggi agiografici,* ed. Paolo Golinelli. Rome, 2000.

———. *La leggenda dell'ebreo assassino,* Roma, 2007.

Canonici, Claudio. "Condizioni ambientali e battesimo degli ebrei romani nel seicento e nel settecento," *Ricerche per la storia religiosa di Roma* 10 (1998): 234–71.

Caranza, Scipio. ASCER, 1Ud 2 inf. 2, fasc. 05.

Carlebach, Elisheva. *The Death of Shimon Abeles: Jewish-Christian Tension in Seventeenth-Century Prague*. The Berman Lecture, Queens College, New York, 2001.

———. *Divided Souls: Converts from Judaism in Germany, 1500–1750*. New Haven, 2001.

Carreti, Ludovico. *Epistola Ludovici Caretti ad Iudaeos*. Paris, 1554.

Casanova, Cesarina. "Patria potestas. Due nuovi contributi alla storia del diritto di famiglia," *Storicamente* 3 (2007), online journal. http://www.storicamente.org/04_comunicare/casanova.htm, visited May 29, 2013.

Cattaneo, Carlo. *Ricerche economiche sulle interdizioni imposte dalla legge civile agli Israeliti, estratto dal vol. xxiii degli Annali di Giurisprudenza pratica, compilati ed editi dall'Avvocato ZINI*. Milan, 1836.

Cavallar, Osvaldo, and Julius Kirshner. "Jews as Citizens in Late Medieval and Renaissance Italy: The Case of Isacco da Pisa," *Jewish History* 25.3–4 (2011): 269–318.

Cavanna, Adriano. "Mito e destini del Code Napoleon in Italia," in *Excerptiones iuris: Studies in Honor of André Gouron*, ed. Bernard Durand and Laurent Mayali. Berkeley, 2000.

Caviglia, Stefano. *L'identità salvata*. Bari, 1995.

Christopoulos, John. "Abortion and the Confessional in Counter-Reformation Italy," *Renaissance Quarterly* 65 (2012): 443–84.

Chrysostom, John. *Homilies against the Jews 1.11.1–2*, in *Jews and Christians in Antioch in the First Four Centuries of the Common Era*, trans. Wayne Meeks and Robert Wilken. Missoula, Mont., 1978. Also "John Chrysostom," *Internet Medieval Sourcebook*, ed. Paul Halsal, https://legacy.fordham.edu/halsall/source/chrysostom-jews6.asp.

Clement XIII. ASCER, 1Ui 2 inf. 2, fasc. 03. *Chirografo della santità di nostro signore Papa Clemente XIII, con cui si costituisce Monsig. Viceregente di Roma giudice privativo di tutte le cause passive de' neofiti, e si confermano i loro privilegi*. 27 October 1766.

Codex iuris Canonici. Rome 1917. http://www.intratext.com/X/LAT0813.HTM, visited December 5, 2013.

Cohen, Jeremy. *Living Letters of the Law*. Berkeley and Los Angeles, 1999.

Colet, John. *John Colet's Commentary on First Corinthians*, ed. Bernard O'Kelley and Catherine Jarrott. Binghamton, 1985.

Collins, James. *The State in Early Modern France*. Cambridge, 1995.

Collins, Jeffrey. *Papacy and Politics in Eighteenth-Century Rome: Pius VI and the Arts.* Cambridge, 2004.

Colzi, Roberto. *"Che ora è?"* Privately distributed.

Corcos, Tranquillo Manoah. ASCER, 2VH 10 sup 2. Fasc. 01. See ASCER, 1Ql inf. 5; 2ZD 10 sup 2. Fasc 02, Jan 23, 1708; 1Ud 2 inf. 2, fasc. 05; 2Va 10 sup. 2; 1Ul 2 inf. 2, p. 519, 1756.

Costanzi, Giov. Antonio. *La verità della Cristiana Religione contro le vane lusinghe de' moderni ebrei.* Rome, 1749.

Cusumano, Nicola. "I papi e le accuse di omicidio rituale: Benedetto XIV e la bolla Beatus Andreas," *Dimensioni e problemi della ricerca storica* 1 (2002): 7–35.

Dacanáy, Adolfo N. "Disputed Questions Concerning Those to Be Baptized: Comments on Cc. 868, 870, 871, and 913," *Diwa* 33 (2008): 36–57.

D'Arco, Giambattista Gherardo. *Della influenza del Ghetto nello Stato.* 1782; reprint, Bologna, 1981.

Davis, Natalie Z. *Fiction in the Archives: Pardon Tales and Their Tellers in Sixteenth-Century France.* Stanford, 1990.

De Becchettis, Antonio Maria. ASCER, b. 1Un 01, 2 inf. 2, 1702. *Sacra Congregatione Sanctissimae Inquisitionis, Romana Tutelae pro Davide de Castro Novo et Gratia Vidua Relicta q. Iosephi de Anticulo Hebraei contra D. Ioannem Baptistam Pauli Neophitum.* Rome, 1702.

De Cesaris, Valerio. "I Cattolici, gli ebrei e l'ebreo.' Note su antigiudaismo e filogiudaismo in Italia," in *Ebrei, minoranze e Risorgimento,* ed. Beer and Foa, 163–76.

De Luca, Jo. Baptistae. *Venusini . . . Theatrum veritatis et justitiae . . .* 19 vols., 1669–77; 12 vols., Cologne, 1689–99.

De Robertis, F. M. *Storia delle corporazioni e del regime associativo nel mondo Romano.* Bari, 1973.

De Susannis, Marquardus. *De Iudaeis et Aliis Infidelibus.* Venice, 1558.

Deutsch, Yaacov. *Judaism in Christian Eyes.* New York, 2012.

Di Nepi, Serena. "Un'anticipazione del Ghetto? Modelli di conversion e strategie di proselitismo nel Libellus del 1513," in *Conversos, marrani e nuove comunità ebraiche in età moderna,* ed. Myriam Silvera, 93–108. Florence, 2015.

Di Segni, Riccardo Shmuel. "L'attacco alla shechità nell'Europa di oggi," *Rassegna Mensile di Israel* 78 (2012): 157–65.

———. *"Provare per credere,"* in *Kolot-Voci,* June 28, 2013, http://www.kolot.it/2013/06/28/provare-per-credere/.

Dohm, C. W. *Concerning the Amelioration of the Civil Status of the Jews,* trans. H. Lederer. Cincinnati, 1957.

Domenico de S. Geminiano. *Liber Sextus,* marginal Commentary to 5, 2, 5.

Donato, Maria Pia. "Cultura dell'antico e cultura dei Lumi a Roma nel Settecento. La politicizzazione dello scambio culturale durante il pontificato di Pio VI," *Mélanges de l'École française de Rome, Italie et Méditerranée* 104 (1992): 503–48.

————. "Roma in rivoluzione 1789, 1848, 1870," in *Storia d'Italia, Annali 16, Roma, la città del papa: Vita civile e religiosa dal giubileo di Bonifacio VIII al giubileo di papa Wojtyla,* ed. L. Fiorani and A. Prosperi, 907–33. Turin, 2000.

Dubin, Lois. *The Port Jews of Habsburg Trieste, Absolutist Politics and Enlightenment Culture.* Stanford, 1999.

Duff, P. W. *Personality in Roman Private Law.* 1938; repr. New York, 1971.

Duffy, John M. "The Jewish Boy Legend and the Western Twist," in *Byzantine Religious Culture,* ed. D. Sullivan et al., 313–22. Leiden/Boston, 2012.

Duns Scotus. Commentary to the Sentences of Peter Lombard, 4 Sent. Dist. 4, q. 9, n. 2. *Opera omnia,* 16:487–89. 26 vols., Paris, 1891–95.

Duso, Giuseppe. *Il contratto sociale nella filosofia politica moderna,* 2nd ed. Bologna, 1998.

Elbel, Benjamin. *Theologiae moralis sacramentalis, per modum conferentiarum casibus practicis applicatae, & illustratae . . . Editio tertia / ab autore revisa & correcta,* vol 3. Augustae Vindel; Graecii : Sumptibus Philippi, Martini, & Joannis Veith, 1733–.

Elliott, Dyan. *Fallen Bodies: Pollution, Sexuality, and Demonology in the Middle Ages.* Philadelphia, 1999.

Elton, G. R. *Reform and Reformation, England, 1509–1558.* Cambridge, MA, 1977.

Esposito, Anna. "Sefarditi a Roma all'inizio del '500, una nota dai testamenti," in *Studi sul mondo sefardito in memoria di Aron Leoni,* ed. Pier Cesare Ioly-Zorattini, Michele Luzzati, and Michele Zarfati, 35–50. Florence, 2012.

Farinacci, Prospero. *De haeres.* Quest. 178 par 6 n. 128.

Feci, Simona. "The Death of a Miller: A Trial contra Hebreos in the Baroque Rome," *Jewish History* 7.2 (1993): 9–27.

————. "Tra il tribunale e il ghetto: Le magistrature, la comunità e gli individui di fronte ai reati degli ebrei romani nel seicento," *Quaderni storici* 99 (1998): 575–99.

Fermosinus, Nicolas Rodriguez. *Tractatus Secundus Criminalium.* Lyon, 1670.

Ferrara, Piera. "Lungo i percorsi della conversione: i neofiti romani nel XVIII secolo," in *Città e campagna: Un binomio da ripensare, Annali del Dipartimento di Storia dell'Università degli studi di Roma Tor Vergata*, ed. R. Morelli and G. Fiocco. 4/2008, Rome, 2009.

Ferrara degli Uberti, Carlotta. *Fare gli ebrei italiani: Autorappresentazioni di una minoranza, 1861–1918*. Bologna, 2011.

Ferraris, Lucio. *Bibliotheca canonica juridico-moralis theologica*. Rome, 1756.

Finestein, Israel. "Anglo-Jewish Opinion during the Struggle for Emancipation (1828–1858)," *Transactions (Jewish Historical Society of England)* 20 (1959–61): 113–43.

Fiorani, Luigi, and Domenico Rocciolo, *Chiesa romana e rivoluzione francese, 1789–1799*. Ecole française de Rome. Rome, 2004.

Fiorelli, Dominico. *Dominicus Caesar Florellus A.C. in criminalibus Locumtenens Generalis, S. Officii Consultor, et Reorum Advocatus. Consultation super dubio an et quomodo sit procedendum com infidelibus denunciatis, quod velint, sed per se nequeant comparere et petere Baptismum, ex quo praepeditur eis aditus, ne fidem Christi amplectantur. Monaldi, 1721*. ASCER, 2Zd 10 sup. 2, fasc. 06; and 1Ue 2 inf. 2, fasc. 03.

Flesch, H. "An Eighteenth-Century Narrative of the Attempted Conversion of a Jewish Girl in the Time of Maria Theresa," *Jewish Quarterly Review*, n.s., 15.3 (1925): 389–407.

Flint, Valerie. *The Rise of Magic in Early Medieval Europe*. Princeton, 1991.

Foa, Anna. *Giordano Bruno*. Bologna, 2011.

Fosi, Irene. *Papal Justice: Subjects and Courts in the Papal State, 1500–1750*, trans. Thomas V. Cohen. Washington, D.C., 2011.

Fram, Edward. "Perception and Reception of Repentant Apostates in Medieval Ashkenaz and Premodern Poland," *AJS Review* 21 (1996): 299–339.

Francesconi, Federica. "From Ghetto to Emancipation: The Role of Moisè Formiggini," *Jewish History* 24 (2010): 331–54.

Gasperoni, Michael. "Note sulla popolazione del ghetto di Roma in età moderna: Lineamenti e prospettive di ricerca," in *Gli abitanti del ghetto*. Ed. Groppi, 69–116.

Ghisalberti, Carlo. *Unità nazionale e unificazione giuridica in Italia: La codificazione del diritto nel Risorgimento*. Rome/Bari, 1982.

———. "Sulla condizione giuridica degli ebrei in Italia dall'emancipazione alla persecuzione; spunti per una riconsiderazione," *Italia Judaica* 4 (1993): 19–31.

Gilchrist, John. "The Perception of Jews in the Canon Law in the Period of the First Two Crusades," *Jewish History* 3.1 (1988): 9–24.

————, ed. *Diversorum patrum sententiae sive Collectio in LXXIV titulos digesta.* Vatican City, 1973.

Gioberti, Vincenzo. *Rinnovamento civile d'Italia.* Paris and Turin, 1850.

Giustiniani, Paolo, and Pietro Querini. *Libellus ad leonem decem.* 1513; reprint, Artioli, 1995.

Gratian. *Decretum, in Corpus iuris canonici,* ed. E. Friedberg, 2 vols. Leipzig, 1879, 1881.

Gratianus, Stefanus. *Disceptationes forenses.* Rome, 1625.

Grayzel, Solomon. "The Confessions of a Medieval Convert," *Historia Judaica* 17 (1958): 89–120.

————. *The Church and the Jews in the Thirteenth Century,* ed. Kenneth Stow, vol. 2. New York and Detroit, 1989.

Greco, Gaetano. *Benedetto XIV: Un canone per la Chiesa.* Salerno, 2011.

Gregory the Great. *Decretum C. 23, q. 6, c. 4, iam vero.*

Groppi, Angela, ed. *Gli abitanti del ghetto.* Rome, 2015.

————. "*Numerare e descrivere gli ebrei del ghetto di Roma,*" in *Gli abitanti del ghetto,* ed. Groppi, 37–68.

Güde, Wilhelm. *Die rechtliche Stellung der Juden in den Schriften deutscher Juristen des 16. und 17. Jahrhunderts.* Sigmaringen, 1981.

Guido de Baysio. *Archidiaconus Super Decreto, clarissimi sacrorum canovm interpretis Gvidonis de Baiisio . . . ennarationes Super Decreto, autor ipse Rosarium appellari maluit.* Lyon, 1549.

Gunzberg, Lynn. *Strangers at Home: Jews in the Italian Literary Imagination.* Berkeley and Los Angeles, 1992.

Guy, J. A. "Henry VIII and the Praemunire Manoeuvres of 1530–1531," *English Historical Review* 97 (1982): 481–503.

Hanley, Sarah. "Engendering the State: Family Formation and State Building in Early Modern France," *French Historical Studies* 16.1 (1989): 4–27.

————. "The Jurisprudence of the Arrêts: Marital Union, Civil Society, and State Formation in France, 1550–1650," *Law and History Review* 21.1 (2003): 1–40.

Harrán, Dan. *Jewish Poet and Intellectual in Seventeenth-Century Venice: The Works of Sarra Copia Sulam in Verse and Prose, along with Writings of Her Contemporaries.* Chicago, 2009.

Harrington, James. *The Commonwealth of Oceana and a System of Politics,* ed. J. G. A. Pocock. Cambridge, 1992.

Haverkamp, Eva. "Martyrs in Rivalry: The 1096 Jewish Martyrs and the Thebean Legion," *Jewish History* 23 (2009): 319–42.

Herculano, Alexandre. *History of the Origin and Establishment of the Inquisition in Portugal*, trans. John C. Branner. Stanford, 1926; repr. New York, 1972, with a Prolegomenon by Yosef H. Yerushalmi.

Holywar.org. https://www.google.com/search?q=holywar.org&oq=holywar .org&aqs=chrome.69i58j69i57j0j5l2.20645jo&sourceid=chrome&espvd =210&es_sm=93&ie=UTF-8, visited March 3, 2013.

Hsia, R. Po-chia. *Trent 1475: Stories of a Ritual Murder Trial*. New Haven, 1992.

Hudon, William. "Religion and Society in Early Modern Italy," *American Historical Review* 101 (1996): 783–804.

Iacuzzi, Alfred. *John Adams, Scholar*. Ragusa, 1952.

Inscrutabile. English Papal Encyclicals Online, http://www.papalencyclicals.net/ Pius06/p6inscru.htm, visited Sept. 15, 2012.

Interesting Letters of Pope Clement XIV, translated from the French, vol. 2. London, 1781.

Ioly-Zorratini, Pier Cesare. *Processi del S. Uffizio contro ebrei e giudaizzanti*, 16 vols. Florence, 1982–92.

Jaher, Frederic Cople. *The Jews and the Nation: Revolution, Emancipation, State Formation, and the Liberal Paradigm in America and France*. Princeton, 2002.

Jefferson, Thomas. "1786 Virginia Act for Establishing Religious Freedom," drafted originally by Jefferson in 1779. http://religiousfreedom.lib.vir ginia.edu/sacred/vaact.html, visited August 15, 2013.

———. A Bill for Licensing Counsel, Attorneys at Law, and Proctors, 18 June 1779 [Main Series 2:589], *The Papers of Thomas Jefferson Digital Edition*, ed. Barbara B. Oberg and J. Jefferson Looney. Charlottesville, 2008.

Johnson, Willis. "Before the Blood Libel: Jews in Christian Exegesis after the Massacres of 1096," MA thesis (typescript), Cambridge University, 1994.

Jewish Culture and History, 4.2 (2001). *Special Issue: Port Jews: Jewish Communities in Cosmopolitan Maritime Trading Centres, 1550–1950*.

Jordan, William Chester. *The French Monarchy and the Jews*. Philadelphia, 1989.

———. "Learning about Jews in the Classroom: A Thirteenth-Century Witness; UCLA Library, Rouse MS 17," in *Envisioning Judaism: Studies in Honor of Peter Schaefer on the Occasion of His Seventieth Birthday*, ed. Ra'anan Boustan, Klauss Herrmann Reimund Leicht, Annette Yoshiko Reed, and Giuseppe Veltri, 1247–60. Tübingen, 2013.

Justinian. *Novel 118*, http://webu2.upmf-grenoble.fr/DroitRomain/Anglica/ N118_Scott.htm.

Justinianic Code. *Corpus iuris civilis*, ed. Paul Krueger and Theodore Mommsen. Berlin, 1888.

Jutte, Daniel. "Interfaith Encounters between Jews and Christians in the Early Modern Period and Beyond: Toward a Framework," *American Historical Review* 118 (2013): 378–400.

Kantorowicz, E. H. *The King's Two Bodies*. Princeton, 1957.

Kaplan, Benjamin. *Divided by Faith: Religious Conflict and the Practice of Toleration in Early Modern Europe*. Cambridge, 2010.

Kaplan, Zvi Jonathan. "A Marital Dilemma: French Courts, Foreign Jews and the Secularization of Marriage," *Journal of Jewish Studies* 64 (2013): 365–82.

Karp, Abraham J. *From the Ends of the Earth: Judaic Treasures of the Library of Congress*. Washington, D.C.: Library of Congress, 1991.

Karp, Jonathan. *The Politics of Jewish Commerce in Europe, 1638–1848*. Cambridge, 2008.

Katz, Dana E. "'Clamber not you up to the casements:' On Ghetto Views and Viewing," *Jewish History* 24 (2010): 127–53.

Katz, Jacob. "Even though a sinner, he is still of Israel" (in Hebrew), *Tarbiẓ* 27 (1958): 203–27.

Kedar, B. Z. "Canon Law and the Burning of the Talmud," *Bulletin of Medieval Canon Law* 9 (1979): 79–82.

Kertzer, David. *The Kidnapping of Edgardo Mortara*. New York, 1997.

Kirshner, Julius. "*Sibi Faciat Civem:* Bartolus of Sassoferrato's Doctrine on the Making of a Citizen," *Speculum* 48 (1973): 694–713.

Klapisch-Zuber, Christiane. "Zacharias, or The Ousted Father," in *Women, Family, and Ritual in Renaissance Italy,* trans. L. Cochrane. Chicago, 1985.

Klar, Benjamin, ed. *Megillat Ahimaaẓ*. Jerusalem, 1974.

Kuttner, Stephan, and Gilbert Fransen, eds., *Summa "elegantius in iure divino" seu Coloniensis,* New York, 1969.

Lampronti, Isaac. *Pahad Yitẓhaq*. Lyck, 1869.

Leo XIII. *Immortale dei.* http://www.vatican.va/holy_father/leo_xiii/encyclicals/documents/hf_l-xiii_enc_01111885_immortale-dei_en.html, visited July 18, 2013.

———. *Immutabile.* http://www.vatican.va/holy_father/leo_xiii/encyclicals/documents/hf_l-xiii_enc_01111885_immortale-dei_en.html, visited August 10, 2013.

Liberles, Robert. "The Jews and Their Bill: Jewish Motivations in the Controversy of 1753," *Jewish History* 2 (1987): 29–36.

Linder, Amnon, ed. *The Jews in the Legal Sources of the Early Middle Ages*. Detroit and Jerusalem, 1999.

Luti, Carlo. *Romana Oblationis Puerorum ad Fidem super Epistola Benedicti XIV edita Anno 1751* (handwritten copy).

———. ASCER, 1Ul, 2 inf. 2, fasc. 07.

Luzi, Laura. "Dallo status civitatis alla cittadinanza. La crisi del diritto comune attraverso il mutamento dello statuto dell'ebreo," *Mediterranea: Richerche Storiche* 5 (2008): 527–66

———. "Inviti non sunt baptizandi: La dinamica delle conversioni degli ebrei," *Mediterranea: Ricerche storiche* 4 (2007): 225–70.

———. "Octo sunt permissa, Controllo dei nuclei ebraici," *Mediterranea: Ricerche Storiche* 5 (2008): 95–132.

———. "'Tanquam capsari nostri': Il ruolo del giurista di diritto comune nei confronti degli ebrei," *Mediterranea: Ricerche Storiche* 9 (2012): 111–42.

Luzzatti, Luigi. *God in Freedom*. New York, 1930.

MacCulloch, Diarmaid. "Henry VIII and the Reform of the Church," in *The Reign of Henry VIII: Politics, Policy and Piety,* ed. Diarmaid MacCulloch. London, 1995.

Madison, James. *Memorial and Remonstrance against Religious Assessments, 1785.* http://religiousfreedom.lib.virginia.edu/sacred/madison_m&r_1785.html

Madison to Mordecai Noah. http://www.jewishvirtuallibrary.org/jsource/loc/madison.html

Malkiel, David. "Ebraismo, tradizione e società: Isaaco Lampronti e l'identità, ebraica nella Ferrara del XVIII secolo," *Zakhor* 7 (2005): 9–42.

Mancini, Massimo. *"Pier Gaetano Feletti e l'affare Mortara,"* in *Dominikaner und Juden/Dominicans and Jews,* ed. Elias H. Fuellenbach and Gianfranco Miletto, 421–37. Berlin, 2015.

Mann, Michael. "The Autonomous Power of the State: Its Origins, Mechanisms and Results," *Archives européennes de sociologie* 25 (1984): 185–213.

Marchino, Philipo. *De Bello divino* (cited by Benedict XIV in *Postremo mense*).

Marcocci, Giuseppe, '. . . *per capillos adductos ad pillam.' Il dibattito cinquecentesco sulla validità del battesimo forzato degli ebrei in Portogallo (1496–1497),* in *Salvezza delle anime, disciplina dei corpi: Un seminario sulla storia del battesimo,* ed. Adriano Prosperi, 339–423. Pisa, 2006.

Marconcini, Samuela. "The Conversion of Jewish Women in Florence (1599–1799)," *Zeitsprünge: Forschungen zur frühen Neuzeit* 14 (2010): 532–48.

Marti, Federico. *Il "favor fidei" nella Decretalistica*. Rome, 2011.

Martin, Dale. *The Corinthian Body*. New Haven, 1996.

Mazzacane, Aldo. "Diritto e giuristi nella formazione dello Stato moderno in Italia," in *Origini dello Stato,* ed. Giorgio Chittolini, Anthony Molho, and Pierangel Schiera, 331–49. Bologna, 1993.

Menniti, Ippolito. *Il governo del papa nell'età moderna.* Rome, 2007.

Merchant, J. H. *A Review of the Proposed Naturalization of the Jews.* London, 1753.

Miccoli, Giovanni. "Santa Sede, questione ebraica e antisemitismo fra Otto e Novecento," in *Gli ebrei in Italia, Annali 11,* vol. 2: 1371–1574. Turin, 1997.

Milano, Attilio "L'impari lotta della comunità di Roma contro la Casa dei catecumeni," *Rassegna Mensile di Israel* 16 (1950): 355–68 and 408–19.

———. *Il Ghetto di Roma.* Rome, 1964.

Militi, Manuela. "Gli ebrei 'fuori dal Ghetto': Incontri e scontri con il Lazio durante la Repubblica romana (1798–1799)," *Archivie Cultura* 40 (2007): 195–215.

———. "Il costo della Repubblica 'sorella' per gli ebrei di Roma (febbraio 1798–settembre 1799)," *EuroStudium,* La Sapienza, Rome. April June 2012. http://www.eurostudium.uniroma1.it/, visited August 7, 2014.

———."Descriptio Hebreorum, Trascrizione," in *Gli abitanti del ghetto,* ed. Groppi, 189–285.

Moro, Renato. "Antigiudaismo e antisemitismo: Continuità e/o rotture," in *Ebrei, minoranze e Risorgimento,* ed. Beer and Foa, 199–205.

Morosini, Giulio. *Via della Fede.* Rome, 1683.

Natta, Marc. Aton. Astensis. *Consiliorum seu responsorum, 2, Lyons 1566, and 3, in Monte Regali ex officina Torrentiniana, 1566.*

Newman, Sharan. *The Devil's Door.* New York, 2004.

Nichols, Aidan, O.P. *Abortion and Martyrdom.* Herefordshire, UK, 2002. http://www.christendomawake.org/pages/anichols/abortion&martyrdom1.htm, visited August 3, 2013.

Noonan, John T., Jr. "Indissolubility of Marriage and Natural Law," 14 *The American Journal of Jurisprudence* 79 (1969): 82–93.

Nussdorfer, Laurie. *Civic Politics in the Rome of Urban VIII.* Princeton, 1992.

Oryshkevich, Irina. "*Roma sotterranea* and the Biogenesis of New Jerusalem," *RES: Anthropology and Aesthetics* 55/56 (2009): 174–81.

Padoa-Schioppa, Antonio. "A Common Law of Europe, Reflections on the Decline and Rebirth of a Model," in *Towards a New European Ius Commune,* ed. A. Gambaro and A. M. Rabello, 21–40. Jerusalem, 1999.

———. "La storia del diritto italiano: Una identità problematica," in *Excerptiones iuris: Studies in Honor of André Gouron,* ed. Bernard Durand and Laurent Mayali. Berkeley, 2000.

Panormitanus. *Quartum et Quintum Decretalium Commentaria.* Lyon, 1559.

Parente, Fausto. "The Index, the Holy Office, the Condemnation of the Talmud, and Publication of Clement VIII's Index," in *Church, Censorship and Culture in Early Modern Italy,* ed. Gigliola Fragnito. Cambridge, 2001. = Parente in *Storia d'Italia: Annali 11; Gli Ebrei in Italia,* ed. Corrado Vivanti, vol. 1. Turin, 1996.

Pariseo, Pier Paolo. *Consilia.* Venice, 1570.

Parker, David. "Sovereignty, Absolutism and the Function of the Law in Seventeenth-Century France," *Past and Present* 122 (1989): 36–74.

Parma, Marcelo Fernando. *El favor fidei en el Decretum Gratiani.* Rome, 2009.

Pascal, Philippo. *De iuribus patriae potestatis.* Cosenza, 1669.

Patton, Pamela. "Constructing the Inimical Jew in the *Cantigas de Santa María:* Theophilus' Magician in Text and Image," in *Beyond the Yellow Badge: Anti-Judaism, Anti-Semitism and European Art before 1800,* ed. Mitchell Merback, 233–56. Leiden, 2008.

————. "The Little Jewish Boy: Afterlife of a Byzantine Legend in Thirteenth-Century Spain," in *Images and Afterlife: Essays in Honor of Annemarie Weyl Carr,* Ed. Lynn Jones. Aldershot, in press.

Penn, William. "Frame of Government, 1682." http://www.constitution.org/bcp/frampenn.htm, visited August 8, 2013.

Pignatelli, Iacobi. *In Salentinis sacrae Theologiae acI.V. Doctoris Consultationum canonicarum . . .* 14 vols. Venice, 1687.

Pignatelli, Nicolò. ASCER, 1Ud 2 inf. 2, fasc. 08, case of Ercole Servi; and 1 UB 02 inf. 1, fasc 04.

Pio XII, *Discorso di sua santità Pio XII al tribunale della Sacra Romana Rota.* http://www.vatican.va/holy_father/pius_xii/speeches/1946/documents/hf_p-xii_spe_19461006_roman-rota_it.html#top *Domenica, 6 ottobre 1946.*

Pittella, Raffaele. "Labirinti archivistici e contesti istituzionali," in Groppi, *Gli abitanti.*

Pius V, *Hebraeorum gens, Bullarium Diplomatum et Privilegiorum Taurensis editio.* Turin, 1857–1872, 7:740–42.

Prodi, Paolo. *The Papal Prince: One Body and Two Souls: The Papal Monarchy in Early Modern Europe.* Cambridge, 1987.

Prodi, Paolo, and Adriano Prosperi, ed. *Disciplina dell'anima, disciplina del corpo e disciplina della società tra medioevo ed età moderna.* Bologna, 1994.

Prosperi, Adriano. "L'Inquisizione romana e gli ebrei," in Ed. M. Luzzatti, *L'inquisizione e gli ebrei in Italia,* Bari, 1994, 67–120.

————. *Tribunali di Coscienza,* Turin, 1996.

————. *Dare l'Anima: Storia di un infanticidio,* Turin, 2005.

Pullan, Brian. "A Ship with Two Rudders: Righeto Marrano and the Inquisition in Venice," *Historical Journal* 20 (1977): 25–58.

Ravid, Benjamin. "Cum nimis absurdum and the Ancona Auto-da Fé Revisited: Their Impact on Venice and Some Wider Reflections," *Jewish History* 26 (2012): 85–100.

————. "'Contra Judaeos' in Seventeenth-Century Italy: Two Responses to the 'Discorso' of Simone Luzzatto by Melchiore Palontrotti and Giulio Morosini," *AJS Review* 7 (1982): 301–51.

————. "The Forced Baptism of Jewish Minors in Early-Modern Venice," *Italia* 13–15 (2001): 259–301.

Regis, Pietro. *De iudaeo cive.* Turin, 1793.

Revel, Jacques. "Juifs et citoyens: Les incertitudes de la Révolution française," in *From Florence to the Mediterranean and Beyond,* ed. Diogo Ramada Curto et al. Florence, 2009.

Ricciulli, Antonio O.I.C. Roblanense, Patritiae Rhegino, in Aula Romana Advocato, *Tractatus de iure personarum extra ecclesias gremium existentium, cui propter argumenti similitudinem annexus est alter Tractactus De Neophytis, Romae, sumptibus Io. Angelo Ruffinelli et Angeli Manni,* 1622, *lib. 2, cap. 32. n.3 et sequen.*

Rigano, Gabriele. "Antigiudaismo e antisemitismo: Elementi per un dibattito storiografico," in *Ebrei, minoranze e Risorgimento,* ed. Beer and Foa, 177–97.

Riganti, Io. Baptista. *Io. Baptista Riganti Adv. Pro Juliana Falconeria, Josepho Ercolani et litis Neophitis,* ASCER, 1Ul 2 inf. 2.

————. *Contra Perlam Vid. Rel. Salomonis Narni et litis etc. . . . . Hebreos.* Rome, 1751. ASCER, 1UB 2 inf. 1, fasc. 04.

Rigau-Pérez, José G. "Surgery at the Service of Theology: Postmortem: Cesarean Sections in Puerto Rico and the Royal Cedula of 1804," *Hispanic American Historical Review* 75 (1995): 377–404.

Riley-Smith, Jonathan. *The First Crusade and the Idea of Crusading.* Philadelphia, 1986.

Rocciolo, Domenico. "Catecumeni e neofiti a Roma tra '500 e '800: provenienza, condizioni sociali e 'padrini' ilustri," in *Popolazione e società a Roma nel Medioevo all età contemporanea,* ed. Eugenio Sonnino, 711–24. Roma, 1998.

Rosa, Mario. "La Santa Sede e gli ebrei nel Settecento," in *Gli ebrei in Italia,* ed. Vivanti, 740–86.

————. "Tra tolleranza e repressione: Roma e gli ebrei nel '700," *Italia Judaica* 3. Rome, 1989.

Roth, Cecil. "The Forced Baptisms of 1783 at Rome and the Community of London," *Jewish Quarterly Review,* New Series, 16.2 (1925): 105–16.

————."Forced Baptisms in Italy: A Contribution to the History of Jewish Persecution," *Jewish Quarterly Review,* n.s. 27.2 (1925): 105–16. http://www.jstor.org/stable/1451786 visited May 20, 2013.

————. "The Jews of Malta." Paper read before the Jewish Historical Society of England, March 28, 1928. http://www.jhse.org/book/export/article/14560, visited March 29, 2013.

————. *The Ritual Murder Libel and the Jew: The Report by Cardinal Lorenzo Ganganelli, Pope Clement XIV.* London, 1934.

Rowan, Steven W. "Ulrich Zasius and the Baptism of Jewish Children," *Sixteenth Century Journal* 6.2 (1975): 3–25.

Ruch, C. "Baptême," in *Dictionnaire de théologie catholique.* Paris, 1908.

Rudt de Collenberg, W. H. "Le baptême des juifs à Rome de 1614 à 1798 selon les registres de la 'Casa dei catecumeni.'" *Archivum Historiae Pontificiae* 24 (1986): 91–231; 25 (1987): 105–262.

Sanchez Thomae. Cordubensis ex societate jesu. *de Sancto Matrimonii sacramento disputationum,* vols. 7 and 10. Venice, 1712.

Sarna, Jonathan. "God Loves an Infant's Praise: Cultural Borrowing and Cultural Resistance in Two Nineteenth-Century American Jewish Sunday-School Texts," *Jewish History* 27 (2013): 73–89.

Schechter, Ronald. *Obstinate Hebrews: Representations of Jews in France, 1715–1815.* Berkeley and Los Angeles, 2003.

Schilling, Heinz. *Early Modern European Civilization and Its Political and Cultural Dynamism.* Hanover, 2008.

Schmitt, J. C. *La Conversion d'Hermann le juif: Autobiographie, histoire et fiction.* Paris, 2003.

Schutte, Ann Jacobson. "Review of Marina Caffiero, *Battesimi Forzati,*" *Sixteenth Century Journal* 37.1 (2006): 282.

Sefer Ha-yashar (attributed to R. Tam), ed. S. Rosenthal. 1898.

Segre, Renata. *The Jews in Piedmont, 1297–1723.* Jerusalem, 1986-88.

Sereni, Enzo. "L'assedeo del Ghetto di Roma del 1793 nelle memorie di un contemporaneo," in *Scritti in Memoria di Enzo Sereni,* ed. D. Carpi and A. Milano. Milan and Jerusalem, 1970.

Sermoneta, Giuseppe. "Jewish Culture at Rome in the XVIII Century as Seen through New Documentation" (in Hebrew), *Italia Judaica III*. Rome, 1989.

———. *Ratto della Signora Anna del Monte*. Rome, 1989.

Sessa, Giuseppe, *Tractatus de iudaeis*. Turin, 1716.

Shoval, Ilan. "'*Servi Regis*' Re-examined: On the significance of the earliest appearance of the term in Aragon, 1176," *Hispania Judaica Bulletin* 4 (2004): 22–69.

Siebenhuener, Kim. "Conversion, Mobility, and the Roman Inquisition in Italy around 1600," *Past and Present* 200 (2008): 5–35.

Simonsohn, Shlomo. *The Apostolic See and the Jews*, 8 vols. Toronto, 1988–91.

Solomon ibn Verga, *Shebet Yehudah*, ed. A. Shohat, intro. Y. Baer. Jerusalem, 1947.

Sorkin, David. *The Religious Enlightenment: Protestants, Jews, and Catholics from London to Vienna*. Princeton, 2008.

———. "Beyond the East-West Divide: Rethinking the Narrative of the Jews' Political Status in Europe, 1600–1750," *Jewish History* 24 (2010): 247–56.

———. "Is American Jewry 'Exceptional'? Comparing Jewish Emancipation in Europe and America," *American Jewish History* 96 (2010): 175–200.

———*The Count Stanislas de Clermont-Tonnerre's "To the Jews as a nation . . .": the career of a quotation*. Jerusalem, 2012.

Spannocchio, Francesco Maria. ASCER, 2Zd 10 sup. 2, fasc. 06.

Spizzichino, Giancarlo. "Tra controllo e repressione: L'Università degli ebrei di Roma e il Sant'Uffizio (1731–1741)," in *Gli abitanti del ghetto*. Ed. Angela Groppi, 117–160.

Stephani, Heinrich. *Ueber die absolute Einheit der Kirche und des Staates*. N.p., 1802. Stern, Moritz, *Urkundliche Beitraege ueber die Stellung der Paepste zu den Juden*. Kiel, 1893.

Stone, Suzanne Last. "The Intervention of American Law in Jewish Divorce: A Pluralist Analysis, " 34 *Israel Law Review* 170 (2000).

Stow, Kenneth. "The Burning of the Talmud in 1553, In the Light of Sixteenth Century Catholic Attitudes Toward the Talmud," *Bibliotheque d'Humanisme et Renaissance* 34 (1972): 435–59.

———. "Conversion, Christian Hebraism, and Hebrew Prayer in the Sixteenth Century," *Hebrew Union College Annual* 47 (1976): 217–36.

———. *Catholic Thought and Papal Jewry Policy, 1555–1593*. New York, 1977.

———. "Jewish Approaches to the Papacy and the Papal Doctrine of Jewish Protection, 1050–1150," in Hebrew. *Studies in the History of the Jewish People and the Land of Israel* 5 (1981): 75–90.

———. *Taxation, Community, and State: The Jews and the Fiscal Foundations of the Early Modern Papal State*. Päpste und Papsttum. Stuttgart, 1984.

———. "Delitto e castigo nello Stato papale: ebrei e carceri a Roma alle fine del Cinquecento e agli inizi del Seicento. Primi sondaggi," *Italia Judaica II*, 173–92. Rome, 1986.

———. "The Letter of Maestro Andrea," in *Community and Culture: Essays in Jewish Studies in Honor of the Ninetieth Anniversary of the Founding of Gratz College*, ed. Nathan M. Waldman. Philadelphia, 1987.

———. "Expulsion Italian Style: The Case of Lucio Ferraris," *Jewish History* 3.1 (1988): 51–63.

———. "The Good of the Church, the Good of the State: The Popes and Jewish Money," *Christianity and Judaism: Studies in Church History* 29 (1992): 237–52; in Hebrew, revised, in *Economics and Religion*, ed. Menahem Ben-Sasson. Jerusalem, 1994. Reprint, *Jewish Life in Early Modern Rome* (Aldershot, 2007).

———. "Sanctity and the Construction of Space: The Roman Ghetto as Sacred Space," in *Jewish Assimilation, Acculturation and Accommodation*, ed. Menahem Mor, 54–76. Lanham, MD, 1992.

———. "Sisto V, the Jews, and their Ghet," in *Essential Papers on Jewish Culture in Renaissance and Baroque Italy*, ed. David Ruderman, 386–400. New York, 1992.

———. *Alienated Minority: The Jews of Medieval Latin Europe*. Cambridge, MA, 1992, 1994.

———. "A Tale of Uncertainties: Converts in the Roman Ghetto," in *Shelomo Simonsohn Jubilee Volume*, ed. D. Carpi et al. Tel Aviv, 1993.

———. "Ebrei e inquisitori," in *L'Inquisizione e gli ebrei in Italia*, ed. M. Luzzati, 3–18. Bari, 1994.

———. *The Jews in Rome*, 2 vols. Leiden, 1995, 1997.

———. "Marriages Are Made in Heaven," *Renaissance Quarterly* 48 (1995): 445–91.

———. "Church, Conversion, and Tradition: The Problem of Jewish Conversion in Sixteenth-Century Italy," *Dimensioni e problemi della ricerca storica* 2 (1996): 25–34.

———. "Corporate Double Talk: Kehillat Kodesh and Universitas in the Roman Jewish Sixteenth Century Environment," *Journal of Jewish Thought and Philosophy* 8 (1999): 283–301.

———. "La storia degli Ebrei italiani: Approcci contrastanti," *Rassegna storica italiana* 61 (1999): 250–64.

―――. "The Jewish Woman as Social Protagonist: Jewish Women in Sixteenth-Century Rome," in *Le donne delle minoranze*, ed. Claire Honess and Verina Jones. Turin, 1999.

―――. "Conversion, Apostasy, and Apprehensiveness: Emicho of Flonheim and the Fear of Jews in the Twelfth Century," *Speculum* 76 (2001): 911–33. Reprinted in *Popes, Church, and Jews in the Middle Ages*. Aldershot, 2007.

―――. *Theater of Acculturation, The Roman Ghetto in the Sixteenth Century*. Seattle, 2001.

―――. "*Neofiti* and Their Families: or, Perhaps, the Good of the State." *Leo Baeck Year Book* 47.1 (2002): 105–13.

―――. "Papal Mendicants or Mendicant Popes: Continuity and Change in Papal Policies toward the Jews at the End of the Fifteenth Century," in *Friars and Jews in the Middle Ages and Renaissance,* ed. Stephen McMichael. Leiden, 2004.

―――. "The Church and the Jews," in Italian in *Atlante del Cristianesimo,* ed. Roberto Rusconi. Turin, 2005. Revised English version in *Popes, Church, and Jews in the Middle Ages*. Aldershot, 2007.

―――. *Jewish Dogs: An Image and Its Interpreters*. Stanford, 2006.

―――. Review of "The Medici State and the Ghetto of Florence: The Construction of an Early Modern Jewish Community by Stefanie B. Siegmund," *American Historical Review* 112 (2007): 302–3.

―――. *Jewish Life in Early Modern Rome: Challenge, Conversion, and Private Life*. Aldershot, 2007.

―――. "Medieval Jews on Christianity," *Cristiani, ebrei, musulmani nell'Occidente medievale=Rivista di storia del cristianesimo* 4 (2007): 73–100.

―――. "Jews in the Middle Ages," in A *Companion to the Medieval World,* ed. Carol Lansing and Edward English. Oxford, 2009.

―――. "Jews and Christians, Two Different Cultures," in *Interstizi: Culture Ebraico-Cristiane a Venezia e nei suoi domini tra basso medieovo e prima epoca moderna,* ed. Uwe Israel, Robert Juette, and Reinhold Mueller. Rome, 2010.

―――. "Equality under Law, the Confessional State, and Emancipation: The Example of the Papal State," *Jewish History* 25.3–4 (2011): 319–37.

―――. "From Civil Society to the Family: Transformations in Early Modern Jewish Confraternal Structure," in *Brotherhood and Boundaries/Fraternità e barriere,* ed. Stefania Pastore, Adriano Prosperi, and Nicholas Terpstra. Pisa, 2011.

―――. "Jewish Pre-emancipation: Ius commune, the Roman Comunità and

Marriage in the Early Modern Papal State," in *Tov Elem: Memory, Community and Gender in Medieval and Early Modern Jewish Culture, Festschrift in Honor of Prof. Robert Bonfil*, Jerusalem, 2011. Reprinted in *Jewish Life in Early Modern Rome*. Aldershot, 2007.

———. "Was the Ghetto Cleaner?," in *Rome, Pollution and Propriety: Dirt, Disease and Hygiene in the Eternal City from Antiquity to Modernity*, ed. Mark Bradley with Kenneth Stow. Cambridge, 2012.

———. "The Cruel Jewish Father: From Miracle to Murder," in *Studies in Medieval Jewish Intellectual and Social History: Festschrift in Honor of Robert Chazan*, ed. D. Engel, L. H. Schiffman, and Elliot R. Wolfson. Leiden, 2012.

———. Review of Marina Caffiero, *Forced Baptisms*, in *Journal of Religion* 93.2 (2013): 239–42.

Strakosch, Henry. *State Absolutism and the Rule of Law*. Sydney, 1967.

Surdi, Pietro. *Consiliorum sive Responsorum D. Ioan Petri Surdi Casalensis J.C. Praeclariss. et Montisferrati Senatus praesidis Dignissimi, Liber Secundus*. Venice, 1600.

Symcox, Geoffrey. *Victor Amadeus II: Absolutism in the Savoyard State, 1675–1730*. London, 1983.

Tama, M. Diogene. *Transactions of the Parisian Sanhedrim, or Acts of the Assembly of Israelitish Deputies of France and Italy convoked at Paris by an Imperial and Royal Decree, Dated May 30, 1806*. London, 1807.

Teter, Magda. *Sinners on Trial: Jews and Sacrilege after the Reformation*. Cambridge, MA, 2011.

Theodosiani libri XVI cum Constitutionibus Sirmondianis, ed. Th. Mommsen and Paul M. Meyer. Berlin, 1905. http://droitromain.upmf-grenoble.fr/Constitutiones/codtheod.html, visited December 3, 2013.

Thomas Aquinas. *Summa Theologica*. http://www.newadvent.org/summa/3010.htm#article1, visited August 4, 2013.

Toschi, Domenico. *Practicarum conclusionem iuris in omni foro frequentiorum*. Rome, 1606.

Tosti, Mario. "Force of Arms, Force of Opinions: Counterrevolution in the Papal States, 1790–1799," in *Republics at War, 1776–1840. Revolutions, Conflicts, and Geopolitics in Europe and the Atlantic World*, ed. Pierre Serna, Antonino de Francesco, and Judith A. Miller. Houndsmills, 2013.

Trasselli, Carmelo. "Un ufficio notarile per gli Ebrei di Roma," *Archivio della R. Deputazione Romana di Storia Patria* 60 (1938): 231–44.

Trenca, Carlo. ASCER, 1Ui 2 inf. 2, fasc. 03.

Trigano, Shmuel. "The French Revolution and the Jews," *Modern Judaism* 10 (1990): 171–90.

Trivellato, Francesca. *The Familiarity of Strangers: The Sephardic Diaspora, Livorno, and Cross-Cultural Trade.* New Haven, 2009.

Ullmann, Walter. *The Growth of Papal Government in the Middle Ages.* London, 1962.

———. "Juristic Obstacles to the Emergence of the Concept of the State in the Middle Ages," in *The Church and the Law in the Earlier Middle Ages.* London, 1965.

Van Caenegem, R. C. *An Historical Introduction to Private Law.* Cambridge, 1988.

Virgulti, Lorenzo. *L'ebreo catecumeno istruito ne' principali misterj della santa fede cristiana, e cattolica dalla legge di Mosè, e dalle scritture de' profeti. Opera utile anche a i cristiani, che desiderano di sapere i fondamenti della loro fede . . .* In Roma, Per Gio. Zempel e Gio. de Meij, 1728.

Voghera, Gadi Luzzatto. *Il prezzo dell'eguaglianza. Il dibattito sull'emancipazione degli ebrei in Italia (1781–1848).* Milan, 1998.

Wacks, David A. *Double Diaspora in Sephardic Literature: Jewish Cultural Production Before and After 1492.* Bloomington, 2015.

Washington, George: "Letter to the Jews of Newport," August 18, 1790, Washington Papers, 6:284–85, cited in http://www.tourosynagogue.org/index.php/history-learning/gw-letter, visited August 28, 2013.

Wendehorst, Stephan. "The Roman Inquisition, the Index and the Jews: Sources and Perspectives for Research," *Jewish History* 17 (2003): 55–76.

Wirszubski, Chaim. *Three Studies in Christian Kabbala* (in Hebrew). Jerusalem, 1975.

———. *A Christian Kabbalist Reads the Law* (in Hebrew). Jerusalem, 1977.

Wood, Carolyn, and Peter Iver Kaufman. "Tacito Predicatore: The Annunciation Chapel at the Madonna Dei Monti in Rome," *Catholic Historical Review* 90.4 (2004): 634–49.

Wright, Dudley. *Roman Catholicism and Free Masonry.* Whitefish, MT, 2003.

Zacour, Norman. *Jews and Saracens in the Consilia of Oldradus de Ponte.* Toronto, 1990.

Index

Illustrations are indicated by italicized page numbers.